WITHDRAWN

ENGLISH SCHOLARS

GULIELMUS DUGDALE
Ætatis. 50. A. MDCLVI.

WILLIAM DUGDALE
An engraving by William Finden of the original plate by Wenceslaus Hollar, 1658

ENGLISH SCHOLARS

1660-1730

by

DAVID C. DOUGLAS

*Fellow of the British Academy, and
Professor of History in the University
of Bristol*

GREENWOOD PRESS, PUBLISHERS
WESTPORT, CONNECTICUT

85542

Library of Congress Cataloging in Publication Data

Douglas, David Charles, 1898-
    English scholars, 1660-1730.

    Reprint of the 1951 ed. published by Eyre & Spottis-
woode, London.
    Includes bibliographical references and index.
    1. Historians--England. 2. Scholars--England.
3. Learning and scholarship--England. I. Title.
DA3.A1D6 1975   942'.007'2022   75-3865
ISBN 0-8371-8093-7

First edition 1939
Second, revised, edition 1951

Originally published in 1951 by Eyre & Spottiswoode, London

Reprinted with the permission of Eyre Methuen, Ltd.

Reprinted in 1975 by Greenwood Press,
a division of Williamhouse-Regency Inc.

Library of Congress Catalog Card Number 75-3865

ISBN 0-8371-8093-7

Printed in the United States of America

To
My Father
JOHN DOUGLAS
in proud memory

CONTENTS

ILLUSTRATIONS

PREFACE

T HE subject of this book is a learned group of worshipful men. Its object is to recall their adventures, to indicate their pervasive influence, and to illustrate the manner in which their corporate achievement was left as an abiding legacy to the nation which they taught. But to make the scholars live again, and to assess their work, were aims too high to invite more than partial fulfilment, and no attempt at a comprehensive history of English medieval scholarship between 1660 and 1730 has here been made. The more restricted purpose of my book will be apparent to readers of its first chapter.

Certainly, a pious excuse may be found for the venture, and, perhaps for that reason, I have been abundantly fortunate in the most generous help I have received. First among my obligations must be placed those to Professor F. M. Stenton of the University of Reading. It is difficult for me to avoid monotony in recording once more a debt which has long ago grown too large ever to be repaid, but, in connection with this book, it was surely an especial privilege to receive guidance from a medievalist who reproduces in himself so many of the qualities of his seventeenth-century predecessors, and in a library which perfectly expresses the spirit of their work. Dr. John Murray, Principal of University College, Exeter, added to the numerous kindnesses I have received from him by reading the bulk of the text in manuscript and by spending many hours in improving my exposition. To others, also, I have been variously indebted: I owe much to the constant interest of the Rev. W. E. Brown of Glasgow; Mr. Charles Johnson gave me valuable information respecting Dugdale; the late Sir Charles Firth supplied me with some important references relating to Hickes; and I was most courteously given permission to reproduce in these pages a few paragraphs which had previously appeared in *The Times Literary Supplement* and in *History*. My wife's share in the production is not to be described in a sentence. She would not wish her share in our common work to be acknowledged in detail. It will suffice to say that without her it would never have been concluded.

The greatest debt, however, still remains unrecorded. This volume was the last of several to be planned by me in the company of my father, and continued with his encouragement. Whatever may be found

9

of value in my writing is in a sense but an imperfect reflection of our association. He died on June 12th, 1935. Now therefore that the book is completed, albeit so very different from what it might have been, it is seemly that even its unworthiness should be dedicated to his memory.

D. C. D.

Exeter, 1939

PREFACE

TO THE SECOND EDITION

This book, which originally appeared a few months after the outbreak of war in 1939, has now for some years been out of print. The preparation of a new edition has given me the opportunity of making a thorough revision of its contents, and while I have found no reason to modify any of its main conclusions, I have been able to make some alterations in detail which, I hope, have improved both its accuracy and its exposition. One chapter has been entirely re-cast, and illustrations have been added in order that the reader may be enabled to form a more intimate acquaintance with some of the chief personalities to whom he is here introduced. I gratefully acknowledge the permission given to me by the Authorities of the National Portrait Gallery and the British Museum to have photograghs taken of pictures and books in their possession. Finally, my very sincere thanks are due to my reviewers in 1939 for their generosity and helpful suggestions, to the Electors to the James Tait Black Memorial Prize in 1940, and to all those who have so kindly stood friends to this book from the time of its original conception down to the present.

D. C. D.

Bristol, 1950

ENGLISH SCHOLARS

CHAPTER I

ENGLISH SCHOLARS

What condynge graces and thanks ought men to gyve to the writers of
historyes, who with their great labours have done so moche profyte to
the humayne lyfe - Albeit that mortall folke are marveylously separated
both by lande and water, and right wonderously sytuate: yet are they and
their actes (done peradventure by the space of a thousande yere) compact
togyder by th'histographier as it were the dedes of one selfe cyte and in
one mannes lyfe.

LORD BERNERS: *Introduction to Froissart.*

B ETWEEN 1660 and 1730 a long succession of highly distinguished
Englishmen brought to its proper culmination the best sustained
and the most prolific movement of historical scholarship which
this country has ever seen. To-day, they are known to professed students of history mainly through stark references to their names in the
footnotes of learned works, and to others of their countrymen they are
known scarcely at all. Yet they were themselves as notable as their
works, and many of them would have achieved distinction even if they
had written nothing. Vigorous in their humour, encyclopaedic in their
interests, they were driven by their abundant vitality not only into the
hidden places of obscure learning but also out into the world of perilous endeavour, and some among them made their choice of causes for
which they were prepared to suffer or to die. Through the energy of
their very strenuous lives they gave to the age in which they lived some
of its most distinctive qualities and in their books they established the
foundations of our present knowledge of medieval England. They
challenge attention therefore both for what they wrote and for what
they were. And it is the aim of this book to penetrate in some measure
into their intimacy; to display their achievement in scholarship as a
triumph of character; and to claim for the scholars themselves a definite, if a modest, place among the architects of England.

No interpretation either of the epoch they adorned, or of the Middle
Ages which they studied, can, in truth, afford to neglect them. For
they not only explored the part history of their country, but did so in
such a manner as to contribute substantially to its development. They
lived at a time of crisis and in its hazards they were directly, and often
distressfully, involved. They saw the deposition of a king and the over-
throw of a time-honoured dynasty; and they were themselves en-

meshed in religious disputes which they regarded as penetrating to the roots of life. Nevertheless, amid all the circumstances of change, they never allowed England to forget the importance of her own history, or to become oblivious of her own traditions. During the decades in which their work was done England twice experienced a political upheaval which cruelly divided her people and threatened a break with her history. Yet throughout this period a great movement of historical research was vigorously sustained, and never perhaps have statesmen of all parties, and the leaders of all opinions, turned more instinctively to the past in order to discover therein a solution to the problems of the present. The two facts are not unconnected. It was not for nothing that a pervasive enthusiasm for antiquity coloured this age. It involved the rectories and vicarages of England; it infected squires, lawyers and doctors; it stretched up to government itself. Historical contemplation, it might almost seem, was to become a mainspring of political action, and the work of the scholars was to be made the weft on the loom of English public life.

A community may at any time be judged by the manner in which it regards its own past, and, if the test be here applied, the result is impressive. Certainly, the conscious attempt of the scholars of this period to impart a sense of continuity to a people in the throes of change could be amply illustrated by their own declarations. 'Man without learninge, and the remembrance of thingse past,' it was remarked in 1655, 'falls into a beastlye sottishnesse and his life is noe better to be accounted of than to be buryed alive'',[1] and the same sentiment persisted into the great controversies of the ensuing period. The autocracy of James II was both attacked and defended by reference to the reign of William the Conqueror; and ejected ministers who refused to take the oaths to William III cited the examples of 'Non Complyers after the coronation and establishment of William I, King Stephen, Edward III and Henry V'.[2] In 1714, again, when England was faced with a new constitutional change, a lawyer who was much concerned with the establishment of George I declared that 'History and Antiquity is the Glass of Time' and added: 'To know nothing before we were born is to live like children, and to understand nothing but what directly tends to the getting a Penny is to live the Life of a sordid Mechanick'.[3] It is little wonder that knowledge prized so highly should have been

---

[1] W. HAMPER: *Life, Diary, and Correspondence of Sir William Dugdale* (1827), Plate iii.

[2] *A Seasonable and Modest Apology on behalf of the Rev. Dr. Hickes* (1710) (by HILKIAH BEDFORD), p. 13.

[3] *The Difference between an Absolute and Limited Monarchy*, ed. John Fortescue-Aland (1714), Introduction, p. lxxii.

eagerly sought, and a widespread interest in the very technicalities of research persisted even into the age of Addison.

> I have heard [said he] one of the greatest geniuses this age had produced, who had been trained up in all the polite studies of antiquity, assure me, upon his being obliged to search into several rolls and records, that notwithstanding such an employment was at first very dry and irksome to him, he at last took an incredible pleasure in it, and preferred it even to the reading of Virgil or Cicero.[1]

The scholars of this age were divided on almost all the questions which sundered contemporary society, but they were strangely and notably united in this: that they went to the past for their arguments, and it was from historical doctrine that they derived the impulse which ruled their vigorous lives. During an era tense with revolution, they proclaimed their lively conviction that Truth is the daughter of Time.

Their influence upon their contemporaries, and upon posterity, would never, however, have been exercised merely through the expression of pious sentiments. Many of these men were, in a sense, public figures, and many more were embittered partisans. But they were also scholars in the strictest sense of the term, and it was their achievement to bequeath to posterity a legacy of learning that is of positive and abiding value. Thus it would not be difficult to defend the opinion that Anglo-Saxon studies have never progressed with greater rapidity than in the period which elapsed between the publication of William Somner's *Dictionary* in 1659 and the death of Humphrey Wanley in 1726,[2] and the endeavour which ensured this notable advance was very widely spread. At Oxford, during these years Edward Thwaites and his friends were eliciting from Queen's College, that 'profluvium of Saxonists' which (as was said) 'poured forth from the House of Eglesfield', and this flood was to include William Nicolson, later Bishop of Carlisle, and Edmund Gibson, successively Bishop of Lincoln and London. At Cambridge, there had been established about 1640 an Anglo-Saxon lectureship whose first holder, Abraham Wheloc, produced the first edition of the vernacular version of Bede's Ecclesiastical History, and his work was later to be developed by another Cambridge man, John Smith, whose magnificent edition of the same work appeared in 1722. Nor was this endeavour confined to the Universities, or to the ranks of the successful. It was not as Fellow of Lincoln, nor yet as Dean of Worcester, but as a hunted fugitive that George Hickes

[1] *Spectator*, No. 447. [2] See below, chaps. iii-v.

was to make the massive contribution to Old English scholarship embodied in his monumental *Thesaurus* of 1703-1705, and when Humphrey Wanley, Hickes's pupil, who perhaps taught his master more than he learnt from him, came to London from Oxford in 1700, it meant that Anglo-Saxon studies were being successfully inaugurated for the first time in the metropolis itself.

Simultaneously, a consistent interest was maintained both in Anglo-Norman history, and in the constitutional developments characteristic of English history during the later Middle Ages.[1] Sir Henry Spelman's great essay on *Feuds and Tenures by Knight Service*, originally written in 1639, was published in a corrected form by Edmund Gibson in 1698, and to this period also belongs the later work of Fabian Phillips on feudalism. Meanwhile, Robert Brady, physician in ordinary to Charles II, was making his own notable contribution to these studies both in his *Compleat History* and also in more specialized works. Matthew Hale, Chief Justice of the King's Bench, devoted to the Norman Conquest no less than fifty pages of his *History of the Common Law*, and when Sir William Temple, already famous both as diplomat and man of letters, issued, in 1695, his *Introduction to the History of England*, it was found that five-sixths of the work was concerned with the same theme. Nor was the subsequent history of medieval England neglected in the constitutional debates of the age. Much of the erudite work of William Prynne, who was a greater scholar than ever he was a politician, was produced during these years, and before the period closed there had appeared the standard Whig histories of Tyrrell and Echard.

Many of the constitutional investigations undertaken at this time were of ephemeral interest, being designed in the first instance to serve the needs of contemporary controversy, but many more although undertaken in the same spirit embodied the result of substantial research. It was, in fact, becoming realized that the paramount need in these studies was to examine the sources themselves not as providing material for later arguments, but in the light of their meaning to the men who made them. When all due qualifications have been made therefore it remains true that the chief contributions made in this period to historical scholarship lay in the discovery, the criticism, and the editing of materials. The great chronicles of medieval England for instance received in this sense an elaborate attention.[2] Most of the monastic annals later edited in the nineteenth century by H. R. Luard were, for example, printed between 1684 and 1691 by William Fulman

---

[1] See below, chap. vi.   [2] See below, chap. viii.

and Thomas Gale, while in his *Anglia Sacra* of 1691 Henry Wharton
made an enduring mark on all subsequent study of ecclesiastical history.[1] The example was infectious, and all over England men such as
Joseph Sparke at Peterborough and Thomas Rud at Durham began to
devote themselves to the annals of the particular sees they served. It
was, in short, a period during which the narrative sources of English
medieval history were assiduously edited; and the effort, carried on in
so many quarters, moved forward to its proper climax. Despite occasional back-slidings into inaccuracy, a more faithful reproduction of
the manuscript texts than had before been attained on such a scale was
offered to the public in the long series of chronicles edited by Thomas
Hearne before his death in 1735.[2]

Even more important than the editing of chronicles was the discovery and publication of a vast quantity of those record sources of
English history whose transcendent value it has been a special object of
modern scholarship to assert. Indeed, the books in which this endeavour
was enshrined have remained of such importance that they still continue to be cited in almost every serious work devoted to the antiquities of medieval England. Thus it was between 1655 and 1673, that
there first appeared the massive volumes of the *Monasticon Anglicanum*,
usually attributed to William Dugdale, and that great corpus of
monastic charters embodied only a part of the labours of this indefatigable scholar.[3] He was, in a sense, to set the pace to those who
followed after, and during the next seventy years there was a vast output of works devoted to the documentary materials which must always
form the basis of the exact study of English history in the Middle Ages.
Indeed, the stupendous production of the age could hardly be better
summarized than by saying that it began with the *Monasticon Anglicanum*, and did not end until after there had appeared Wanley's catalogue of Anglo-Saxon manuscripts (1705); the *Formulare Anglicanum*
(1702) and *Exchequer* (1711) of Thomas Madox; and the original fifteen
volumes of Rymer's *Foedera* (1702-1711).[4] Even the great *Concilia* of
Wake and Wilkins, which was at last issued in 1737 was, in the main,
the result of work carried out before 1730.[5] The fact that all these
famous books still remain standard and indispensable works of reference, that they are used (and criticized) almost as if they had been
written yesterday, is itself an indication of the monumental achievement in scholarship of the age in which they were produced.

[1] See below, chap. vii.   [2] See below, chap. ix.
[3] See below, chap. ii.   [4] See below, chaps. xi.
[5] See below, chap. x.

B

Thus from the time of Dugdale, who after the Restoration instructed his younger contemporaries in the erudition of their predecessors, until that of Madox who before his death in 1727 anticipated some of the most modern developments of documentary criticism, the continuous study of medieval England never flagged. Nor was this a movement confined to few specialists or to a fortunate constellation of outstanding men. The strength of English medieval scholarship in this age derived also from the fact that it was served by many devoted hands.[1] It was from a large company of diverse abilities, but of common interests, that the great scholars of the time – and the great books – stood out. The particular aims which directed a work, so widely undertaken, were naturally, therefore, very various. Anthony Wood, the Oxford historian, 'could never give a reason why he should delight in those studies more than in others, so prevalent was nature mixed with a generosity of mind and a hatred for all that was servile, sneaking, or advantageous for lucre sake', and 'the Society of Merton would not let him live in college for fear he should pluck it down in search of antiquities'.[2] This was the curiosity that was described as 'the direct incontinency of the Spirit', which, as Halifax remarked, 'hath a pleasure in it like that of Wrestling with a fine Woman'.[3] Certainly, it was an unqualified lust for the past which sent Thomas Hearne a-whoring after antiquities. But such a simple impulse was rare, and it was widely condemned as characteristic of those 'unhappy people who were so greedy after materials that they seem to have forgot at last for what end they collected them'.[4] It was unnecessary for Pope to sneer:

> With sharpened Sight pale antiquaries pore
> Th' Inscription value but the Rust adore
> This the Blue varnish that the Green endears
> The Sacred Rust of twice two hundred years,

for men trained in the very discipline he despised had already condemned such perversions. 'I do not understand', wrote William Nicolson in 1693, 'the humour of making discoveries purely for a man's own private information.'[5] The vast majority of these men regarded all history as 'contemporary' in the sense that they were sought in the past the answers to questions which were for them of

---

[1] See below, chap. xii.
[2] WOOD: *Life and Times*, i, p. 183.
[3] JEREMY TAYLOR: *Holy Living* (1654), p. 129; HALIFAX: *Works* (ed. Raleigh), p. 249.
[4] E. Gibson to Ralph Thoresby, July 23rd, 1696 (*Letters of Eminent Men addressed to Ralph Thoresby*, ed. J. Hunter – 1832 – i, p. 241).
[5] WILLIAM NICOLSON: *Epistolatary Correspondence* (ed. John Nichols – 1809), p. 39.

contemporary urgency. They expressed in historical terms the philosophy which informed their careers.

The chief of the immediate pre-occupations which thus inspired the scholars of this age was undoubtedly religion. The antiquarian bias which had from the start been characteristic of the English Reformation was to pervade the seventeenth century and to survive its close. It may, for instance, be seen in the learned work of those numerous Anglican scholars who after the Restoration were concerned, by learned argument, to defend their Church against both Pope and Presbyter; and it informed the historical production of the Nonjurors. More especially did it stimulate Anglo-Saxon studies whose progress during these years was in large measure assured by their being associated with the most vital argument of the age. Thus George Hickes, in this sense, employed the accumulated resources of his stored erudition against his Popish adversaries. 'I know not', he wrote in 1714, 'any work an antiquary can do more serviceable to the Church than this, which will show the faith and other chief doctrines of the English-Saxon Church to be the same as ours, and perfectly answer that never ending question: "Where was your church before Luther?" '[1] Even into the Hanoverian age, the same sentiment continued to appear in the work of those who explored the Anglo-Saxon past. 'By the ancient Saxon Monuments', wrote one of these, 'we are able to demonstrate that the Faith, Worship and Discipline of our Holy Church is in great measure the same with that of the primitive Saxons.' 'This is no small satisfaction', remarked another, 'that we reap from Saxon Learning: that we see the Agreement of the reformed and ancient Saxon Church.'[2] The reiteration becomes monotonous. But this controversial ardour directed into antiquarian channels produced astonishing results when men of exceptional industry ransacked the writings of antiquity for their arguments, and, like Hickes and Wharton, Gibson and Wake, published whole texts upon which they might base their contentions.

There can be little doubt that the close connection between medieval research and ecclesiastical polemic which persisted, though in a diminishing degree, down to the first quarter of the eighteenth century, was in the long run to prove detrimental to the true interests of history. But it is equally certain that the great positive achievements of the age in medieval scholarship would never have been attained had the

---

[1] Hickes to Bishop of Bristol, May 22nd, 1714 (*Hist. MSS. Comm. Portland MSS.*, vol. v, p. 445); cf. E. ELSTOB: *English Saxon Homily* (1709), pp. xxx, xxxi.
[2] FORTESCUE-ALAND, op. cit., p. lxviii; E. ELSTOB, op. cit., p. xiv.

scholars not been urged to their work by motives derived from religious conviction. Nowhere, for instance, could this stimulus be better observed than in the work of those who, for religious reasons, suffered for refusing to take the oaths to William III and George I. The Non-jurors had a special interest in patristic literature and in Byzantine history. They were keenly concerned with English ecclesiastical tradition. Moreover the circumstances of their lives, and the controversies in which they engaged, turned their attention particularly towards the early history of their country. Much of this book will therefore be a commentary upon their work, for the distinction of the Non-jurors in all fields of medieval investigation was one of the most striking phenomena of the time. To name such as Hickes and Hearne, William Lloyd and Jeremy Collier, is alone sufficient to indicate the work which was zealously undertaken by many of this company. This small minority of disinherited, and often penurious, men doubtless in many respects invited the criticism which they have received, but in their learned works they compelled a respectful attention even from their ecclesiastical opponents. They remained a scholarly leaven in English society, and their contributions to historical studies were out of all proportion to their numbers. Isolated by their opinions, and scattered over the land, they yet maintained an intellectual unity among themselves. They achieved a fertile collaboration, and sent out to each other, across a hostile world, their learned missives like balloons from beleaguered cities.

Closely connected with the ecclesiastical controversies of the age was the exuberant nationalism which had once been sung by Shakespeare, and here was to be found the second great motive which stimulated the historical scholarship of the time. When, for instance, William Camden, whose *Britannia* was later to be so influential, announced in the preface to that work his entrance into the learned world, he did so in a manner which left no doubt about the impulse which had prompted his research.

I hope – he remarked – I shall not appear too presumptuous in this venturing as an author from the lowest rank of antiquaries, where I might as well have remained concealed, on the theatre of this learned age, among the variety of tastes and opinions. But, to speak the truth ingenuously, the love of my country which includes all other affections, the glory of the British name, and the advice of my friends have done violence to my modesty, and forced me against my will to undertake this task. . . . There are some who despise and scout the whole pursuit of antiquity as an impertinent inquiry into past things. Their authority I neither totally reject, nor do I much regard, their judgment. I want not arguments to recommend this undertaking to honest and worthy men who wish to see their native country illustrated or to prove that these studies afford the most agreeable and liberal entertainment. If there are any who wish to remain strangers in their own country and city, and children in knowledge, let them enjoy their dream. I have neither written nor laboured for such men.[1]

The example was never forgotten; and it was this sentiment which, after the Restoration, sent politicians, under the cloak of patriotism, to investigate the origins of Parliament, and impelled lawyers to study history for the purposes of politics. Even the more abstruse scholars of this age felt themselves deeply moved in their labours by the promptings of a national loyalty. 'What!' exclaimed one of them in 1714, 'is the Antiquity of the Laws of the English Nation which is the Honour of it of no moment? And is the Honour of the English Nation to be disregarded?'[2] Indignant antiquaries found no difficulty in lashing with their scorn the pretensions of those who considered their culture to be too exquisite to be concerned with the history of their own country,[3] and it was without great difficulty that towards the close of the seventeenth century the erudition of England was mobilized once more to remodel the *Britannia*.

Strong tides of sectarian zeal, of pristine patriotism, and of political conviction, thus swept through these scholars and gave to their research an ardour which it would never otherwise have possessed. This fact alone will serve to explain their vast productivity. The works of medieval erudition produced in England during these seventy years would fill a small library, and the range of the reading of some of the individuals most concerned in this output was well nigh incredible. It defies explanation how some of them could have amassed their immense erudition in the midst of careers consistently devoted to practical affairs unless the spur of immediate enthusiasm was such as to permit no respite in men capable of an industry hardly to be paralleled in any later age. For the same reason, the political and religious upheavals in which they were concerned did not distract them from their learned labours, but rather gave to their inquiries an added zest. The struggle of Charles II with his later Parliaments, the Revolution of 1688, the Non-juring schism, the Convocation Controversy, all in their several ways inspired fresh studies of the Middle Ages. To these scholars, the sense of the past was the foundation of wisdom, and the English past in

---

[1]Preface to *Britannia* as rendered by R. Gough in his edition of 1806.

[2] FORTESCUE-ALAND, op. cit., pp. xiv–xv.

[3] Cf. E. ELSTOB: *English-Saxon Homily*, pp. v, vi; *Rudiments of Grammar*, pp. ii, ix, xxxiv.

particular the prime object of their loving study. A dominant characteristic of English medieval scholarship during the seventy years which
followed the Restoration – perhaps, even, the chief reason for its
remarkable progress – was the close inter-relation which then existed
between historical research and the problems of contemporary life.
This association was capable of inspiring an immense energy in men
who held that in their study of medieval England, they were probing
questions which concerned their personal honour, and sometimes even
their personal salvation.

There was thus an heroic element in their enterprise which is to be
discovered alike in their research, and in the public adventures which
led many of them to risk death and to suffer persecution. The tough-
ness of their minds and bodies gave them an inexhaustible vitality, and
the solemnity of purpose which they shared, brought together in a
common research scholars who were widely different in character, and
bitterly opposed in politics. The zeal which animated them forbade
compromise, so that their learning was ever ready to flash out like a
sword from its scabbard, and they imparted into every controversy the
ardour of a crusade. Their anger supplied sinews to their erudition, and
their diatribes blew like a fine wind through the fustiness of secluded
studies, leaving behind an air cleansed by sincere conviction. Their
exuberant virility relaxed upon humour rather than upon wit. They did
not shrink from bawdy, and in quality of their boisterous laughter there
was nothing of the don.[1] They dwelt among books, and they counted
saints among their number; but their scholarship needed no meretri-
cious advertisement, and their laborious piety no sanctimonious cloak.
Their learning was in touch with life, and eminent as scholars, they
played their masculine part in the world of men.

Their world therefore received them, and their pre-occupation with
its problems has made it difficult for later students adequately to appreciate their great achievement in scholarship. For they lived in an atmosphere which later generations have found hard to breathe, and their
work was informed by fierce personal emotions in which their successors have had little share. The form in which they presented their
research has also contributed to the neglect from which it has some-

[1] DR. PRICE, the Anniversarist, was made Dean of Hereford. But 'Dr. Watts Canon of
that Church told me that this Deane was a mighty Pontificall proud man, and that one
time when they went in procession about the Cathedral Church he would not doe it the
usually way in his surplice hood etc, on Foot, but rode on a Mare thus habited, with the
Common Prayer Booke in his hand, reading. A Stone Horse happened to break loose and
smelt the Mare, and ran and leapt her, and held the Reverend Deane all the time so hard
in his Embraces, that he could not get off till the Horse had done his bussinesse. But he
would never ride in procession afterwards' (AUBREY: Life of Richard Corbet).

times suffered. They built for posterity an enduring mansion of the mind, but they did not trouble to make it easy of access. Scorning dust-less laurels for themselves, they did not spare their readers, deeming none worthy to sup with Clio that had not shared in the labour of their Parnassus climb. And now, as the eloquence of their long empty pulpits resounds strangely from a half-forgotten world, the lapse of time has made ever more difficult of approach their uncompromising fervour. Nevertheless, the work of these men is in no sense to be regarded merely as the antiquated product of outworn faction. They wrote from conviction, and sometimes they allowed the intensity of their beliefs to distort their use of evidence. But they were well aware that history is not the art of stating a case in antiquarian terms, and they avoided the more modern fallacy that the purpose of the historian is the accu-mulation of endless detail terminating in a stalemate of suspended judgment. The intrinsic integrity of their research thus survived the particular controversies it was designed to embellish; and their dis-coveries, founded on meticulous inquiry, have remained of importance long after many of the theories based upon them have crumbled away.

It deserves, indeed, considerable emphasis that, not only the great works of learning which were produced by the scholars of this age, but also many of their lesser books still retain their interest, not as curiosities of outworn erudition but as valuable contributions to present-day knowledge. A considerable number of the sources of English medieval history which were first edited (perhaps for polemical purposes) at this time have never been reprinted, and sometimes the early editions have been given a fortuitous importance by the subse-quent destruction of the manuscripts upon which they were based. Our knowledge of the chronicle ascribed to 'Benedict of Peter-borough' – a cardinal source for the reign of Henry II – thus owes much to the fact that one of its manuscript versions was transcribed by Wanley and edited by Hearne before it was burnt in 1731;[1] and the edition of Bede issued by John Smith in 1722 preserves in an appendix the text of several very early charters the originals of which have since been lost.[2] Furthermore, much that is of immediate value to scholar-ship to-day may be discovered in works of this period which might themselves seem, on first consideration, to be of purely polemical sig-nificance. A suggestive discussion of the medieval English baronage is,

[1] See W. STUBBS: Introduction to *Gesta Regis Henrici Secundi* (Rolls Series, 1867), vol. i, pp. xxi-xl. And see below, chap. ix.
[2] See below, pp. 62-64.

for instance, embedded in Archdeacon Hody's contribution to the Convocation Controversy,[1] and the same debate elicited Wake's *State of the Church* of 1703 which served to prepare the way for the *Concilia* of 1737.[2] Again, some very modern views respecting Anglo-Norman feudalism were foreshadowed in a purely political tract written by Robert Bruce Cotton in 1621 which was printed posthumously in 1657.[3] Such examples, cited haphazard from among many, may at least suggest how rash it would be to dismiss as 'antiquated' the erudition in books which are seldom read. They also illustrate afresh how the controversial ardour of a disputatious age served to stimulate, from men profoundly conscious of the past, a scholarly production of permanent importance.

The two motives were, in truth, hardly to be distinguished. George Hickes[4] was to be brought at his peril to console his friends on the scaffold by the same dedicated energy which led him to compose the wonderful treatises which are found in his *Thesaurus*; and some insight into the circumstances of historical production in this period might be obtained from the mere contemplation of Prynne's ear-marked head bent over his interminable pamphlets on Parliamentary antiquities. In one sense, indeed, the special fervour which such men exhibited, alike in their research and in their public acts, might be said to reflect an older notion of scholarship. It derived in part from an earlier age when all learning had been regarded as a unity, and had been sought above all as being necessary to the spiritual needs of man. According to such ideas, history itself could hardly be visualized as a separate subject, being regarded rather as forming part of a general adventure into the humanities, and as but one of the means whereby a man might be helped to acquire knowledge necessary to his own fundamental welfare, and to that of the world in which he lived.[5] This belief in the unity of learning, and of its purpose, which was characteristic of the sixteenth, and early seventeenth, centuries died in England very hard, and even at the time of the Restoration the boundaries between history and theology, between history and philology, between history and political speculation, were in no sense as yet clearly drawn. It was part of the work of the ensuing period, in some measure, to define them.

It is precisely for this reason that the Restoration can be regarded as

---

[1] H. HODY: *A History of English Councils and Convocations* (1701), pp. 287, 288. Cf. F. M. STENTON: *English Feudalism* (1932), p. 86.

[2] See below, chap. x.

[3] *Cottoni Posthuma* (ed. 1672), p. 14. Cf. D. C. DOUGLAS: *Norman Conquest and British Historians* (1946), pp. 27, 28.

[4] See below, chap. iv.

[5] Cf. F. M. POWICKE: in *English Studies* (1948), p. 71.

marking the beginning of a new epoch in historical scholarship, and more particularly in the development of English medieval studies. A new specialization began at this time to appear. The earlier scholars had allowed their unqualified energy to operate over the whole field of learning, so that while many of them made most important contributions to historical erudition, it would often be difficult to define them simply as historians. James Ussher, Archbishop of Armagh from 1625 to 1655, was, for instance, a very notable investigator of early British history, but he was primarily a theologian and a biblical scholar. John Selden again, whose edition of *Eadmer* printed in 1623 is still of value, was, first and foremost, a lawyer and politician, and his collected works reveal the astonishing range of his learning which stretched to the study of Hebrew language and antiquities. And Sir Henry Savile, who was responsible for the valuable collection of English medieval chronicles which appeared in 1596, not only edited the work of St. John Chrysostom, but displayed an instructed interest in mathematics to such purpose that he became the founder of two famous University Chairs in that subject.[1] This riot of learning frequently entailed an erudition so diversely profound as almost to baffle credence, and (as will be seen) many of the scholars after the Restoration had good reason to be grateful in their particular studies to the work of their predecessors.

After the Restoration, however, it became clear that a stricter discipline was necessary. Much of the older universality of interest was to remain but some limitations now began to impose themselves upon individual curiosity, though not on individual effort. History was becoming circumscribed as a separate study, and even within historical scholarship some distinctions were beginning to be made. The point could, in fact, be well illustrated by a simple comparison between two of the greatest scholars of seventeenth-century England. At the beginning of the century William Camden would undoubtedly have deemed it inappropriate to make any rigid division between ancient and subsequent history: his *Britannia* is essentially Roman Britain as seen in relation to its later growth; and the first holder of the Camden Chair of History in Oxford lectured not only on the ancient authors but also those of later times.[2] By contrast, William Dugdale, who appeared in print in 1655, was perhaps the first man in England who could be strictly called a medievalist, and the term could be applied even more appropriately to several of his immediate successors. The emergence of

[1] Cf. H. STUART JONES in *Oxoniensia*, vol. ix, p. 171.
[2] See DEGORY WHEARE: *Method and Order of Reading History* (ed. 1698).

such distinct categories of scholars was itself a mark of a new and a more modern era of scholarship.

Even more characteristic of this period was the increased objectivity in English historical scholarship which then became manifest. Throughout these decades, the close connection of antiquarian investigations both with theology and politics continued to give to the historical inquiries of the age a greater profundity than they would otherwise have possessed. But as the period advanced many of these men became, so to speak, increasingly enamoured of the historical theme itself, and of the evidence which might give it substance; and this temper checked advantageously, and at a critical moment, the tendentious impulse which might have made historical learning the handmaid merely of faction. Thus, at this time, Old English studies became more independent of ecclesiastical polemic, and while the constitutionalists continued to bandy medieval precedents, the seventy years which followed the Restoration saw not only the continuation of their debate, but also a widespread publication of the authorities themselves. A man like Edmund Gibson could plead his erudite case in the Convocation Controversy without the smallest sacrifice of his scholarly integrity, and Humphrey Wanley's great catalogue of manuscripts revealed scarcely a trace of the religious disputes which had inspired so much of the movement of Anglo-Saxon learning which his career triumphantly closed. But perhaps the tendency of the age in this regard could best be illustrated in the two scholars who, respectively at the beginning of this period and towards the end, issued the two greatest books on medieval charters which the epoch produced.[1] The passionate royalism of Dugdale is latent in nearly everything he wrote, but it would be hard to discover from the learned work of Madox to what political party he belonged. In the disciplined nature of their inquiries, and in the more detached character of their investigations, many scholars of this age seem much nearer to the spirit of modern scholarship than were their immediate predecessors.

The scientific revival characteristic of Restoration England doubtless here exercised its own influence upon historical scholarship in this country by directing attention more to the dispassionate examination of evidence and less to the possible consequences to conduct which might ensue therefrom; and it is noteworthy that in its early days the Royal Society did not exclude historical scholars from its membership or disdain contributions from their pens. In this company even ecclesiastics might be heard to boast of the purely secular nature of their

[1] *Monasticon Anglicanum* (1655-1673); T. MADOX: *Formulare Anglicanum* (1702).

interests, and to claim that 'the two subjects of God and the soul being only forborne, in all else they wander at their pleasure'.[1] Such contacts must have provided a further check to the polemic which had marred some of the antiquarian work hitherto produced in England. But it may none the less be doubted whether this new influence was here to be wholly beneficial. Historical scholarship has never, at its best, been able to neglect problems relating to 'God and the soul', and there was a more vital danger that the new scepticism might shrivel the very motives which had prompted the scholars to their important achievement. The rejection of scholasticism, the development of the Baconian method, and the growth of experimental science, fostered a habit of mind which sharply distinguished between a 'fact' and a metaphysical truth, and this distinction cut at the root of that connection between historical and ethical inquiry which in the past had provided the main stimulus to historical research, and which after the Restoration still continued to do so. When this was weakened, medieval scholarship was itself, as a consequence, for a considerable time, to languish.

Thus, during the latter part of the eighteenth century there can be discerned a slackening in the endeavour which it had been the aim of the earlier scholars to sustain.[2] After Wanley's death in 1727, no 'Saxonist' of his stature was to appear in England for nearly a hundred years, and only one book was issued in the later eighteenth century about Saxon scholarship worthy to stand beside the multifarious production of the previous decades. Similarly, it was to be long before the study of English ecclesiastical antiquities was again to proceed with the momentum it had attained in the time of Henry Wharton, and during the Convocation Controversy. The assiduous editing of medieval chronicles, which had proceeded with scarcely an interruption down to the death of Hearne in 1735, was, likewise, not to be resumed on anything like the same scale until the middle of the nineteenth century. Any rigid division between epochs of learning must, in some sense, be arbitrary, but when all allowances have been made for individual exceptions, it will be hard to escape the conclusion that the movement of historical scholarship, which is here surveyed, came to a close about the fourth decade of the eighteenth century. It had commenced when, after the Restoration, men developed, and began to modify, the learned tradition they had inherited. It declined in the secular atmosphere of an Age of Enlightenment when the earlier motives for inquiry

[1] T. SPRAT: *History of the Royal Society of London* (ed. 1734), p. 83. Cf. B. WILLEY, *Seventeenth Century Background* (1934), p. 211.
[2] See below, chap. xiii.

were disdained, and when elegance was rated above research, and interpretation above discovery. Here also is displayed the scholarly unity of
the intervening epoch, set as it was between a period of preparation and
one of reaction. The flight of James II, and the advent of George I, had
divided the opinions of English learned men, but had not altered the
fundamental character of their approach to the past. But the leaders of
English culture as they appear in the connections of Samuel Johnson
adopted towards historical scholarship in general, and towards medieval studies in particular, an attitude so different from that of their erudite predecessors, that it is permissible to discern in the transition between them the end of an age.

During the decades which followed the Restoration English
medieval scholarship advanced to a climax in an age that was uniquely
propitious to its growth. The solemn fervour which had previously
inspired a relentless search through the past was not evaporated. The
more modern ideal of objective research was beginning to be understood. Zeal still untired was harnessed to criticism, the scholars rose to
their opportunity, and a large section of educated England was eager to
welcome their work. Nor was their achievement due merely to the
surrounding influence of a friendly culture. They were themselves
conspicuous. Dominant figures in a notable age, they carried into their
investigations of the past the same quality of adventure which marked
their public lives. Thus it was that they kept alive that intense and pervasive interest in the history of their country which had been fostered
by their predecessors. But their learned performance was, none the
less, to be distinct. For it was their special task to claim for their subject
an independent position as a separate branch of learning, and they provided for Clio at last a distinctive dwelling within the English House of
Wisdom.

In 1658 – a bare two years before the Restoration – there appeared
the most remarkable historical monograph in the English language. It
was *A Brief Discourse of Sepulchral Urns lately found in Norfolk*, and in it
Sir Thomas Browne discussed *Hydriotaphia* through eighty-four short
and memorable pages. Like every genius, Browne escapes classification,
and the approach to eternity through the past may have been incidental
to the achievement of this man who wandered so strangely through
the garden of Cyrus, and plied his eident curiosity so diligently among
the buried antiquities of the East Anglican fields. But he could not
escape the prevailing temper of his generation. 'We were hinted by the
occasion, not catched the opportunity, to write of old things, or in-
trude upon the Antiquary. We are coldly drawn into discourses of

Antiquities, who have scarce time before us to comprehend new things, or make out learned Novelties. But seeing they arose as they lay, almost in silence among us, – we were very unwilling they should die again and be buried twice among us.'[1] The result was an historical essay which only began 'when the Funeral Pyre was out and the last Valediction over', and then moved with set purpose over diverse tracts of miscellaneous learning until it culminated in its own magnificent climax of superb rhetoric. There need be no suggestion that *Hydriotaphia* was a work of unchallengeable historical research; nor were the urns as old as Browne thought them. But the author of *Vulgar Errors* did not need to be told that inquiry can disprove a tradition of misconception; nor was his critical scepticism unaware that there were 'uncertainties' which must still be regarded as 'dubious'. And there is no escaping the conclusion that in him there was exemplified that special type of erudite curiosity which after the Restoration transformed a great tradition of learning into a pregnant movement of medieval research.

The curtain thus rises upon this drama of erudition to the congenial music of his familiar prose. ' 'Tis opportune to look back upon old Times, and contemplate our Forefathers. Great examples grow thin, and are to be fetched from the passed world. Simplicity flies away, and Iniquity comes at long strides upon us. We have enough to doe to make up our selves from present and passed Times, and the whole stage of things scarce serveth for our instruction.' 'What Song the *Sirens* sang, and what name *Achilles* assumed when he hid himself among Women, though puzzling questions are not beyond all conjecture. What time the persons of these Ossuaries entered the famous Nations of the Dead and slept with Princes and Counsellors might admit a wide Solution.' 'Consideration of Times before you – so runs up your thought upon the Ancient of days, the Antiquaries truest object, unto whom the eldest parcels are young, and Earth itself an Infant.' ' 'Tis time to observe Occurences and let nothing remarkable escape us. The Supinity of elder days hath left so much in silence, or time hath so martyred the Records, that the most industrious Heads do finde no easie work to erect a new *Britannia*.'[2] It was precisely the temper which inspired the lives, and made possible the work, of the English Scholars who are to be commemorated in this book.

[1] *Hydriotaphia* (1658). Preface.
[2] Ibid., p. 71.

CHAPTER II

THE GRAND PLAGIARY

IN June 1667, Anthony Wood, the Oxford antiquary, paid his first visit to the Tower of London, and there, amid the records, he found an older scholar at work. This was William Dugdale. The two men became acquainted, and as long as Wood remained in London they were wont to dine together at a Cook-house within the Tower where sometimes they had 'a boon blade' for their company.[1] In these conversations which took place beside the ruins of a City, recently blackened by the Fire, may be seen, fittingly symbolized, the beginning of a new era in English medieval scholarship. For Wood, who at the Restoration had been a young man of twenty-eight, belonged in 1667 to the new generation of antiquaries, whilst Dugdale, twenty-seven years his senior, had been reared in the discipline of its predecessor. Yet the latter's name had not appeared on a title page until he was fifty, and before his death at an advanced age in 1686 he was to find himself the venerated pattern of younger medievalists. Dugdale's long career of scholarly endeavour thus serves to illustrate the close connection between two ages of antiquarian scholarship, and the character of the transition which divided them. It is therefore seemly that a study of English medieval scholars between 1660 and 1730 should begin with his great and honoured name.

The days of the Popish Plot, and of the Oxford Parliament, wherein Dugdale was to be attacked, were however very remote when in September 1605 a swarm of bees in a Warwickshire garden presaged an industrious future to a babe that had just been born.[2] His father was John Dugdale, who had come from Lancashire, and had later migrated with some pupils to Oxford, where for fourteen years he had been bursar of St. John's College, until at last he sold such property as he possessed, and settled at Shustoke in Warwickshire. Despite the academic connections of the master of the house, conditions at Shustoke were typical of those prevailing in many English country houses of the period where an informed interest in antiquities existed, and where country gentlemen were taking a prominent part in investigating the history of their estates. The same class which filled the Parliaments of

[1] Wood: *Life and Times*, II, p. III.
[2] Ibid., II, pp. 494, 563.

the early Stuarts with men eager to vindicate the privileges of their order also took its full share in proving its historical importance. These men turned as if naturally to the history of the shires they ruled, to family pedigrees, and to the exploits of their ancestors, and in a similar fashion, they became familiar with the ancient laws of inheritance and entail which held their society together. It was probably, therefore, with a combination of motives not wholly distinct that John Dugdale instructed his young son in Littleton's tenures, and also insisted on his early marriage. At the age of eighteen William Dugdale took to wife Margery Huntbach, the daughter of a Staffordshire gentleman, and in 1626 he set up house with her at Blythe Hall in Warwickshire which ever afterwards remained his home.[1]

It is indeed a striking illustration of the intellectual atmosphere of the period that everything seems to have been done to foster proclivities to historical scholarship in this heir to a small but considerable estate. Before he was ten Dugdale was being instructed in antiquities by Samuel Roper, a neighbouring scholar, and very soon after he had settled with his young wife at Blythe Hall, he made another acquaintance which was yet more valuable. This was William Burton, the elder brother of the author of *The Anatomy of Melancholy*, and himself the author of a valuable *Description of Leicestershire* which had appeared in 1622. Burton, who was later to make a further contribution to scholarship by presenting the MSS. of John Leland to the Bodleian Library, immediately exercised an inevitable influence upon a young man of Dugdale's tastes, and he added thereto by introducing him to Sir Simon Archer of Tamworth, 'a gentleman much affected to antiquities', who became the first of Dugdale's close friends. A scholarly circle was thus being formed in the Midlands with young Dugdale at its centre, and though this connection was by no means exceptional in contemporary England it was none the less particularly active. Archer had already made extensive collections relating to Warwickshire and he now communicated these to Dugdale to the end that 'being desirous to preserve the Honour of their Families by some such publiq' worke as Mr. Burton had done by those in Leicestershire'[2] they might eventually produce a still more elaborate history of their own county. Through Archer's influence[3] the neighbouring gentry became sympathetic to a scheme designed to do them honour, and emulation fired the

[1] Dugdale *Autobiography* (HAMPER: *Life, Diary, and Correspondence of Sir William Dugdale* – 1827 – pp. 5, 7, 8). [2] Dugdale *Autobiography* (HAMPER, p. 9).
[3] On Sir Simon Archer, and the part he played in antiquarian studies during the earlier half of the seventeenth century, see Philip Sykes in *Dugdale Society: Occasional Papers* No. 6 (1946).

energy of the chief participants. The shires of England were one after
another receiving their historians. Some fifty years earlier for example
Lambarde had issued his *Perambulation of Kent*, and Sampson Erdes-
wicke's description of Staffordshire was well known though still unprinted. In such work, it was doubtless felt that the gentlemen of
Warwickshire should not lag behind.

The Warwickshire circle, moreover, speedily enlarged its connections, and the year 1638 brought about two meetings, which were to
be decisive in Dugdale's life, and to have profound results upon the
later development of English medieval scholarship. In the spring of
that year Archer, who had 'some acquaintance' with Sir Henry Spelman, brought Dugdale to the London house of that most famous
scholar. It was a meeting pregnant with significance. Spelman had
known Elizabethan England, and in a notable company he had sponsored English antiquarian learning in its first period. Now, nearly
eighty years of age, and the greatest survivor of an earlier age of
scholarship, he must have looked with an intimate curiosity upon the
eager and industrious young man who was so signally to enhance a
great tradition. Certainly, he did more than vaguely praise, and by his
influence he brought about one of the most prolific unions in the whole
history of English erudition, telling Dugdale 'that one Mr. Roger
Dodsworth, a Yorkshire gentleman, had taken much paynes in search
of Records, and other antient Memorialls, relating to the Antiquities
of that County; but especially touching the Foundations of Monasteries there, and in the Northern parts of the Realme, which worke he
did not a little commend to the paynes and care of some industrious and
diligent searchers into Antiquities'. He added that he had himself,
'being a Norfolk man', 'got together the Transcripts of the Foundation
Charters of divers Monasteries in Norfolk and Suffolk'; and he ended
by 'much importuning Mr. Dugdale to joyne with Mr. Dodsworth in
that commendable worke, which by reason of his youth and forward-
nesse to prosecute those Studies might in time be brought to some perfection'.[1] It was a notable piece of advice, and the old scholar was fully
aware of its real purpose. 'He knew', remarks his own biographer, 'that
Mr. Dodsworth had got together a vast collection of Records' and he
'thought that these might be very well improved into a *Monasticon
Anglicanum* and lest the design should miscarry by Mr. *Dodsworth's*
death he prevailed upon Mr. *Dugdale* to join him in so commendable
a Work.'[2]

[1] Dugdale *Autobiography* (HAMPER, p. 10).
[2] E. GIBSON: *Life of Spelman* in *Reliquiae Spelmannianae* (1698).

William Dugdale and Roger Dodsworth met for the first time in that summer of 1638 at the lodging of Samuel Roper in Lincoln's Inn, and the younger man showed himself eager to collaborate with his senior. Dodsworth, at the age of fifty-three, had already made great progress in those labours of transcription which make his vast collections (to-day in the Bodleian Library) a fitting monument to one who may justly be termed the father of topographical studies in the North of England. He had much to offer Dugdale, and the latter was quick to see the value of the association. The two scholars, therefore, 'acquainting each other what they were then in hand with as to their farther progresse in those Studies readily engaged themselves to prosecute the gayning what Transcripts they could obtaine from any Leiger-bookes, publiq' Records, original Charters or other Manuscripts of note ... but still with this reservation that Mr. Dugdale would not neglect his Collections touching the Antiquities of Warwickshire.'[1] The proviso was perhaps significant as indicating the direction in which Dugdale's main energies would for some time still be turned. But the contact with Dodsworth was none the less immediately productive. At the age of thirty-three Dugdale was fully involved in the two great enterprises upon which his fame was later to rest. By the inspiration of William Burton he had joined with Simon Archer in the preparation of a History of Warwickshire, and by the influence of Henry Spelman he had formed with Roger Dodsworth his connection with the project of an English *Monasticon*.

The labour entailed in this scheme of study was immense. About the time of his first association with Dodsworth, Dugdale may, for example, be watched at work in the Tower 'busy among the Fynes, having run through the reigns of Richard I, K. John and parte of Henry 3rd'; and after his mornings' work in the City he would proceed in the afternoons either to the library which had been collected by Sir Robert Bruce Cotton or to Westminster to 'fall upon the Pipe Roule' or on 'the Wills of the Prerogative Court.'[2] Research of this character, sustained with little intermission, imposed a heavy burden on a scholar whose energies it threatened to absorb in unremunerative or even expensive labour. Dugdale was no pauper, but on the other hand he was never a wealthy man, and later he was reluctant to accept the honour of knighthood because of the exigency of his means. In these early days his devotion to a profession which produced no income might well have overtaxed his resources. But this difficulty was also in

[1] Dugdale *Autobiography* (HAMPER, pp. 10, 11).
[2] Dugdale *Correspondence* (HAMPER, p. 177).

C

some measure met by those in high places who valued his research and the objects to which it was directed. At Spelman's instigation, Christopher Hatton, comptroller of the household of Charles I and himself a member of a family which was to produce great scholars and great patrons of learning, took Dugdale under his protection and secured for him a place in the Heralds' College. He became a pursuivant in 1638, and, except for the period of the Interregnum, he was always to remain in the College, rising at last to its highest dignity of Garter King at Arms.[1] He always took his duties very seriously, and later he was to complain that they interfered with his studies. But he owed much to his appointment.[2] The College of Arms in the seventeenth century has often been condemned by those who have had to expose the results of its venality. Its appointments, however, might be used to endow historical scholarship, and Dugdale's was not the only case in which they were fortunate. His office gave him in time a London residence; it provided him with perquisites and with a small income; and finally it brought him into contact with records and with those who owned them.

The early career of William Dugdale exhibits the zeal of an enthusiastic student fostered by the favour with which this was greeted in the age in which he lived. It also displays to the full the multitudinous energy of his generation of learned men. Dugdale was a self-devoted student, but he was also a zealous royalist and his research was throughout intermingled with a stormy political life. In 1641 for example at the instance of Hatton he journeyed with a feverish energy throughout England to make notes of those ecclesiastical memorials which might be destroyed in the political storm he saw approaching,[3] but in the very next year, with a virile versatility not usually associated with the denizens of public reading rooms, he appeared before Banbury 'in his Coat of Armes with Trumpets sounding before him', and successfully called upon its castle to surrender to the King.[4] He was present at Edgehill, and he shared the royal sojourn at Oxford, but despite political disasters he yet found time in 1644 to pay a hurried visit to Worcester to examine the treasures of the cathedral muniment room. Later, he suffered heavily for his political convictions. His estates were sequestrated and his salary was unpaid. He was fined £168, and his

[1] Dugdale *Autobiography* (HAMPER, pp. 10, 34); M. NOBLE: *College of Arms*, pp. 302-310; F. R. RAINES: Introduction to Chetham Soc. Publications, vol. LXXXVIII.
[2] POWICKE: *Notes on the Hastings Manuscripts* in *Huntingdon Library Quarterly*, vol. I, pp. 247, 248.
[3] Dugdale *Autobiography* (HAMPER, p. 14).
[4] Ibid., p. 16.

movements were closely restricted.[1] But when proscribed, he visited France and there obtained transcripts of charters relating to alien English priories.[2] Dugdale was at once a scholar and a public servant; his vitality was only matched by his devotion; and both surprise an astonished admiration. He took his full share in a Civil War, suffered mulcting and persecution, begat nineteen children in twenty-four years,[3] and pursued with 'unspeakable energy' his antiquarian researches in the midst of a Revolution which vitally affected him.

The intermingled enthusiasms of this fervent life were shared by Dugdale's associates in scholarship, and as a result, the first volume of a *Monasticon Anglicanum* was at last ready in 1654 for the press. Still, however, there were difficulties to be overcome, for the booksellers were reluctant to undertake the venture, and Dodsworth and Dugdale were forced to pawn MSS. to ensure publication. As a result of their efforts the first volume of this notable book actually appeared in print in 1655. It contained a vast mass of original documents relating to the Benedictine, Cluniac, Cistercian and Carthusian monasteries of England, and it was at once recognized by scholars as marking an epoch in the study of charters as a source of English history. Sir Edward Walker, Garter King at Arms, for example, who managed to obtain the book for three days during his exile in Holland, made himself 'almost blind with perusing it',[4] and other students were equally enthusiastic. Nevertheless the volume aroused hostility. Puritans affected to see in the book an attempt to reintroduce Catholicism into England, and many country gentlemen feared that an extensive printing of monastic charters might impair their own title deeds, for such was the authority of the *Monasticon* that its publication entailed suits at Westminster Hall.[5] Moreover the book was a financial failure,[6] which, since Dodsworth died in 1654, Dugdale was left to face alone, and in spite of the praise of competent critics there were still copies on his hands after five years. For these reasons, the second volume did not appear until 1661, and it was not until twelve years later that a third volume at last completed one of the most remarkable productions of English medieval learning.

[1] Dugdale *Autobiography* (HAMPER p. 20); *Diary* (ibid., pp. 46-83); DUGDALE: *View of the Late Troubles* (1681), passim.
[2] Dugdale *Autobiography* (HAMPER, p. 23).
[3] See Chart-pedigree in HAMPER, op. cit., p. 474.
[4] Dugdale *Correspondence* (HAMPER, p. 293).
[5] WOOD: *Life and Times*, II, p. 76.
[6] KENNETT: *Life of Mr. Somner*, p. 84. (This originally appeared in SOMNER: *Treatise of the Roman Ports and Forts in Kent* (1693), and it reappeared 'revised and much enlarged' in the second edition (1726) of Somner's *Treatise of Gavelkind*. It is this latter version which is here quoted throughout.)

Like all pioneer works of scholarship the *Monasticon* is easy to criticize on points of detail. In the accuracy of their literal reproduction of medieval texts its compilers were not in advance of their age, and they were not aware of the importance, in dealing with early charters, of producing a collated text, or at least a version derived from a good cartulary source. Many documents whose originals were available were thus inserted into the *Monasticon* in copies derived from late and inferior manuscripts. Nor was a proper discrimination always exercised as to what should be included. Sir Roger Twysden, who had recently proved himself a notable editor of medieval chronicles, pointed out on the morrow of its publication that the *Monasticon* contained many spurious deeds which were inserted without comment alongside the genuine charters.[1]

A production which has become a standard work of reference to every serious student of medieval antiquities is not however to be appraised by means of a catalogue of its incidental faults. The *Monasticon* was based upon most extensive research, and, with a lavish wealth of illustration, it demonstrated as had never before been possible the historical importance of the English monasteries. It made known for the first time a whole range of documents whose true significance had hitherto been unappreciated, and by so doing it illustrated almost every phase of English social and economic history in the Middle Ages. More than a decade before the appearance in France of Mabillon's great book on medieval charters, the *Monasticon* taught English scholars the importance of charters for history, and it published these in such numbers that a comparative study of them became for the first time possible. Thomas Madox for instance was to work from originals rather than from cartulary texts, but his own work would hardly have been possible apart from the publication of this book, and Thomas Tanner derived his productive interest in monastic studies partly from the same source.[2] Later scholars in their turn have been indebted, one after another, to the material contained in the *Monasticon*, and it has now become an accepted doctrine that in the charters of the twelfth century 'the characteristics of Anglo-Norman feudalism find their most authentic expression'.[3] The *Monasticon* made possible the scientific study of English social history in the Middle Ages; it became essential to all future students of English feudalism; and it provided the materials upon which a knowledge of English diplomatics might in time be based.

[1] Twysden to Dugdale (HAMPER, p. 335).
[2] HEARNE: *Collections*, IV, p. 301.
[3] STENTON: *English Feudalism* (1932), p. 6.

This work, which has exercised such a profound influence upon English medieval scholarship, is now almost universally known, quoted and referred to as 'Dugdale's Monasticon'. Nevertheless, it is very necessary, as several critics have shown, to consider what was in fact Dugdale's own share in the production. There can be no doubt that the original idea of the book belonged to Dodsworth and Spelman, and that the collections of the former scholar had attained a vast size before ever Dugdale became associated with the undertaking. Even after Dugdale's meeting with Dodsworth it appears certain that the energies of the former were still for a time primarily devoted to the collection of materials for the history of his county, and that Dodsworth's was the driving force in the co-operation which was later to produce the Monasticon. For these reasons Anthony Wood asserted that the first and second volumes of the Monasticon were 'both collected and totally written by Dodsworth'. 'The chiefest now of the College of Arms', he added, 'have several times informed me' of this 'as the original which they had seen do testify.'[1] Richard Gough and T. D. Whitaker, who were both highly competent critics, later accepted Wood's statement.[2] It is certain that Dodsworth always regarded the book as being in a special sense his own, and alluded to it as such to Lord Fairfax. Moreover, in 1651, three years before Dodsworth's death, Dugdale himself admitted that the work was 'Mr. Dodsworth work of Monasterye foundations',[3] and at about the same time he regarded it as almost ready for the press. In view of this it is probable that, by later claiming for himself even one third of the book, Dugdale exaggerated his personal contribution, for Dodsworth (as his will shows) continued to the end of his life to consider the Monasticon as his own work over which he had sole and absolute control.[4] It is hard to resist the conclusion that if one single name alone is to be affixed to the Monasticon it should be that of Roger Dodsworth.[5]

This verdict is just. But though the labour which produced the Monasticon was primarily Dodsworth's, it may, none the less, be doubted whether single handed he would ever have succeeded in publishing the book which ought to be his greatest memorial. Dodsworth was a man of wonderful industry who was always collecting material but never able to bring his work to the point of publication,[6] and it

[1] WOOD: Fasti (ed. Bliss), pt. II, col. 24.
[2] GOUGH: British Topography, II, p. 395; T. D. WHITAKER: Richmondshire, I, p. 299.
[3] Bodleian Quarterly Record, vol. VII, p. 412.
[4] NICHOLS: Literary Anecdotes, IV, p. 62.
[5] J. HUNTER: Three Catalogues (1838), p. 249.
[6] GIBSON, op. cit.; WOOD: Fasti, pt. II, col. 25.

was probably here that, as Spelman anticipated, Dugdale made his greatest contribution to the enterprise, bitterly complaining the while of the labour involved, 'soe great a taske have I had to bringe Mr. Dodsworth's confused collections into any order'.[1] Perhaps it was the memory of that drudgery which permitted him later to accept the sole attribution of the work. At all events, as early as 1655 with Dodsworth scarcely a year dead, the Vice-Chancellor of Cambridge was sending to Dugdale the thanks of the University for 'your Monasticon',[2] and in 1656 Hollar's fine portrait of Dugdale showed him with the *Monasticon* before him as his own production.[3] Dugdale's name appeared with that of Dodsworth on the title pages of the first two volumes, and from the third, in which Dugdale had a greater proportionate share, the name of Dodsworth was inexcusably omitted.

The *Monasticon* was, in truth, a great co-operative work. Dodsworth's vast collections, especially for the northern counties, were the basis of the book; Dugdale added documents of his own finding, particularly from Warwickshire and from France, and took the greatest share in the final editing. But other scholars were also concerned. Henry Spelman supplied some East Anglian material,[4] and William Somner, who was already at work on his Saxon Dictionary, not only sent transcripts from Canterbury but placed his special knowledge of Anglo-Saxon at the disposal of the chief compilers.[5] Anthony Wood contributed documents,[6] and Sir John Marsham, the Egyptologist, turned surprisingly from his own studies to survey the whole field of English monasticism in an elaborate introduction. The *Monasticon* thus represented not only the learning and the labour of Dodsworth, not only the editorship of Dugdale, but the generous scholarship of many others, and a grievous literary injustice has been committed in assigning its authorship to a single individual and that not the man who made the chief contribution to its production.[7]

The very strange history of the *Monasticon* did not, however, end with Dugdale's death, and its concluding chapters supply a pungent commentary upon the character of seventeenth-century scholarship, and upon its treatment by some more modern inquirers. The book has had many commentators.[8] As early as 1693, 'J.W.', who was probably

[1] Dugdale to William Vernon, Jan. 29th, 1652 (HAMPER, p. 266).
[2] Lightfoot to Dugdale (HAMPER, p. 290); cf. Dugdale to Reppes (ibid., p. 284).
[3] See frontispiece to this book.
[4] Gibson: op. cit.   [5] Kennett: *Somner*, p. 83.
[6] WOOD: *Life and Times*, II, p. 113.
[7] HUNTER: *Three Catalogues*, p. 62; *Bodleian Quarterly Record*, VII, pp. 409-414.
[8] Dugdale himself in 1682 brought out a new edition of vol. 1. It was identical with the first edition except for a slightly enlarged index.

James Wright, the historian of Rutland, in defiance of instructions left by Dugdale, issued an English epitome of the whole book, and twenty-five years later there appeared a more elaborate translation with a few additions. This is usually attributed to John Stevens, a Catholic, whose main interests were in Spanish literature.[1] This man was also an industrious antiquary, and in 1722 four years before his own death he produced two supplementary volumes to the *Monasticon* which contained a valuable appendix of five hundred additional charters some of which are of great value. During the remainder of the eighteenth century nothing more was added to the book, but early in the nineteenth a lavish new edition of the whole work was planned and issued between 1817 and 1830 under the editorship of John Caley, Henry Ellis and Bulkeley Bandinel in eight large folio volumes at unprecedented expense with elaborate plates and most extensive footnotes. Immediately upon its appearance this edition was greeted with a chorus of praise, and critics described it as 'a laborious and truly national work' and as 'one of the most splendid works that ever issued from the English press'.[2] It is through this edition that nine out of ten of the modern students of the *Monasticon* are acquainted with the work, and it is this edition which is generally supposed to have modernized the labours of the seventeenth-century scholars, corrected their errors, widely supplemented their discoveries by a new investigation, and added a vast quantity of new material to the whole collection.

To disturb a reputation which is thus based upon a century of eulogy might seem a bold venture, but, in truth, it is difficult to discover what were in fact (apart from binding and print) the contributions made to learning by this famous emendation of seventeenth-century learning. The short accounts of particular religious houses, and the separate entries of the *Valor Ecclesiasticus* which were now included were, it is true, innovations, but neither of these was of substantial importance: the former were probably derived from eighteenth-century works, while the latter were very often inaccurate. The extracts from Domesday which were introduced into this edition were derived verbatim (save for omissions) from the great edition of that record which appeared in 1783, and the enormous footnotes which now graced the book for the first time were mostly taken from the printed catalogues of the Harleian and Cottonian collections. The increased bulk of the book did not (as is sometimes supposed) imply that large quantities of

[1] Cf. THORESBY: *Diary*, II, pp. 270, 309. Stevens also prepared an Irish *Monasticon*.
[2] HAMPER, p. 480. The edition of 1846 was a verbatim reissue; cf. *Notes and Queries*, 4th series, vol. X, p. 18.

new matter had been added to this edition. Relatively few new texts were inserted (as for example in the Glastonbury and Gloucester series) which had not appeared before, either in the original volumes or in Stevens's additions, and, as if to compensate for these, all the Nuneaton charters[1] were omitted without any good cause. Finally, the actual presentation of the texts was inexcusable. Many of the charters of Holy Trinity, Aldgate, for instance, were left in the English version given by Stevens in 1722,[2] and in general the new editors seldom seem to have checked the versions printed in the seventeenth century by comparing them with the manuscripts from which they were derived. Certainly, they made no attempt to supply a better version through an examination of more reliable sources. Even the references to authorities were deplorable, for whilst these were sometimes modernized, they were more frequently left in their seventeenth-century form, which through the changes in manuscript collections had often become obsolete, and which, according to modern standards, were usually unsatisfactory. Dugdale's valuable indexes were omitted and the index which took their place was not adequate to satisfy what is still felt by all students as a great want.[3]

The time has perhaps come when it must be admitted that in the nineteenth-century edition of the *Monasticon*, now lovingly cherished in the public and private libraries of England, modern scholars have been prone to accept at its face value an edition which, for all its convenience, is something of a literary imposture. It is fortunately unnecessary to inquire where its editors bought their scissors or concocted their paste, for in all the essentials of scholarship the book which they produced added nothing to that which it was supposed to improve. These editors, neglecting the opportunities afforded them by the improved conditions of research, reproduced old errors without the excuse which must be given to pioneer work, and they added new ones of their own. Popularizing an erroneous attribution of a great work of seventeenth-century learning, they imposed upon their contemporaries and upon their successors, as an original contribution to scholarship, a book which was almost entirely derivative. It is the paradox of William Dugdale that the popular reputation of this great scholar derives to-day not only from a book which in the main he did not write but also from an edition whose significance has been misconceived.

---

[1] *Monasticon*, vol. I (1665), pp. 518-520.
[2] STEVENS: op. cit., I, pp. 74-95.
[3] 'A.O.V.P.' contemplated making a full index in 1872. (*Notes and Queries*, 4th series, vol. IX, p. 506.)

Dugdale himself had little need to accept this attribution of work which was not wholly his own. His own productions were in very truth themselves sufficiently extensive. Only a year after the publication of the first volume of the *Monasticon* there appeared *The Antiquities of Warwickshire illustrated from Records, Leiger-Books, Manuscripts, Charters, Evidences, Tombes and Armes*. It was in every way a remarkable performance and it won immediate praise. 'I cannot but congratulate the happiness of this County', wrote Thomas Fuller in his *Worthies of England*, 'in having Master *William Dugdale* whose *Illustrations* are so great a work ... A well chosen *County* for such a Subject because lying in the *Center* of the *Land* whose *Lustre* diffuseth the *Light* and darteth *Beames* to the *Circumference* of the *Kingdome*. It were a *wild wish* that all the *Shires* in *England* were described to an equall degree of perfection as which will be accomplished when each *Star* is as *big* and *bright* as the *Sun*.'[1] Anthony Wood, whose 'tender affections and insatiable desire for knowledg were ravished and melted downe by the reading of that book', found his life turned thereby into 'a perfect Elysium'.[2] And William Somner, a critic whose opinion was far more valuable, praised the work as being 'so copious and well stored for the matter; so curious and well contrived for the forme: a piece indeed (without all flattery I speake it) to whose composure an industrious hand and an ingenious head have both so well concurred as to render it (in one word) a Masterpiece'. 'Seriously', he added to Dugdale, 'you have drawne the bridge after you and left it impossible for any man to follow you.'[3]

These encomiums were well deserved. Dugdale's *Warwickshire* has remained, in its original and revised editions, a most valuable work of reference. Its production must be regarded as its author's main claim to fame as an historian. Dugdale was well fitted to develop the tradition of local history in England. Like his predecessors he approached his subject in the interests of his class, and he dedicated his book 'to my honoured friends the gentry of Warwickshire', observing that they were 'the most proper persons to which it can be pretended'. 'In it' (he added) 'you will see very much of your worthy ancestors to whose memory I have erected it as a Memorial Pillar and to show in what Honour they lived in those flourishing ages past'.[4] The dedication reflected the strong genealogical interest of the book whilst its distinction derived from its copious and accurate use of authorities. Dugdale in his preoccupations may be compared to the great topographical collec-

[1] FULLER: *Worthies of England* (ed. 1662), pt. IV, p. 134.
[2] WOOD: *Life and Times*, I, p. 209.
[3] Somner to Dugdale, May 9th, 1656 (HAMPER, p. 309).
[4] DUGDALE: *Warwickshire*, Preface.

tors of an earlier generation, but the neatness and method of his work
enabled him to bring to completion labours which other students had
been wont to leave unfinished, and he presented his results in a form
vastly superior to that of any previous history of a similar nature. The
nineteenth century thus found the book as satisfying as did Dugdale's
contemporaries. Neither Richard Gough nor T. D. Whitaker were
unwavering friends to Dugdale's reputation, yet the latter termed the
Warwickshire a book 'which scrupulous accuracy united to stubborn
integrity has elevated to the rank of legal evidence', and the former
considered that 'Dugdale must stand at the head of all our county historians'. Time has since done little to modify this verdict. Modern
criticism has succeeded in correcting points of detail, but one investigator declared that 'after thirty years' acquaintance with its contents
and after following Dugdale through most of his authorities', he was
'filled with admiration at the general correctness'. The book has served
as a model, and the only work of its age comparable with it was constructed deliberately after its example. Dugdale's *Warwickshire* must
take its place with Thoroton's *Nottinghamshire* as one of the two really
important county histories that the seventeenth century produced in
England.[1]

Between 1655 and 1661, Dugdale thus won for himself a permanent
place among the great English medievalists. Within these six years two
volumes of the *Monasticon* had appeared, and also the *Warwickshire* –
three large tomes which have ever since been profitably used by generations of students. Nor did even these exhaust his production at this time.
About 1656 when the *Warwickshire* was on the verge of publication
there came into Dugdale's hands a large number of documents relating
to St. Paul's Cathedral, and he resolved immediately to prepare a book
from these in case any of the memorials of the church should be destroyed in the political troubles which had overtaken the country. The
volume appeared in 1658, and circumstances soon made it of great
value. For the Great Fire of 1666 was to accomplish what the Puritans
had refrained from doing, and in consequence Dugdale's book, with
its descriptions, and in particular with its fine engravings by Hollar,
has remained in its various editions[2] the best account extant of old St.
Paul's before its destruction. As a contribution to scholarship it is not
to be compared either with the *Monasticon* or with the *Warwickshire*.

[1] T. D. Whitaker. Advertisement to *History of Craven*; GOUGH: *British Topography*, II,
p. 299; F. R. RAINES, op. cit., p. 21; HAMPER, p. 483.
[2] HAMPER, pp. 489–91. The edition of 1716 included *An historical Account of the Northern
Cathedrals*, which was not, as there stated, the work of Dugdale. The edition of 1818 is,
particularly in its large-paper form with the proof plates, a magnificent book.

It may better be regarded as a fitting pendant to a prolonged effort of learned endeavour which within a year of the Restoration had been brought at last to a triumphant conclusion. Dugdale had been in no haste to publish; and if he had died at the age of fifty he would have been remembered as but one of the most industrious of seventeenth-century collectors. He had been intimate with many of the scholars of an earlier age, but it was only after the Restoration that his own great reputation became established. Then, his two greatest books had recently appeared, his party was triumphant in the state, and he entered into his own, as an acknowledged leader among the historical scholars of England.

It would be interesting to contemplate him at this time of his honoured maturity. But, grave and somewhat pompous, he exhibited very little of his private life even to his contemporaries, and to-day he tends to remain hidden behind the bulk of his own folios. His public appearances were usually those of a herald, for in 1660 he had spontaneously resumed his duties, and he enjoyed the trappings of his historic office. His integrity here was sometimes subject to temptations as when he was offered five pounds to embellish a coat of arms which showed too clear an evidence of bastardy, but there can be little doubt of the force and content of Dugdale's reply. He discharged his heraldic obligations with ardour, and his later years were in consequence filled with disputes and at least one lawsuit. During his visitations of the northern counties between 1662 and 1670 he dealt severely with what he regarded as usurpations of this authority, and his zeal sometimes burned too bright in so small a cause. His prestige was however enhanced, and he himself would have savoured the praise that 'his loyalty and courage were displayed in his conduct to his royal master, and in his publicly disclaiming such as took upon them the titles of Esquire and Gentleman without just right'.[1]

There was a severity in Dugdale which accorded well with the gravity of his literary pursuits, and perhaps at times he was unduly conscious of a personal dignity that was none the less real. The keen eyes which peer out of his portraits seem not merely critical but capable also of seeking affronts, and the set of the straight mouth betokens obstinacy as well as strength. His correspondence, however, though it seldom condescends from the formal is nearly always urbane, and he was capable of inspiring strong friendships. His numerous letters to Simon Archer, for example, show cordiality and many of the more

[1] M. NOBLE: College of Arms, p. 309; cf. Dugdale Correspondence (HAMPER, pp. 357, 358); F. R. RAINES: op. cit., pp. 22-34.

eminent literary men of the day wrote to him in terms of intimacy and admiration. In younger men also he could inspire affection. The great respect in which his character was held was well deserved, for he had achieved his eminence by long endeavour, and his grave simplicity was well calculated in that age to vindicate the dignity of serious scholarship. Something of the quality of his character emerges from the account of a notable dinner at Magdalen when he talked 'very seriously about some Antiquities as he thought he might properly do among Scholars', and 'one of the Company (who was in Orders) laughed at and made a Jest of what he said'. The uneasy pause following the impertinence can be felt across two centuries. But 'Sir William took no other notice' but 'only asked him: "Sir, are you a Clergyman?"' A proleptic echo of Dr. Johnson repeated after a generation from Hearne's malicious print: Sir William Dugdale, 'the great retriever of our English antiquities'.[1]

For more than a quarter of a century following the re-establishment of the Monarchy he served, Dugdale thus lived on into a new world, producing a series of books which of themselves would have made the reputation of a lesser man. In 1661 he was in correspondence with Lord Gorges, the Surveyor-General of the Great Level, and preparing a work which contained a history of the Fens, and a minute topographical description of them. The importance of this treatise, which appeared in 1662, was not inconsiderable; it was later to be re-issued by the Corporation of the Bedford Level, and it has within recent years served as the basis of a valuable study of medieval intercommoning.[2] Its merits, however, were not so conspicuous as those of a book on judicial antiquities which Dugdale produced in 1666. His *Origines Juridiciales* contains much material which is still not to be found elsewhere, and it is particularly illuminating in respect of the history of the Inns of Court. It passed through several editions, and it supplied the material for other books published at a later date.[3] Finally, at the very end of his life Dugdale issued 'a perfect copy of all Summons of the Nobility to the Great Councils of this Realm'. This contended with justice that the regular summons was at any rate of 'no higher date' than 1265, and that even then 'though it was issued out in the King's name, it was neither by his Authority nor by his Direction'. The whole treatise was to exercise an important influence upon the development of the study of the English medieval constitution made between 1660 and 1730,

[1] HEARNE: *Collections*, IV. p. 371; SOMNER: *Dictionary*.
[2] DUGDALE: *History of Imbanking* (1662); HAMPER, pp. 491, 492; NEILSON: *Terrier of Fleet* (Brit. Acad. Records, vol. IV).
[3] HAMPER, pp. 492, 493.

and, if fully assimilated, it might have prevented the spread of some Whig falsifications of medieval history at a later date.

Besides his printed books, Dugdale also left behind him a mass of manuscript collections some of which have been published,[1] but among all his later productions none was so important as his *Baronage* of *Historical Account of the Lives and most Memorable Actions of our English Nobility*. The project had for long been in Dugdale's mind, and the materials had been slowly accumulating during the many years when the *Warwickshire* and the *Monasticon* were in preparation. After the Restoration it began to absorb the greater part of his energies, so that when he first met Anthony Wood in 1667 he was already fully engaged upon it,[2] 'being' (as he informed another correspondent) 'every day at the Tower little less than twelve hours for that purpose'.[3] Dugdale himself remarked that not many readers could well judge 'with what difficulty, length of time, and expence the Materials for this Work have been got together': 'a task of such importance and weight' (he added) 'I could hardly be perswaded to undertake'.[4] By 1673, however, he could express the hope that the first volume would appear before the year was out, but it was not until two years later that the printed sheets were ready for his final inspection. The *Baronage* at last appeared in 1675 and 1676.

This was the third of the great works of historical learning with which Dugdale was associated. It had not the scope of the *Monasticon*, and it could not boast the same accuracy of scholarship as the *Warwickshire*. But it marked the beginnings of the comprehensive study of English feudal history and it was to prove the starting point of a long series of studies which still continue. The plan of the book was very wide. The first volume was concerned with the aristocracy before the reign of Henry III; the second dealt (less fully) with the nobility which had its rise between 1272 and 1358; and the third (which is shorter again) embraced subsequent creations down to 1676. The subject was probably too large for any single scholar adequately to cover, and the work in consequence contained many inaccuracies which laid its author open to attack. Members of the College of Arms complained that they could not rely upon the book in cases of disputed pedigrees, and a virulent invective, launched against Dugdale, asserted that his 'numberless errors and defects', his 'negligence and ignorance', and his 'gross and complicated blunders' had produced 'a masterpiece of

[1] Cf. *Chetham Society Publications*, vol. LXXXVIII.
[2] WOOD: *Life and Times*, II, p. III.
[3] POWICKE: *Huntington Library Quarterly*, vol. I, p. 247.
[4] DUGDALE: *Baronage*, Preface.

stupidity'.[1] No criticism could have been worse informed. Certainly the *Baronage* had faults, and subsequent scholars who have suffered from them have paid the book the compliment of criticizing it as if it were a modern work. Mature judgment may however confidently conclude that its inaccuracies were far less than might reasonably have been expected in a pioneer enterprise of this magnitude.[2]

Dugdale based his book upon a great mass of original authorities. These he sought not only in the great repositories of public records but also among the archives of noble families with whom his frequent visitations as a herald had given him a considerable acquaintance. His association with the family of Hastings has for example been described in a mass of surviving correspondence, which illustrates how useful such connections could be made for an historian of Dugdale's assiduity.[3] With such materials at his disposal he set himself resolutely to demolish 'legendary fictions and fables cunningly devised to flatter either the fond fancies of old families or the unwarranted assumptions of new'. He sought, in fact, to free peerage history from the distortions of panegyric which had hitherto been its especial bane, and in large measure he succeeded in his object. For that reason alone his book was to have a wide influence upon later studies, and both because of its scope and because of its dependence upon original authorities it still remains indispensable to every modern student of English historical genealogy. Moreover, Dugdale was the first man comprehensively to emphasize the connection of 'questions of descent and family relationship' with 'the changing feudalism of the Middle Ages',[4] for the very nature of feudal organization depended in his view upon the great families which were responsible for its operation. Since he wrote to solve wide general problems by a detailed examination of their particular applications, he produced a book that, for all its shortcomings, has remained a standard work of reference which is only now with the appearance of the new edition of the *Complete Peerage* being at last superseded. No single work has ever done so much for the history of the English aristocracy as the *Baronage* of William Dugdale.

The size and number of the publications with which Dugdale was associated were such that a suspicion is created that he was wont to profit unduly by the labours of others. It was with a proper acknow-

---

[1] *A Small Specimen of the Many Mistakes in Sir William Dugdale's Baronage* (1730 and 1738). Sometimes ascribed to Charles Hornby; cf. *Biographia Britannica* (Kippis), sub. Dugdale.

[2] Cf. J. HUNTER: *Hallamshire* (1819), p. 30.

[3] POWICKE: op. cit., pp. 247-260.

[4] STENTON in *History*, vol. XIX, p. 291.

ledgment that in 1672 he issued Selden's tract upon the office of the
Lord Chancellor; but it was in his own name that ten years later he
produced a book on 'the ancient usuage of bearing arms'. This was
almost entirely derivative, and its publication gave rise to a general
charge of constant plagiarism which was trenchantly expressed in 1713
in a letter which John Anstis, himself a herald and genealogist of note,
addressed to Dr. Charlett, then Master of University College, Oxford.
He roundly termed Dugdale 'that GRAND PLAGIARY', and announced
that he could 'trace the fellow's guilt through every book he hath
printed . . . getting himself a good estate and character among such as
did not know his talent of stealing, with his grave countenance'.[1]

In respect of the three greatest books ascribed to him there is indeed
good reason to believe that Dugdale used with success the labours of
men whose work has failed to be properly acknowledged by posterity.
The *Monasticon* was, as has been seen, largely the work of Dodsworth;
but even the *Warwickshire* which was far more exclusively Dugdale's
own production owed much to other scholars. William Burton had
originally intended that Archer should write the book and had supplied him with materials, whilst Archer and others in their turn had
made very large collections, which, as Dugdale very properly admitted, embellished almost every page of the printed work.[2] Here, however, the acknowledgment was probably adequate, and apart from the
Monasticon, it is perhaps in connection with the *Baronage* that the
charge of plagiarism may most plausibly be preferred against Dugdale.
The idea of such a book had long been in the air and many scholars had
contemplated writing it. Dodsworth moreover had gone further and
and spent long years collecting materials for the work.[3] As early as
1647 he notified a friend 'of my intended and *almost finished* worke of
the Baronage of England',[4] and by 1650 Dugdale himself was alluding
to the fact that Dodsworth had 'taken much paynes in getting together
materialls for the Baronage'.[5] Others, also, testified to the good progress which Dodsworth was making, so that if the book had been
'almost finished' in 1647, it must really have been nearly ready for the
press in 1654, the year of Dodsworth's death. Consequently it becomes
of interest to learn that in 1666 Dugdale borrowed from Lord Fairfax
eighteen volumes of Dodsworth's collections just at the time when he
was working on his own *Baronage*;[6] and it is at any rate beyond dispute

[1] Quoted by HAMPER, p. 497.   [2] See P. SYKES, op. cit., p. 40.
[3] *Bodleian Quarterly Record*, VII, p. 413.
[4] HALLIWELL: *Autobiography of Sir Simondes D'Ewes*, II, p. 313.
[5] Dugdale to W. Vernon, June 22nd, 1650 (HAMPER, p. 238).
[6] Dugdale *Diary* (HAMPER, p. 124); HUNTER: *Three Catalogues*, p. 75.

that of the references to authorities which form the most valuable part
of the *Baronage*, a very large number are to texts in the *Monasticon*
which we know that Dodsworth had collected. In view of this, it was
hardly adequate for Dugdale in his preface to state among various
obligations to patrons, that he had made use of the 'elaborate Collection from the Pipe Rolls made by Mr. Roger Dodsworth whereunto
my quotations do refer'.[1] For the 'quotations' are meagre, and the debt
was far greater.

The use made by Dugdale of the work of other scholars could hardly
be better illustrated than in his treatment of Henry Spelman. In 1627
Spelman had published under the title of *Archaeologus* his fine historical
glossary as far as the letter L, and there was a general desire that the
remainder might also be made available. Dugdale therefore deserved
all credit for undertaking this meritorious work. He complained, however, that his labours were excessive in that the manuscript copy was
'not at all fitted for the Presse'. The truth was apparently rather different. Many years later Edmund Gibson, himself an acute scholar, saw
fit to investigate the whole matter, and discovered that 'the very Copy
from which it was printed is in the Bodleian Library . . . in Sir Henry
Spelman's own hand and agrees exactly with the printed book'. 'So
far then', he concludes, 'as this copy goes (for it ends with the word
'Riota') it is a certain testimony that Sir William Dugdale did no more
than mark it for the printer and transcribe here and there a loose
paper.'[2] A critic in 1684 was, therefore, right to conclude that the vast
bulk of the *Glossarium*, as the new edition was called, was 'the true,
genuine and proper work of Sir Henry Spelman':[3] and Dugdale's own
additions to the remaining letters were by no means always happy, as
Ducange and others were quick to point out. Nevertheless, Dugdale's
editorship here gave to the world a valuable book which it might
otherwise have lacked: and it deserves also to be noted that to the
second volume of Spelman's *Concilia* which he edited in 1664 he contributed a far larger share of the work. It is true that this volume was
inferior to its predecessor and contained numerous mistakes which
William Somner, the 'Saxonist,' began forthwith to correct; but of
the two hundred sheets which it contained, not more than fifty-seven
were of Spelman's collecting.[4]

A later tradition certainly assigned to Dugdale a larger share than
was his due in many of the most important historical productions of

[1] DUGDALE: *Baronage*, Preface.
[2] Dugdale *Autobiography* (HAMPER, p. 29); GIBSON, op. cit.
[3] BRADY: *Introduction to the Old English History* (1684), pp. 229, 230.
[4] HEARNE: *Collections*, XI, p. 221; POWICKE: *Sir Henry Spelman and the 'Concilia'*, p. 13.

his age. But no charge of 'plagiarism' however 'grand' can explain the position to which he attained in the contemporary world of scholarship. He had a special skill in bringing to the point of publication work which other men had left in the form of disordered notes, and there is no doubt that he here performed in many cases a signal service to scholarship. An enemy might say of him that 'he had a greedy appetite to Antiquities but like an Ostrich swallowed whatever came his way unchewed, and it passed through him undigested'. The truth, however, was the exact opposite. Dugdale employed a methodical scheme of study which directed his work always towards ends of publication, and it was this controlled energy which accounted for his own production and for the extent to which he profited by the work of others. Moreover, this was a scholar who was ready to give as well as to receive assistance, so that throughout his life distinguished men were ready to stand his friends, and his juniors freely acknowledged their debt to him. Henry Spelman had sponsored his entrance into the learned world, and Thomas Blount was to question him about tenures, whilst Anthony Wood, who owed him much, repaid him not only with a bitter quarrel but also with his help and friendship. Even the very different intelligence of Thomas Browne found pleasure in communication with Dugdale, and sometimes his scholarly interests could transcend the bounds of party and make him the intimate of his Puritan adversaries. His influence was pervasive, and it stretched into unexpected quarters. Thus, Dugdale was never himself a Saxon scholar, but he was none the less in close sympathy with a movement which was here to open up new avenues of medieval investigation. And it is not the least of his claims upon the gratitude of posterity that, as its author expressly stated, the first printed Saxon Dictionary would never have appeared had it not been for his 'most active and effectual assistance'.[1]

Dugdale's correspondence reveals the symbolic relation in which he stood to the antiquarian culture of his time. His accomplishment was fulfilled in the Restoration world and then his reputation flowered. But he moved therein as an old man full of memories, and he was fully conscious that his was the special task of handing on a tradition which he himself had helped to form. Theophilus Hastings, for example, the seventh Earl of Huntingdon, might suggest to him that he should turn his attention to the antiquities of Leicestershire. 'This is the seventieth year of my age,' he replies. 'It must be a much younger man – whose

---

[1] Dugdale *Correspondence, passim* (HAMPER); *Collections,* III, pp. 54, 55; F. R. RAINES, op. cit., pp. 34-36; cf. L. C. LOYD and D. K. STENTON, *Sir Christopher Hatton's Book of Seals* (1950), pp. xxi *sqq.*

D

genius totally inclines thereto; for money cannot hire any other to take the pains as I have done.' 'Where such a one is to be found,' he adds, 'passes my skill to tell you.' Dugdale was not immune from the characteristic foible of the old scholar who sees among his juniors no one capable of following the giants who had instructed his own youth, and he lost few opportunities of emphasizing to the younger men the high standards of that noble school of learning wherein he had himself been trained. Works of scholarship he insists are not to be undertaken lightly for materials 'cannot be got together in a few years'.[1] 'In matters of Antiquity to be in haste does make the blinder birth.' 'Lett me be bold to give you this caution', he had once written, 'that to depend on any mens collections or transcripts without comparinge them with the originalls will but deceive you.'[2]

He was a fit preceptor because his own achievement reflected many of the best qualities both of the scholars who had taught him and those he was to teach. The energy which linked his research to his political life, and merged in a common endeavour his scholarship and his heraldic zeal, belonged to the past. But the man who had been born before the death of Shakespeare lived on to cross swords with Gilbert Burnet,[3] and there was in him much that could best be appreciated by those who followed after. His scholarship had that disciplined specialization which was later to become an ideal, and he was an adept in those methods of research which are proper to medieval study. The fine actuality which pervaded all his work was a pattern to his successors. So it still remains. Like his seniors he was ardently concerned with general historical principles, but he was fully aware of the dangers of theories divorced from their particular examples. He cultivated a detached inquiry into specific instances without thereby allowing his research to be unduly circumscribed. Thus the principles of tenure were related by him to the charters in which they were severally expressed, and feudalism to the families which controlled its operation. His *Warwickshire*, which was his finest performance, was not the only one of his books wherein it was triumphantly demonstrated how arbitrary is the line that separates national from local history. From him, in no small measure, did his immediate successors derive their characteristic conviction that the development of England is mirrored in her countryside, and that the history of England is rooted in her soil.

Surrounded thus by an ever increasing veneration, Dugdale ad-

---

[1] POWICKE in *Huntington Library Quarterly*, vol. I, pp. 252, 253.
[2] Dugdale to Archer (HAMPER, p. 182).
[3] HAMPER, p. 424.

vanced into his stately old age, himself active to the last. In May 1685,
John Evelyn had the privilege of dining in his company, and heard him
boast that at the age of eighty-one he had 'his eyesight and his memory
perfect'.[1] But a year earlier he had complained that 'the cole smoake
ayre of London'[2] was destructive to his health, and he retired more and
more to the seclusion of Blythe Hall, his Warwickshire home. There,
one February evening in 1686, he lingered too long in the damp
meadows near the house, and a few days later they found him dead in
the chair in which most of his writing had been done. It was a fitting end
to a remarkable career, and it robbed the company of English scholars
of a familiar and prominent figure. Dugdale was inferior in industry
to Dodsworth; he lacked the critical power of Thomas Madox; he was
less original than Humphrey Wanley. But his services to scholarship
were scarcely less than those of any of these outstanding men. His
special achievement was to amass materials; he 'gave originals'; and
that, as Hearne remarked, was his 'chief excellency'.[3] The objective
character of his work and his specialized interest in medieval antiquities
provided a most apposite stimulus to those who followed in his foot-
steps. He linked together two most learned generations, and made the
antiquarian erudition of the one the starting point in the achievement
of its successor. 'What Dugdale hath done', cried Anthony Wood, 'is
prodigious: his memory ought to be had in everlasting remembrance.'[4]
If modern criticism can disturb the popular reputation of Dugdale, it
cannot reverse this verdict, pronounced by one who knew the man
and understood his work.

[1] EVELYN: *Diary*, May 21st, 1685.
[2] Dugdale to Robert Brady, Oct. 6th, 1684 (HAMPER, p. 438).
[3] HEARNE: *Collections*, VIII, p. 268.
[4] WOOD: *Fasti*, pt. II, col. 28.

CHAPTER III

THE SAXON PAST

THE career of William Dugdale serves as a symbol of that transition in English historical scholarship whereby a great tradition of medieval learning was made at once more specialized and more objective. In no department of antiquarian investigation was this development more notable than in the sphere of Anglo-Saxon studies, for nowhere had the earlier activity been more various and constant, and nowhere was the later progress to be more marked. Between 1660 and 1730 students of Old English history built upon mighty foundations, but the edifice which they erected was notably of their own design. In the short space of seventy years they transformed the study of the Saxon past. They gave to the world its first comprehensive Anglo-Saxon dictionary whose appearance in 1659 might fitly be taken as marking the beginning of a new epoch in the study of English philology. They set up new standards of editorship that produced works which still have an intrinsic importance. They made Old English studies the loving concern of important groups in the universities, and, as never before, a living interest for educated England. For all these reasons, the period 1660-1730 must be regarded as a great epoch in the history of Anglo-Saxon scholarship. During these years a long succession of devoted students sustained a continuous endeavour to retrieve the Anglo-Saxon past, and their efforts (which are to be considered in this chapter) formed the essential background to the personal achievements of George Hickes and Humphrey Wanley.

Despite its originality, the work of these men cannot be wholly separated from that of their predecessors since they were throughout influenced by an earlier tradition.[1] The beginnings of Old English scholarship derived from the English Reformation. Matthew Parker, in his collecting of manuscripts, and in the important, if corrupt, series of editions which he sponsored in company with his secretary John Josselin, must have been moved in part by a predilection for historical study; but the chief impulse which inspired his work was undoubtedly a polemical hope that perhaps he might find in the primitive ecclesiastical polity of the Anglo-Saxons a prototype of the reformed church over which he had been called to preside. In like man-

[1] Cf. WÜLKER: *Grundgriss sur Geschichte der Angelsächsischen Litteratur* (1885), pp. 1-34.

ner, Laurence Nowell, who was perhaps the first man adequately to realize the essential contribution which English topography could make to Anglo-Saxon study,[1] was himself deeply affected by the ecclesiastical changes of the time. It was characteristic alike of the English Reformation and of the origins of Old English studies that in 1571 Foxe the Martyrologist should pray that the text of the Saxon gospels 'Imprinted thus in the Saxone letters may remaine in the Church as a profitable example and president of olde antiquitie . . . how the religion presently taught . . . is no new reformation . . . but rather a reduction of the Church to the Pristine State of olde conformitie'.[2] The same motives persisted in many of the greatest scholars of the age. Before he became Archbishop of Armagh in 1625, James Ussher had taken a leading part in the ecclesiastical controversies of his age, and it was a polemical urge which impelled him to embrace Old English studies so profitably in his encyclopaedic learning. And it was partly at the instance of Ussher that about 1640 Henry Spelman founded his lectureship at Cambridge to promote the study of 'domestique Antiquities touching our Church and reviving the Saxon tongue'.[3]

The work of such men inevitably influenced the future, and the motives which had inspired it were not easily forgotten, the more especially as the political controversies of the early seventeenth century had also generated an interest in the Saxon past. The Common Lawyers, for example, had found it easy to draw attention to the legal system of primitive communities whose 'freedom' they were concerned to praise. Sir Edward Coke was no historian, but he was ever ready to seek the origin of the Common Law in Saxon antiquity, and John Selden, whose knowledge of pre-Conquest history was perhaps exaggerated by his admirers, displayed in his *Analecta Anglo-Britannica* a genuine interest in Anglo-Saxon institutions. 'To refer the original of our English laws to the (Norman) Conquest', he remarked, 'is a huge Mistake, for they are of far more distant Date,' and the need for a text of Anglo-Saxon laws less defective than that which had been prepared by Laurence Nowell and William Lambarde was widely felt by many who aspired to be learned in the law. As late as 1714, Judge Fortescue-Aland was to declare that 'to a lawyer, even a Practicer at the Bar, this Language cannot but be of great use; since the very Elements and Foundations of our Laws are laid in this Tongue'.[4]

[1] R. FLOWER: *Laurence Nowell and the Discovery of England* (1937).
[2] Cf. ADAMS: *Old English Scholarship* (1917), p. 32.
[3] Henry Spelman to Wheloc, Sept. 28th, 1638 (ADAMS: op. cit., p. 52).
[4] FORTESCUE-ALAND: *Monarchy*, pp. xiv, xv, xlix; E. ELSTOB: *Rudiments o Grammar*, p. viii; GIBSON: *Life of Spelman (Reliquiae Spelmannianae*, 1698).

The supreme achievements of the Saxon scholars after the Restoration was that, while keeping alive the extraneous enthusiasm of the earlier generation, they set up new standards of criticism independent of contemporary controversy. Early in his life, the man who was, more than all others, to be responsible for the inauguration of the new epoch stated the fresh ideal with force and dignity. 'Loving Truth (the end of all Science) for itself,' wrote William Somner, 'altogether unbyassed with any by-respects . . . I have made it my constant endeavour . . . that Truth alone might triumph over Falshood, Antiquity over Novelty.'[1] It was an emphatic statement of the motives which should animate all historical research, but it was particularly significant coming from such a quarter at the beginning of a movement on Old English learning which was to make these studies more objective than they had ever been before.

The fulfilment of these aims depended from the first upon the solution of certain practical problems. Even before the Restoration it had become apparent that no advance in Old English scholarship could be made secure until steps had been taken to lay the foundation of a working knowledge of Saxon philology. Critics, in particular, 'observed it impossible to cultivate any language or recommend it to the industry of learners without the help of some Dictionary for a standing oracle in obscure and dubious words'.[2] It was in fact partly to remedy this defect in English scholarship that Henry Spelman had founded his Lectureship at Cambridge. 'We have', he remarked, 'some Dictionaries MS. already of very good use, done by skilful men in that language, all which I endeavour to get drawn into one Body', and he therefore instructed his first Lecturer, Abraham Wheloc, to occupy himself in this task, though (he added) 'in the mean tyme you would applie your self to the antientest Authors of our Church and Church History'.[3] Spelman was precisely correct in his diagnosis of the situation. There was in truth much scattered material waiting to be assimilated. Apart from the glossaries and word lists which had been added to a few printed works, collections in manuscript had been prepared (among others) by Laurence Nowell, John Josselin, and by the great continental scholar, Francis Junius, who was to exercise a profound personal influence upon many of his successors in England. But in the middle of the seventeenth century the need for a complete dictionary none the less remained urgent. 'This was yet wanting to the *Saxon* language, and

---

[1] SOMNER: *Gavelkind*, Preface.
[2] KENNETT: *Life of Mr. Somner*, p. 85.
[3] Spelman to Wheloc, Sept. 28th, 1638 (ADAMS, op. cit., p. 53).

was the reason why so few were masters of it. For men care not to travel without a guide in lands unknown.'[1]

The first comprehensive Anglo-Saxon Dictionary was completed in 1659 by the industry of a great and simple-minded man whose life was afterwards finely written by Bishop White Kennett as an example to the medievalists of his own time. William Somner belonged to the generation of Dugdale and he shared its interests. Born at Canterbury, he had been appointed by Laud to the office of Registrar of the ecclesiastical courts of that diocese, and zealous in the service of his master, he had suffered much in the cause of the King, for whom he wrote an elegy which at last appeared as a commentary to the royal portrait in Εἰκὼν Βασιλική. His personal tastes, however, lay always with antiquities, 'and when he had any hours reliev'd from the business of his calling, those he devoted to his beloved search into the mysteries of time'. Like Dugdale, again, it was the history of his native county which chiefly engaged his attention, and among other books relating to Kentish antiquities, he had produced in 1640 his history of Canterbury which later was to prove the model and the starting-point of further studies in the local history of the south-east. In Somner's *Canterbury* there was moreover already to be discovered that interest in Anglo-Saxon which was to lead its author to his most important achievement in scholarship, and this line of research he rapidly developed in other works. By 1647, for example, he had completed his treatise on *Gavelkind*, and four years later the appearance of his notable glossary which was added to the edition of chronicles that Roger Twysden produced in 1651 showed him conclusively to be the man who was best fitted to supply what was the greatest need in Anglo-Saxon scholarship. In these circumstances he received much encouragement. Meric Casaubon, the classical scholar, the worthy son of a greater father, for example, 'ceased not to importune him that he would think of compiling a Saxon dictionary, by which means he would best cultivate that language and receive infinite thanks from all those who were desirous of studying it.'[2] The family of Spelman rendered more material assistance when after the death of Wheloc in 1653 it was arranged (albeit with some difficulty) that the stipend of the Cambridge Lectureship should be transferred to endow Somner's research. By the good will of other scholars much of the manuscript material which had already been collected came into his hands. But even so, great labour was required in a work of synthesis demanding such originality. Not

[1] KENNETT: *Somner*, p. 85.
[2] Op. cit., p. 86.

until 1659 did there appear at last the *Dictionarium Saxonico-Latino-Anglicum* which is the most worthy memorial of the fine and self-effacing student who made it.[1]

Somner's Dictionary was not of course free from the defects inseparable from a pioneer work of this nature. Its standards of definition were inadequate according to modern notions, and 'the Author had this peculiar disadvantage that while the abundant sense of words can be gathered only from a multitude of writers in all different times and all different professions, he could procure but few books and those of a short and ignorant age'. With his inherent modesty Somner was himself acutely conscious of the shortcomings of his book, and though he never lived to complete the emended edition which he contemplated he 'was alway improving the stock and soliciting all Scholars whom he thought could be beneficial to him'.[2] He had no need to apologize for what he had accomplished. His book opened a new path to the Old English philologist, and at the same time it made his subject less esoteric. It initiated also a new period in the study of Anglo-Saxon history by supplying students with an instrument of which they had stood in sore need. About a year before its publication Roger Twysden had expressed to Dugdale the concern with which he was awaiting its publication, confessing: 'I am not so good at the Saxon as I wish I were.'[3] He spoke for many of his fellow scholars who, when Somner's book appeared, found that their hopes had not been disappointed. The Dictionary in consequence soon became scarce. When in 1699 Edward Thwaites, Fellow of Queen's College, Oxford, was busily engaged in building up the first School of English Language and Literature in that university, he gave forcible expression to the need for the book and to the difficulty of obtaining it. 'We want Saxon Lexicons,' he cried. 'I have fifteen young students and but one Somner for them all.'[4] In truth, the book unique in its character, had proved indispensable, and in consequence Thomas Benson, one of Thwaites's junior colleagues, prepared a new epitome of it which it was hoped might satisfy a persistent demand. The attempt was abortive (as appears from the single printed sheet which passed with Hearne's manuscripts into the Bodleian Library), but in 1701 this *Vocabularium Anglo-Saxonicum* actually appeared. 'It bears the name of Mr. Thomas Benson,' remarked Hearne, but it was 'done chiefly by Mr. Thwaites. Mr. Todhunter . . . had some hand in it as had also two or three more young gentlemen

[1] KENNETT: *Somner*, pp. 75-103. TWYSDEN: *Decem Scripoures* (1652), Preface.
[2] KENNETT: *Somner*, pp. 99, 101.
[3] Twysden to Dugdale, Nov. 11th, 1658 (HAMPER, op. cit., pp. 336, 337).
[4] NICHOLS: *Literary Anecdotes*, IV, p. 141.

of the same College . . . Tis a compendium of Mr. Somner, the additions being taken from Mr. Junius's papers in the Bodleian Library.'[1]
Whatever the authorship of the book, the circumstances in which it
appeared abundantly testified to the part that was already being played
by Somner's Dictionary in the development of Old English study.

From one point of view the publication of Somner's Dictionary may
be regarded as a partial fulfilment of the purpose of Spelman's Lectureship at Cambridge, and certainly the period of Old English research
which it introduced was marked by the gradual absorption of these
studies by the universities. This development was so characteristic of
the growth of Anglo-Saxon scholarship in the latter part of the seventeenth century, and so productive of future progress, that it deserves
an especial emphasis. Earlier investigations in this field had been non-
academic; they had been conducted by divines, by lawyers and by
country gentlemen in their own several interests. Now a change took
place; and for a short period the English universities became the especial homes of Old English learning. At first the centre of such studies
tended to be at Cambridge, and, as if naturally, the first endowed
academic office in this subject had been set up in the university of
Matthew Parker. After the Restoration, however, it is chiefly (though
not exclusively) in Oxford that must be sought the greatest figures
among the Anglo-Saxon scholars. Indeed, the efflorescence of Old
English studies at Oxford between 1660 and 1730 was so remarkable
that perhaps less than justice has been done to the fine work which
continued to be produced at Cambridge during these years. The Cambridge men were mostly modest about their performance. They had
no Wood or Hearne to record their achievements, and in many cases
posterity has been too ready to pass them by. But the possession of
such treasures of material as Matthew Parker had left to Corpus could
hardly fail to stimulate interest in an intellectually vigorous society.
And Cambridge, whose researches into pre-Conquest history during
this period are sometimes hastily assumed to have been completely
overshadowed by those of Oxford, produced in fact a body of work
that was impressive both for its quality and for its bulk.

This activity might be watched in a group of Cambridge men whose
productions, though not individually important, testified to the interest taken within the University in the problems of Old English
history at this time. At Caius, for example, there was Robert Sheringham, who had brought back from his recent exile as a royalist in Holland a lively interest in Teutonic mythology. 'A person of great

[1] HEARNE: Collections, I p. 248.

modesty and learning', and (in Hearne's view) 'endowed with an accurate judgement', he was to continue his antiquarian studies at Cambridge until in 1677 he 'died of an apopletical fit which caused him to fall on the fire in his chamber at Caius College in the winter time'.[1] His book on the origins of the Anglo-Saxon race[2] which was issued at Cambridge in 1670 was particularly well received by historical scholars. William Nicolson in his *English Historical Library* hailed it as 'the very best performance that I know of relating to the prime antiquities of the Saxons', and another contemporary critic declared that here were to be found 'many curious antiquities searched for in the most antient Saxon German and Danish Authors'.[3] Such eulogies were however hardly deserved. Sheringham made little attempt to distinguish between fact and fable or (as in the case of Geoffrey of Monmouth) between legend and history. He was 'always very loth to part with anything of an old Story that looks gay and is even tolerably well contrived'.[4] His book, in short, contained a mass of laboriously collected, and misapplied, learning, but the labour which went to its compilation may at least bear witness to the interest for the subject which prevailed in the University from which it came.

An even greater enthusiasm restrained by perhaps yet smaller critical power marked the work of Aylett Sammes, who had come from an Essex home to a Fellowship of Christ's College, and who in 1676 argued through five hundred erudite pages for the Phoenician origin of the English race.[5] After the treatment which had been meted out to Sheringham, the reception accorded to this volume was surprising in its venom. There was apparently something in Sammes which stimulated the spleens of his contemporaries, so that he had the distinction of uniting in a rare harmony of abuse inveterate enemies among his critics. Thus the Non-juror, Hearne, thought Sammes 'a very ignorant silly fellow', and William Nicolson, who became a Bishop after the Revolution, poured scorn on his linguistic pretensions, dubbing him 'the most unaccountable and ridiculous Plagiary and Buffon that ever had his name upon the title page of any book what so ever'. Some critics went yet further, and after condemning the book asserted as an additional crime in Sammes that he never wrote it. This calumny was refuted by Myles Davies the bibliographer in 1716, but it still re-

---

[1] WOOD: *Fasti* (ed. Bliss), pt. I, col. 445.
[2] SHERINGHAM: *De Anglorum Gentis Disceptatio* (1670).
[3] NICOLSON: *English Historical Library* (1736), p. 50; EDMUND BOHUN: in Wheare, *Method and Order of Reading Histories* (1698), pp. 135, 136.
[4] NICOLSON: op. cit., p. 37.
[5] *Britannia Antiqua Illustrata* (1676).

mained difficult to pass judgment in such an atmosphere of aspersion. Aylett Sammes, whose erudition at least impressed Henry Oldenburg, secretary to the Royal Society, was undoubtedly harshly treated by his contemporaries. His book, although in some sense a literary curiosity, is not even to-day without interest. The Phoenicians were undoubtedly 'his only darlings', but he none the less composed a pioneer work on comparative mythology which contains frequent references to Bede and other early writers, and which includes in an appendix a remarkably accurate edition of the Laws of Ine.[1]

The bepraised fervour of Sheringham and the castigated enthusiasm of Sammes might be matched among other productions of Cambridge scholarship during the period as evidence of the culture of Old English antiquities then sustained at that University. But the investigations of this group paled into insignificance by comparison with the production of another scholar who played a far more prominent part in the social life of the time, but who must be included among their number if only from the fact that he took his Master's degree at Cambridge from Trinity College in 1662. This was Thomas Gale, who became successively Professor of Greek at Cambridge in 1666, High Master of St. Paul's School in 1672, and Dean of York in 1697. Gale's influence upon his contemporaries was manifold, and the range of his interests was immense. An edition of classical texts had procured him his Chair; the flourishing condition of St. Paul's School under his rule suggests that he was a good Headmaster; he was an important member of the Royal Society; and as Dean of York he adorned the edifice over which he presided. As a scholar, he established for himself a European reputation before ever he turned to English antiquities, and Huet justly described him as pre-eminent in his generation for versatility of learning.[2] He was in many ways almost a Renaissance figure, a successor to Isaac Casaubon and Scaliger rather than to Dodsworth and Spelman. But no survey of the Saxon students trained at this time in Cambridge can afford to exclude him, if only because the edition of chronicles which he completed in 1691[3] contained as its first three items the texts of Gildas, Nennius, and Eddi.

From the earliest days of English historical scholarship the strange narrative of Gildas had attracted much attention and no less than fifteen

[1] HEARNE: *Collections*, III, p. 231; NICOLSON: *English Historical Library* (1736), pp. 26, 39; MILES DAVIES: *Athenae Britannicae*, I, p. 335. PETHERAM: *Historical Sketch of Anglo-Saxon Literature*, 1840, considers that Somner was the author of the translation of Ine's Laws. I have been unable to confirm this.
[2] NICHOLS: *Literary Anecdotes*, IV, pp. 536-555; *Biographia Britannica*, sub. T. Gale.
[3] See below, pp. 170-171.

publications of it had taken place before Gale turned his interests to this perplexing author. Of these earlier editions those of Polydore Vergil (1525) and John Josselin (1567) were the most notable, and the work of these men had left Gale with a specific task to undertake. For Josselin, who had set himself to correct the acknowledged inaccuracies of Vergil's text, had based his work on two manuscripts, of which one is to-day in the Cambridge University Library while the other is now lost, having been destroyed in the fire at the Cottonian Library in 1731. Gale in his turn discovered a third MS. (now also in the Cambridge University Library), and by this means he was enabled to produce a more reliable text of Gildas than had hitherto appeared.[1] Some of the results of his criticism, which was not uniformly happy, have survived into nineteenth-century editions of this indispensable record,[2] and Gale must be regarded as among the chief agents whereby one of the principal sources of our knowledge of the Anglo-Saxon invasions passed into the canon of English historical criticism.

It was an achievement for a scholar who had many other interests to have taken this part in the elucidation of a cardinal text, but it was perhaps a greater distinction for him to have prepared the first edition of the *Historia Brittonum* ascribed to Nennius, and the first English edition of Eddi's *Life of Wilfrid*. In both these undertakings he had illustrious associates. The *Historia Brittonum* had already been subjected to the careful criticism of James Ussher who had examined no less than eleven MSS. of the work,[3] while Eddi's *Life of Wilfrid* had attracted the attention of continental scholars. Heinsius, when in 1675 he was editing for the Bollandists that part of the *Acta Sanctorum* in which Wilfrid's name occurs, regretted that he had not been able to discover the *Life by Eddi*, which, being acquainted with the abridgment that is given by William of Malmesbury, he rightly supposed to exist in some English library. Mabillon in his turn, when engaged on his great work on the history of the Benedictine Order, actually traced the text to a manuscript in the Cotton collection and eagerly sought for a transcript. Through the medium of Edward Bernard, the Savilian Professor of Astronomy at Oxford, he obtained one from Gale, and this he published. In the meantime, however, Gale had himself discovered a second and more complete manuscript in the library of Salisbury Cathedral, and by means of this he produced his own superior edition

[1] HARDY: *Catalogue of Materials*, I, pp. 132-137; POTTHAST: *Bibliotheca*, sub. Gildas; GILDAS: *De Excidio*, etc. (ed. J. Stevenson – 1838 – pp. xvii-xxi).
[2] His division of the *Epistola* from the *Historia* was due to a faulty criticism of the manuscripts. It was accepted, however, as late as 1838 by J. Stevenson.
[3] Cf. W. H. STEVENSON: *Asser's Life of King Alfred* (1904), p. xl.

in 1691, whilst the additional matter derived from the Salisbury manuscript was sent through Bernard to Mabillon, who published it sepa-
rately and with due acknowledgment in a subsequent portion of the
Acta of the Benedictine Order.[1] The whole transaction deserves note
not only as illustrating the influential part played by Thomas Gale in
the development of Anglo-Saxon history, but also as revealing the
close connection between English and European historical learning at
this time. There was little that was insular in this work except its
subject, and here the results were commensurate with the effort which
was expended. The *Historia Brittonum* has been the object of a most
extensive critical literature in modern times, and Eddi's *Life of Wilfrid*,
has taken its place as an important source for the history of seventh-
century England.

Gale's production helped to elucidate many of the problems of
Anglo-Saxon history, but it did not contribute except indirectly to
those linguistic studies which were, in this period, to be especially
characteristic of the new investigations into the Old English past.
Nevertheless to this endeavour too a notable contribution was made
during these years by Cambridge scholars, and indeed the new advance
which was to be made in these studies after the Restoration would
hardly have been possible at all, had it not been for the publication in
1644,[2] from the University Press, of a remarkable volume which was
dedicated comprehensively 'to God, the Church of England and the
University of Cambridge'. It was the work of Abraham Wheloc who,
after a distinguished career at Cambridge as an orientalist,[3] had come,
in his old age, under the notice of Henry Spelman, and had been
appointed by him as the first Saxon lecturer of the new Foundation.
Spelman had employed Wheloc in earlier days at transcription from
Anglo-Saxon manuscripts, and he knew his man. The appointment,
despite Wheloc's earlier interests in other subjects, was a good one, and
the book which resulted therefrom was the best possible justification
of the new endowment, and of the first man to enjoy it. Its importance
may be judged by the bare statement that it contained the first English
edition of the Latin text of Bede's *Ecclesiastical History*, the first edition
of the Saxon version of that work, the first edition of the Anglo-Saxon
chronicle, and an edition of the Old English Law better than any that
had hitherto appeared. It thus called attention to a group of fundamental sources for the early history of this country, and by so doing it

[1] RAINE: *Historians of the Church of York* (1879), I, pp. xxxv, xxxvi; HARDY: *Catalogue of Materials*, I, pp. 396, 397.
[2] Some title pages apparently have the date 1643.
[3] PETHERAM: op. cit., p. 57; ADAMS: op. cit., p. 52.

proved the starting point of a whole series of investigations which took place during the seventy years which followed the Restoration.

Wheloc's work on Bede was to an especial degree important. His version of the Latin text was superior to its predecessors, and, by publishing for the first time the Saxon version as well, he made available for scholars in its complete form the cardinal authority for the history of England during the early Anglo-Saxon period. He worked in both instances from several manuscripts, and in view of the difficulties which faced him his performance was notable.[1] But the book here had defects. The Latin text depended too much upon earlier continental editions, and the Saxon version was, despite many valuable notes, inadequate as a critical edition. Both James Ussher and Thomas Gale realized that much more work on the Ecclesiastical History was still needed, and it was here that the greatest contribution of Cambridge to Old English studies during this period was made. It took the form of long years of devoted work which at last reached its fulfilment when in 1722 there appeared the first truly critical edition of Bede's *Ecclesiastical History* produced by a scholar who had been trained at St. John's College, Cambridge, and printed with types that had been specially cut for the purpose by the Cambridge University Press. This edition was the result of fourteen years' labour by John Smith whose achievements in scholarship have been somewhat overshadowed by those of his Oxford contemporaries. In virtue of his performance he must, however, be placed among the founders of English medieval scholarship since he produced what was perhaps the most perfect single book of the greatest age of Anglo-Saxon historical learning.

He was a native of Lowther born in 1659; and when he was fifteen years old "the nearness of the place and the company of a young student who was going thither suggested Glasgow University as a suitable place for his education'. But when the day fixed for the journey arrived, 'it proved so rainy and tempestuous that his father would not venture him away from home', and St. John's College, Cambridge, was selected as a second choice. The family came afterwards to look upon the event 'as a providential escape from the Scottish religion', and certainly English historical scholarship derived great benefit from the Westmorland rain. John Smith speedily became 'a good Historian who would talk of the most remarkable passages with great Acuteness being well versed in the septentrional literature, and having a fertility of genius joined to an uncommon penetration and solidity of judgement'. He won in consequence golden opinions from his fellows, and

[1] Cf. C. PLUMMER: *Baedae Opera Historica* (1896), I, p. xxix.

only in one matter does the accuracy of his judgment appear to have been impugned. He was noted as being 'a very rare example of temperance, abstaining from all sorts of strong liquors'. 'He imagined' – it was added – 'this great abstemiousness made his head clearer and better for study which too he thought his constitution required. But in this he was mistaken: for by that and too intense study he broke the vigour of it.' This eccentricity, however, did not prevent him from corresponding with almost all the leading antiquaries of the time. He contributed to the new edition of Camden's *Britannia* that appeared in 1695; he made collections for a History of Durham for which undertaking, it was observed, he was 'the most proper person'; and he started work upon a corpus of Anglo-Saxon charters. But all his interests were subordinated to his studies on the text of Bede, and he carried this enthusiasm through a career which led him to be chaplain to the Embassy in Madrid and back again to be treasurer of the Church of Durham. It was to Cambridge at the last that he returned to finish his work and to die.[1]

His death occurred just before his large and beautiful folio appeared, and it was seen through the final stages of publication by the pious energy of George Smith, his son. It was 'a truly monumental work,' observes a modern critic, and 'its execution deserves all praise'. It contained the majority of Bede's historical works, and it incidentally preserved in an appendix the text of a valuable series of Anglo-Saxon charters from Mercia whose originals have since been lost. But the main function of the book was to present, by means of a most efficient critical apparatus, a complete and reliable text of Bede's *Ecclesiastical History* in both its versions. The Latin text was founded upon the famous Moore manuscript, but variant readings were carefully given in the admirable footnotes, and since Smith worked from three out of the five oldest manuscripts[2] of the *Ecclesiastical History* it was natural that his text based upon such a judicious selection should have marked an enormous advance upon all previous editions. His scholarly accuracy was apparent upon every page of his book, and his comments and collations were so revealing that it is even now difficult to find points for criticism. In certain cases, yielding too much to a laudable predilection, he may have paid excessive deference to the Moore manuscript, and in some of the notes he was indebted to Ussher and to Thomas Gale. But in general his book was both original and definitive; and his

[1] *Biographia Britannica*, pp. 3724-3726.
[2] The fifth of these has only been recently discovered and was unknown even when the best modern edition was produced in 1896. Cf. Lowe in *English Historical Review*, vol. XLI, p. 245.

text of the *Ecclesiastical History* was so good that for nearly two centuries after its appearance editors were content practically to reproduce it. It is the measure of the achievement of John Smith that scarcely anything was done for the textual criticism of Bede between 1722 and 1896; and when in the latter year the latest editor of the *Ecclesiastical History* published his work, he was constrained to remark that he was offering to the public 'the first critical edition since Smith's of 1722'.[1]

During the period subsequent to the Restoration there was thus maintained at Cambridge a continuous interest in the problems of Anglo-Saxon history. It inspired the curious work of Sheringham and Sammes; it was worthily expressed in the editions of Thomas Gale; and it found its proper culmination in the magisterial performance of John Smith. This was a continuous movement of research of which any university might be proud, and the Cambridge 'Saxonists' of this age have probably received less eulogy than is their due. But while their achievements demand emphatic and grateful notice, it still remains true that the most notable sign of the progress of Old English studies during this period was in the production of a brilliant group of scholars who had been trained at Oxford. Contemporaries themselves appear to have been conscious that the centre of Anglo-Saxon scholarship at this time was shifting gradually to the banks of the Isis. An observer could remark as a matter of surprise that John Smith had not gone to Queen's College, Oxford, and it was hardly a coincidence that so many of these Cambridge scholars after they had achieved distinction as students of Old English history formed connections with Oxford. Sammes and Thomas Gale, for example, were both incorporated as Masters of Arts at Oxford, and Hearne proudly noted that for a little while George Smith was a pupil of Thwaites. Despite the fine work which was continually devoted at this time to Anglo-Saxon studies at Cambridge, it was Oxford which progressively produced the leaders among contemporary students of Old English history.[2]

There were many reasons for this, but probably first among them was that the splendid legacy of learning which was bequeathed by the younger Francis Junius came to England through the medium of Oxford. Junius had been born at Heidelberg in 1589, but in 1621 he had entered the household of Thomas Howard, Earl of Arundel, and after thirty happy years in that service he had become almost an

---

[1] PLUMMER: op. cit., vol. I, Preface and p. lxxx; J. STEVENSON: *Bedae Historia Ecclesiastica* (1838), p. xxxiii.

[2] WOOD: *Fasti* (ed. Bliss), pt. II, cols. 204, 363; HEARNE: *Collections*, IX, p. 342; cf. ibid., VII, p. 327.

WILLIAM SOMNER
Engraving by Michael Burghers

English figure, so that it was in this country that he laid the foundations of his wonderful erudition. Having discovered in England many Anglo-Saxon manuscripts he had used these not only to acquire the greatest knowledge of that tongue possessed by any contemporary scholar, but also to form the basis of his studies in comparative philology. Throughout his long life his activities were informed with a passion for pure scholarship, and his intimate contact with Oxford had served to promote a change in the attitude of the University towards the studies of which he was an acknowledged master. The beginnings of that change may perhaps be dated from the time when Junius found his favourite pupil in Thomas Marshall of Lincoln College, for Marshall, who had also studied under James Ussher, was himself an enthusiastic 'Saxonist', and he strove that the powerful external stimulus of the example of Junius should be continually brought to bear upon the University. Consequently, though Junius was away from Oxford between 1651 and 1674, his influence upon Oxford was never allowed to flag, and his work during these years although mostly published abroad bore none the less the marks of English collaboration and in particular of the co-operation with Marshall. It was fitting therefore that Junius should in 1674 return to England to spend his last years with his friend and pupil. In 1676 he finally settled in Oxford, and on his death, two years later, the University acquired his noble fount of type, and his annotated collection of manuscripts which have ever since provided a starting point of research.[1]

It would be difficult exactly to assess the influence of Francis Junius upon the University of his adoption, but there can be no question that, partly owing to him, Anglo-Saxon studies became after the Restoration something of a fashion at Oxford. In the early part of this period, the leadership of this Saxon movement still remained at Lincoln College where Marshall became Rector in 1672, and where already for seven years there had been acting as tutor a young man who was later to exercise over Anglo-Saxon scholarship an influence for which it would be hard to find a parallel. His name was George Hickes, and the Oxford revival of Old English studies was to owe him an incalculable debt. If the work of Junius had been in part the mainspring of this movement, its leader was to be Hickes, and the enthusiastic scholars who were to surround him all wore in some measure the livery of his majestic mind.

[1] FIRTH: *School of English Language and Literature* (1909); WOOD: *Ath. Oxon.*, IV, col. 170; GOLLANCZ: *The Caedmon Manuscript of Anglo-Saxon Biblical Poetry* (1927), pp. xiii-xv; cf. NICHOLS: *Literary Anecdotes*, IV, p. 146.

E

Marshall and Hickes gave to Lincoln College an honoured pre-eminence at the beginning of the Oxford revival, but after the departure of Hickes to spheres of more public activity, its centre in the University passed to Queen's. This College not only produced a 'profluvium of Saxonists' which astonished contemporary observers, but also by utilizing the talent of its Fellows it inaugurated in Oxford the development of an organized school of English language and Literature. William Nicolson, who was later to be Bishop of Carlisle, became the first collegiate lecturer in this subject at Oxford, and in a letter dated November 27th, 1679, he was already described, at the age of twenty-four, as 'so well skilled in the Saxon language that Sir Joseph Williamson has founded a Saxon lecture in our College which he reads every Wednesday in term time'. But it was not until after the Revolution that the influence of Queen's College upon Old English studies reached its climax under yet more notable direction. The advent of Edward Thwaites to Queen's in 1689, and his appointment as Anglo-Saxon 'preceptor' ten years later, marked the period when the dissemination of Old English learning in the University proceeded from Queen's College with especial rapidity under the stimulus of a teacher of outstanding charm.[1]

Thwaites, who came from Westmorland to Oxford at the age of twenty-one, was to typify the spirit of Anglo-Saxon teaching at that University at its most productive period. His successive appointments as Lecturer in Moral Philosophy and Professor of Greek testified to the wide range of his activities, but until his death in 1711 his real interests, at the inspiration of Hickes, were always in Old English studies. His *Heptateuchus* for example which appeared in 1698 marked an important stage in the publication of the work of Ælfric, and would alone be sufficient to establish his reputation as a scholar.[2] His best work, however, was done through the medium of other men whom he inspired or assisted. Thus, the edition of Alfred's Boethius which his pupil, young Christopher Rawlinson, issued in 1699 from the transcripts of Junius, owed much to his instruction, and it is possible that its Latin preface came directly from his pen.[3] Benson's revised edition of Somner's Dictionary was also initiated at his inspiration and completed through his laborious supervision; and it was fitting that his portrait should grace the edition of Ælfric's *Homily on the Birth-day of St. Gregory* which the Elstobs produced in 1709, since both the editors were

[1] FIRTH, op. cit., p. 8; MAGRATH: *Flemings at Oxford* (1903), I, p. 302.
[2] *Heptateuchus, Liber Job et Evangelium Nicodemi Anglo-Saxonice* (1698).
[3] SEDGEFIELD: *King Alfred's Old English Version of Boethius* (1903), p. xxi.

deeply indebted to Thwaites for their success in scholarship.[1] There
was, in truth, an innate generosity in Thwaites which enabled him to
make his contribution to many of the most important works on Old
English history which were issued during his lifetime, and the sensitive
dignity which in his portrait illuminates his phthisis-ridden face only
in part explains his influence over his younger contemporaries. He was,
without doubt, one of the most inspiring teachers which Oxford has
ever produced.

This editor of learned texts was 'of a cheerful merry temper' and 'his
parts were quick'. But the quality of the devotion which he was able
to excite may more readily be understood by his conduct in adversity:

Of its own accord came a growing on one of his knees, attended, as supposed, with great pains; though in his conversation, reading lectures etc., he
showed no tokens of them by wry faces or complaints. When all advices and
means used at Oxford proved ineffectual, and an amputation above the knee
was the last reserve, he went to London to Charles Bernard, the Queen's
serjeant-surgeon, to perform it.

Mr. Bernard thought the operation so hazardous and desperate that he
would have declined it.

Says Mr. Thwaites: 'I came to London on purpose to have my leg cut
    off, and off it shall go; and if you will not do it, lend
    me your tools and I will do it myself'
Says Mr. Bernard: 'I believe I can do it better than you'
So sat to work.
He would not suffer himself to be tied down: and during the whole opera-
tion not one distortion or ho.

Mr. Bernard leaves him and goes abroad about his business but not out of
call. The arteries burst the cauteries and set a bleeding: Mr. Thwaites takes
his handkerchief, and with a bed staff twists it as hard as he could upon the
end of the stump, rammed his fingers into the mouths of the arteries like
spickets: then knocked for Mr. Bernard who was called back and seared up
the veins.[2]

---

[1] HEARNE: *Collections*, I, p. 248; XI, p. 432; ELSTOB: *English Saxon Homily*, p. vii. The
portrait is in the initial 'L' on page I of the latter book; cf. NICHOLS: *Literary Anecdotes*,
IV, p. 131.
[2] Brome to Charlett quoted in NICHOLS: *Literary Anecdotes*, IV, pp. 148, 149. Thwaites's
adventure might be paralleled in a nineteenth-century experience of Robert Liston, the
surgeon, though here it was the operator and not the patient who dealt with the crisis: 'At
an amputation of the thigh by Mr. Russel then the Professor of Clinical Surgery an artery
in the cut bone bled violently, and in consequence of its osseous surroundings, could not
be secured. Liston with the amputating knife at once cut off a chip of wood from the
operating table, formed it into a cone and drove it into the bleeding orifice and in this way
immediately arrested the haemorrhage' (ROBERT PATERSON: *Memorials of James Syme –
1874 – p. 212*).

As far as can be gathered Thwaites's excursion to London involved little interruption of his learned labours. He died in 1711, having been 'reduc'd to a meer Sceleton'.[1]

The extraordinary enthusiasm which made possible the corporate achievement of the Saxon scholars at Queen's College during these years must in great part be attributed to Thwaites's magnetic personality. The affection of his pupils broke out into natural and artless phrases of admiration. He was (they said) 'beautiful in his personage', 'pleasant in conversation', 'agreeably natural', and (it was added) 'he wrote the fairest hand that I ever saw'. Such devotion was well deserved, for Thwaites gave the best years of his life to the young men who under his direction were initiating a new School in Oxford. Now he is clamouring for more Dictionaries for their use, and now he is exhorting them to further labours. Scholars from elsewhere might come to Oxford to sit at his feet. But it was to his pupils at Queen's that Thwaites gave his most whole-hearted attention, and the fifteen young students to whom he lovingly alludes were the beginning of a flourishing School which transformed Queen's College into 'a nest of Saxonists'.[2]

As the mantle of Junius descended upon Hickes, and that of Marshall fell upon the shoulders of Thwaites, so did the activities of the Oxford 'Saxonists' increase in volume and in intensity. Their positive achievements can best be surveyed in connection with the performance of Hickes and Wanley, but it is here particularly noteworthy that they took a prominent share also even in enterprises which had originally been Cambridge undertakings. Thus while John Smith was bringing the labours of Wheloc on Bede to something near perfection, the development of Wheloc's work in respect of the other historical material which he had used – the Old English Laws and the Anglo-Saxon Chronicle – was being profoundly influenced by the endeavours of two young members of Queen's College, each of whom was to have a notable future in the Church.

The senior of these was William Nicolson who later, as Bishop of Carlisle and subsequently of Londonderry, was to play a notable part in the political and learned life of his age, co-operating effectively (especially with Hickes) in many of its most important enterprises, and leaving to posterity in his extensive correspondence and in his *Historical Libraries* a precious record of the literary society which he adorned. He

---

[1] HEARNE: *Collections*, III, p. 287.

[2] NICHOLS: *Literary Anecdotes*, IV, pp. 141-149; *Letters* (from the Bodleian) *written by eminent persons . . . and lives* (by AUBREY) *of Eminent Men* (1813), I, p. 247. This publication is here afterwards referred to as *Bodleian Letters*.

was admitted into Queen's in 1670 when he was about fifteen years of age, and he started his distinguished career by philological study reinforced by foreign travel, and in particular by making collections for a Saxon grammar. But the manner in which he was to be instrumental in bringing the influence of his College to bear upon the development of Saxon learning in his time could hardly be illustrated better than in the part which he played in the study of the Old English codes of Laws. The text of these Laws which Wheloc had published had virtually been that which Lambarde in 1568 had printed from the transcripts of Laurence Nowell, and with the lapse of years it had become clear that it was wholly inadequate.[1] Scholars, therefore, loudly voiced the need for a new edition, and Nicolson throughout took an active part in the preparatory studies which were directed to this end. The amended edition which appeared at last in 1721 was to be produced by David Wilkins the Prussian exile whose notable contribution to English historical scholarship must be considered in another connection. His edition of the laws, however, which collated much new manuscript material and superseded that of Wheloc, was the result of the efforts not only of its titular editor but also of other scholars, and in particular of Nicolson, who took a large share in the enterprise,[2] and contributed thereto a long Latin preface which is not the least valuable part of the book. By so doing he was to be partially responsible for bringing the study of the legal antiquities of Teutonic England to a stage which was not to be passed until the nineteenth century.[3]

Another young scholar at Queen's who at this time performed a notable service in developing the earlier work of Wheloc was one whose subsequent career was to be even more brilliant than that of Nicolson. Edmund Gibson, later to be Bishop successively of Lincoln and London, and to be one of the most notable ecclesiastical writers and editors of his day, arrived at Queen's from the north country in 1689 at the age of twenty. Immediately, he submitted himself with such zeal to the dominant interest in his College that three years later he was able to make his own contribution to a branch of Saxon scholarship which had hitherto been cultivated mainly at Cambridge. Among the materials in Wheloc's book was not only Bede and the Laws, but a version of the Anglo-Saxon Chronicle itself. Wheloc did not discover the Anglo-Saxon Chronicle nor was he the first man to work upon it, but, as was later remarked, he has the distinction of 'having rescued

[1] SISAM in *Modern Language Review*, xx, p. 253; FLOWER, op. cit., pp. 23, 24.
[2] NICOLSON: *Epistolatory Correspondence* (1809), pp. 456-462, 469, 476-480, 490, 492-496, 505.
[3] LIEBERMANN: *Gesetze der Angelsachsen* (1898), I, pp. xlv-l.

from moths and worms this monument of our national history'.[1] He
constructed his text primarily from an eleventh-century manuscript
which passed later into the Cottonian collection, and he collated this
with the manuscript which Matthew Parker had given to Corpus
Christi College, Cambridge, and which still remains the oldest known
version of the Chronicle.[2] In spite of its incidental inaccuracies,
Wheloc's text was in essence a good one, and through it, both as a
pioneer[3] and as a critic,[4] he influenced all subsequent work upon the
Chronicle.

But, as is now well known, the Anglo-Saxon Chronicle exists in
six principal recensions, which are to-day usually designated by the
first six letters of the alphabet.[5] Of these only one, the Parker manuscript ('A') was (through one of its derivatives) represented in Wheloc's
book. There was thus here room for much supplementary study, and
it was with these ideas in his mind that Gibson in 1692, at the age of
twenty-three, produced his own edition. It was based upon Wheloc's
but it also included matter derived from MS. 'E' (the so-called 'Peterborough Chronicle[6]) and also additions taken from the transcripts
which Josselin and Junius had made from two of the other recensions.
The inquiries which had made these additions possible correctly
indicated the lines upon which research here needed to proceed, but it
was a fatal defect in Gibson's book that the new matter was introduced
in such a manner as to create confusion in the future. Wheloc's text had
been based upon a single recension of the Chronicle derived from two
related manuscripts, and thus for all its shortcomings it remained in the
main a trustworthy guide to scholars. Gibson, in seeking to create a
continuous narrative from several distinct sources of varying importance, produced, by means of conflation, a hybrid text which was in
reality less valuable than its predecessor; and from this time there dates
the prevalent fallacy of regarding the Anglo-Saxon Chronicle in its
diverse forms as if it were a single homogeneous authority derived

[1] Cf. SYKES: Gibson, p. 10.
[2] EARLE and PLUMMER: Two Saxon Chronicles parallel, II, pp. cxxviii-cxxix.
[3] Wheloc's work has an additional importance in that the Cottonian manuscript which
he used was almost totally destroyed in the fire of 1731. Portions of this MS. supplemented
the Parker MS. from which it was derived, and subsequent scholars have thus in these
instances to rely upon Wheloc's printed text or on the transcript of the MS. independently
made by Laurence Nowell (cf. FLOWER: op. cit., p. 25).
[4] The reading of the revised annals in the Parker MS. for the years 892-929 were reproduced in Plummer's edition. They were criticized by ARMITAGE ROBINSON, Times of Saint
Dunstan, 1923, p. 20.
[5] Cf. EARLE and PLUMMER, op. cit., I, pp. x-xiv; ARMITAGE ROBINSON, op. cit., pp.
17-24. Cf. STENTON, Anglo-Saxon England (1943), pp. 679-683.
[6] In the sixteenth century Laurence Nowell had made transcripts from this and supplemented them by collations from other texts.

from a single mind.[1] The work of these two scholars, however, taken together, brought the Anglo-Saxon Chronicle as a cardinal course of early English history for the first time properly into the orbit of criticism. Thanks to their editions, which were not to be superseded until the nineteenth century, the Parker version of the Chronicle could be studied, and the existence of four out of the six chief versions of the Chronicle became known to scholars.

The influence of Nicolson and Gibson upon the scholarship of their age – and upon its political life – is not to be appraised parenthetically by reference to but one of their manifold interests. But it deserves an immediate emphasis that they both began their careers as exponents of Anglo-Saxon antiquities. Not the least important result of the prevailing enthusiasm at Queen's College during these years was that many men who were later to rise to high positions in the State carried with them into wider spheres of influence a recollection and an affection for the studies to which they had been attracted in their youth. English scholarship was to be profoundly affected, and Anglo-Saxon learning notably enhanced, when men like William Nicolson and Edmund Gibson, the one a prime factor in stabilizing the Revolution settlement in the north, and the other perhaps the most influential of Georgian prelates, retained in the midst of their practical activities an abiding interest in the learning in which they had been initially trained. When those who had been thus nurtured reached the most exalted places in the Church they were able and willing to use their influence to secure for Old English learning a place in the intellectual interests of England such as it had never before possessed. 'For the honour of the Clergy', exclaimed a shrewd observer in 1714, 'I can't help taking Notice that the World is obliged to those of that Order for the reviving of this ancient Language and the Northern Literature; and that they are chiefly possessed of this Knowledge; and that it is owing also to them, under the kind and generous Influence and Encouragement . . . of the University of Oxford that the way to the attaining of this Language is now made easy.'[2]

This eulogy of Oxford-trained prelates was well deserved, and it exactly summed up the characteristics of the last general phase in the cultivation of Old English studies during this period. The movement which had begun with the publication of Somner's Dictionary had swept through the Universities so that at Cambridge a long succession

[1] EARLE and PLUMMER: op. cit., I, pp. cxxviii-cxxxi. Cf. N. SYKES: Edmund Gibson (1926), pp. 11-12, and GIBBON: Misc. Works, III, pp. 597, 598.
[2] FORTESCUE-ALAND: Monarchy, p. lxxx.

of scholars had advanced Old English learning at the same time as Oxford was becoming the more especially affected by Anglo-Saxon erudition. But by the beginning of the eighteenth century, it was becoming clear that the energy which was transforming these studies could not be confined to either of the Universities, or even to both. The movement which George Hickes inspired when he was himself a political proscript was almost national in its scope, and, as Herley's librarian, Humphrey Wanley was to make London a centre of this research. Characteristic of this endeavour was, moreover, the actuality, which inspired it, and in particular the refusal of these scholars to make any rigid distinctions between Old English archaeology, philology and history. To them it seemed that the Anglo-Saxon past should be studied in the monuments and coins of that age, in its manuscripts, and especially in its language, as well as in its records and annals. This close connection between linguistic and more specifically historical studies was undoubtedly to the advantage of both, and their later separation was to be deplored. Indeed, the chief reply of the twentieth century to the nineteenth in these matters has perhaps been to reassert the claim of the earlier scholars that the language of the Anglo-Saxons cannot be adequately studied with reference to the life they led, whilst an insight into the history of the Anglo-Saxons can only be obtained through an acquaintance with the tongue in which they spoke and wrote.

Thus was the influence of the 'Saxonists' carried throughout England, and whilst the chief agents in this process were undoubtedly the great scholars themselves there must also be cited, as an example of this missionary endeavour, the career of perhaps the strangest member of this remarkable company: a young girl who in 1715 was able to boast that she was well versed in a tongue which 'few men and none of the other sex have ventured to converse with since the time when it was the current language'.[1] Elizabeth Elstob[2] produced an Anglo-Saxon grammar, an edition of Ælfric's homily on the birthday of St. Gregory, and an unfinished folio which was to have contained a collection of Old English sermons. But though these books had some individual importance, it was, in reality, the circumstances of their production which made them influential, and contemporary students (and some of their successors) were in consequence led even to exaggerate the part played by Elizabeth Elstob in the development of Old English learning. There was doubtless a romantic piquancy in the discovery that a young

[1] E. ELSTOB: *English-Saxon Homily* (1709), Dedication.
[2] For Elizabeth Elstob see in particular NICHOLS: *Literary Anecdotes*, IV, pp. 112-140; and *The Saxon Nymph* in *Times Literary Supplement*, Sept. 28th, 1933.

woman was engaged in such adventures of scholarship, and it might certainly have been enhanced by a glance at the strange domestic interior in which they were conducted. When 'for example' Ralph Thoresby from Yorkshire on July 8th, 1712, visited the London lodging of Elizabeth Elstob and her brother William, he surprised a revealing privacy. For Elizabeth (as he notes)

> showed me a delicate copy of the Textus Roffensis, wrote by a poor boy she keeps, most of it before he was quite ten years of age; his name is (James) Smith. I saw the boy who has imitated the Saxon and other antique hands to a wonder; what Latin and Saxon he has was from her reading him the grammar.[1]

Some commiseration may perhaps be felt for young James Smith who was apparently compelled to proceed from the humblest domestic tasks to the transcription of Anglo-Saxon manuscripts, but his work was to survive in a transcript[2] which at the time won august praise, and which even now owing to the omissions in Hearne's edition of 1720 has some intrinsic interest.[3] Here, at any rate, was unaffected simplicity informing strenuous lives, and while there is no need to overrate the performance of Elizabeth Elstob as a pure scholar, it is permissible to pay some special deference to a lady who was claimed by Hickes as his 'Saxon mistress', and hailed by others as 'the Saxon nymph'.[4]

It was as a propagandist of Old English studies that Elizabeth Elstob, without ever herself attaining to the front rank in scholarship, was able to take her place among a most distinguished company of scholars. Her grammar, for example, sought avowedly to explain Anglo-Saxon to those 'whose Education hath not allowed them an Acquaintance with the Grammars of other languages', and in an attempt to appeal to a wide public she 'resolved to give them the Rudiments of that Language in an English Dress'. Nor was she slow to see the importance of her own decision. 'I have chosen', she added, 'rather to use such English as would be both intelligible and best express the Saxon: that as near as possible both the Saxon and the English might be discerned to be of the same Kindred and Affinity'.[5] It would be difficult to impeach the critical principle thus expressed, and it was a distinction in this writer

[1] THORESBY: *Diary*, II, p. 131.
[2] Stowe MS. 940.
[3] D. C. DOUGLAS: *Odo Lanfranc and the Domesday Survey* in *Essays presented to James Tait* (1933), p. 49.
[4] Portland MSS. Rep., vol. v, p. 451; THORESBY: *Diary*, II, p. 131.
[5] *English-Saxon Homily*, p. ix; *Rudiments of Grammar*, p. ii.

to have asserted in such a practical manner the essential 'continuity of English prose'.

The books produced by this remarkable young woman are chiefly interesting for the lively and witty introductions which they contained, for these represented a highly original endeavour to stimulate the more widespread cultivation of Old English studies, and in particular to defend such learning from the attacks of those who contended that it was nothing more than 'barbarous antiquated stuff'. She was, in this work, already vindicating medieval erudition against the 'polite' taste of the ensuing generation which was to retard its development in England. But if the immediate future was to be with her opponents there was a strictly modern ring about her conclusions. 'I fear', she exclaimed, 'if things were rightly considered that the charge of Barbarity would rather fall upon those who while they fancy themselves adorned with the Embellishments of foreign Learning are ignorant even to barbarity of the Faith, Religion, the Laws and Customs, and the Language of their Ancestors.'[1] 'But to leave these Pedagogues to huff and swagger in the heighth of their Arrogance,' she added, 'I cannot but think it great pity that in our consideration for The Refinement of the English tongue so little Regard is had to the Antiquity and the Original of our present Language.'[2] It was in a sense the reply of the twentieth century to the eighteenth in such matters, and if Elizabeth Elstob might fear that 'ill Treatment of our Mother Tongue has led me to a Stile not so agreeable to the Mildness of our Sex',[3] the work which she was performing was as useful as it was original. She knew, moreover, how to vary her invective with humour, as when she concluded her attack with the disarming plea:

> If any think fit to take up Arms against me, I have great confidence in the Protection of the Learned, the Candid, and the Noble; amongst which from as many as bear the Ensigns of St. George, I cannot doubt of that help that true Chevalrie can afford to any Damsel in Distress, by cutting off the Heads of all those Dragons that dare but to open their Mouths or begin to hiss against her.[4]

The 'Damsel in Distress' was in truth a formidable opponent. And Elizabeth Elstob took her full share in vindicating the new Saxon studies against interested opponents, and in making them known to a far wider public than that to which the scholars themselves in the first instance had appealed.

---

[1] *English-Saxon Homily*, p. vi.   [2] *Rudiments of Grammar*, p. ix.
[3] Ibid., p. ix.   [4] Ibid., p. xxxiv.

It was however not enough for her thus to inculcate an interest in Old English history among those who might even be ignorant of Latin, or to withstand the onslaughts of a 'polite' prejudice. The barriers of sex had themselves if possible to be broken down, and Anglo-Saxon learning introduced to the women of England. At the age of eight she had encountered the exasperation of a guardian who protested that 'surely one tongue was enough for a woman',[1] and in her maturity she returned to the charge. 'It will be said', she wrote, 'what has a Woman to do with Learning? This I have known urged by some Men with an Envy unbecoming that Greatness of Soul which is said to dignify their Sex.'[2] She thus proceeded to a general claim for woman's share in medieval scholarship, and here again she seems to speak more for the twentieth century than for her own. For she battled against an intractable opposition which considered that such education for women would 'make them Impertinent and neglect their household Affairs'. 'Perhaps', however, she added, 'these persons mean no more than that it makes them neglect long sittings at Play or tedious Dressings and visiting Days', which are enjoyed by those 'who despairing to arrive at any laudable degree of Knowledge seem totally to abandon themselves to Ignorance contenting themselves to sit down in Darkness as if they had not Reason'.[3] A lady who had herself won high distinction in a difficult branch of scholarship could yield to such impatience without loss of dignity; and while there is no need to exaggerate the originality of the particular opinions here expressed, Elizabeth Elstob must none the less be regarded as a pioneer in the plea that historical scholarship should not be confined to men.

The need for propagandist work such as Elizabeth Elstob undertook was well illustrated in the melancholy story of her later life. For she lived on into an age which had become a stranger to her enthusiasms, and in consequence she was left to experience for forty years the afflictions of sordid poverty. 'Being shocked by the cold respect of some and the haughty scorn of others', she strove to make a living by starting a dames' school at Evesham.[4] Its failure was perhaps inevitable; but there was perhaps something shameful in mid-eighteenth-century society which forced this woman to apologize: 'There are some things to be taught in such a school which I cannot pretend to; I mean the two accomplishments of spinning and knitting. Not that I would be thought to be above doing any commendable work proper to my sex. And as

[1] NICHOLS: Literary Anecdotes, IV, p. 128.
[2] English-Saxon Homily, p. ii.
[3] Ibid., p. iii; cf. Rudiments of Grammar, p. ii.
[4] TINDAL: Antiquities of Evesham (1794), pp. 276-277.

an instance of the truth of this the gown I had on when you gave me the favour of a visit was part of it my own spinning, and I wear no other stockings but what I knit myself.'[1] At all events contemporary cynicism swallowed the easy bait: 'She was a northern lady of an ancient family and a genteel fortune; but she pursued too much the drug called learning and in that pursuit failed of being careful of any one thing necessary.'[2] An elegiac note appeared inevitably in the remarks of her remaining admirers. 'We visited her in her sleeping room surrounded by books and dirtiness. But if any one desires to see her as she was they may view her portraiture in the initial G. of the English-Saxon homily.' A youthful and buxom face smiles somewhat complacently out of a severe framework of Anglo-Saxon type – Elizabeth Elstob, once 'the favourite of Dr. Hudson and the Oxonians'.[3]

The strange career of Elizabeth Elstob was in fact symbolical of the conscious effort which, during the early years of the eighteenth century, was made to render available to a wider public the results of the Saxon research so assiduously cultivated at Oxford, and to make certain that its value would be appreciated by the nation at large. Others took part in this endeavour, and the fine preface which in 1714 John Fortescue-Aland added to his ancestor's work on the *Difference between a Limited and an Absolute Monarchy* was in itself a notable defence of Anglo-Saxon learning. In a world in which the canons of scholarly criticism and the demands of public taste were both rapidly changing, propaganda of this nature was necessary and valuable. But, in general, the scholars were themselves the best apologists for their subject, and the dissemination of their teaching derived from its own inherent fertility. The full achievement of the Oxford Saxonists was not made possible, nor was its abiding influence assured, until Hickes began to gather his followers from all over England to lead them to their astonishing performance, and Humphrey Wanley carried his genius for the study of manuscripts from Oxford to London, and from the Bodleian into the houses of the Great.

[1] E. Elstob to George Ballard, March 7th, 1734/5 (NICHOLS: *Literary Anecdotes*, IV, p. 139).
[2] *William and Elizabeth Elstob, the Learned Saxonists* in *Reprints of Rare Tracts* (ed. M. A. Richardson, Newcastle upon Tyne, 1847), vol. I, p. 73.
[3] ROWE MORES: *Typographical Founders* (1778), p. 30.

CHAPTER IV

GEORGE HICKES

GEORGE HICKES, who was born at Moorhouse Farm near Kirby Wiske in Yorkshire in 1642, and who died in 1715, was probably the most remarkable figure among the English historical scholars of his time, and certainly no other member of that very distinguished company exercised a learned influence which was more potent or more widely spread. It was not merely that his erudition, in its profundity and scope, was a wonder to his contemporaries. It was also that his stormy life was itself so dramatic in its misfortunes, and so steadfast in its purpose that it attracted to him an attention which might otherwise never have been his. The authority of Hickes over his fellow-scholars was pervasive, but it derived from his character as well as from his learning. And the courage which he displayed in adversity must also be held to explain the astonishing fact that among the historical scholars of this age, it was this persecuted ecclesiastic who, as a pro-scribed rebel and as a hunted fugitive, exercised over them all for a quarter of a century an hegemony which was none the less real because it was unofficial.

The quality of this extraordinary man might be guessed from a glance at the remarkable portrait which adorns his greatest work. A face of pronounced features confronts the world with resolution, and whilst the direct gaze bespeaks an uncompromising courage, the compressed mouth, set in a straight line, betokens determination and even obstinacy. The eyes display a stern intrepidity not devoid of harshness, but with a hint that on occasion they might soften into sympathy. The whole countenance suggests a man who, fully conscious of his own worth, is so mindful of the value of his own convictions as to be proof against both criticism and applause. He radiates the strength of leadership and something of its loneliness. He repels an easy familiarity, and the detachment of his forceful isolation has so survived his death that even now he is difficult to approach. Despite his scholarly importance, despite even the dramatic epic of his career, he still lacks a biographer.

This neglect may be partly attributed to the fact that the technical scholarship of Hickes was both in form and matter hard to master, and partly to his extreme versatility. He wrote on so many subjects with a uniform depth of erudition that no single critic has found it possible to survey the total product of his pen without serious misgiving. There is perhaps, even to-day, no scholar who could for example appraise the treatise in which Hickes ransacked the Greek and Latin Fathers to vindicate the 'Dignity of the Episcopal Order', and then turn with an equal confidence to criticize the huge folios of the 'Treasury of the Northern Tongues'. Even if but one aspect of his work is considered – his medieval erudition – a similar difficulty is experienced, for he possessed to a marked degree the qualities which remove him furthest from the atmosphere of modern scholarship. He belonged in a sense to an age earlier than that in which he lived, since his mind, encyclopedic in its range, refused to specialize and so entangled his learning with his life, that it is difficult to regard him solely as an historian or philologist, or solely as a divine. 'The Letters which passed between Hickes and a Popish Priest' are, for example, redolent of outworn controversy, but they include fifty-six not unimportant pages of Anglo-Saxon print, and it was characteristic of Hickes that he should study the fate of a Theban legion in connection with the problems of the English Revolution. To superficial critics such a habit of mind has seemed to imply in Hickes a doctrinaire inability to cope with practical life. But the man who barely escaped murder by Scottish rebels in 1679, who contemplated a brother's execution in 1690, and who for long years after led a proscribed party against the State cannot be judged as an academic recluse. Hickes's historical scholarship, technical in its character and objective in its results, was intertwined with a life as adventurous as that of any of his more mundane fellows.[1]

There was little in his early career to suggest more than the rapid rise of an industrious youth of ability who won his way from a Yorkshire farm-house to a distinguished position in the south. Hickes came of yeoman stock, and if perhaps he owed his tenacity to his north-country parentage, he derived his monarchical principles in the first instance from Thomas Smelt, an alcoholic schoolmaster of charm and genius, who sent many of his pupils from Northallerton into the paths of eminence. His career, however, Hickes fashioned for himself. It was intended that he should enter commerce and he was actually apprenticed to a merchant in Plymouth. But his literary promise at seventeen was already so great that interested friends urged that he should go to

[1] WOOD: *Ath. Oxon.*, IV, col. 565; T. D. WHITAKER: *Richmondshire*, I, pp. 290-294: OVERTON: *Non-Jurors*, pp. 91-112; J. KETTLEWELL: *Works* (1719), vol. I, *passim*; MAYOR: *Cambridge under Queen Anne*, p. 445; MACAULAY: *History of England*, chap. XIV.

Oxford. In 1659 therefore he arrived at St. John's, still recalcitrant in his royalist sympathies and greedy for study. The Restoration gave to such a youth his opportunities. He became Fellow of Lincoln in 1664, and after a short tour on the continent with one of his pupils in 1673, he was appointed, three years later, as Lauderdale's chaplain in Scotland where he had full scope for denouncing the Presbyterian opposition. He became a Doctor of Divinity of St. Andrews in 1679, and after his return to England in the same year it was almost inevitable that promotions should come to him in quick succession. By 1683 he was established as Dean of Worcester, and it was widely felt that a man of such principles and of such ability might aspire to the highest ecclesiastical honours.[1]

Before the death of Charles II, Hickes was thus well launched on the familiar and prosperous career of a successful cleric with high-church views. He had already poured out a stream of tracts on the favourite theme of passive obedience whereby might be displayed 'the Harmony of Divinity and Law about not resisting Sovereign Princes'. The type was recognized; Authority smiled; and the door of advancement opened wide on a prospect of commonplace distinction. But already a shrewd observer might have discerned something exceptional, something perhaps disquieting, in this sombre Yorkshireman heavily presiding over his west-country Chapter. A hard vein of resistance had already begun to show. The royalist undergraduate at Presbyterian St. John's in 1659 had confronted his seniors with a refusal to take sermon notes or to 'frequent the meetings of the young scholars for spiritual exercises'. The chaplain of Lauderdale had declined to take office until he had been satisfied that the Duke's moral character had been unduly aspersed. His party was now triumphant in the State; devotion to his principles demanded rejoicing; but even so compliance seems to have come almost hardly to the Dean of Worcester. After 1685 the new King himself seems to have discovered an unwelcome capacity for independence in this favoured prelate, for 'as soon as Dr. Hickes's *Jovian* came out it pleased King James very well . . . but soon after he showed some dissatisfaction upon account of the doctor's having asserted that 'tis lawful for the Subjects to say anything in opposition to an arbitrary prince tho' not justifyable to take up Arms against him'. The royal misgivings about the man, who was later to give up everything for James II, were fully justified. Hickes became one of the most prominent Anglican opponents of the Declaration of Indulgence, and when in 1687 the illness of Bishop Thomas of Worcester threatened a

[1] KETTLEWELL: op. cit., I, pp. 4-6; *Portland MSS. Rep.*, IV, pp. 37-41.

vacancy in the See, Hickes publicly declared that, were a Romanizing prelate to be nominated by the Court, he would endure any penalty rather than summon the Chapter to elect.[1]

The principles of Hickes were those of the majority of the Seven Bishops, and he shared their perplexity in seeking to reconcile his loyalty to the Anglican Church with a sanctified allegiance to the Catholic king who was attempting to subvert its constitution. But, even in such company, Hickes was exceptional in the extent to which the passionate rigidity of his convictions transformed every one of the political crises of these years into a personal torment which raised up a spiritual conflict within him, and bitterly annealed a character that was by nature unyielding. Torn by the rival claims of opposing loyalties, the year 1685 in particular subjected him to an ordeal that left an enduring mark upon him. His elder brother, John, who was already identified with western non-conformity, pushed his resistance to the point of rebellion and came to ruin with Monmouth, bringing down Alice Lisle with him in a common destruction. In the Dean of Worcester this set up an uncompromising struggle of deciding between a deep natural affection and an unflinching conception of moral justice. By all his deepest beliefs his brother had committed not only a capital offence against the State but also a deadly sin against God. Even the intercession which he was constrained to make must have appeared a condonation of evil. 'My brother', wrote John from prison, 'went to London to try what could be done for me.' But the concession to affection was in vain, and George Hickes returned to Worcester to overcome his outraged sorrow in the justice of cold condemnation. Two days after the execution he wrote as a priest dealing with a soul in peril. 'I pray you to let me know', he asked, 'whether he left any message to his children that they should live in the communion of our Church, and whether he desired and received the holy sacrament, and, if not, whether he refused it or it was refused to him as might justly have been done to a man persisting in schisme ... and if he acknowledged his punishment to be the righteous punishment of God for the sin of rebellion.' The tone of this letter – it has been noted – 'may seem somewhat hard', but anyone who can find the phrases facile must be strangely lacking in imagination. They were the tragic utterance of a strong man subordinating deep personal feelings to the hard demands of rectitude, and it was scarcely surprising that there was afterwards observed 'in the countenance of his portrait an harshness and

---

[1] HEARNE: *Collections*, I, pp. 211, 268; *Orthodox Churchman's Magazine* (1802), vol. II, p. 321; *Life and Character of Nathaniel, Lord Crewe* (1790).

GEORGE HICKES

Drawn from life by Robert White in 1703, and engraved by him.

acerbity of expression which indicate no very amiable disposition within'.[1]

This personal disaster magnified the sacrifice made by Hickes in giving up everything for the King who had executed his brother. He was no sycophant, and for the sake of the Church he had pushed passive resistance to its limits. But he would not violate allegiance or condone usurpation. Consequently, after the Revolution, he did not hesitate to refuse the oath of William, and without alarm he awaited the inevitable penalties of obduracy. When his deposition was announced, and his successor appointed, he saw fit once more to give the whole world the assurance of his indomitable independence. As the populace of Worcester assembled for morning prayer on May 2nd, 1690, they were confronted with a strange document nailed securely to the choir gates of their cathedral:

Whereas the Office, Place and Dignity of Dean of this Cathedral Church of Worcester was given and granted unto me for a Freehold during my Natural Life by Letters Patent under the Broad Seal of King Charles II of happy memory who had an undoubted Right to confer the same . . .

And whereas I George Hickes . . . have for several Years peaceably enjoyed the same . . .

And whereas I am given to understand that my Right to the said Office and Dignity has of late been called in question, and that one Mr. Talbot M.A. pretends a Title to the same . . .

Now know ye therefore, and every one of you,

That I the said George Hickes . . . do hereby publickly PROTEST and declare, that I do claim Legal Right and Title to the said Office and Dignity of Dean – and that I am not conscious of any Act or Misdemeanor the Conviction whereof, if any such were, should or can determine my said Right; but do conceive that I was, and still do continue, the only Rightful and Legal Dean of this Cathedral Church of Worcester; and that I do not any way relinquish my said Title, but shall, God willing, use all just Means which the Laws of this Realm allow for the Preservation and Recovery thereof . . .[2]

Such a challenge could not be ignored by the Government. Before nightfall Hickes was a hunted fugitive in peril of death.

The crises in the personal career of Hickes take on so much of the character of a tragic sequence that in contemplating them it is easy to forget that this man, as he battled with inexorable circumstance, was at the same time laying the foundations of an erudition scarcely sur-

---

[1] *Eng. Hist. Review* (1887), p. 752; *Western Martyrology* (1705), pp. 190 *sqq.*; OVERTON: op. cit., p. 98; WHITAKER: *Richmondshire*, p. 294.
[2] KETTLEWELL: op. cit., I, p. iii; cf. *Bodleian Letters*, I, p. 69.

passed in Europe. His theology was based upon a wide and detailed use of Patristic literature; he was well acquainted with Hebrew; and after his appointment at Worcester he had, at the King's suggestion, plunged into a study of the Patent Rolls. He had also become famous as a prolific, forceful and weighty controversialist against both Puritans and Papists. But his main interests, apart from religion, were beginning to centre in those Old English studies to which he had been introduced by Marshall in his Oxford days. In 1689 he published the first Anglo-Saxon grammar, and dedicated it characteristically to the deposed Sancroft.[1] It was not however until after his personal ruin in 1690 that he began to prosecute these investigations with such unexampled vigour that he was at last after many years to produce the work which entitled him to an honoured place among any company of English scholars.

The life of Hickes during the nine years which elapsed between his flight from Worcester and the withdrawal of the proceedings against him by Lord Chancellor Somers in 1699, displayed to the full his energy and courage. It was his intrepid determination that, in circumstances of utter adversity, set him apart from his fellows and placed him in the forefront of every cause of scholarship or politics with which he was connected. This was the period when Hickes became a 'Bishop' of the Non-jurors, and conducted their negotiations with the exiled James; but it was during these same years that by the force of his zealous learning he became pre-eminent in those linguistic studies for which the Oxford school was already famous. The ardour of the research which led to this achievement, and the labours which it entailed, would be wellnigh incredible in a man not otherwise occupied, and assured of tranquillity. But the investigations which were later to produce the most elaborate treatise of historical philology that was ever devoted to the Anglo-Saxon language, were carried on by a political refugee busy with the constant preparation of pamphlets, and risking his neck in negotiations with a deposed prince.[2]

Obscurity naturally descends upon Hickes during the time when he was persecuted. But occasionally the curtain lifts upon perhaps the strangest conditions under which an epoch-making work of technical scholarship was ever produced. Shortly after his departure from Worcester, Hickes was to be found at the house of White Kennett, then Vicar of Ambrosden, 'where he wore a Lay-Habit and affected to be unknown till a Fellow of a College in *Oxford* coming over and

---

[1] HICKES: *Institutiones Grammaticae Anglo-Saxonicae et Maeso-Gothicae* (1689); HEARNE: *Collections*, VI, p. 264.
[2] HICKES: *Records of the New Consecrations*, Introduction; OVERTON: op. cit., p. 84.

calling the Doctor by his Name he thought there was a Danger in staying and so he went off immediately to some more obscure retreat'.[1] Perhaps this was the home of William Brome of Hereford where he stayed for more than a year, so that his host ever afterwards thought of this time 'as the best part of his Life'.[2] But he passed on from there, doubtless under duress, and in the summer of 1695 he was with Francis Cherry of Shottesbrook, the Non-juring patron of Hearne. There 'he went under the name of Dr. Smith being forced to disguise himself', and he 'used to take great delight in walking upon Mr. Cherry's *terras* and meditating there by himself'. But this also was a brief respite; for 'it being at length understood that the Dr. was at Mr. Cherry's, the house was one night beset on purpose to apprehend him, but he got out at a back door, passed through the Gardens into the Church-Yard and escaped safe to Bagshot'. There too it was the same story: while he was deep in his studies the house was suddenly surrounded by a mob that had heard of an alleged plot against King William, and once again Hickes was compelled to take refuge in precipitate flight, after which 'falling into a long sickness he remained unsettled for some months'.[3] These were the conditions in which the immense contribution of Hickes to scholarship was confidently made.

He was of the stuff of the martyrs. Conscious in 1696 – and not without reason – of the uncertainty of life, he solemnly declared: 'I bless God who gave me courage and constancy to refuse the oath, making me to stand in the time of Trial when so many others to my astonishment fell . . . thinking me worthy to suffer in so righteous a cause as that under which I have been engaged.' Conscientious, almost to the point of fanaticism, he carried into his controversies a crusader's zeal. To his opponents he appeared a bigot, but to his friends the consistent champion of principles from the support of which no earthly power could make him flinch. Refluent as water within him, the twin passions of his life met and merged, and he pursued the long pathway of his erudition with the same inexhaustible energy that controlled his conduct in political adversity. He struck hard and suffered much, for, without pliancy, he led a lost cause against men who were ready to forgive but could not afford to condone. His tenacity excites admiration, but he lacked the statesmanship of the trimmer. Such was his hardness of belief that 'nothing could teach him moderation'.[4]

Nevertheless, it would be easy to sketch in too rigid outlines the por-

[1] *Life of Kennett* (1730), pp. 12-14; cf. HICKES: *Thesaurus*, Preface to Ottley, p. xlv.
[2] HEARNE: *Collections*, VIII, p. 211.
[3] Ibid., X, p. 237.
[4] OVERTON: op. cit., p. 102; Noble's Grainger, I, p. 120.

trait of a man whose character was the reserve of simple. Hickes was too large minded to harbour petty animosities, and the universality of his vast learning itself implied a liberality of soul that sometimes seemed to be in odd contrast to the rigour of his constant struggles. In particular, the 'republic of letters' was for him a living state, and unlike many of his contemporaries he did not allow his political principles to warp his judgment of fellow scholars, or to interfere with his generous contributions to the labours of others. As time went on, this proscript took his place ever more notably as the leader of English linguistic studies in a manner that would have been impossible to a narrow partisan. The encouragement which he gave to lesser men appeared remarkably in comments scattered through the correspondence of the age. Thus Wanley laconically noted how one scholar was 'set on' by Hickes to work at Alfred's version of Orosius,[1] and in July 1705 Hickes 'communicated' to another 'a folio book in French containing the History of the Deposition of Richard the Second', whilst on December 5th, 1711, yet a third 'came to the Bodleian on purpose to look over Junius's MSS., he having had a letter from Dr. Hickes (whose Advice he asked about the Matter) that an edition of Chaucer was there in great Measure done to his Hands'.[2] But these were themselves Non-jurors, and the character of Hickes's beneficence was perhaps better illustrated in his treatment of Ralph Thoresby the Dissenter who broke into prim phrases of gratitude to the man who 'having courteously perused several sheets of my manuscript Topography obliged me with variety of readings from some rare Dano-Saxon authors'.[3] The work of Elizabeth Elstob was similarly derived from his 'ample encouragement' and she rightly gave him thanks for his 'great Assistance'.[4] The sympathy expressed by Hickes even for foreign scholars of opposed opinions showed that his erudite appreciation could transcend the limitations of nationality,[5] and his praise of the work of political opponents aroused the displeasure of some of his own friends who thought it 'a Piece of Indiscretion to cringe to low Fanatical Fellows', and insinuated that Hickes's judgments in this respect were 'very often wrong'.[6]

The quality of his influence on the contemporary world of scholarship was as remarkable as its strength, for whilst his relations with lesser known men were always stimulating and exacting, they were

---

[1] Wanley's Diary (Lansdowne MS. 771, fol. 5b).
[2] HEARNE: Collections, I, p. 6; III, p. 273.
[3] THORESBY: Diary, II, p. 32. Cf. I, p. 343; II, p. 23; HEARNE: Collections, v, p. 88.
[4] E. ELSTOB: Rudiments of Grammar (1715), p. xxxv; Portland MSS. Rep., v, pp. 445, 451.
[5] HEARNE: Collections, III, p. 384; v, p. 196.   [6] Ibid., II, p. 334.

also normally benevolent. He seems indeed to have regarded the maintenance of such connections as an important duty to be performed despite the special difficulties it entailed. 'Though I thank God,' he wrote
to one of these students, 'the change in my fortune is no trouble to me
upon my own account, yet it is often a great trouble to me to reflect
that I am incapacitated by it to help my friends.' But the assistance was
none the less vigorous and constant. 'I give you hearty thanks,' wrote
Hickes to another in 1699, 'for your good intentions of adorning my
book . . . You shall have all the credit without arrogating anything to
myself of all you do, and my book shall do you I hope much credit as
well as justice . . . I am now in the chapter *De Dialecto Normannico-
Saxonico* which furnishes me with pleasant theories about the alteration
of the Saxon upon the Norman Conquest and particularly of the
change of the *Manus Saxonica*, as Ingulf calls it, into the *Manus Gallica*.
This makes me resolve to give the world a specimen of the many
Gallica out of Domesday Book and the red book of the Chequer. I
know you have them in your book of alphabets and if you will let me
have them described by your hand, you will oblige me and give me
the best opportunity of recommending you and your work to our
great men, and do what is acceptable to all Learned Men.' Such an
association must have been in the highest degree advantageous to a
rising scholar, and the interest of Hickes in the men who were following his leadership sometimes stretched into the most intimate personal
details of their lives to become almost paternal in its tone. When a
young gentleman of University College contemplated matrimony,
Dr. Hickes seemed the most proper person to consult, and the reply
sent without delay was characteristic: 'As marriage is of divine institution and honourable upon the account both of its author and its end, so
I have always observed the blessing of God to attend it when it was
undertaken considerably and in the fear of God . . . The married state
I am sure does not hinder but promote studies. And since you have so
discouraging a prospect at Oxford, go in God's name to gain your
virtuous Cosin's affection for you may live upon her fortune independent of any man . . . I beg you to send me a copy of your specimen of
Domesday Book.' The encouragement of research could hardly go
further; but the lady's comments upon the letter are unknown.[1]

To this constant solicitude many young men who were later to
achieve great eminence in scholarship owed a heavy debt. In the early
grammar which he published in 1689 he took pains to address 'our
young gentry who adorn the Inns of Court', and hoped 'that if pos-

[1] Harl. MS. 3779, fols. 79, 82b, 83, 84.

sible they would not spare their pains to learn the Saxon tongue and
run over the many monuments of venerable Antiquity in that language and character – the peculiar treasure of the Nation'. But though
such exhortations may have had an effect on rising young lawyers,
who, like John Fortescue-Aland,[1] were afterwards to prosecute their
studies in Old English antiquities, it was mainly to professed scholars of
the younger generation that Hickes directed his attention. Thus he not
only appreciated the character of Hearne but also was among the first
to realize wherein lay the true greatness of that self-centred eccentric
who was even then starting his stormy career at Oxford. 'Dr. Hickes',
remarked Hearne, 'was for having me print what MSS. I could in my
Life Time and to leave Improvements to others.'[2] The advice was
notable, for Hearne was to win the gratitude of scholars, not for his
critical opinions which were often childish, but for the fine accuracy of
his numerous editions,[3] and he owed much to the older scholar who,
with discrimination and constant sympathy, encouraged him, despite
ridicule, to continue the work for which he was best fitted. Nor was
even this the most productive example of Hickes's care for the interests
of younger scholars. Humphrey Wanley himself was to owe more to
Hickes than to any other man,[4] and he was so nobly to repay the debt
that the association between them was to prove a partnership in learning comparable in its results to that between Dodsworth and Dugdale.
Wanley was later to become perhaps the greatest critic of medieval
manuscripts that England has ever known, and he was to instruct even
his preceptor. But some of the credit of his astonishing performance
must be attributed to the older scholar who fostered his early career by
constant and firm direction. In the achievements of Wanley may be
seen perhaps the greatest reflection of the stimulating force of Hickes.

The remarkable career, and the still more remarkable character, of
George Hickes gave him an extraordinary influence, and by the last
decade of the seventeenth century the work of all the other members
of the Oxford school was becoming more and more closely related to
his. Hickes's grammar of 1689 had shown the direction in which his
research was moving, and it was well known that under the greatest
difficulties he was pursuing his investigations so that a much larger
book was now eagerly awaited by interested scholars.[5] In October 1698

---

[1] HICKES: *Institutiones Grammaticae*, Introduction; FORTESCUE-ALAND: *Monarchy*, p. lxxx.
[2] HEARNE: *Collections*, VIII, p. 21; cf. ibid., V, pp. 52, 53, 62, 138; *Bodleian Letters*, II, p. 1.
[3] See below, chap. ix.   [4] See below, chap. v.
[5] On the details of the production of the *Linguarum Veterum Septentrionalium Thesaurus*,
the reader may now be referred to the admirable essay by J. A. W. BENNET: 'Hickes's
"Thesaurus": a study in Oxford Book Production' (*English Studies* – 1948 – pp. 28–45).

William Nicolson remarked that 'the Doctor meets with far more encouragement than his own circumstances and those of the times seemed to allow him to hope for', and subscriptions came in from unexpected quarters. By November, Gibson declared that he had actually seen in print fifteen sheets of the book which was to be 'a very beautiful folio', and a little later he gleefully announced that it would be 'as much a book of criticisms as grammar rules', and so 'would give us insight into many customs etc. about which we were wholly in the dark before'.[1]

The folio volume of which fifty-four sheets were actually in print in 1699 did not appear as Nicolson hoped in the spring of that year. Two years later Hickes was still carrying on the work in an atmosphere of eager anticipation. 'I am really afraid to go into company,' he declared, 'I am so catechized everywhere about my book.' The delay was easily explicable. As the work proceeded its scope widened until it came to be regarded not only as the major project of Hickes but almost as the corporate undertaking of the school which acknowledged his leadership. The 'Saxonists' one after another were drawn into its orbit. William Elstob supplied a Latin translation of the Saxon homily of Wulfstan, and William Hopkins, Prebendary of Worcester, sent an annotated Anglo-Saxon commentary on saints buried in England. Edmund Gibson contributed a transcript of the laws of Ethelbert, Hlothere and Edric, and William Nicolson gave his continuous advice. Bartholomew Shower, the vigorous High Tory Recorder of London,

> reputed long
> For strength of lungs and pliancy of tongue,

gave the undertaking his steady support, and others helped in a material manner. Adam Ottley, Canon of Hereford and later Bishop of St. David's, provided financial assistance, the Dean and Chapter of Durham sent a gift of twenty pounds, and Oxford University lent their famous Junian types which were here used with perhaps their greatest effect.[2]

Of all Hickes's collaborators three need a special mention. 'I think I formerly told you', wrote Hickes to Thoresby in 1703, 'that the Numismatica Saxonica would be one part of my great work . . . The gentleman that undertook that part is very fit for it being as otherwise a general scholar, so particularly a great nummist.' The connection was strange, for the reference was to Sir Andrew Fountaine who was above all else a virtuoso living in a world of metropolitan 'politeness' far

[1] THORESBY: *Correspondence*, I, pp. 331, 332, 340.

[2] ELLIS: *Letters of Eminent Literary Men*, p. 283; THORESBY: *Correspondence*, I, pp. 331, 348; HICKES: *Thesaurus*, Preface to Ottley, p. iv; Harl. MS. 3779, fol. 155; GARTH: *Dispensary*.

removed from the temper of Hickes or the Saxonists with whom he worked. Nevertheless, Fountaine,[1] the intimate of Addison who could 'pun scurvily' with Swift, and correct the designs for the *Tale of a Tub*, was stimulated by Hickes into constructing an illustrated catalogue of Anglo-Saxon coins, and by his social connections both at home and abroad he brought the whole undertaking to the notice of men who might otherwise have been indifferent to it.[2] Far more valuable in its results was the co-operation of Thwaites, who with the generosity which characterized his whole career, 'being zealous that the *Thesaurus* might at last come abroad perfect, used his utmost Application in revising and correcting with constant Care and Pains the Sheets as well before they went to the Press as while they were in it'. Hickes himself 'gratefully acknowledged' that Thwaites, *auctoris adjutor maximus*, 'had a very great hand' in the final production.[3] Lastly Humphrey Wanley was to add to the work a large critical catalogue of manuscripts which, occupying near a whole folio of print, is probably to-day the most valuable section of the book. It must however be regarded in the first instance as the most remarkable achievement in its author's own career as a scholar.[4]

In 1703 the work upon which so much scattered labour had been expended began at last to appear, in huge folio volumes, under the forbidding title of *Linguarum Veterum Septentrionalium Thesaurus* – the 'Treasury of the Northern Tongues'.[5] It was a book (as was remarked

[1] His own copy of the *Thesaurus* is a large paper one having emblazoned on its spine the elephants noted by De Ricci (*English Collectors of Books and Manuscripts*, p. 42) as being characteristic of his books.
[2] *Thesaurus*, loc. cit.; THORESBY: *Correspondence*, II, p. 36; Leibnitz to Fountaine (SHELTON: *Short View*, pp. 89, 90, 115, 116); *Bodleian Letters*, I, p. 266.
[3] *Thesaurus*, Preface to Ottley, pp. iv, vii; SHELTON: *Short View*, p. 6; HEARNE: *Collections*, X, p. 317; NICHOLS: *Literary Anecdotes*, IV, p. 147.
[4] See below, chap. v.
[5] It is an inchoate book whose arrangement subsequent binders have sometimes further confused. The main headings of the *Thesaurus* in the order in which they are usually bound are as follows:

Vol. I.	1. Dedication
	2. General Preface addressed to Adam Ottley, pp. l-lxviii
	3. Anglo-Saxon Grammar (with a special Preface to John Pakinton), pp. 1-239
	4. Frankish Grammar (with a special Preface to William Nicolson), pp. I-III
	5. Icelandic Grammar, pp. 1-91
Vol. II.	Sive De Linguarum Veterum Septentrionalium Usu Dissertatio Epistolaris)
	1. Prefatory Letter to Charlwood Lawton
	2. Dissertatio Epistolaris (addressed to Bartholomew Shower), pp. 1-161
	3. Appendix on Coins by Andrew Fountaine
Vol. III.	(Liber Alter seu Hunfredi Wanleii Catalogus Historico-Criticus)
	1. Preface to Robert Harley
	2. Wanley's Catalogue of Anglo-Saxon Manuscripts
	3. Sundry Appendices by e.g. Peringskiöld
	4. Brome's Indexes to the whole *Thesaurus*

in 1708) 'to which the learned world never yet saw anything like or comparable in this kind of literature'.[1] And if by its very size it repelled a facile perusal, nevertheless it cannot be regarded (even to-day) as in any sense merely a literary curiosity. In two branches of Anglo-Saxon scholarship – the linguistic and the historical – this 'elaborate and incomparable treatise' marked an epoch. Joseph Ritson, the great eighteenth-century critic, was right in declaring that the *Thesaurus* 'never had nor will have its equal'.[2]

The book was in the first instance a study of comparative philology, seeking not only to elucidate the Anglo-Saxon language but also to place it in its proper setting among kindred tongues. 'Since men of all Nations', wrote Hickes, 'naturally love their own Native Languages and endeavour eagerly to fetch them from their originals, and to search out the Etymologies of Words which after many attempts they have learnt at last to speak, the knowledge of the old Northern Tongues is not only useful but necessary.'[3] The first volume therefore began with an enlarged reissue of the grammar which Hickes had published in 1689, proceeded to a comprehensive grammar of Frankish, and concluded with an edition of the Icelandic grammar of Runolph Jonas. The bare enumeration of these sections gives no indication of their erudition. This book embraced all the dialects of the old Teutonic stock, each of which had hitherto afforded sufficient occupation for its own national grammarians and antiquaries.[4] The labour of collecting the materials was itself immense, and Hickes made himself acquainted with almost every Teutonic manuscript in northern Europe. 'The force of learning', remarks Dr. Nicol Smith, 'could no further go.'[5] After the *Thesaurus*, Anglo-Saxon studies were to make no appreciable advance until the development of the new philology in the nineteenth century.

Since Hickes was undoubtedly the most powerful influence on Old English scholarship during a fruitful period in its growth, and since his own grammatical work remained a pattern for more than a century after his death,[6] it is of interest to learn the course of reading which he

---

[1] W. WOTTON: *Brevis Conspectus* (1708), Preface.
[2] RITSON: *Observations* (1782), p. 48; cf. D. N. SMITH: *Warton's History of English Poetry* (1929), p. 8; SHELTON: *Short View*, dedication.
[3] HICKES: *Thesaurus Diss. Ep.*, p. 148 (trans.).
[4] WHITAKER: *Richmondshire*, I, pp. 292-294.
[5] D. N. SMITH: op. cit., p. 8.
[6] His one violent critic was Samuel Henshall whose own 'ignorance and self-conceit' were exposed by Richard Gough. Henshall in 1798 'relying little on his own knowledge but confident in the errors of his opponents' attacked Hickes in company with 'many Antiquaries, Blackstonians, Electioneering Oxonians . . . and other herds of animal that follow their leader's tail'. His strictures need not be taken seriously (HENSHALL: *Saxon and*

prescribed for any student of Anglo-Saxon. First, the Saxon grammar itself was to be read, and afterwards the Old English gospels as presented by Marshall, and the *Heptateuchus* as edited by Thwaites. Ælfric's Easter homily and his Discourse on the Old and New Testaments were to follow, and the learner was then to proceed with the Saxon Bede. These books were to be supplemented by Wheloc's edition of the Laws. Even this was not all, for it was the essence of Hickes's teaching that Anglo-Saxon was not a language to be studied in isolation. A knowledge of the *Heimskringla* and of the Icelandic *Edda* must therefore be added before the student could consider that he had covered the groundwork of his subject. Then, and only then, would 'all Things in the Northern Monuments be made plain and manageable'.[1]

The two years which were allotted for this preliminary study[2] seem scarcely adequate, and in truth the grammars as presented in the *Thesaurus* have never offered an easy road to students in a hurry. They were moreover based upon a linguistic criticism which was later to be discarded, so that it became easy for subsequent scholars to excuse their neglect of a difficult book. But there can be little doubt, that even in this field, nineteenth-century scholarship would itself have been more productive if the labours of Hickes had been properly utilized. J. M. Kemble, perhaps the greatest of Victorian 'Saxonists', termed the grammatical work of his predecessor 'a miracle of mistaken energy and learning', but he was fully aware of the true greatness of Hickes. 'Though modern attention', he wrote, 'has detected so many errors as to render his Grammars rather dangerous than useful, we owe to him great and hearty thanks for his labours. The enthusiasm which he brought to his task spread far beyond himself; a host of Saxon students rose around him, and his Grammar answered all the needs of which they were conscious.'[3]

Despite their discursive erudition, the Grammars in the *Thesaurus* are probably the least valuable section of that monumental book. The 'Treasury of the Northern Tongues' was a cardinal work not only on Old English philology but also on Old English history. Hickes brought his study of language to bear upon every department of Anglo-Saxon

English Languages, p. 1; *Gentleman's Magazine*, vol. LXVIII, pt. 2, pp. 861-865). Large paper copies of the *Thesaurus* have always been a prize for collectors (see *Bodleian Letters*, I, p. 267), as may be illustrated by the extensive correspondence on this subject between the fourth Viscount Charlemont and Malone towards the end of the eighteenth century (*Charlemont MSS. Rep.*, II, pp. 45, 52, 61).

[1] *Thesaurus*, Preface to Saxon Grammar *versus finem*.

[2] HEARNE: *Collections*, II, p. 248.

[3] J. M. KEMBLE: Letter to F. Michel in *Bibliotheque Anglo-Saxonne* (1837), p. 13; PETHERAM: op. cit., p. 83.

life and culture, and an improved mastery of Anglo-Saxon opened the
door to a fresh understanding of the whole Old English past. In the
Thesaurus the intimate connection between these branches of study was
worked out with an elaboration of learned detail in a wonderful preface
of forty-eight folio pages which Hickes addresses to his friend Adam
Ottley, Canon of Hereford. But the most remarkable exposition of the
theme was in the still longer treatise which in the same book Hickes
directed to Bartholomew Shower under the title of *Dissertatio Episto-
laris*. The *Dissertatio* was a monument of constructive research; it still
remains both stimulating and valuable; and by itself it would entitle
Hickes to a prominent place among the great English medievalists.

The treatise sought to expose the critical foundations of the study of
Old English antiquities. Since it combined an intensive investigation of
language with an exhaustive examination of the sources of Anglo-
Saxon history, it threw a flood of new light upon the materials themselves and upon the institutions which they illustrated. The learning of
the *Dissertatio* thus found expression not only in connection with its
main theme but also in numerous digressions which, even to-day, carry
the full weight of the magisterial scholarship that informed them. The
contributions thus made to knowledge are not to be assessed in a para-
graph. Even in its main arguments the scope of the treatise was comprehensive. It opened with an elaborate description of Anglo-Saxon
government in which for the first time the operations of the primitive
Teutonic courts in England were systematically discussed. It went on to
describe the basis and procedure of Anglo-Saxon law[1] in such a way
that if the evidence here amassed and correctly interpreted (for instance
on the origin of the jury)[2] had been properly studied some of the difficulties of nineteenth-century historians might have been removed. To
select from many topics, it was in this treatise that the proper study
of Teutonic names was inaugurated, and its value indicated for the
purposes of historical investigation.[3]

The main importance of the *Dissertatio* was in its treatment of Anglo-
Saxon charters as a fundamental source of Anglo-Saxon history. It was
only in 1681 that Mabillon had first issued his great book which laid the
foundation of the modern study of medieval charters, but Hickes had

[1] *Thesaurus: Diss. Ep.*, pp. 3-16.
[2] Ibid., pp. 33-44. Hickes rightly (p. 35) dissociated the jury from the usage described in
the Laws of Ethelred, and his conclusions (p. 41) harmonized with those elaborated later
by Brunner and Maitland: 'De origine et primordiis duodecemviralis judicii, apud
Anglos, quod a Nortmannis e Scandia potius quam a Saxonibus e Germania profectis
accersendum puto.'
[3] Ibid., pp. 23-29.

found time to master his teaching. In the *Dissertatio* he brought his linguistic knowledge to bear upon a new series of highly important texts. Every aspect of these charters was profitably discussed, their palaeography, their detailed structure, their form and their language; with the result that it began for the first time to be possible to set up standards of authenticity in respect of them. Very many of these instruments which had hitherto been accepted as genuine were now (like the famous series contained in the history of Crowland by the pseudo-Ingulf) rightly pronounced to be spurious. As time passed, students of Anglo-Saxon history came more and more to realize the importance of these charters as a prime object of their research, and J. M. Kemble was to inaugurate in the nineteenth century a new movement in their study. But it was Hickes who began the proper investigation of Anglo-Saxon charters, and, in collaboration with his pupil Wanley, he set subsequent research moving upon lines from which it has never profitably deviated. His linguistic knowledge coupled with his familiarity with all branches of Old English erudition enabled him confidently to apply tests which had before been unknown, and in consequence he succeeded in establishing canons of diplomatic criticism, in respect of these charters, which (speaking generally) have been accepted and developed by all those of his successors who were competent to carry on his work.[1]

The major portion of the *Thesaurus* thus contained the grammars, the preface to Ottley, the invaluable *Dissertatio*, and the much lauded treatise of Fountaine upon coins. The final volume of this vast undertaking – a catalogue of manuscripts – was mainly the work of Wanley, and it must therefore be discussed later as part of the accomplishment of that great scholar. Viewed as a unity the *Thesaurus* serves as an abiding memorial of the men who collaborated in its production – 'a Treasury which contains in itself all the Customs and Manners of our country, or will at least illustrate whatever is elsewhere contained in Books that have hitherto been scarce if at all understood'. The only danger was that this 'incomparable' work might be buried under its own weight, and, doubtless with this apprehension, Thwaites rounded off his own contribution to the great undertaking by extracting therefrom a smaller Anglo-Saxon grammar which he published in 1711 a few months before his death. Another epitome of less value had already been produced by William Wotton in 1708, and this book, which was stigmatized by Hearne as 'a trivial, mean Performance', derived some merit from the fact that it received the approval of Hickes himself who

---

[1] *Thesaurus: Diss. Ep.*, pp. 45-108; Preface to Ottley, p. xxxiii.

was probably the author of some of its footnotes.[1] Doubtless originally intended as an advertisement of the larger work, this summary was translated in 1735, and with the reissue of this translation in an enlarged edition two years later, the supplementary literature relating to the *Thesaurus* was completed.[2]

No summary, however, could do justice to the magisterial importance of the *Thesaurus* which marked the climax of the work of the Oxford school of 'Saxonists'. The movement had swept through a long course since Somner had published his Dictionary, and the advance which had been made was illustrated in the essay which Hickes included in his book to show the inevitable defects arising in the work of earlier historical scholars from their lack of linguistic knowledge.[3] The progress had, indeed, been so rapid that now students were starting their work almost at the point where the great men of the past had left off, and the linguistic limitations of men such as John Selden and Henry Spelman were becoming a commonplace of undergraduate criticism. The immense difficulties which had before surrounded these studies were now gradually disappearing as the result of the labours of the later generation. Materials were being collected and classified, canons of criticism were being set up, an atmosphere of objective inquiry was coming to prevail, and the facilities of grammars and dictionaries were beginning to serve the needs of students. Not only was it recognized that a knowledge of Anglo-Saxon was the correct preliminary for the study of Old English history, but the opportunities for such knowledge were being provided for all serious students of the subject. By the end of the first quarter of the eighteenth century it could be said for the first time that to be ignorant of Anglo-Saxon was no longer the misfortune of a scholar but his fault.[4] And this exactly summed up the achievement of the movement whose performance culminated in the *Thesaurus*.

The publication of the *Thesaurus* was an event also in the progress of linguistic studies in Europe. It swung the work of the Oxford school into the tide of continental learning. With all his marked individuality there was nothing provincial in the scholarship of Hickes. The dedication of the *Thesaurus* to Prince George of Denmark, who both before and after his marriage to Anne Stuart had connected his name with these studies in Europe, was concerned to link up English and continen-

---

[1] THWAITES: *Notae in Anglo-Saxonum Nummos* (1708); WOTTON: *Conspectus*, dedication; HEARNE: *Collections*, II, p. 92; NICHOLS: *Literary Anecdotes*, IV. p. 147.
[2] MAURICE SHELTON: *Short View* (1735 and 1737).
[3] *Thesaurus:Diss. Ep.*, pp. 148-155.
[4] KENNETT: *Somner* (1726), p. 34.

tal studies in philology. Hickes's desire to remove from his work any trace of insularity was fully realized in his performance, and the extent to which foreign learning was used by him is one of the most remarkable features of his book. The incorporation of the Icelandic grammar of Jonas was but one example of this, for Leibnitz had assisted Fountaine with his friendship, and a yet more valuable association was that between Hickes and John Peringskiöld, the Danish scholar, who sent to his English friend a catalogue of Scandinavian books that was duly included in the *Thesaurus*.[1] But of all the connections made by this book perhaps the most interesting was that with Mabillon. For the Benedictine monk was ideally qualified to pass judgment on the *Dissertatio*, and he was loud in its praise. Though he had himself been criticized in the treatise he recommended it to his pupils, and he pronounced Hickes to be 'one of Ten Thousand', 'a truly learned Person and not one of those Writers who did not understand their Subject to the Bottom.'[2] The *Thesaurus*, in short, embraced the relevant learning of the Latin as well as the Scandinavian and Teutonic countries. It won admiration in Paris and it was acquired by the Escurial Library. Even the Duke of Tuscany sent for a copy and, after perusing it, summoned a special meeting of learned men, who with a delightful facility of understatement reported that 'they believed the author to be a man of a particular head'.[3]

Hickes had, indeed, 'a particular head'. The *Thesaurus* was his individual creation not only in the sense that his personal erudition informed the whole work, but also because he was able to express in its volumes the solidarity of the group of scholars whom he had so strangely come to lead. There are few more moving episodes in the whole history of English scholarship than this endeavour of the Oxford 'Saxonists' to sustain around Hickes a corporate movement of learning despite the political forces which threatened to tear it asunder. The proscribed Non-juror confidently appealed not only to his political friends but also to fellow-scholars among his bitterest opponents. He was not disappointed in the response he elicited from men trained in his own University. Thwaites risked his place in order to dedicate his work to his master, and Edmund Gibson whose career was already bound up with the Whig regime watched every stage in the preparation of the *Thesaurus* with sympathetic encouragement.[4] White Ken-

---

[1] *Thesaurus*, Dedication; Preface to Ottley, p. v; *Gram. Franc.*, p. 5; *Diss. Ep.*, pp. 123 sqq.; *Testimonia* (Palthenius to Hickes, Feb. 18th, 1699), *Bodleian Letters*, I, p. 267.

[2] E. ELSTOB: *Rudiments of Grammar*, pp. xxxiv, xxxv; cf. *Thesaurus*: Preface to Ottley, pp. xxxi, xxxii; NICOLSON: *Epist. Corr.*, p. 159.

[3] *Bodleian Letters*, I, p. 267; NICHOLS: *Literary Anecdotes*, I, p. 18.

[4] *Thesaurus: Diss. Ep.*, p. 155; THWAITES: *Heptateuchus* Dedication; NICHOLS: *Literary Anecdotes*, IV, p. 143; THORESBY: *Correspondence*, II, pp. 340, 357.

nett, soon to be Whig Bishop of Peterborough, sheltered Hickes in his exile and was influential in fostering his work.

> Having contracted an intimate Acquaintance with Dr. *Hicks* [Kennett] received him freely into his Vicarage-House, and finding that by his Condition of Suffering for the cause of King *James* his Head and Thoughts were too much determined to Politicks . . . Mr. Kennet to divert him from that Mischief (as well for other reasons) desired his Instruction in the *Saxon* and *Septentrional* Tongues. While Dr. *Hicks* was thus pleased by the Country Vicar, it gave the latter an Opportunity to intreat the Doctor to look more upon those Studies, to review his *Saxon* and *Islandic* Grammar. It was upon this frequent Discourse and Importunity of Mr. *Kennett* that Dr. Hicks then and there laid the Foundation of that noble Work which he brought to Perfection in about seven Years after.[1]

In those seven years much happened to Hickes besides the preparation of the *Thesaurus*, but, when the book appeared, the earlier conversations were not forgotten, and though intimacy with Kennett was no longer possible, Hickes paid generous tribute

> to that reverend and most learned man who seven years ago often urged me to gird myself to this work . . . In his house I began without delay books in which, now that they are at length brought to a close – if I have in any way helped the republic of letters – to him as the begetter of all that I have done it is to be attributed.[2]

William Nicolson, again, who became one of the foremost of the Revolution prelates continued even after his advancement to look to Hickes as his leader in scholarship – 'the greatest Master of his Subject that ever yet appeared in Print',[3] whilst Hickes cited the Whig Bishop as a man

> to be honourably named for his manifold erudition, and especially illustrious on account of his knowledge of the Northern literature – a highly reverend prelate who when many times consulted by us, answered quite as an oracle in difficult and obscure matters, and gave us replies that were full of light, and with the utmost courtesy.[4]

These phrases cannot here be regarded merely as the formal language of learned compliment. They were, on the contrary, the expression of a highly remarkable magnanimity among contemporary English

---

[1] *Life of Kennett* (1730), p. 12.
[2] *Thesaurus*: Preface to Ottley, p. xlv (trans.).
[3] NICOLSON: *English Historical Library* (1736), p. 42; cf. *Epist. Corr.*, pp. 78-81.
[4] *Thesaurus*: Preface to Ottley, p. iv (trans.); cf. ELLIS: *Letters of Eminent Literary Men*, p. 267.

scholars. They were also an extraordinary tribute to the personality of Hickes himself. Hickes had tasted to the full the bitterness of civil strife. He had steeled himself to regard his brother's death as a just retribution, and for another cause he had himself suffered long years of persecution. He had worked under the shadow of the scaffold and consoled his friends upon its steps. When in 1691 John Aston the Jacobite was executed at Tyburn –

> he would not permit the Ordinary to pray with him, but desired Sir Francis Child to let him have the divine that went along with him, to perform the last ghostly offices, which was permitted . . . It was Divine Hicks, and after him came little Cook of Islington. And so he went into the other world.[1]

The scholars from whom Hickes was to exact collaboration were, many of them, active and prominent members of the party which had ordered this execution, and at its hands Hickes had seen his own career blasted and his possessions scattered. They, on their side, sincerely regarded the political opinions, which he consistently held, as subversive to the Church and dangerous to the State. And it was a fine achievement in English scholarship when a learned co-operation prevailed amid such stress, and, with such honourable forbearance, brought to fruition a great movement of historical research.

The achievements of the Oxford school of Saxon scholars were thus in a sense also those of Hickes, for his influence was profound and pervasive, and, while life lasted, it never waned. The painful disease, which for long years ravaged his health, succeeded no better than persecution in abating his manifold energies. As early as November 1708 he could write to Thoresby: 'I have been very ill of a fever and strangury, and my constitution is quite broken',[2] and though in the next year he professed himself in moderate ease,[3] the relapses became more frequent, and so severe that in 1712 Hearne was constrained to pray that God would 'continue the Life of this Great and Good Man upon whom so much depends'.[4] The end did not come until December 1715,[5] and to the last the same solemnity of purpose informed the career of this 'truly venerable, learned and pious Christian minister of a primitive spirit,

[1] E. C. to Robert Harley, Jan. 29th, 1691 (*Portland MSS. Rep.*, III, p. 458).
[2] THORESBY: *Correspondence*, II, p. 124.
[3] Ibid., II, p. 209.
[4] HEARNE: *Collections*, III, p. 496; cf. ibid., p. 195.
[5] H. Bedford to Hearne, Dec. 15th, 1715: 'It is Sir to acquaint you that after a long indisposition from which we hoped he was now rather recovering our excellent friend the late Dean of Worcester was at about 12 last night taken speechless and dyed this morning soon after ten. I pray God support us under this great loss and all our afflictions, and remove them, or us from them, when it is his blessed will' (HEARNE: *Collections*, V, p. 153).

patience and resolution'.[1] Born into a changing world, his standards were incapable of change, and it was his limitation as well as his misfortune that he lived to some extent an exile amid his own generation. Nevertheless, his erudition was massive in its honesty, and his enthusiasms were single in their strength. The vassal of suffering, wedded to a lost cause, austerely devoted to an integrity of steadfast purpose, and battered by circumstances to which he never yielded, George Hickes seems almost drawn into the orbit of classical tragedy. His learning and his character combined to make him a unique influence. There was a root of authority in him. He lived and died a leader of men.

[1] *Lives of the Norths* (1890), I, p. 412.

CHAPTER V

HUMPHREY WANLEY

TWO portraits, the one in the Students' Room of the Manuscript Department in the British Museum, and the other in the Gallery of the Bodleian Library at Oxford, look down to-day upon those who study medieval documents in the two greatest libraries of England. The subject of both pictures is the same, and from them can be compositely constructed a countenance that is in many ways remarkable. Here is to be found neither the dedicated force of Hickes nor the somewhat peevish austerity which appears in the portraits of Dugdale. This face, on the contrary, is rubicund with good living, and 'peppered with variolous indentations'. The features are slightly blurred, perhaps by dissipation, but the want of spirituality is counterbalanced by evidence of saturnine strength. This was Humphrey Wanley,[1] and to-day as of right he contemplates with a cynical detachment the toil of his successors in the libraries to which he devoted the greater part of his productive life.

Humphrey Wanley was born in 1672, and both his parentage and his boyhood were a curious preparation for the particular career in which he was to win distinction. His father, Nathaniel Wanley, who had become Vicar of Holy Trinity, Coventry, in 1662, was a man of immense and indiscriminate reading whose tastes found an apt expression when in 1678 he published his *Wonders of the Little World* wherein the prodigies of human nature were displayed with an uncritical zeal that has delighted generations of subsequent readers. His son must have been reared in a strange household, but a desultory interest in the marvellous was early tempered by his being apprenticed to a draper in the city. Here he doubtless encountered a healthy discipline, the more especially as the boy managed to combine his duties with an ardent study of manuscripts, devoting himself particularly to the investigations of ancient handwritings, and it was in the draper's shop that he

---

[1] The best appreciations of Wanley are to be found in the course of Mr. SISAM's fine articles on *Ælfric's Catholic Homilies* (*Review of English Studies*, vol. VII, p. 7; vol. VIII, p. 51; vol. IX, p. 1), and in Professor TURBERVILLE: *History of Welbeck Abbey and its Owners* (1938), vol. I, pp. 364-377. Wanley left behind him a most remarkable collection of literary remains. For example, his Diary (Lansdowne MSS. 771, 772) is of the highest interest, and his surviving correspondence, some of which is contained in Harl. MSS. 3777-3782, is also extremely valuable.

began his studies by transcribing Somner's Dictionary. His successes in salesmanship have not been recorded, but his interest in palaeography speedily attracted a discriminating patronage which is itself a testimony to the intellectual temper of the age in which he lived. William Lloyd, the Bishop of his diocese, sought out the draper's assistant, and it was with his help that Wanley found his way to Oxford in 1695 where he matriculated at St. Edmund's Hall. About the same time Thomas Tanner, another eminent medieval scholar who was to rise to the episcopal bench, was also standing his friend, and after being an undergraduate for a year Wanley attracted notice in yet a third distinguished quarter. Dr. Charlett, then the influential Master of University College, took a special liking to the young man, and gave him a lodging in his own house.[1]

The patronage of Lloyd, the friendship of Tanner, and the kindly interest of Charlett might have seemed a sufficient guarantee that a youth of Wanley's parts would rise smoothly to a position of academic eminence. But something in the young man apparently prevented him from submitting tamely to the prescribed curriculum at the University. Logic he found a particular source of irritation. 'By God Mr. Milles,' he exclaimed to his tutor after attending his first lecture in that subject, 'I do not and cannot understand it', and so 'he came no more'. The result was that Wanley was never able to graduate in the University which had once refused a B.A. to William Camden, and a certain antagonism grew up between him and academic authority. Though by his training and connections Wanley belonged to the Oxford Saxonists, he never became a vital force in the life of the University, and, not unnaturally, having failed to receive recognition in a society which he did not trouble to placate, he sought his fortune elsewhere. London was to gain by Oxford's loss, and scholarship by the resulting expansion of the influence of Old English studies. Wanley suffered duly for his temerity, but in later life he was provided with ample compensations for his lack of academic distinctions. As his reputation for fine erudition grew, the doors of the learned societies of the capital opened wide in his honour, and fashionable poets did not disdain to proclaim him as an accession to the culture of the metropolis. He received respectful letters from Pope, and Matthew Prior made play of a learning which had become proverbial:

[1] NICHOLS: *Literary Anecdotes*, I, pp. 530-542; *Portland MSS. Rep.*, VI, p. 27; *Bodleian Letters*, II, p. 118.

    If to be sad is to be wise
    I do most heartily despise
    Whatever Socrates has said
    Or Tully writ, or Wanley read.[1]

It would be as easy as it would be unjust to blame the University authorities for their treatment of Wanley. They gave the young man his chance, demanding as a condition of further advancement only the acceptance of conventions which were by no means rigid. They placed him in a position to follow profitably a normal academic course, and they even provided him with scope for his special abilities by making him an Assistant in the Bodleian Library under Edward Hyde. Wanley, however, who possessed even more than the usual self-assurance ascribed to brilliant undergraduates was not amenable even to this lax discipline. His sudden transference to Oxford from the draper's shop at Coventry, and the injudicious favours of the great, fed, perhaps too lavishly, the self-esteem of a precocious youth, and Wanley's under-graduate behaviour supplies more entertainment for posterity than it can have afforded to the senior members of his university. Dressed foppishly in a long wig he emerged 'strutting mightily about', and 'talking big'. Nor was Mr. Milles the only don who suffered from his tongue, for he was observed to be 'very impudent' with Dr. Charlett himself whom he regarded as his 'friend and crony'. The picture of youthful impertinence which was thus sketched so eagerly in Hearne's venomous ink[2] bears all the marks of authenticity. It is not difficult either to explain or to excuse. But it is hardly surprising that such a youth made enemies, or that his conduct provoked the outraged pro-tests of his elders.

Throughout a chequered career Wanley at least never lacked the advice which his many mentors were always delighted to supply. 'As I allow you to have a good opinion of yourself,' wrote Thomas Smith, the learned and venerable librarian to the Cotton family, in 1697, 'so the friendship which I profess to have with you prompts mee to advise you not to graspe at too much and to think as well of other men's in-dustry and understanding as your owne.'[3] Two years later a yet more vigorous reprimand came from Lloyd. 'It is said', remarked the Bishop, 'that you live at the rate of most other foolish young men that affect to be gentlemen and to live above their rank and loiter away

---

[1] SISAM: op. cit., VII, p. 7; HEARNE: *Collections*, IX, p. 161; POPE: *Works*, ed. Courthope VIII, pp. 206-207; X, pp. 115, 116.

[2] HEARNE: *Collections*, II, p. 181; VII, p. 276.

[3] ELLIS: *Letters of Eminent Literary Men*, p. 248.

their time in idle company. If this be true you must look to yourself and take up betimes before the habit be grown too strong for you. You must tie yourself strictly to study and duty . . . that God may enable you to subdue your affections and lusts and to bridle your roving imagination.'[1] There seems little reason to suppose that the admonition was not well deserved.

At this critical period in his career it was Wanley's good fortune to fall under the influence of Hickes, who at once recognized the abilities of the younger man and sought to stabilize his character by bringing him into the scheme of study which was slowly creating the *Thesaurus*. Wanley responded with an immediate enthusiasm, and as early as 1697 Hickes was already acknowledging his 'many and great obligations' to him,[2] and in return bringing him under the notice of influential men who might be willing to foster his research.[3] Some estimate of the value to Wanley of such a friend may be guessed by the advice which Hickes in his turn felt periodically constrained to give to his wayward and brilliant pupil. In 1699 he wrote:

> I advise you to keep company with none but men of learning and reputation; to let your conversation be with an air of respect and modesty to them; to behave yourself upon the place with candor caution and temperance; to go to bed in good time and rise in good time; to let them see you are a man that observes houres and discipline . . .[4]

This theme in their correspondence was not to disappear even after Wanley had gone to London, when metropolitan delights might induce the young man to neglect the correction of proof sheets. 'I can admit no further delay,' writes Hickes. 'You are so unfortunate in putting my business off that I am at a loss what to call this misfortune.' Or again: 'This is the last complaint I intend to make to you. The next shall be to your friends to try if they can oblige you to deal with me as you expect all the world should deal with you, that is with faith, truth, and honest fair dealing.'[5] Hickes was, in truth, no man to trifle with. And Wanley who was subsequently to teach Hickes as much as he learnt from him later complained that his master used his work without due acknowledgment.[6] But on the whole Hickes's admonition was kindly, and at many of the crises in Wanley's career he stood by him. He placed his pupil under an immeasurable debt.

---

[1] *Bodleian Letters*, I, pp. 100, 102.　　　　　　[2] Harl. MS. 3779, fol. 59.
[3] Cf. Hickes to Charlett, 1700 (Harl. MS. 3779, fol. 127).
[4] Hickes to Wanley 1699, (ELLIS, op. cit., p. 283).
[5] Harl. MS. 3779, fols. 92, 156, 161, 178, 192.
[6] TURBERVILLE: *Welbeck*, I, p. 365.

Wanley's association with Hickes gave his University some further grounds for complaint which were more to his credit than those supplied by his personal behaviour. The fervour with which Wanley entered into his new work was such that his routine duties now became almost as irksome to him as the preparation for a degree. He was not the first – or the last – man to complain that the tasks allotted to an academic office unduly trenched on the higher interests of research, and the struggle which followed is a familiar one in the history of all Universities. The autumn of 1699 he spent largely at Cambridge collating the Anglo-Saxon manuscripts he found there,[1] and in the next spring he announced his desire to pursue these researches in the Cotton Library in London. The Bodleian authorities may be excused for objecting to this continual absence of one of their assistants, and it did not add to Wanley's popularity that both he and Hickes tried to brush aside their protests as negligible. 'It is a great trouble and discouragement to me,' wrote the latter, 'to hear that the Curators of the Publick Library have denied Mr. Wanley leave to take the Catalogue of the Saxon MSS. in the Cotton Library.'[2] The situation, indeed, was not without its humour, and the comments of those occupied in discharging the errant librarian's duties in his absence may well have been illuminating. Even Wanley deep in his studies far afield sometimes complained that 'Sir Thomas Bodley's bell' 'rang so loudly'[3] in his ears as to disturb the tranquillity necessary to research. Thomas Smith was inevitably there to point the moral: 'You would do well', he wrote to Wanley, 'to examine and transcribe whatever is of this nature in the Publick Library where you are fixed . . . without seeking for materialls abroad.'[4]

Wanley's habits and the range of his interests were, in short, of such a character that he could not conform to the exigencies of academic routine, and he had no real reason for complaint when his applications to succeed Hyde as Bodley's Librarian in 1698 were refused. By the end of the century it was becoming clear that he would have to seek his fortune outside Oxford. But he had gambled so recklessly with his chances of material advancement that the future was bleak. The recommendations from the Bodleian could hardly be cordial, and in 1699 he failed to become Bentley's deputy in the King's Library. Later he was to suffer a similar disappointment in the Library of the Cottons. Wanley, however, was always fortunate in his friends, and help now came from an unexpected quarter when Robert Nelson the saintly

[1] ELLIS: op. cit., p. 283.
[2] Hickes to Charlett, 1700 (Harl. MS. 3779, fol. 127).
[3] Wanley to Charlett, 1699 (ELLIS: op. cit., p. 291).
[4] T. Smith to Wanley, June 8th, 1697 (ELLIS: op. cit., p. 248).

Non-juror (possibly at the instigation of Hickes) secured for him the post of assistant to the secretary of the newly-founded Society for Promoting Christian Knowledge.[1] The appointment at a salary of £40 a year was 'thankfully accepted', but it was none the less a strange one, and it became the more openly incongruous when Wanley sought to justify the choice of his employers by translating pietistic literature from the French. The sharp pens of contemporary malice lost no time in giving point to the situation. 'Besides what hath been mentioned (Mr. Wanley) published one Book, a Translation for the use of the Religious Societies. He was a very loose debauched Man, kept Whores, was a very great Sot, and by that means broke to Pieces his otherwise very strong constitution.'[2]

Hearne hated Wanley for many reasons, and his aspersion of a man whom he regarded with a jealous disapproval need not be taken too seriously.[3] But he was right, at least, in considering that a post with the S.P.C.K. was unsuited to Wanley's special talents. Wanley's transcendent abilities were always to be displayed in Anglo-Saxon research, and during the eight years he served the Society he kept them alive so that, during this period, he not only collaborated in a valuable report on the Cottonian manuscripts but also produced his own greatest work, the invaluable final volume of Hickes's *Thesaurus*. It was just that such consistent industry should in time bring its proper reward. At this time, again through the efforts of Hickes, Wanley formed his connection with the Harleys. In particular he succeeded in making himself indispensable to Robert Harley who was then building up his magnificent collection of manuscripts. As early as 1701 he was in communication with him; five years later he notified him of the possibility of acquiring the famous D'Ewes collection; and in 1708 mainly through Wanley's agency the purchase was actually effected. Shortly afterwards Wanley was definitely installed as Library-Keeper in the Harleian Library, and this office he held until his death in 1726, serving not only the first Earl of Oxford but also his son.[4]

As Librarian to the Harleys, Wanley at last found employment which was to the last degree congenial, and the energy which he expended on his duties enabled him to make an indelible mark upon the Harleian collections. At the command of his master he kept a Diary of

[1] SECRETAN: *Robert Nelson* (1860), pp. 104-112; *Bodleian Letters*, I, p. 99.
[2] HEARNE: *Collections*, IX, pp. 161, 162.
[3] He accused him (with equal lack of justification) of theft, of perpetual drunkenness, and of incompetence (*Collections*, I, pp. 175, 180; III, p. 434; IV, pp. 421-427; VI, p. 132; IX, pp. 161-162).
[4] Hickes to Robert Harley, April 1701 (*Portland MSS. Rep.*, IV, p. 16); TURBERVILLE: *Welbeck*, I, p. 366.

his activities, and when it is published it will throw a flood of light not only upon the circumstances in which this noble Library was formed but also upon the provenance of some of the most important medieval codices in the national collection. Wanley's unending search for manuscripts also of itself makes entertaining reading. The early summer of 1720 for example found him as ever hard at work. At the end of April 'a young man unknown brought MSS to sell but would not declare whose they are or how he came by them or to whom he belongs. Only that they came out of the country . . . He asked ten guineas for them. But I, finding the owner was desirous of being concealed, and the Messenger in several stories, would make no bargain about them.'[1] It may be surmised that the texts were of little value, for Wanley was not always so squeamish, and the acquisition of a treasure was always an event to be recorded with exuberant joy. June 27th, 1720, was for instance a notable date, for 'this day the Codex Aureus Latinus was cleared out of the King's Warehouse and delivered into my custody'. But before evening there was more work to be done and so Wanley went 'to Mr. Warburton and offered him 100 guineas for his old MSS etc. . . . But he flew back on his word as so many others have done and protested that two of the books cost him about that sum . . . and that therefore he would not part with them under three hundred guineas,' 'a price', adds the diarist, 'in my poor opinion much too horribly exorbitant.'[2] If Wanley's diary thus shows the character of his search for manuscripts, his correspondence displays its extent. His quest took him into the humblest as well as into the most exalted quarters, and the illiterate hands to be seen in many of the letters he received suggest that he was sometimes successful in eliciting his treasures from cottage homes. Nor was he more scrupulous than some of his successors. In August 1723, for instance, it was discovered that certain MSS. were in the hands of an Oxford farmer's wife where 'they cannot be highly valued', and it was further ascertained that Wanley might perhaps claim cousinship with her. The result of the transaction can hardly remain in doubt. Modern collectors would have little to teach Humphrey Wanley.[3]

As Harley's librarian,[4] Wanley was brought into contact with nearly all the historical scholars of the time. His good will was now something to be sought for, and it was not too easily obtained. It was a bold man who for example sought to bribe with a guinea one who had been once 'impudent' with Dr. Charlett, and Wanley was incorruptible in

[1] Lansdowne MS. 771, fol. 20b.   [2] Ibid., fol. 25.
[3] Harl. MS. 3777, fols. 42 sqq.; cf. Portland MSS. Rep., v, p. 251; VII, pp. 364-366.
[4] Cf. G. F. Barwick in The Library (1902) pp. 24-35; 243-255; (1910) pp. 166-171.

the service of his lord.[1] A real affection grew up in time between him and his noble patrons, and the intimacy actually became a source of jealousy to interested parties. William Stratford, the canon of Christ Church whose letters to Edward Harley supply an illuminating commentary upon the scholarly connections of his time was, for example, always faintly disparaging in his references to Wanley, and expressed the wish that his noble friend could be 'bound prentice' to someone else. 'I suppose you are now happy,' he added with a sarcasm that was but lightly concealed, 'for I take it that Mr. Wanley must be with you.'[2] The Harleys knew, however, that they had the best librarian in Europe, and Wanley on his side, fully conscious of his own worth, was not afraid on occasion to chide his master for neglecting his advice. He was unimpressed by rank, and for the sake of the library he was always ready to withstand the exalted or the importunate. Thus, in 1718 Edward Harley complacently learned that 'the great Mr. Wanley has used the Bishop of Chester very unkindly not to say rudely in refusing flatly to consult some papers for him in your father's library'.[3] Wanley had shown himself able to exchange successful repartee with Hearne – no mean achievement – and he was fully capable of guarding efficiently the treasures committed to his charge. But his zeal for scholarship mitigated his uncertain temper, and, in general, any genuine investigator could count upon his reasonable assistance. He had become a person of consequence. Happily married to a devoted wife,[4] he had settled down to be an influence upon the contemporary world of learning. He was a considerable figure in the Royal Society, and as the friend of Pepys, the pupil of Hickes, and the protégé of the Earl of Oxford he could afford to choose his acquaintance. His learning had at last received its due meed of recognition, and his position brought him into contact with the most distinguished medievalists of his time.

He was a great librarian; and his conception of his duties was so wide that he became a natural centre of antiquarian culture. It was, for example, almost his personal achievement to have crystallized his scholarly connections into an organized form; and the revival of the Society of Antiquaries at the beginning of the eighteenth century owed more perhaps to him than to any other man. Before the end of the sixteenth century such a Society had been formed in England,[5] and its

[1] Lansdowne MS. 771, fol. 31.
[2] *Portland MSS. Rep.*, VII, pp. 216, 272, 302.
[3] Ibid., p. 238.
[4] Cf. TURBERVILLE: *Welbeck*, I, p. 370.
[5] *Archaeologia*, vol. I, pp. i-xxiv. L. VAN NORDEN, in *Huntingdon Library Quarterly*, vol. xiii, No. 2 (1950), pp. 131-160, has some useful observations as to the date when this Society was formed, and as to its activities.

'curious discourses were later to be lovingly collected by Hearne'.[1] But this Society had failed to survive. London was not then sufficiently a centre of English antiquarian learning which was cultivated mainly by gentlemen upon their country estates, and by prelates in their several sees. Thus while the original Society of Antiquaries continued for 'diverse years' nevertheless 'as all good uses commonly decline, so many of the chief supporters hereof either dying or withdrawing themselves from London into the Country this among the rest grew – to be discontinued'.[2] The association had also to face a positive opposition. The Universities were jealous lest it might detract from academic prestige, and a more powerful opponent was found in the Crown which was then suspicious that such assemblies of gentlemen might cloak the operations of 'a treasonable cabal'. When between 1614 and 1617 Henry Spelman and others sought to restore the Society of Antiquaries they expressly avoided this danger by making it a rule of the Society 'that we should neither meddle with matters of State nor of Religion'. The caution, however, went unrewarded, for 'His Majesty took a little mislike of our Society, not being enform'd that we had resolved to decline all matters of State, and so all our labours lost'.[3] Not until the early years of the eighteenth century was the atmosphere again favourable to the formation in London of a Society of Antiquaries, and it was fortunate that in Humphrey Wanley there was to be found a man well fitted in every way to take advantage of the opportunity.

The conditions of English learning were changing, and a need had arisen in its organization. Historical scholarship was becoming more regulated, but the universities shackled to an older curriculum were unwilling or unable to undertake its co-ordination. Experimental science had led the way with the establishment of the Royal Society, and though, at the beginning, this body included among its transactions several antiquarian discourses of which Wanley's were the most important, nevertheless it was already submitting to its more modern limitation of interest. In these circumstances, many historical scholars in England began to desire a society which might represent their interests and facilitate their work. In 1694 William Nicolson, when writing to Thoresby, had urged the establishment in England of a 'College of Antiquaries' similar to that already existing in Sweden, and two years later he publicly reiterated his plea.[4] It was left, however, to

---

[1] HEARNE: *Curious Discourses* (1771), II, pp. 421-499.
[2] HENRY SPELMAN, preface to *Original of the Four Terms* printed in *Reliquiae Spelmannianae*, ed. 1698, pp. 69-70.   [3] Ibid.
[4] THORESBY: *Correspondence*, I, p. 162; cf. NICOLSON: *English Historical Library* (ed. 1696), Preface.

Wanley to be the chief agent in developing the idea. 'Such a Society',
he wrote in 1707:

> will bring to light and preserve all old Monumental Inscriptions etc. Archi-
> tecture Sculpture Engraving Musick will come under their consideration;
> and the ancient methods being restored many things may be used afresh.
> They will explain obscurities not only in our own but in Greek and Roman
> authors. A correspondence might be maintained through England and
> abroad and fit persons sent to travel over England and abroad to inspect
> Books and MSS to draw ancient Fortifications Castles Churches Houses
> Tombs Inscriptions Epitaphs Painted Glass etc. and if need be to buy up
> the most curious for the Society. This Establishment their Library and
> Repository would be an ease and satisfaction to the Officers of State and to
> Foreigners that attend their Meeting; a seminary and school for learning the
> ancient constitution laws and customs of this Kingdom.[1]

The ambitious project started to take shape almost immediately, and
the genesis of the Society of Antiquaries may perhaps be seen when on
December 5th, 1707, Wanley noted that he and two of his friends,
John Bagford and John Talman, had

> met together and agreed to meet together every Friday in the evening by
> six of the clock upon pain of forfeiture of six pence.

A week later it was further agreed

> that the business of this Society shall be limited to the object of Antiquities
> and more particularly to such things as may illustrate or relate to the History
> of Great Britain.

These meetings of 1707 took place at the Bear Tavern in the Strand
where Wanley and his friends were soon joined by others, among
whom were Peter le Neve, the herald, William Elstob, and Thomas
Madox who was even then engaged upon his monumental history of
the Exchequer. In the course of 1708 with Peter le Neve as their President and with Wanley as their Secretary they moved to Fleet Street,
first to the *Young Devil*, and then to the Fountain Tavern. They collected other members in their transit, and by 1717 the Society was firmly
established, and its continuous series of minute books begun.[2]

It is fitting that most of the documents relating to the revival of the
Society of Antiquaries should be in Wanley's handwriting for he
appears to have been the prime agent in its re-establishment. But both

---

[1] NICHOLS: *Literary Anecdotes*, VI, p. 149.
[2] ELLIS: *Letters of Eminent Literary Men*, p. 100; cf. *Archaeologia*, I, pp. xxvi-xxxiv.

the formation of the new society and more particularly the spread of its later influence owed a great deal also to one of his associates in the venture. Maurice Johnson, who was born at Spalding in 1688, and who had become a barrister of the Inner Temple, was with Wanley one of the original members of the Society and an active agent in its growth,[1] and in 1717 he became its honorary librarian. But his special distinction was to carry the work of the Society into the provinces of England. Local history in this country was later to owe much to the man who founded the *Gentlemen's Society* at Spalding as a 'cell' to the Society of Antiquaries,[2] for it was mainly owing to Johnson and his friends that 'the spirit of emulation and communication which prevailed among the Revivers of the Society of Antiquaries' produced elsewhere other 'Establishments whose object was to extend their inquiries in the History and Antiquities of this Kingdom by mutual correspondence'. Thus an antiquarian society was founded at Peterborough in the early eighteenth century, and in 1721 the Stamford Society was created on the model of that of Spalding. Other 'literary' societies were similarly established about the same time at Wisbech, Lincoln and Worcester.[3] By the third decade of the eighteenth century such societies had indeed become something of a fashion and one which penetrated even into the Universities to take shape in the creation of such curious institutions as 'Antiquity Hall' at Oxford or the Zodiac Club of St. John's College, Cambridge, wherein each member represented either a Sign or a Planet, and Samuel Pegge the Elder, the historian of Rochester, occupied the chair dedicated to Mars.[4] Such clubs only came to be characteristic of English learned life at a later period, and it was only then that their proper contribution to English erudition was made. But the movement itself began before the death of George I, and perhaps its chief inspirer was the tireless librarian of the Harleys who was even then establishing his own reputation as one of the most important figures in the whole history of Old English scholarship.

Humphrey Wanley is chiefly to be honoured for the magnificent contribution which he made to Anglo-Saxon learning, but his investigations took him into many fields of inquiry. Thus in 1705 he was apparently contemplating an edition of the Anglo-Saxon Bible. Later he considered writing a history of printing, and in 1708 by a strange transition he was reported to be engaged upon a life of Wolsey. The elaborate notes to be seen in his copies of Gibson's edition of the *Anglo-*

---

[1] KORTHOLT: *Ep. ad Kappum de Soc. Antiq. Lond.* (1730), p. 6.
[2] NICHOLS: *Literary Anecdotes*, VI, pp. 1-162.
[3] *Reliquiae Galeanae* (Bibl. Top. Brit.), p. 1.
[4] NICHOLS: *Literary Anecdotes*, VI, p. 228.

Saxon Chronicle and in Godwin's *De Presulibus*[1] show the assiduity of his private studies. But a better idea of his energy and the extent of his interests could be formed by a contemplation of his vast correspondence which fills many manuscript volumes in the British Museum, and which, when it is published, will illuminate the conditions of contemporary learning. This correspondence was by no means confined to the business of the Harleian Library since it dealt at length with controversial points of technical scholarship, and many contemporary scholars had good reason to appreciate the weight of Wanley's critical judgment. For example, he gave to Thomas Tanner valuable help for the revised edition of his *Notitia Monastica* which appeared in 1695; he wrote an account of the Harleian Collection for Nicolson's *English Historical Library*; and he added to Chamberlayne's *State of England* a description of the Bodleian. The *Philosophical Transactions* of the Royal Society were in their turn adorned by contributions from his pen. Wanley as late as 1721 might complain that his duties as Harleian Librarian left him no time for writing, but the record of his production does not justify the grievance.[2]

Wanley was a great critic of manuscripts, a great palaeographer, and a great Anglo-Saxon scholar. And these combined qualifications enabled him to render to Old English history a peculiar service to which scholarship is still indebted. For it was his especial virtue that he based his work upon a detailed study of the manuscripts themselves, observing their several peculiarities with an imaginative curiosity perfectly disciplined by critical caution. To Wanley an Old-English manuscript was something whose individuality might of itself suggest lines of valuable inquiry quite apart from the varied topics which might be discussed therein, and he gave, therefore, special attention to the composition of each MS. which he examined: to its make up, its handwriting, its variations and its addenda. The very success with which he did his work led in later years to a certain neglect of the manuscripts which he catalogued in such numbers and with such care. But there was nothing antiquated in his methods, and among scholars best versed in such matters there is now a tendency to revert to something like the technique which he employed.[3] In so far as Wanley emphasized the importance of studying the individual characteristics of the manuscripts upon which Old-English scholarship must be based, his work has an immediate interest in the present state of Anglo-Saxon learning. Inasmuch

[1] Marked *c* 60 *n l* and c 60 h l in the British Museum Library.
[2] HEARNE: *Collections*, I, pp. 44, 131; II, p. 137; VI, p. 27; NICOLSON: *English Historical Library* (1736), pp. vi, vii; *Philosophical Transactions* for 1705, pp. 1993-2008.
[3] See SISAM, *Ælfric's Catholic Homilies* (op. cit., loc. cit.).

as he succeeded in criticizing such manuscripts with a natural acumen that approached genius, his conclusions have even to-day an abiding importance.

In one sense all the achievements of Wanley were off-shoots of a vast project which was never completed. For in 1697 Thoresby informed Gibson that 'a young gentleman in Oxford, Mr. Wanley, is laying the foundation of a *Res Diplomatica* for England particularly. He designs and draws admirably well; having besides an unaccountable skill in imitating any hand whatsoever. His great curiosity in books printed and manuscript has recommended him to the University to be one of their under Library Keepers; and the command he has of everything there gives him the best opportunity he could wish of carrying on this honourable design.'[1] The design was indeed honourable, but its magnitude might have daunted even a young scholar in the seventeenth century. 'My intent', wrote Wanley to Thomas Smith in the same year, 'is to trace the Greek and Latin letters from the oldest monuments of antiquity now extant as the marbles and medals to the MSS and so down to the present age. When any other language derives in character from these as the Coptic or Russian from the Greek; the Francic Irish Saxon etc. from the Latin; I shall consider them in their several times, but the Saxon I would especially bring down from the oldest charters to the present English hands. The Charters I believe may be older than the Books and may determine the age of all the Saxon MSS . . . I am not in haste with my design which I know will cost many years time . . . and yet after all I may have a second volume *De Re Anglorum Diplomatica*.'[2]

It is hardly surprising that two years later this portentous book had not yet safely 'passed the pains and perils of its birth', or that Mr. Wanley appeared 'almost fatigued with the work'.[3] Nevertheless he persisted and later we find him noting as among the necessary subjects of his investigation:

1. The state of the *Runic* and *Roman* hands as they were at the time when our Saxon ancestors are supposed to have taken their letters from them.

2. All the Anglo-Saxon hands as well in the Latin as in the Saxon tongues from the oldest monuments extant down to the Conquest with all the alphabets, cubical and great uncial letters, ligatures, abbreviations, and occult ways of writing used in those ages.

3. All the same variety of Normanno-Saxon hands to the time of Edward III.

---

[1] THORESBY: *Correspondence*, I, p. 305. [2] *Bodleian Letters*, I, pp. 80-81.
[3] THORESBY: *Correspondence*, I, p. 355.

4. All the English hands thence to 1700 particularly the Pipe, Exchequer, Chancery court, text and other set hands with date remarks and observations.[1]

When Wanley's other pre-occupations during these years are remembered, the scope of this research seems the more remarkable. And it is evident that he made great progress in his design and that his advance was being sympathetically watched by distinguished critics. As late as 1702, William Nicolson could write to him: 'I heartily agree with those worthy promoters of the knowledge of our English antiquities who press you to go on with your *Res Diplomatica*, and I am extremely well pleased that you resolve to listen to their good advice.'[2] The *De Re Anglorum Diplomatica* never appeared in that form. But it is no mere paradox to observe that a great advance in English medieval studies was made by this notable book that was never written. For the researches undertaken by Wanley in its preparation were embodied in three books issued by other men, and Wanley's contributions to them entitle him to a place in the very first rank of English historical scholars.

The first of these productions was the great catalogue of manuscripts which the University of Oxford produced in 1697, and which is commonly spoken of as *Bernard's Catalogue* owing to the fact that it was supervised by Edward Bernard who, for eighteen years, had been Savilian Professor of Astronomy at that University. This extraordinary man whose life was written by his admiring contemporary, Thomas Smith, was born in 1638, and he was to play an important part in the development of scientific studies at Oxford. But his interests were encyclopedic, and he turned easily from mathematics to ancient oriental literature, even going so far as to prepare an edition of Josephus and to seek a Chair in this subject in the University of Leyden. Bernard's reputation as a scholar extended far beyond the boundaries of Oxford, or even of England, and, the friend of Mabillon, it was said of him by a continental critic that 'few in his time equalled him in learning and none in modesty'. It was fortunate for historical scholarship that such a man as this began in 1692 to prepare a comprehensive catalogue of the Bodleian MSS., and it was still more fortunate that before he had been many years at his task he found in Wanley the young scholar who in all England was the best qualified to assist him.[3]

'I conceive it as part of a Library-Keepers duty', wrote Wanley

---

[1] NICHOLS: *Literary Anecdotes*, I, pp. 103, 104.

[2] Nicolson to Wanley, July 23rd, 1702 (Harl. MS. 3780, fol. 261).

[3] T. SMITH: *Vita Edwardi Bernardi* (1704), esp. pp. 61-63; BROGLIE: *Vie de Mabillon*, I, pp. 128 *sqq*.

about this time, 'to know what books are extant in other Libraries besides his own', and here he indicated what was to be the primary virtue of the critical catalogue in whose construction he was assisting. The compilers of *Bernard's Catalogue* did not confine their attention to MSS. in the Bodleian Library itself but placed contemporary scholarship under a far greater debt by considering also MSS. existing elsewhere in England. Such a labour necessitated wide collaboration, and as the preface to the book showed, many notable scholars took a share in the final production. It would, therefore, perhaps be easy, in view of his later achievements, to ascribe too great a share in the undertaking to Wanley who, after all, during these years was but a novice learning his trade. The account given of the Coventry MSS. was, however, wholly his own, as was also 'the very accurate but too brief' index to the whole book, and it is probable also that the work of his anonymous hand is to be found elsewhere.[1]

It was a distinction for a young man of twenty-five to be intimately connected with a work of co-operative scholarship as important as *Bernard's Catalogue*, for the volume was one of the major achievements of the Oxford school of Saxonists, and it gave a great impetus to medieval, and in particular to Old English, studies. One of the chief difficulties of all previous investigators into the early medieval history of England had been that any proper comparative study of their chief sources was impossible for them owing to their ignorance of what MSS. existed, and where they were to be found. Henry Spelman had for example very rightly pointed out this essential defect in the equipment of Old English scholarship in that 'most of the materials were to be fetched from Manuscripts whereof indeed there were very great numbers both in the Universities and in other parts of the Kingdom: but being neglected by the generality of scholars they lay in confusion and were in a great measure useless'. 'At that time', comments Edmund Gibson, 'this was a just and proper Apologie, but our age is much more curious in these matters. Witness that noble Catalogue of Manuscripts which we daily expect from the Oxford Press.' Gibson's expectations were justified; and it was thus that *Bernard's Catalogue* introduced a new period in the comparative study of Anglo-Saxon texts.[2]

Whatever may have been the exact share of Wanley in *Bernard's Catalogue* there can be no doubt that he was primarily responsible for the success of a similar undertaking of like importance. As early as 1701, Hickes had suggested to Robert Harley that he ought to employ

---

[1] *Bodleian Letters*, I, p. 91; N. SMITH: *Warton's History of English Poetry*, p. 10.
[2] GIBSON: *Life of Spelman* (in SPELMAN: *English Works*).

HUMPHREY WANLEY
From the original portrait by Thomas Hill, 1717

Wanley to make a catalogue of his library, for 'that indeed', he added, 'would be a catalogue worthy of it'.[1] Thus by 1708 Wanley was hard at work on the enterprise which was to occupy him for the rest of his laborious life. The Harleian catalogue, as he visualized it, was to be no mere list, but a critical description of each manuscript with comparative comment and palaeographical information. The method provoked the easy sneers of Hearne, but the descriptions were exactly what made Wanley's work here of permanent importance. No other man in England was better able to appraise the significance of a manuscript, and he had the additional gift of being a most accurate transcriber, being 'so exact a man that his copies are next to originals'. Consequently the extensive quotations which adorned his work in the Harleian catalogue, since they were all from texts hitherto unpublished, were of the greatest value, and they made smooth the path of many of his successors. Wanley never lived to see this catalogue in print. By the time of his death he had ended his work on two thousand four hundred and seven manuscripts. But what he had written was not printed until a completed catalogue of the whole collection began in 1759 to be published, and this work in its turn was to be embodied in the present catalogue of the Harleian Manuscripts which the Record Commission issued between 1808 and 1812. Wanley's influence through the pages of these books has been immense, and it is still exercised. One example only need be given: it is probable that Thomas Warton was moved to write his *History of English Poetry* by the publication in 1759 of Wanley's work on the Harleian manuscripts, and certainly he derived much stimulation from it. All subsequent students of English medieval antiquities have been placed under a similar obligation. 'Wanley', remarks Dr. Nicol Smith, 'is still the greatest of our cataloguers. He may not have been a great critic of poetry but he was a very great critic of manuscripts, and all of us who are interested in the history of our early poetry owe him more than we sometimes know.'[2]

Over half a century separated the publication of *Bernard's Catalogue* from the appearance in print of the Harleian catalogue of 1759–63, and in both of these compilations Wanley's contributions, though sufficient to establish his reputation as a scholar, were to a certain extent anonymous. In 1705, however, there was published as a supplementary volume to the *Thesaurus* of Hickes a folio which bore Wanley's name on its title page and which was the crowning achievement of his career. The 'Critical and Historical Catalogue of Anglo-Saxon Manuscripts' begun

---

[1] *Portland MSS. Rep.*, IV, p. 16.
[2] *Catalogue of Harleian MSS.* (1808), I, pp. 27-28; N. SMITH: op. cit., p. 11.

H

by Wanley as a young man was the most valuable section of the *Thesaurus*. It later acquired fortuitously an additional importance from its detailed description of many manuscripts which perished in the fire which damaged the Cotton Library in 1731. And from the quality of its scholarship and the extent of its range it retains its value as an indispensable work of reference, and is to-day almost as useful as when it was written.

Here, too, it was Wanley's object to make his book as comprehensive as possible. But this, in an age when travel was neither easy nor inexpensive, entailed special difficulties, the more particularly for a student who at first was 'discouraged' from wandering by the Bodleian authorities who still employed him. It was usually impossible to get MSS. sent from Oxford, and though young Wanley did not lack audacity in his demands these were seldom successful. When he asked leave to borrow from the Cotton Library that great portfolio of charters known to all students to-day as *Cotton MS. A.ii*, he was curtly informed that the librarian was 'extremely amazed at the request', and advised that 'if the Mountaine cannot come to Mahomet, Mahomet must condescend to go to the Mountaine'.[1] However, slowly the necessary texts were examined. Cambridge was visited in 1699; later, the Cotton collection was surveyed; and, at another time, Wanley was elsewhere in London being shown for example 'Domesday Book, the continuation of it in a lesser volume, the antient Copy of them, the Pipe Roll with the black and red books of the Exchequer'.[2] Wanley was always conscious of the necessity of making his inquiries extremely wide, and he even noted the possibility that 'the libraries of France Italy and Germany' ought to be visited to discover what books they have illustrating or appertaining to our English history; and particularly to get an accurate account of the English records and Register Books formerly belonging to Monasteries in this Kingdom which 'being carried away to Rome at the dissolution of Abbeys are (as it is said) still preserved there in the archives of the Vatican Church'.[3]

The labour entailed in Wanley's greatest book was conditioned not only by the scattered nature of his material but even more by the exact and exhaustive methods he adopted. It is perhaps the most important feature of Wanley's achievement as a scholar that he carried the comparative study of manuscripts to lengths unknown before in English scholarship. In matters of dating, the excellence of his results was cer-

---

[1] ELLIS: *Letters of Eminent Literary Men*, p. 247.
[2] Ibid., p. 258.
[3] NICHOLS: *Literary Anecdotes*, I, pp. 101, 102; cf. *Bodleian Letters*, I, pp. 80, 81.

tainly due to his expert use of such a method. 'Every Book with a *Date*', he informed the Royal Society in 1705, 'is a *Standard* whereby to know that Age of those Books of the *same* or a *like* Hand and of those that are not very much *older* or *newer*.'[1] From the very first he put these ideas into practice. For example, in 1697, he is to be found writing from Oxford to a friend: 'I extremely want *the true Saxon character of King Alfred's time*; we have in the Publick Library *Pope Gregory's Pastoral Care* in Saxon which for several reasons I take to be as old as King Alfred who translated it or near unto it; but I cannot be certain of this, and I love two strings to my bow. Now Dr. Smith says that in the Cotton Library – there is another copy of the same book which formerly belonged to Plegmund, archbishop of Canterbury. If this be so my curiosity may be easily satisfied if you will get Mr. Sturt to copy me 10 or a dozen lines exactly from the book with the alphabets of the great and small letters and points.' A novel and important principle in comparative palaeography could hardly have been more remarkably illustrated. Wanley's successful adherence to it qualified him as a pioneer, and justified his boast that he 'never entertained any notion or relied upon any observation but as I found it confirmed by the suffrage of concurring circumstances and sufficient authority'.[2]

The initial scope of Wanley's research at the beginning owed much to Hickes who impressed upon his pupil the prime necessity of making his textual descriptions as full as possible. 'In taking the catalogue', he wrote, 'pray put the beginning and ending of every Tract and Homily, the first and last entire sentence, and the whole period when they are not too long.'[3] But Wanley was to become a better palaeographer than his master, and he himself described the methods he employed in preparing his greatest work. It was easy, he remarked, for critics to say that he was proceeding too slowly with his researches in the Cambridge Libraries. 'But, Sir, you ought not to think that there are so many Saxon MSS in this place as to keep a man seven weeks in barely transcribing their Titles. No, Sir, had that been all I had to do I might have done in seven hours. But I have looked over seven score MSS to see if I could find any Saxon words in them . . . I have not contented myself with saying *Liber Homiliarum Saxonicarum*, but noted the day it was proper for the Place of Scripture it treats upon, with some lines of the beginning and end. By this means I have been able to compare one homilie with another to find which do agree, which differ, which

[1] *Philosophical Transactions Abridged* (1731), vol. v, pt. II, p. 4.
[2] W. H. STEVENSON: *Asser*, p. xlv; NICHOLS: *Literary Anecdotes*, I, p. 97.
[3] ELLIS: *Letters of Eminent Literary Men*, p. 283.

copie had more of the same Text and which less etc. For other Saxon books I have copied large pieces of them; on purpose to compare them with other books in other Libraries that I might thereby know how they agree together. For I find we have more copies of the same book than I thought of as I believe I shall make appear. I have further transcribed all manner of Epistles, Wills, Covenants, Notes, Charms, Verses, Catalogues, etc. that I foresee may be of use to the Book. . . . In one word, if Dr. Hickes will accept from me a Catalogue of all the Saxon MSS that I know of in England, I will do my endeavour to restore many hitherto anonymous Tracts to their proper Authors; will specifie particularly what has been printed and what not; with a multitude of Remarks and Observations.'[1] Wanley was twenty-seven when he wrote this letter; and the book which appeared seven years later exactly bore out his prophecies.

Wanley's catalogue of Anglo-Saxon manuscripts remains to-day one of the half-dozen most valuable works of Anglo-Saxon scholarship, and the modern critic best qualified to pass judgment upon it has recently laid a proper emphasis on the abiding character of its influence. 'Plan and execution', he says, 'are alike good; every accessible MS. containing Old English words is described in detail.' Wanley's 'search for material went far beyond the obvious sources; his eye was quick to light on the things that matter; and he combined with the natural aptitudes of a great palaeographer a sureness of method which has made it possible to reconstruct his reasoning from his short conclusions. So when the revival of Anglo-Saxon studies came in the nineteenth century, scholars found the bulk of the manuscript materials collected, described, dated and indexed by an expert. With Wanley's catalogue as a guide they could go straight to the particular materials they required.' 'This facility led to the rapid and efficient printing of the texts.'[2] Such is high praise but it is not exaggerated. Wanley not only surveyed the whole of his vast subject in a manner which has not been possible for any other single scholar, but he brought to his critical task an accuracy and a sureness of judgment which have never been surpassed in any student of Old English MSS. Already in 1701 Hickes declared that 'Mr. Wanley . . . has the best skill in ancient hands and MSS of any man not only of this but of any former age',[3] and if this was the eulogy of a friend, subsequent criticism has found no reason to disturb the judgment. When, in the early years of the twentieth century, W. H.

---

[1] Wanley to Charlett, Oct. 19th, 1699 (ELLIS, op. cit., p. 292).
[2] SISAM: op. cit., VII, pp. 7-9.
[3] *Portland MSS. Rep.*, IV, p. 16.

Stevenson in his researches covered some of the same ground as
Wanley, he found, at the last, that he could only repeat the verdict of
Hickes: Wanley's 'accuracy in dating Old English MSS', he remarked,
'is astonishing to modern palaeographers who with all the advantages
they enjoy for the minute study of handwriting in the shape of accurate
photographic facsimiles seldom find reason to dissent from him'.[1] 'One
can seldom look', concludes Mr. Sisam, 'at an Anglo-Saxon manuscript without thinking gratefully of Humphrey Wanley.'

By 1726 his strange and prolific career was completed. From the
shop at Coventry, through the vagaries of undergraduate extravagance
and the routine of missionary endeavour, Wanley has reached his goal
at last as one of the greatest of librarians, and perhaps the finest critic of
Saxon manuscripts, that England has ever produced. His work was
done: securely embodied in folios which for generations would remain
a storehouse of information for subsequent scholars, and as an honoured
figure in the learned world of London, he might well feel himself far
removed from the storms and stresses of his youth. But, at the very
last, something of the old impetuosity asserted itself once more. Mor-
tally ailing as he was, he suddenly announced his intention of marrying
a second wife, 'a very young Creature who had been his Whore'.
Nothing that could be said would turn him from his purpose. 'Dr.
Hale did what he could to dissuade him on account of his condition.'
Wanley answered that 'he was betrothed and would marry'. 'It is a
pity', adds the clerical commentator with more than a touch of complacency, 'that the man cannot be hindered from such egregious folly
. . . No woman can think of marrying one in his condition but to strip
him.' Within a fortnight of the ceremony, Wanley was dead, and it
was fitting that Edward Harley should be stricken with grief. He did
not need to be told that he had lost 'the completest servant you could
have had in Europe'. Condolences came in to him from many quarters,
but the final comment might rather have been addressed to English
scholarship: *Haud illud invenies parum*.[2]

The methods of Wanley separated him to some degree from the
scholars from whom he had learnt at Oxford, and his interests alienated
him to some extent from the age in which he died. His career has therefore a certain quality of isolation. But he none the less belonged to that
group of 'Saxonists' who between 1660 and 1730 revolutionized the
study of their subject. Exercising perhaps less influence over his contemporaries than Hickes, he left to posterity a yet more enduring legacy

---

[1] W. H. STEVENSON: op. cit., p. xliv.
[2] *Portland MSS. Rep.*, VII, pp. 439, 442; HEARNE: *Collections*, IX, p. 162. Cf. X, p. 377.

of print, and it was his additional function to carry to the metropolis the Oxford tradition of Saxon learning just at the time when a transformation of public taste was threatening the existence of those studies to which he had given his life. The picture of Wanley moving as a respected figure in the London of Swift and Pope has a symbolical significance. Dropsical and dying in 1726, he could look back upon a performance which few English scholars have ever been able to emulate, and he could contemplate all around him the evidence that in his work a great movement in scholarship had reached its proper climax. After Wanley, no scholar of comparable importance addressed himself to the problems of Anglo-Saxon history until the advent of J. M. Kemble in the nineteenth century. The sterility of the intervening years throws into proper relief the magnitude of the corporate endeavour which had begun after the publication of Somner's Dictionary in 1659, and which had progressed so notably when John Smith was working upon his Bede, and when Nicolson and Thwaites were labouring at Oxford to sustain the tradition of Junius and Marshall. It would be difficult to discover a movement in English learning more productive of enduring achievement than that which ended by Wanley's death-bed. From this company the greater men stood out not by reason of the enthusiasm which they shared with their fellows but because of the superlative excellence of their own books. Smith's edition of Bede is still to be consulted as a work of the first importance, the reputation of Hickes probably stands to-day higher than at any period during the past century, and the study of any group of Anglo-Saxon manuscripts still starts inevitably from Wanley's critical catalogue. The work of these men, and of their numerous collaborators, justifies the description of the seventy years which followed the Restoration as the most constructive epoch in the development of Old English studies. During this period the foundations of our knowledge of Anglo-Saxon history were securely laid.

CHAPTER VI

THE NORMAN CONQUEST AND DR. BRADY

THE efflorescence of Anglo-Saxon scholarship in the period following the Restoration exercised an indirect but remarkable influence upon the investigations made during the same period into other problems relating to English medieval history, and in particular into those respecting the Norman Conquest. 'Saxonists' have always found difficulty in approaching the Norman Conquest in a spirit of critical detachment for they justly see in the events of that time a revolution which went far towards destroying a fine vernacular culture, and substituted in its place an alien Latinity which took no root in English soil. From the point of view of such scholars the Norman Conquest must always appear as a disaster of almost contemporary significance, and the zeal with which Saxon studies were pursued in the latter half of the seventeenth century inevitably tended to bias judgment upon the history of eleventh-century England. In 1623 William Lisle had fervently exclaimed: 'Thanks be to God that he that conquered the land could not so conquer the language,'[1] and among his successors he has found many to share his sentiments. Even now students of Old English literature have to resist with apparent difficulty the temptation to denaturalize the history of eleventh-century England.

Such predilections are in themselves deleterious to impartial historical inquiry. In the latter half of the seventeenth century they were moreover strongly reinforced by a potent tradition of political propaganda inherited from the immediate past. This was a legacy from the period when Parliamentarians had zealously invited the support of antiquaries and the Common Lawyers had continually cited medieval precedents in defence of their case against the Crown. Between 1603 and 1660 this literature had grown to a vast size, and claims such as those of Edward Coke that the laws of England had remained unchanged through the five successive ages of the Britons, Romans, Saxons, Danes, and Normans, won a wide acceptance even from well informed men, as did the similar assertions contained in Selden's *History of Tithes*.[2] As late as 1714 lawyers were concerned to keep the same tradition alive. 'Should we allow our Laws to have an uncertain Original,' wrote one of them, 'I fear that some People would of themselves fix their Original from

---

[1] *Saxon Treatise*, Preface.
[2] COKE: *Eighth Report*, Preface; Selden: *Works*, ed. Wilkins, III, pp. 1069 *sqq*.

William the First, and if that should be taken for granted, I don't know what ill use the Champions of Absolute Monarchy may be inclined to make of such a Concession.'[1] In certain quarters it was felt for these reasons to be more decent to speak of the Norman 'acquisition' or even of the Norman 'purchase' of England.[2]

There can be no doubt that the vigour of this polemical tradition derived from the constitutional controversies of the early seventeenth century. As early as 1613 John Hayward had issued his remarkable, if somewhat inaccurate, *Lives of the Three Norman Kings of England*. This was in many respects a notable book but it was begun for political reasons with the express approval of Prince Henry, and about the same time the theme was being also discussed in the *Breviary of the History of England*[3] that was later attributed to Sir Walter Ralegh. Already the study of the Norman Conquest was beginning to be linked up with present politics, and there was a difference in the attitude of these writers to their subject from that exhibited by John Rastell in his *Pastyme of People* nearly a hundred years earlier. It was, however, during the ensuing decades that the polemical approach to the subject was established by a multitude of tracts few of which shared in the merits of Hayward's book. Writers who supported the opinions of Edward Coke 'popularized' the theme in such a tendentious manner that it became almost impossible to undertake a study of the Norman Conquest in a proper spirit of historical inquiry.[4] When in 1701 Archdeacon Humphrey Hody, himself a distinguished investigator of ecclesiastical history, endeavoured to free himself from this net of argument, he did so in words which of themselves fully indicate the strength of the shackles from which he sought to escape:

> I take that Controversie about the Antiquity of our present Constitution to be as little material as that other which usually goes along with it; Whether William the Conqueror was truly a Conqueror? Let us grant he was so: Yet what is that to us who are descended not only from those that are supposed to have been Conquered but also from their Conquerors; and are the Heirs and Inheritors of all their Rights and Liberties.[5]

The Norman Conquest after the Restoration as before remained the sport of political propaganda and the objectivity which was to a great extent achieved in Old English studies between 1660 and 1730 was

---

[1] FORTESCUE-ALAND: *Monarchy*, p. xv.
[2] SPELMAN: *Glossarium* (1644), p. 145.
[3] Printed 1693, but in Hearne's opinion not the work of Ralegh (*Collections*, x, p. 198).
[4] See TEMPLE: *Introduction to the History of England* (1695), p. 312.
[5] *History of English Councils and Convocations* (1701), Preface.

seldom paralleled at the same period in discussions of English history
in the eleventh century.

The vigour of this baleful tradition could hardly be better illustrated
than in the single strictly historical work produced by the greatest
lawyer of Restoration England. Matthew Hale, Lord Chief Justice of
the King's Bench under Charles II, was 'allowed on all hands to be the
most profound lawyer of his time', and his saintly character elaborated
by Gilbert Burnet for the edification of posterity was of such repute,
that 'one good word of his was of more advantage to a young Man
than all the favour of the Court could be'.[1] When therefore he addressed himself to write the History of the Common Law he wrote as a
practical lawyer speaking with the authority of a fine scholar noted for
his impartiality. In these circumstances his treatment of the Norman
Conquest in such a connection is almost as remarkable for its length as
for its character. The book was perhaps the most notable contribution
made to the History of English Law before the appearance of the
volumes of Maitland and Pollock in 1895.[2] But it was singularly disappointing just at the point when to the historian it might have been
most interesting. Matthew Hale's charity did not extend into the
eleventh century, and his elaborate treatment of the Norman Conquest,
instead of marking a new epoch in an important department of English
historical study, carried on into a new period an old tradition of unhistorical controversy.

This tradition has by no means spent its force even to-day, and it too
must be noted in assessing the influence of seventeenth-century scholars
upon their successors. For it is surely wholly remarkable that these
events in a remote medieval past should always have generated such
polemical fervour in those who have discussed them. The treatment of
the Norman Conquest made by a long succession of English writers
between 1600 and 1900 forms indeed one of the curiosities of our
literature, and it affords an illuminating commentary upon the changing habits of the English mind.[3] During these three centuries book
after book has appeared devoted to this theme, but few of these have
succeeded in escaping from prejudices derived from very different
surroundings than those of the first Norman King. It would hardly be
paradoxical to speak here of a link between John Hayward and Edward
Freeman himself. For in the most extensive account of the Norman
Conquest which exists – a book replete with learning and too often

[1] BURNETT: *Life and Death of Matthew Hale* (1681), p. 181.
[2] Cf. HOLDSWORTH: *History of English Law*, VI, pp. 585-587. Contrast MAITLAND:
Collected Papers, II, p. 5.
[3] See DOUGLAS: *Norman Conquest and British Historians* (1946).

disparaged – the nineteenth century crowds in upon the eleventh, and Earl Godwine speaks often with the accents of Gladstone. While the interpretation of Anglo-Norman history clearly entails the solution of problems which are strictly historical, it still proves strangely difficult to dissociate these from extraneous issues of nationality, ecclesiasticism or republican interest.[1]

These preoccupations flourished in England during the seventy years which followed the Restoration, and their effect upon Anglo-Norman studies found expression in an over-large literature. Its character may be exemplified by reference to one book which was by no means exceptional in its tone – a volume with the engaging title of *Argumentum Anti-Normannicum* which appeared appositely in 1680 when the Parliamentary opposition to Charles II was reaching its climax. This anonymous work has been attributed to William Atwood, a Whig barrister who was later to become Chief Justice in New York, where he exercised his office until he was discharged therefrom in 1702 by Lord Cornwallis for gross corruption. But the book was more probably written by Edward Cook who, as a contemporary observed, might be regarded as Atwood 'in masquerade'. Whatever was its authorship, its purpose was made abundantly clear. It was concerned to show that William I never 'made an ABSOLUTE CONQUEST of the Nation'; that he did not 'ABOLISH all the ENGLISH LAWS'; or 'take away the estates of the ENGLISH'; and that there were 'ENGLISH men in the COMMON COUNCIL of the whole kingdom'. The spirit of the treatise was expressed in an allegorical frontispiece which depicted a highly complacent Britannia presenting to a dejected William a sceptre with one hand and the Laws of St. Edward with the other, while William in return gave thanks to his 'Sacred Queen' for the dominion she had thus conditionally bestowed upon him. In case prose and picture were not of themselves sufficient, verse was also added to convince those who still remained sceptical of this social contract of 1066. The sentiments, not unknown to-day, need no elaboration; nor was the book in itself of any importance save as showing the tendency of a large body of pseudo-historical literature. But it is surely a strange commentary on this aspect of seventeenth-century scholarship that such a plea 'to see GREAT CHARLES happy in's Parliament' should thus have taken the form of documented diatribe against William the Conqueror.[2]

[1] In 1936 a large historical congress in London was informed that the Norman Conquest was 'the last wave of barbarian immigration into this country'.

[2] *Argumentum Anti-Normannicum*, 'Explanation of the Frontispiece'; cf. BRADY: *Introduction to the Old English History* (1684), p. 235.

Few historical treatises of the late seventeenth century admit such
easy criticism as the *Argumentum*, but the prejudices which animated
its author appeared to a lesser degree in other works devoted to the
same topic and even in the remarkable essay which no less a personage
than Sir William Temple produced in 1695 under the title of *An Introduction to the History of England*. This work deserves serious consideration if only for the fact that so sound a critic as William Nicolson considered it 'the most excellent account' of the Norman Conquest, and
discovered in it 'such Reflections as become a Statesman'.[1] There was
indeed some reason for this praise, for, after the turgid prolixities of
the controversialists, it is a relief to read a stimulating account of
William the Conqueror written by one of their contemporaries who
justly won for himself a high reputation as a stylist. Nor did the merits
of the book lie solely in the attractive presentation of the theme.
Temple's observations were often original, and on such topics as the
coronation of Harold, the influence of the house of Godwine, and the
use made by the Conqueror of mesne tenures on ecclesiastical lands, his
remarks may even now be read with profit. Indeed, allowing for not
infrequent errors of detail, Temple's interpretation of English history
between 1051 and 1066 was more in keeping with the teaching of
modern scholarship than were the majority of the works produced in
the early nineteenth century.[2]

Despite its merits it is, however, impossible to dissociate even this
book from the tendentious discussions of Anglo-Norman England
which were characteristic of the age in which it was produced. It is true
that at times Temple displayed a healthy scepticism as when he remarked that the legal theories of the Norman Conquest propounded
by Selden and Coke were 'not so easily proved as affirmed'. But
Temple's criticism was seldom truly historical and his work abounded
in blunders. He made no real attempt to understand the ecclesiastical
history of the reign; his treatment of the Anglo-Norman jury was
without excuse dogmatic and inaccurate; and his observations on the
institution of Anglo-Norman feudalism showed that he was unac-
quainted with texts which were familiar to many of his contemporaries. The weakness of Temple's work was, in fact, exactly indicated
when he declared that he had 'not been so particular as other writers
in the Names of Places or of Persons or Distinction of Years'. He had
neither the knowledge nor indeed the inclination to make a proper
examination of the materials for his study, and his essay failed of its

[1] NICOLSON: *English Historical Library* (1736), p. 76.
[2] TEMPLE: *Introduction to the History of England*, pp. 104, 105, 160, 296-298, 312, 313.

purpose for that very reason. The same flavour of extraneous polemic in consequence crept in once more, and his final eulogy of the Conqueror was really as fundamentally uncritical as were the aspersions of his opponents. Not without reason did critics see here a deliberate compliment to William III, especially when they read how elaborately the Conqueror's putting aside of Edgar Atheling was described and condoned.[1]

The extensive literature devoted to the Norman Conquest in the last quarter of the seventeenth century might vary from the stimulating essay of Temple to the fantastic lucubrations of the *Argumentum*, but from the point of view of historical scholarship it was in the main barren of results, since the contentions of both parties were based upon false analogies which warped the critical judgment of the writers. But out of this constitutional debate there emerged at the hands of one man an important work of scholarship whose value has been somewhat obscured by the circumstances of its production. When Dr. Robert Brady issued his *Introduction to the Old English History* in 1694 and followed it up the next year with the first volume of his *History of England*, it might well have seemed merely that two new books were being added to a disputatious literature that was already overgrown. The truth was otherwise. The fatal defect of all the previous controversial work of this nature had been that its producers had made no proper objective study of the relevant documents or any adequate attempt to place these in their correct medieval setting. With Brady there is a change. His political convictions were at least as strong as those of any of his opponents and he wrote avowedly in support of a cause; his treatise of 1690 on the English boroughs was designed to justify the Stuart attack on municipal liberties and even the *Introduction* itself was largely made up of tracts that had previously been written in opposition to William Petyt and others.[2] But while Brady's motives were the same as those of his fellows, his methods were wholly different. Almost alone among his contemporaries in this controversy he made a thorough and remarkably extensive study of the sources of the history of Anglo-Norman England; and, in that he treated his texts as the product of the medieval past and sought to discover their meaning to the men who wrote them, his work has remained of permanent importance after its polemical significance has evaporated.

---

[1] TEMPLE, *Introduction to the History of England*, pp. 130, 131, 155, 166, 172, 188–226, 232, 256, 286.

[2] *An Introduction to the Old English History, Comprehended in Three several Tracts. The First, An Answer to Mr. Petyt's Rights of The Commons Asserted; and to a Book Intituled Jani Anglorum Facies Nova . . . The Second, An Answer to a Book Intituled Argumentum Anti-Normannicum . . . The Third, The Exact History of the Succession of the Crown of England . . . together with an Appendix . . . and a Glossary.*

It is unsatisfactory that so little is known concerning the private life of this scholarly doctor of medicine, for Robert Brady was no inconsiderable figure in Restoration England. In 1660 he was appointed Master of Caius College, Cambridge, and he became not only a professor of Medicine in the same University but also its representative in the Parliaments of 1681 and 1685. His Parliamentary activities are obscure, but the political fervour exhibited in his writings must have made him a recalcitrant member of Whig assemblies, and it comes as no surprise to learn that had the House sat but two days longer in March 1682 it would have ordered his existing tracts to be burnt. Despite his close connection with Cambridge, Brady seems to have been a metropolitan rather than an academic figure. As physician in ordinary both to Charles II and James II he was constantly at court, and in this capacity he was one of those who attested the momentous birth of the Prince in 1688. Nor was the position he won for himself in medicine entirely due to the royal influence. Brady was a Fellow of the College of Physicians, and he dared to bandy argument with Thomas Sydenham himself on the incidence of epidemic disease. It was a bold venture, for Brady's distinction was to be won in other fields. In due course this physician was somewhat strangely appointed to be Keeper of the Records at the Tower, and he forthwith set himself to study and to master the documents committed so unexpectedly to his expert charge.[1]

Brady was a master of record learning, and his achievement in historical scholarship has been regrettably belittled by the faint praise of those who were content silently to profit by his erudition while condemning his political opinions. Even to-day his books are often dismissed by a facile criticism which curtly remarks that they 'show a partisan spirit', or that though 'laborious' they are 'marked by the author's desire to defend the royal prerogative'. Brady's bias is too clear to need such reiterated comment. What requires more emphatic statement is that his learned conclusions are embodied in many standard works of a later date which omit to state the source from which they are derived.[2] In respect of the period which he made the object of his special study, Brady was a pioneer in research. In the world of Restoration learning he fulfilled a function closely comparable to that of J. H. Round in more recent times. Impatient of abstract theories which could not be justified by the detailed evidence, he was especially

---

[1] WOOD: *Life and Times*, II, p. 533; *Ath. Oxon.*, IV, col. 270; T. SYDENHAM: *Epistolae responsoria duae. Prima de Morbis epidemicis ab An 1675 ad An 1680.*

[2] Hume, for example, was much indebted to Brady.

concerned to correct the hasty assumptions of any author who 'made Partial Citations and Expositions by publishing only Ends and Shreds of Records and Histories where he found anything that did but sound like what he thought might maintain his assertion'. 'These Gentlemen', he complained, 'never cite anything particularly or exactly out of Domesday so as it is a great trouble to trace them.' 'You have been partial in your Citations,' he rightly remarked of one of them, 'taking some fragments or parcels of Sentences or sometimes a short sentence you thought might serve your turn, and always leaving what you could not but know would have destroyed your Notion and Argument; and also you have evinced both here and throughout how unjust or ignorant you have been in the Explication and Application of what you have cited, rendering and interpreting the words in several places rather according to their sound than true meaning.' It was exactly the criticism most needed in this branch of historical study, and developed at the hands of a considerable scholar, it was more valuable than any of Brady's own political arguments. The *Introduction* was, for this reason, not only a valuable piece of particular research; it was also a reasoned plea for the scientific study of Anglo-Norman history.[1]

The work therefore proved of permanent value, not as a fragment of political propaganda but as an essay in historical interpretation. Brady's criticism was throughout constructive for he was familiar with his texts and highly skilled in their exposition. 'Before the use of them', he declared, 'I considered again and again whether I might not be mistaken in their true meaning and like wise considered all Circumstances and compared them with other relations of the same Times and Things.' The results showed that this was no idle claim, but one which could be justified by the elaborate documentation which graced the book. 'As to my own Citations,' he added, 'if any Man thinks I have not been in every way faithful in them they are so particularly noted as it may with the greatest possible ease imaginable be discovered.' Francis North was right when he declared that Brady's work was compiled religiously from the very text letters and syllables of the authorities, but the success of the book was due not only to this fidelity, but also to the discriminating care of its author. Brady was careful to distinguish between the various types of evidence with which he dealt and his treatment of his texts in this respect bears comparison with that later adopted by the greater Madox. There was a modern ring about his conclusion: 'The Records I have used are faithfully cited; and likewise the Historians . . . whose Writings in very many things do agree

[1] BRADY: *Introduction*, esp. pp. 270, 280, 315-324, 325.

with the Publick Records; and this I affirm from my own collating and comparing of them.' For the time when it was written, it was a remarkable statement of the comparative use to be made of the record and chronicle sources of history.[1] The best testimony to the value of Brady's *Introduction* lies in the fact that it can still be criticized almost as if it was a modern book. It dealt admirably with just those problems which have in more recent times exercised the minds of students of Anglo-Norman history. Thus Brady's views of feudal election may be considered alongside of those of Chadwick; his description of the feudal basis of William's *curia* may be compared with the theories of G. B. Adams; his discussion of Anglo-Norman litigation formed the essential prelude to the work of Bigelow; and the elaborate and critical glossary which concluded the book may still be advantageously consulted. Dugdale was perhaps swayed by political sympathy when he declared the *Introduction* to have been 'done with much judgement as well as great paines', but he was right in his verdict; and many years later William Nicolson (who shared few of Brady's political opinions) was emphatically to endorse it. Later scholars, however, have not shared either the magnanimity, or the sound judgment, of Nicolson, and after two centuries of Whig disparagement it seems again necessary to assert not only that Brady's *Introduction to the Old English History* was a pioneer work on Anglo-Norman history, but that it remains to-day one of the most valuable extant treatises on the Norman Conquest.[2]

Brady's books inevitably impinged upon many of the particular controversies which continued to agitate contemporary students of history. They concerned for example the old argument as to the origins of feudal tenures in this country which in an earlier generation had exercised the ingenuity of Ralegh, of Selden and of Coke. There can be little doubt that the most valuable essay upon this subject that was written in England before the days of Maitland and Round was that which Henry Spelman had composed in 1631 and which was first published by Edmund Gibson in 1698. In this treatise on *Feuds and Tenures by Knight Service*, Spelman anticipated much of the most recent work which has been done on English feudal origins. In contrast to his fellows he made a clear distinction between the dependencies of Saxon times and the ordered feudalism established by William I; he discussed authoritatively the relation between the fee and the benefice; and he

[1] BRADY: *Introduction*, 'Epistle to the Candid Reader' and 'Advertisement'; *Lives of the Norths* (1890), I, p. 25; HEARNE: '*Hemingford*' (1731), I, p. xvi.
[2] BRADY: op. cit., pp. 21, 237, 281, 303; Dugdale to Brady, Oct. 6th, 1684 (HAMPER, pp. 436-439); NICOLSON: *English Historical Library* (1736), p. 194.

approached the question of the development of hereditary military tenures in England in a manner which may still excite admiration.[1]

By the end of the seventeenth century the immediate heats of the particular controversy in which Spelman had been engaged had passed, and it might therefore have been expected that the late publication of his remarkable essay would have secured for it more critical attention than it has ever received. But though even by 1660 the old argument had passed its fiercest phase, the circumstances of the Restoration, and in particular the abolition of feudal tenures by Charles II, aroused in certain quarters a curious revival of the dispute. In particular, they stimulated into activity a man who was one of the strangest personalities of the age. This was Fabian Philipps, and posterity has done less than justice to the profundity of his learning, and to the fortitude of his life. An essential conservative, even to the verge of eccentricity, he battled without pause for the re-establishment of conditions which had irrevocably passed away. But his erudition was of a permanent character, and his career took on something of the dignity of a rear-guard action fought to the death. Born in the reign of Queen Elizabeth, he carried his enthusiasms into a generation in which he was never at home; and, a survivor from a bygone world, he continuously asserted his principles with scholarly force until as a very old man he died in 1690.[2]

Courage and a native obstinacy were always characteristic of the life and writings of Fabian Philipps, and it was in opposition that he delighted. None the less it must have excited some wonder when, two days before the execution of Charles I, this minor official of the Court of Common Pleas was observed in London, 'causing to be put up on posts and in all common places' a Protestation against the 'Intended Murder' of the King. 'King Charles I', he asserted immediately afterwards, was 'no Man of Blood but a Martyr for his People.'[3] This might, for all its intrepidity, be regarded as, perhaps, but an extreme manifestation of royalist enthusiasm. But after the Restoration, Fabian Philipps advanced into a more isolated position, when, more royalist than the King, he denounced as disastrous the measures which put an end to feudal tenures in this country. He was not quite alone in this

---

[1] SPELMAN: *Feuds and Tenures by Knight Service* (*English Works*, ed. Gibson, 1698, pp. 1-46). His conclusions should be compared with those of Nicolson in his preface to Wilkins's edition of the Saxon Laws (1721), and also with those of such modern works as Stenton, *English Feudalism* (1932), esp. pp. 7-41 and 151-190.

[2] Fabian Philipps seems to be very little known. The best account of him appears to be in *Biog. Britt.* (Kippis). There is a note on him in HOLDSWORTH: *Hist. Eng. Law*, VI, p. 610. A list of his works is given in *Dict. Nat. Biog.*

[3] WOOD: *Fasti* (ed. Bliss), pt. II, col. 6.

unpopular contention since Francis North apparently shared his views.[1] But he was unique in the extent to which he advocated his opinions by means of an exhaustive examination of medieval precedent. The quaint titles of his very lengthy tracts – *Tenenda non Tollenda* (1660) or *Ligeancia Lugens* (1661) for example – concealed a mass of antiquarian learning. His works make up a long list, and his culminating folio on the *Established Government of England* written when its author was eighty-two years old is a mine of learned information.

Most of the books of Fabian Philipps are to-day as rare as they are neglected. In 1849, however, a copy of his *Government of England* was in the fine library of James Crossley, and he wrote within its cover: 'I venerate the Memory of Fabian Philipps and regard this Book as one of the great treasures of my Library ... The volume is full of historical research and seems to be quite unknown to all writers on English history.'[2] It was a just verdict. Fabian Philipps was no mere eccentric, or even merely an Elizabethan antiquary who had strayed unaccountably into the age of Burnet. He was a learned man, and his books, though ill digested, may yet be consulted with profit. They are of exceptional interest because they were concerned with the antiquity of institutions in the maintenance of which the author was himself directly involved.

Fabian Philipps was the last Englishman to write of feudalism as of a body of living institutions. He had been brought up in feudal surroundings; as a lawyer he had studied the legal implications of feudalism; and as an antiquarian he devoted his loving care to exploring the medieval origins of the system whose passing he lamented. He thus possessed for the task he undertook qualifications which have possibly never been combined in any other single writer on English feudalism. He was not a thinker; his powers of criticism were mediocre; 'his parts were never advanced when young by academical education';[3] his literary style was repulsive. But his writings are none the less of considerable importance, and they have been unduly neglected. Convinced that 'if we would not be ingratefull or unjust wee ought to defend that Kingdome and Government which Reason perswadeth us unto, Experiments approve, and Antiquity commendeth',[4] he gave to his work an unflagging industry which enabled him at last to become extremely well versed in medieval texts. His works are fully documented, and his learning is impressive. But his distinction was acquired from the fact that he wrote

---

[1] *Lives of the Norths* (1890), I, p. 31.
[2] MS. note in B.M. copy of *Government of England*.
[3] WOOD: *Fasti* (ed. Bliss), II, col. 5.
[4] *Tenenda non Tollenda* (1660), p. 276.

I

of the evolution of a social system which he had known at first hand, and he studied it with a zeal derived from the conviction that in its maintenance the welfare of England was involved. 'The *Feudall* Laws', he exclaimed, 'have been so fundamentall to our Laws and Customs of England – *velut ossa carnibus* – and so incorporate in the body thereof as it runneth like the life-blood through the veins arteries and every part thereof.'[1] He wrote of feudalism as an antiquary towards the close of the seventeenth century; but he wrote also in the tradition, and in something of the spirit, of Glanvill and Bracton.

The work both of Philipps and Brady reacted upon the contemporary development of research into the history of Parliament. The *Government of England* dealt with Parliament at length, and while Brady's *Introduction* was chiefly devoted to the Norman Conquest it was particularly concerned to answer the arguments of Petyt in his *Rights of the Commons Asserted* and of Atwood in his *Jani Anglorum Facies Nova*. These Whig writers were lawyers of some distinction, and the former made substantial contributions to learning, but in the sphere of constitutional history they took what was worst from the tradition of the earlier seventeenth century. Eager to discover Parliamentary precedents even where they did not exist, they ruthlessly applied more modern theories of constitutional government to the Middle Ages. The familiar legends respecting Magna Carta for example found a place in their books, and the House of Commons was traced back with a disregard for evidence through the twelfth century and even into Saxon times. What had been excusable in the fourteenth-century author of the *Modus Tenendi Parliamentum*, and understandable in editors like Hakewill and Elsynge, was harder to palliate in an age when the documents relating to Parliamentary history were becoming better known. Dugdale in his last book, and Brady and Philipps after him, undoubtedly enjoyed exposing the fallacies of their political opponents, but their arguments were, historically speaking, well sustained, and their conclusions were substantially correct.[2]

These royalist scholars wrote avowedly on behalf of a party, but their research produced results of positive value, and medieval scholarship suffered by later neglect of their work. When Fabian Philipps for example asserted the feudal origins of the English Parliament, and contended that the Commons were not an essential part thereof, when he further argued that the distinction between the greater and lesser

---

[1] *Government of England* (1687), p. 213; cf. *Restauranda* (1662), pp. 1-57; *Necessity of Pourveyance* (1663), p. 52; *Regale Necessarium* (1671), Preface.
[2] BRADY: *Introduction*, pp. 1-162, 166, 167.

tenants-in-chief came about through the practice of the Crown,[1] he was preaching a doctrine which was unpalatable at the time of the 'Glorious Revolution', but one which, through the efforts of very modern scholarship, has been shown to have been historically sound. Similarly, while the conclusions of Brady on this matter were hatched out of polemic, they were, as history, of such value that they deserve re-statement:

1. That the Commons of England represented by Knights Citizens and Burgesses in Parliament were not introduced nor were one of the three Estates in Parliament before the 49th of Henry III.
2. That before that time the Body of the Commons of England or Freemen collectively taken had not any share or votes in making of Laws for the Government of the Kingdom nor had any communication in Affairs of State unless they were represented by Tenants in capite.

And further he added that there is

Nothing to prove that during the British Saxon and Norman governments the Freemen or Commons of England as now called and distinguished from the Great Lords were an essential part of the Witena Gemote, Common Council or Parliament in those Ages.[2]

Modern students of Parliamentary history would probably assent to every one of these propositions, but it has needed the concerted efforts of scholars during the last fifty years to get them accepted as true. If the work of Brady had been properly studied, not as part of an outworn controversy, but for what it was – a substantial contribution to erudition – a long tradition of error in these matters might perhaps have been avoided.

Before he died, Brady wrote *An Inquiry into the Remarkable Instances of Historical and Parliamentary Records*, and this book was to connect his work with yet another of the related controversies of the age. His purpose had been chiefly to disprove the existence of democratic or republican institutions in medieval England, but he was inevitably concerned also with the historical sanctions of the hereditary rights of Kings. After the Revolution the controversies on the Oaths gave to his work a new topical interest, and the Non-jurors read it with avidity, as containing in their belief the answer to the theories which for example William Higden put forward in 1709 in his *View of the English Constitution*. Higden asserted that thirteen of the Kings of England

---

[1] PHILIPPS: *Government of England*, esp. pp. 163, 204, 207 *sqq.*
[2] BRADY: op. cit., *Introduction*.

between 1066 and 1485 were not in the direct hereditary line, and he
proceeded to the conclusion that it was the *de facto* king who alone by
the very reason of his establishment could claim allegiance. As stated
by Higden his thesis was patent of the criticism which it promptly
received,[1] and since he ignored the sanctions imposed during the
Middle Ages upon monarchy, it was not unreasonable for Hearne to
claim that he 'resolved all into Posession and made all Usurpers have a
title to Allegience not excepting even Oliver himself'.[2] Higden however returned to the charge, and in 1710 he issued against his opponents
an elaborate *Defence* of his views.

The whole controversy might well have been allowed to subside as
an unimportant eddy in the contemporary whirlpool of argument; and
it would probably have done so had not Higden's books elicited the
publication in 1713 of a slim and elegant folio with the title of the
Hereditary Right of the Crown of England, under the anonymous authorship of 'A Gentleman'. This argued with considerable ability that the
known facts of English history indicated that a distinction had always
been made between usurpation and legitimate succession, since the
Kings of England had always asserted some claim based upon hereditary or testamentary right. However true this might be, it was perilous
doctrine in 1713, and it became more offensive to Authority when the
book containing it was published in the most ostentatious manner –
'the title pages' (as White Kennett indignantly noted) 'in full half sheets
of good paper appearing on a Sunday morning upon every conspicuous
post and door to draw away the eyes of all that were going to Church'.
Nor was it more pleasing to the Government when Robert Nelson
made it his business to see that a sumptuously bound copy of the work
was presented to the Queen herself.[3]

The author of the book, who had so provokingly asserted his gen-
tility but not his name, was William Harbin, 'a person of uncommon
Learning admirably versed in all Parts of English History'. Suspicion,
however, immediately fastened upon another Non-juror, Hilkiah
Bedford, who had in fact taken some part in seeing the sheets through
the press. The confusion produced a situation that was both amusing
and tragic. For Lord Weymouth supposing Bedford to be the author
sent him a hundred guineas for his pains, and chose as his emissary with
the money none other than Harbin himself! The true author must have

[1] Cf. *A Letter to the Rev. William Higden by a Natural Born Subject*. See also LATHBURY:
Non-Jurors (1845), p. 230.
[2] HEARNE: *Collections*, II, p. 297; cf. ibid., II, pp. 290, 291, 293.
[3] KENNETT: *Wisdom of Looking Backwards* (1715), p. 313; SECRETAN: *Robert Nelson*
(1860), pp. 85-87.

been indeed disagreeably surprised when Bedford accepted the money without further comment, but Harbin was subsequently to have nothing to lament in the transaction. Bedford was fully to earn the fee which he had accepted under false pretences, for when the reckoning came he stood his trial with fortitude and accepted the heavy responsibility of being the author of a book he did not write. Without ever betraying Harbin, he was sentenced to imprisonment for three years, to a fine of a hundred marks, and to go round Westminster with a paper affixed to his breast explaining the enormity of his crime. The last part of the sentence was remitted through the efforts of Robert Nelson and Hickes, but Bedford had to serve his term in prison where 'his righteous soul was vexed from day to day with the filthy conversation of the wicked'. His release from that most grievious durance was as it were 'a deliverance from hell', but he was a broken man when he regained his liberty.[1]

The book which involved this personal tragedy was the climax of a long argument which did not of course end with its publication. White Kennett made a reply confined to the events of the fifteenth century, and he in his turn was advised 'to forbear the character of an Impartiall Historian and to refrain from seeking a Reputation by quoting books he had not read'.[2] But from the point of view of historical scholarship, the *Hereditary Right of the Crown of England* is mainly remarkable for its lively discussion of certain points of medieval constitutional growth, particularly in respect of the reigns of Stephen and Henry II. Otherwise it contained little that was new, and the author of its preface – Theophilus Downes, who had sacrificed a Balliol fellowship for refusing the oaths to William in 1690 – frankly confessed his debt to the concluding essay in Brady's *Introduction*.[3] The new evidence which was here cited from the Harleian manuscripts was of little value, and the book itself can hardly be considered as a substantial piece of historical research.

Even the most cursory survey of the vast literature of constitutional controversy which was produced between 1660 and 1730 illustrates the abiding interest of the age in the problems of medieval politics. A steady output of books was here maintained which ranged from copious historical narratives to short political diatribes couched in antiquarian terms. The elaborate *Life of Edward III*, issued in 1688 by Joshua Barnes, who was a Greek scholar and the son of a London tradesman, was typical of what was best in this production, and it sup-

[1] NICHOLS: *Literary Anecdotes*, I, pp. 167, 168; *Portland MSS. Rep.*, v, pp. 346, 473.
[2] KENNETT: *Letters . . . Upon the Subject of Bishop Merks* (1713, 1716, 1717), EARBURY: *Serious Admonition to Dr. Kennett*, pp. i, ii.
[3] *Hereditary Right* (1713), p. 17.

plied a mass of information which is even to-day not easily to be obtained elsewhere. But at the same time medieval England remained a favourite subject for numerous writers whose interests were engaged only to a secondary degree in the honest investigation of the past. It would be easy to compile a long list of such books produced at this time; and in collections of tracts such as that particularly associated with Lord Somers, it is astonishing to note how many of the papers deal incidentally with medieval politics. These undoubtedly enlivened contemporary controversy. But very few of them contributed to historical knowledge.

Nevertheless the scholarly production of such as Brady, and the mass of controversial literature by which it was surrounded, caused in England a general improvement about this time in a class of work with which this book has no direct concern. The general interest in antiquities prevailing in England had for long given a vogue to general narratives of English history. These had usually few scholarly merits but they were widely read by many who had themselves no pretensions to scholarship. The most important production of this type was probably the compilation of Sir Richard Baker whose *Chronicle of the Kings of England*, first published in 1643, continued to enjoy such popularity that noble ladies entered into prolonged controversy in respect of its statements,[1] and at a later date Sir Roger de Coverley kept it always 'in his hall window' for constant perusal.[2] After the Restoration the apotheosis of English monarchy contained in Winston Churchill's *Divi Britannici* of 1675 attracted a similar but more restricted attention. These books are hardly to be discussed as works of original scholarship but the research of the age was reflected in this class of literature also, and in particular in the Whig histories of James Tyrrell and Laurence Echard. Tyrrell, whose main claim to distinction was perhaps his friendship with John Locke, was a country gentleman of Buckinghamshire, who had been deprived of his offices in that county for refusing to support the Declaration of Indulgence, and in the three volumes of his History of England which appeared before his death in 1718 he set himself to refute the opinions of Brady. The value of his book lay in his quotation from authorities, and his introduction on Anglo-Saxon government may still be read with interest, though the desire of the author to exalt the power of the Witan as a predecessor of Parliament robs it of much of its value. Tyrrell's work in short never subordinated propaganda to inquiry, and somewhat similar criticism could be

[1] Cf. POWICKE in *Huntingdon Library Quarterly*, I, pp. 260 sqq.
[2] *Spectator*, No. 269.

levelled against Echard's long narrative, the first volume of which appearing in 1707, dealt with medieval England. Echard, the son of a Suffolk clergyman, and himself in orders, was also concerned to refute Brady but he never attained the mastery of medieval records enjoyed by the scholar whose political opinions he attacked. His book was to hold the field in 'popular' history until Nicholas Tindal's translation of Rapin began to appear in 1725, but as far as the Middle Ages were concerned it marked little advance upon existing knowledge. In view of its copious citations from original authorities, however, it approached far more nearly to the standards of historical discussion than its predecessors in the same field, and its author frankly acknowledged his debt to the original work of Brady while disputing his conclusions. The histories of Tyrrell and Echard were, in fact, remarkable books of their kind, and though they are not to be considered as works of original historical research, they deserve a cursory mention even in this place. They indicated how the general reader in England was during this period being influenced indirectly by the work of scholars whose books he might never read.

Both in their scope and in their quality these books stand somewhat apart from the huge production of the age in popular and controversial works relating to the history of medieval England. And when the bulk of this literature is considered, its positive contribution to historical knowledge appears disappointing. It was not so much that the stimulus for, of immediate argument destroyed the sense of historical perspective, while this was so, nevertheless in other branches of historical inquiry such preoccupations did not prevent the production of scholarly work of the first importance. It was, rather, that here the argumentation outran the study of authorities, and that most of the participators in the debate came more and more to bandy against each other selected textual extracts known to all the disputants, but whose provenance was imperfectly understood and whose relation to other contemporary material was unstudied. These men, as White Kennett justly observed, were for the most part mere 'pretenders to Antiquity', in that they 'rais'd the apparition of Records to justifie the cause for which they wrote'. Brady was precisely right when he emphasized this weakness in the writings of his opponents. But he was yet more justified in his claim that the whole controversy would remain barren of positive results until the sources themselves were studied for their own sake, and the texts in their entirety printed in more reliable and more accessible form.

The case of Domesday Book was the most notable example of this.

Ever since the sixteenth century the transcendant importance of King William's great survey as a source of English medieval history had been appreciated. Francis Tate, for example, one of the members of the original Society of Antiquaries, 'perused (it) over and over, and extracted many things from it; and to render it the more intelligible to others he explained the abbreviated words in it'.[1] A widespread consciousness prevailed that here was a text that was essential to the understanding of English medieval society. When, for instance, Selden in 1623 produced his edition of Eadmer's *Historia Novorum* he included in the valuable appendices to that book a considerable amount of information derived from Domesday;[2] Dugdale quoted extensively from it; and in a note appended to his own edition of chronicles Thomas Gale suggested that the genesis of the survey and its interpretation could only be appraised by means of a comparison between Domesday Book and the satellite surveys by which it was surrounded.[3] This anticipated in a remarkable manner the trend that has been taken by the most recent Domesday research, and at the same time numerous scholars were utilizing the survey for the purpose of illustrating topographical antiquities. But real progress was impossible so long as no printed text of the complete Domesday Book was available. Domesday Book itself remained at Westminster under three locks, and to consult it the student had to pay a fee of six shillings and eightpence with fourpence extra for every line transcribed.[4] The consequences were disastrous. John Evelyn might commend to William Nicolson the study of history as tending to the discovery 'whence our holding by Knight's Service have been derived, whether from Saxon or from Norman';[5] but how was the scholar to achieve this laudable object when the chief source of his information was withheld from him? The excessive respect in which Domesday was held combined with an ignorance of its general contents to produce the strangest misconceptions of the nature of the great record, so that even so well informed a man as Samuel Pepys was constrained to search in Domesday 'concerning the sea and the dominion thereof'.[6] Whilst nearly all those who disputed about the constitution of medieval England quoted from Domesday Book, they did so by means of isolated extracts which were, successively and uncritically, used by one writer after another, and with the possible

---

[1] HEARNE: *Curious Discourses* (1771), I, p. lxii.
[2] Esp. pp. iii-vi.
[3] *Scriptores*, XV (1691), pp. 795, 796.
[4] THORESBY, *Diary*, II, p. 30; NICOLSON: *English Historical Library* (1736), p. 213.
[5] NICOLSON: *Epist. Corr.*, p. 141.
[6] ROUND: *Feudal England* (1895), p. 229.

exception of Robert Brady himself there was during the decades which followed the Restoration no single scholar who possessed a general knowledge of Domesday.

It was, therefore, with good reason, that Brady loudly voiced the need for a complete edition, and his plea was soon to be supported by many other scholars. 'I have often wished', remarked Hearne, '(it) were printed entirely, there being no survey of any other country whatsoever equal to it . . . There are accounts of some whole counties printed from this book, and they are very good specimens of the intire work, and cannot but make those that are in love with our antiquities the more earnestly to desire all of it. But, it may be, there are private considerations which may hinder an edition as indeed it too often happens that the publick interest of learning suffers by reason of private concerns.'[1] Private interest was not, however, wholly lacking, for Robert Harley, Earl of Oxford, 'often talked' of sponsoring an edition of Domesday Book engraved upon copper plates.[2] But none of his contemporaries was ready to undertake the task, and more than half a century was to elapse before his hopes were in any measure realized. The continuation of interest in the project was reflected in the support it received from Philip Carteret Webb, who took a leading part in the proceedings against John Wilkes, and in 1756 this remarkable lawyer turned from contemporary litigation to produce his notable *Account of Domesday Book with a view to its being published*. But it was not until 1783 that on the instructions of a Royal Commission a great edition of Domesday at last appeared, printed on 'record' types which were specially cut for the purpose and which later were destroyed in the fire at Westminster in 1834. No name appeared at the head of this edition, but it was the production of a scholar whose labours on this task stretched back almost to the days of Hearne himself. The personal accomplishment of Abraham Farley has been shamefully neglected by generations of scholars who have been content without acknowledgment to profit by his work, but 'for more than forty years' he had 'almost daily recourse' to Domesday Book[3] and he produced one of the most accurate and reliable transcripts in the whole history of English scholarship. His is still the sole indispensable edition of Domesday Book and his work has yet to be superseded. His labours marked the continuation of those of an earlier generation, and by reason of them the aspirations of Brady, Hearne and Harley (to name no others) were at last fulfilled.[4]

---

[1] HEARNE: *Curious Discourses* (1771), I, pp. lxii, lxiii.
[2] HEARNE: *Collections*, X, p. 101.
[3] ELLIS: *Introduction to Domesday* (1833), I, p. 360.
[4] Cf. DOUGLAS: *The Domesday Survey* (*History*, vol. XXI, p. 250).

During the seventy years which followed the Restoration, the absence of a complete edition of Domesday was the greatest obstacle to a proper understanding of Anglo-Norman history. It was symptomatic also of the wider deficiency which had been made abundantly manifest in the controversial work of the constitutional historians of this time. In his perpetual insistence that extracts from medieval texts could not be studied in isolation, Brady indicated precisely the only way in which this branch of medieval study could be made to advance. What was needed was not a repetition of the old arguments reinforced by the same quotations, but a new investigation of the sources themselves. For this purpose, scholars needed, above all else, fuller and more complete editions of the English chronicles. In this work, and not in constitutional controversy, was, therefore, to be found the great contribution of the age to this department of medieval study, and it was thus the great good fortune of English scholarship that at this time there appeared a number of outstanding men able to undertake the task of placing the chronicles of England upon a sounder critical basis. In their labours must be sought the explanation of the great advance made in these studies between 1660 and 1730. For, by their research, and through their editorship, they did little less than make possible the growth of the modern knowledge of English history between the Norman Conquest and the coming of the Tudors.

CHAPTER VII

HENRY WHARTON

IN the early autumn of 1688 a remarkable young man might have been observed in the household of Archbishop Sancroft at Lambeth. His name was Henry Wharton, and he was a youth 'of middle Stature of a brown Complexion with a grave and comely Countenance' and a vigorous healthful constitution.[1] His appointment as domestic chaplain to the Archbishop seemed to confirm his exceptional promise, for he already bore a reputation for great learning, and though he had but recently graduated at Cambridge and was still a deacon, he had been given a licence to preach through the whole diocese of Canterbury. He was clearly marked out for rapid promotion, but despite his prospects he must none the less have found the atmosphere at Lambeth charged with vivid and conflicting emotions. This was the brief heyday of Sancroft's popularity, when the Archbishop might fairly regard himself as the leader of a nation in perplexity. But already the coming of William was foreshadowed, and with the same calmness as he had shown in his prosperity Sancroft was making ready to sacrifice everything for the King whose authority he had done so much to destroy. In the intervening months, however, many other things besides politics were doubtless discussed at Lambeth, and young Wharton appears to have gone about his business scarcely conscious of the political developments which were soon to wreck his career.

He was then but twenty-four, and since he had only six more years to live, it is impossible in contemplating his career to escape the feeling of watching exploits of an infant prodigy. The very circumstances of his birth had been portentous. For if an earlier scholar 'fell immediately from the wombe of his Mother into the lappe of the Muses',[2] young Wharton on November 9th, 1664, had almost vied with this feat by being born unmistakably with a gift of tongues. Two of these appendages were found within his puling lips, and the scientists who solemnly gathered together to consider this sport of nature later delivered papers on the subject to the Royal Society.[3] Of such a child almost anything could be expected, and it seems hardly surprising that

---

[1] Anonymous life of Wharton prefixed to the posthumous collection of his Sermons (1697).

[2] G. Langbaine in Preface to JOHN CHEKE: *True Subject to the Rebell* (1641).

[3] Cf. DR. MORTIMER in *Philosophical Transactions*, 1748, p. 232.

when Wharton entered Caius College, Cambridge, in 1680 from the Paston Grammar School he should already have gained the reputation of 'an extraordinary young man'.[1] He immediately set himself to enhance his fame by working twelve hours a day, and he gained distinction not only in classics and theology but also in mathematics in which subject he was Isaac Newton's last private pupil. A faint air of virtuosity had already begun to surround him. But for once undergraduate brilliance portended an enduring achievement. During the nine years which remained to Henry Wharton after he left Cambridge he produced work of permanent importance, amassed vast manuscript collections, and in his *Anglia Sacra* bequeathed to the future a book which has remained indispensable to the study of English monastic chronicles.[2]

It was probably fortunate for Wharton that his versatile brilliance was early subjected to the discipline of controlled research. When in 1686 no Fellowship at Cambridge could be found for him, he was recommended as assistant to William Cave who was then compiling his famous *Historia Literaria* which was designed to contain an account of all European writers between the birth of Christ and the Reformation. Cave worked the young man hard, and Wharton responded to such purpose that many of the articles in the finished book were to bear his initials, and the section of the work which dealt with the period after 1300 was largely written by him. It was an admirable training, and though Wharton claimed that 'his incesant and exhaustive' labours on the book were never properly acknowledged, he probably owed very much to the instruction in method which he received from the elder scholar. Certainly his work for Cave did not prevent him from undertaking other enterprises at this period. He tried his hand at translation, he inveighed against 'the Enthusiasm of the Church of Rome', and he published tracts on points of ecclesiastical history. By the time that he reached Lambeth he had already begun to make himself familiar with the manuscripts at Cambridge, at Lambeth, and in the Royal Library at St. James's; and under Sancroft's special patronage he was ready to begin the individual research which made ever afterwards significant his brief and thwarted life.[3]

The character and the circumstances of Wharton's achievement would be harder to judge if in the midst of his labours he had not found time to jot down in the form of Latin notes the materials of an auto-

[1] C. R. FORDER: *History of the Paston Grammar School* (1934), pp. 167-170.
[2] *Biog. Britt.* (Kippis), sub. Wharton.
[3] Sermon Life; D'OYLY: *Sancroft*, II, pp. 154-174.

biography whose contents and subsequent history are one of the curiosities of literature. Known to be of exceptional interest, the text of this Latin diary was eagerly sought by scholars after Wharton's death, and Thomas Tanner who had apparently seen the original tried to get possession of it from Wharton's father. He was referred however to a younger brother who – alas! – was discovered to be 'an Apothecary and great Rake' so that already in 1729 it was feared by Hearne and others that the diary together with 'other things of great value' had been 'utterly destroyed'.[1] Nevertheless in 1752 the diary was still in existence, and it was then in the possession of Edmund Calamy, one of the family of Puritan historians. Since then, however, time has apparently accomplished what even the rakish apothecary failed to achieve, and the full text of Wharton's diary has disappeared. But extracts made therefrom by Thomas Birch, the biographer of Tillotson, survive to supply evidence of what must have been a most unusual composition.[2] From it the extraordinary features of Wharton's character emerge from his own description.

He was consumed with that immense energy which was characteristic of seventeenth-century scholarship in England, and no scholar of the age – not even Hickes or Hearne – contrived a larger production within the same space of time. The long stretches of his undergraduate application were increased in later life, and in confidence of his strength 'he was too little regardful of himself and too intent on his studies', so that he would often 'deny himself the Refreshments of Nature; and sometimes in the coldest weather would sit so long at them as to have his hands and feet so chilled as not to be able to feel the use of them for a considerable time'.[3] 'His Method of writing', it was remarked, 'was standing, and when he sat down it was in a great Chair but very close.'[4] The picture needs no elaboration. All that need be added is that these labours produced commensurate results. The Diary shows works begun and completed in a few months which might have employed others for years. It is sufficiently remarkable that *Anglia Sacra* was the work of one man: that it should have been but one of the productions of a short life almost baffles explanation.

An explanation must, however, be sought, if a true conception is to be formed either of Wharton or his work, and it is to be found perhaps in the influence of the peculiar atmosphere of seventeenth-century

[1] HEARNE: *Collections*, x, p. 165.
[2] BIRCH: *Tillotson* (1753), p. 132. Birch's excerpts are contained in a Lambeth MS. and were printed by D'Oyly (*Sancroft*, II, pp. 105 *sqq.*).
[3] Sermon Life; cf. DUCAREL: *Palace of Lambeth* (1785), p. 66; D'OYLY: *Sancroft*, II, p. 160.
[4] HEARNE: *Collections*, VII, p. 164.

scholarship upon a nervous young man of extraordinary abilities.
There can be no doubt of Wharton's extreme piety; nor can there be
any question that the chief motive that inspired his immense labours
was the desire to discover in the past a justification of the ecclesiastical
system that he served. The disputatious fervour of the age of Hickes so
wrought upon the superabundant energies of a receptive youth as to
goad him into a frenzy of emulous endeavour. A vein of sectarian propaganda runs in consequence through Wharton's writing. Since he
never lacked self-assurance, it was natural that he should enter early
into controversy by assisting Tenison, and by being the special means
of bringing back into the Anglican fold 'one of excellent parts'. When
he was twenty-four he made a spirited reply to Thomas Ward, 'the
Roman Catholic soldier', and four years later he produced his learned
'Defence of Pluralities' against the critics of Anglicanism. Among the
last of his works to be published was his edition of Laud's prison diary
which was re-edited in order to defend the memory of the Archbishop
from the attacks and the innuendoes of Prynne.[1]

It was characteristic both of Wharton and his age that this missionary
ardour should impel him to historical research and provoke an immense production of works of pure scholarship whose importance has
long survived the arguments which inspired them. In Wharton, as in so
many of his contemporaries, the controversialist always imparted
energy to the scholar, and the connection, maintained throughout his
life, may be clearly seen in many of his minor writings. In 1687, for
example, he went to Cambridge to work on medieval texts and to
make transcriptions because 'times now grew warm and the Papists
began to be very confident of their cause in so much as there was a fear,
and accordingly care taken about some choice manuscripts lest they
should unhappily fall into the Enemies hand.'[2] The same double motive
may be seen perhaps in the fine edition of Ussher's *Historia Dogmatica*
which Wharton brought out in 1680, wherein the young man not
only collected the scattered observations of one of the most formidable
of British scholars, but filled up certain gaps with his own pen, added
important footnotes, and supplied the Greek passages with an admirable Latin translation. It is hard to say whether the defender of Anglicanism or the antiquarian scholar is here predominant, and the anonymous editor of *A treatise proving Scripture to be the Rule of Faith writ by
Reginald Pecock, Bishop of Chichester before the Reformation* may be termed

[1] WHARTON: *Enthusiasm of the Church of Rome* (1688); '*Speculum Ecclesiasticum*' *considered*
(1688); *Defence of Pluralities* (1692); *History . . . of William Laud* (1695 and 1700).
[2] Sermon Life.

either an extremely able historical scholar, or a highly skilled disputant in a living ecclesiastical issue. His learned preface, which fills up forty pages, not only portrayed one who in his own time had been eminent if unfortunate in controversy, but also attempted to show that 'tradition neither is nor can be the Rule of Faith'. It is surely remarkable that this fine piece of editorship which produced an important historical text equipped with an early glossary of Middle-English words should have been issued as a natural move in a campaign of ecclesiastical propaganda.[1]

Sancroft was exactly the man to dominate a youth of this nature. The saintly character of the Archbishop won his respect, and a zeal for scholarship displayed in high places provided additional inspiration. Sancroft was the correspondent of Dugdale and Hickes, and his influence upon contemporary learning was pervasive, but it was his special distinction to be successful in kindling the enthusiasm of younger men. His chaplains, carefully chosen for their erudition, were devoted to him and several of them besides Wharton were to make contributions to medieval scholarship.[2] It was the wish of the Archbishop that this should be so. Though he excelled in all kinds of learning he was most eminent in the study of English history,[3] and though he had an extreme distaste for publication he left behind him vast collections in manuscript.[4] To such stimulus Wharton immediately submitted. 'It was shameful', he wrote to his patron, 'for a young man to be otherwise than diligent in his studies and to be remiss in doing the greatest possible service to the Church when he saw most unwearied diligence as well in reading as in writing in so dignified a prelate.'[5] By 1688 this susceptible young man had, in fact, found his hero, and he was ready to pour out his labour in unrestrained devotion. 'Your other virtues', he wrote, 'I can only admire; that of diligence I can imitate.'[6] Wharton was undoubtedly of unbalanced energy, and too easily influenced. But the description on his tomb exactly expressed the blended enthusiasms of his life: 'He laboured much to increase and to illustrate letters. He wrote much and toiled more for the Church of Christ.'[7] Literature, scholarship and the Church were inseparably intertwined in the fervent service of this remarkable youth, and in this he was a characteristic product of the age in which he lived.

---

[1] USSHER: *Historia Dogmatica* (ed. Wharton 1689). The Pecock treatise was issued in 1688.
[2] D'OYLY: *Sancroft*, II, pp. 72, 159.   [3] Cf. D'OYLY: op. cit., II, p. 76.
[4] Some of these were printed by Gutch in *Collectanea Curiosa* (1781).
[5] *Anglia Sacra*, I, 'Epistola Dedicatoria', p. vii (trans.).
[6] Ibid.   [7] Sermon Life.

It is possible, however, that a less charitable inquirer looking at the odd face which smirks from the frontispiece to Wharton's sermons might suspect an additional explanation of the almost morbid energy which informed his life.[1] The portrait sends the curious investigator not to the homilies which it introduces but to the autobiography in which this astonishing young man fills up whole pages of Latin diction with the praise and the explanation of his own virginity. In 1678 despite the exuberance of virile propensities which he deplores he cannot recall any lapse or indulgence 'nay not even such as might involve the lips'. Five years later he was, apparently, 'repeatedly sollicitied to vice' by a young girl so that he 'only just escaped making a shipwreck of his own modesty'.[2] There seems here, however, to have been more than one cause for pride for (as he adds) the young lady 'possessed considerable good looks and an untarnished reputation'.[3] In these circumstances it was natural to search history for methods used in the past to frustrate 'thoughts of uncleanness and to prevent the circles of an Inward Fire'. Consequently it was a peculiar gratification for him to be able to describe at some length in 1686 the means by which he managed to resist the attacks of a Romish priest who 'burning with lust no less than theological zeal sought to corrupt not only his soul but his body'.[4] Complacency seems to have blunted the sense of humour. But it is little wonder that with these preoccupations young Wharton flung himself the next year with an especial enthusiasm into his learned treatise against celibacy, and began those labours which led in 1693 to the publication of *Aldhelm, his Eloquent Book on the Praise of Virginity*. Sex suppression has had curious results but perhaps few more strange than *Anglia Sacra*.

Wharton's *Treatise of the Celibacy of the Clergy*, 'wherein its Rise and Progress are historically considered', was remarkable among productions of this type not only for the motives which inspired it but also for the learning with which it developed a theme usually provocative of other qualities than erudition. It may have been congenial to Wharton

[1] The portrait was by R. White. (WOOD: *Ath. Oxon.*, IV, col. 333n). It was perhaps a coincidence that the anonymous life attached to the sermons should have been written by Thomas Green, afterwards Bishop of Norwich, who was 'usually called from his Effeminateness Miss Green' (HEARNE: *Collections*, X, p. 337).

[2] Id maxime vero notandum venit, quod, cum ob athleticum corporis robur, et calorem plus justo vigentem, in mulierum amorem sim perquam pronus, nulli tamen unquam mulieri, nisi perquam invitus, in colloquium descenderim – Nulli unquam lasciviae muliebri, ne osculis quidem, me indulsisse memini. Id certo novi, me ad hunc usque diem virginitatem illaesam et intactam conservasse (Autobiography – D'OYLY, II, pp. 106, 107).

[3] 1683. Sub id circiter temporis a juvencula quadam virgine, formae satis liberalis et illibitae hactenus famae, summis blanditiis ad stuprum saepe invitatus, parum abfuit quin pudicitiae naufragium fecerim (Ibid., p. 109).

[4] Ibid., pp. 112, 113; *Celibacy*, p. 16.

HENRY WHARTON

From a drawing by Henry Tilson, engraved by Robert White, 1700

to brood on 'Virginity as a thing so plausible and if true so venerable, so countenanced by Antiquity and admired by the Unthinking Multitude, so highly subservient to the Secular Interest and outward Grandeur of the Clergy', but his treatise which embarked early upon a critical examination of the writings of Tertullian and Montanus was none the less of considerable value. In it according to Anthony Wood, 'with nervous reasons and variety of reading is made manifest that it was one of the most admirablest vindications of the marriage of the clergy that ever was set out'.[1] Burnet might permit himself the easy sneer: 'this author has very probably examined the Monastick Writers and especially on the point of the Celibacy of the Clergy more minutely than I have done . . . I own it.'[2] The modern student of medieval history, however, can hardly doubt that, judged by results, Wharton's attitude was the more productive, the more especially as he added to his edition of Aldhelm's treatise a first edition of Bede's commentaries on Genesis.

By 1689 Wharton was deeply involved in the great work of his life. In an illuminating letter[3] written at this time he described at length the aims of his endeavour, and recounted the methods of research which were to make Anglia Sacra the abiding memorial of its compiler:

Considering that the history of our church before the Reformation was little known, and that great numbers of the civil antient histories were already published, and more designed; . . . I resolved to make a collection of histories purely ecclesiastical, and publish them together; believing that otherwise they might be for ever lost, and that this might contribute much to an exact ecclesiastical history of our church, if ever it should be undertaken. When I had gained many of these histories and caused them to be transcribed out of several libraries, I found that they were all particular of some one church, relating almost wholly to the affairs of that church of which the writer was a monk or canon. Hence I immediately conceived, that if such histories could be found of every episcopal see, a perfect history of our bishops would then arise. I thereupon resolved to dispose them in such order as might effect the design; leaving out miracles, fables, and such like; but retaining their words and correcting their errors, and supplying omissions by notes at the bottom of the page. Further, because so few of them reached to the Reformation, I found it necessary to continue all of them to that period; and because of some sees no histories could be found, to write a particular history of them: but in both cases would not undertake to give a large elaborate account of the lives and actions of the several bishops but only such

[1] WOOD: Ath. Oxon., IV, col. 330.
[2] BURNET: Letter to the Bishop of Coventry and Litchfield (1693), pp. 16, 17.
[3] Wharton to Hugh Todd, Oct. 28th, 1689 (NICOLSON: Epist. Corr., pp. 12-16).

K

a short account as might make up the whole succession entire; but especially
fix their times more certainly than hath hitherto been done. For my primary
design was the edition of ancient ecclesiastical histories. The contriving it in
such a method as might form an history of the several sees was but a secondary design . . . I first considered the design in October last and before the
next October hope to see it published. In this time I have turned over innu-
merable registers, histories etc. and procured much from other persons; so
that although the work will be far short of what might be hoped, yet, I per-
suade myself that . . . very little will remain to be known concerning our
bishops before the Reformation.

The modern scholar hardly knows at which to marvel most: the assurance of the young man, the magnitude of the task he set himself, or the
speed at which within the space of two years he successfully completed
an undertaking that might more properly have occupied a committee
for a generation.

Anglia Sacra is, to-day, a book more praised than handled, and more
quoted than read. A full use of its accumulated erudition has perhaps
not yet been made. Two folio volumes made their appearance in 1691.
The former was concerned 'with cathedral churches possessed at one
time by monks', and it contained materials relating to the dioceses of
Canterbury, Winchester, Rochester, Norwich, Coventry and Lichfield, Worcester, Bath and Wells, Ely, and Durham. By far the greater
portion of the book consisted of editions of chronicles, but these were
sometimes abridged, and the story was often concluded by Wharton
himself. The latter volume was filled entirely with miscellaneous
medieval texts relating to the lives of bishops and the history of their
sees. The two volumes together contained over fifteen hundred folio
pages of Latin print and the majority of these are still of importance to
every serious student of English medieval antiquities. Even this however did not complete Wharton's design, for having thus ended his
work as far as it concerned those sees which were served by monks he
wished to compile a third volume relating to the bishoprics which had
been served by regular or secular canons, and though this labour was
never finished, a small quarto representing his collections for the sees
of London and St. Asaph was published in 1695 after the death of its
author.

This immense production constituted pioneer work of the first
importance. First and foremost it made a notable addition to knowledge of the chronicle sources of English history, not only by bringing
many new texts for the first time into print, but also by illustrating their
provenance and delimiting their scope. The comparative study of

English medieval chronicles for the first time became possible, and an opportunity was at last provided for the realization of Brady's dream that each narrative source might be carefully examined in connection with the circumstances of its origin, and in relation to other productions from other areas. Before Wharton's day, each chronicle tended to be regarded as a record in isolation which for the most part could only be criticized by means of internal evidence. Now, the whole monastic contribution to medieval chronicles began to be surveyed as a whole. Since the book, with this aim in view, traversed a very wide field, co-ordinated the earlier labour of scattered scholars and made extensive new discoveries, it could be used with profit by successive generations of students investigating the chronicles of England.

Anglia Sacra thus brought together a collection of materials that might subserve a scientific history of the medieval Church in England. The great English sees were here severally displayed in their proper historical setting, and the ecclesiastical contribution to medieval life and letters was emphasized in a manner which had never before been attempted. The importance of the early biographies of English prelates was made clear, and though Wharton's transcriptions were often faulty and his texts sometimes unjustifiably abbreviated, the first presentation of many of these in print gave a new turn, as Stubbs discovered, to the investigation of medieval chronology. Here were to be found for example first editions of William of Malmesbury's Life of Wulfstan, of John of Salisbury's Life of Anselm and of Eadmer's lives of Bregwin and St. Oswald. Here also were to be found (among other narratives) the Life of Bishop Gundulf of Rochester, one of the makers of the Tower of London; the Canterbury Chronicle of Stephen Birchington; the Norwich history of Bartholomew Cotton; and William of Wycombe's twelfth century Life of Robert of Bethune.[1]

Wharton's originality may be measured both by the general plan of his book and by the discoveries which were involved in its execution. His methods, if sometimes hasty, were admirable in that he attempted to adapt to his purpose what was best in contemporary scholarship, and so brought into the orbit of English learning much of the material which was scattered in the great continental collections. His work stands in close relation therefore to that of many of the European scholars. At the same time, for example, as he was editing Eadmer's Life of Odo from a late Lambeth MS., Mabillon was also preparing an independent edition of the same work from a thirteenth-century text which had belonged in succession to De Thou and to Colbert. The

[1] *Anglia Sacra*, I, pp. 1-48, 397-402; II, pp. 151-176, 191-210, 239-270, 293-320.

later Bollandist edition in consequence owed something both to the French and to the English scholar, and when in 1773 Langebek, the Danish scholar, prepared yet another version, he was rightly obliged to make full acknowledgment of his debt to Wharton.[1] Wharton, again, was probably the first man to bring to the notice of English scholars the historical importance of Dunstan, though here too this work was part of a large co-operation of scholars. For Osbern's Life of Dunstan, which appeared in *Anglia Sacra*, had already been edited six years earlier by Mabillon,[2] whilst Eadmer's life of the same prelate had been printed (but with a wrong attribution) as early as 1573 by Surius and had since engaged the attention of both Benedictine and Bollandist scholars. But it was the Englishman whom Migne folllowed in his nineteenth-century patrology, and the work of Wharton on Dunstan cannot truly be said to have been superseded until Stubbs edited the 'Lives' afresh in 1874.[3]

No better example of the detailed character of Wharton's work could be found than his treatment of the chronicles of the See of Ely.[4] By far the most precious of these is the remarkable narrative which goes by the name of *Liber Eliensis*. This chronicle interspersed with charters was in the main the work of Thomas of Ely (fl. 1170).[5] It is divided into three books, the first being chiefly concerned with the life of St. Etheldreda, the second carrying the story to 1107, and the third continuing to 1169. When Wharton began his work he found in print a Life of St. Etheldreda taken by Mabillon from Book I of the *Liber Eliensis*, and he also discovered that Thomas Gale had begun to print Book I of the text and that part of Book II which related to pre-Conquest history. Wharton treated the text properly as a whole though, in view of what had already been done, he unfortunately epitomized much of it. But he added much of what had been omitted by Mabillon from Book I, and his long extracts from Book III were especially valuable, partly because this section had never before been edited at all,

[1] *Anglia Sacra*, II, pp. 78-87 (cf. p. xii); MABILLON: *Acta SS. Ben.* Saec. v, pp. 288-296; *Acta Sanctorum* (Bollandists), July 4th; LANGEBEK: *Scriptores Rerum Danicarum* (1773), II, pp. 401-411.

[2] *Anglia Sacra*, II, pp. 88-121; MABILLON: op. cit., Saec. IV, pp. 659 *sqq. Acta Sanctorum* (May, vol. IV, pp. 359 *sqq.*).

[3] *Anglia Sacra*, II, pp. 211-221 (containing large extracts from Eadmer's life of Dunstan); Surius Vitae SS., II, pp. 231 *sqq.* (assigning this life to an imaginary 'Osbert'); MABILLON (op. cit., Saec. v, pp. 689-712) and the Bollandists (Acta SS. May, vol. IV, pp. 689-712) give large extracts from the text of Surius; cf. STUBBS: *Memorials of St. Dunstan,* pp. xlii-lii.

[4] *Anglia Sacra*, I, pp. xxxix-xlvi, 593-691.

[5] The section of the chronicle printed by Wharton in *Anglia Sacra*, I, pp. 615 *sqq.,* is attributed by him to an earlier 'Richard of Ely'. It is, in fact, by Thomas who, however, acknowledges his debt to his predecessors; cf. D. J. STEWART: *Liber Eliensis* (1848), Preface.

and partly because the chronicle is here dealing with events within the personal knowledge of its author.[1] It is remarkable that even to-day in spite of a modern edition of Books I and II of the *Liber Eliensis*, there does not exist anywhere save in *Anglia Sacra* a printed version of the whole of this most important twelfth-century chronicle.[2]

The publication of *Anglia Sacra* gave Wharton, at the age of twenty-seven, an assured place among the founders of English medieval scholarship. He had received help in his undertaking from scholars such as Matthew Hutton, Rector of Aynhoe, and Hugh Todd, the Cumberland antiquary, but he alone was responsible for the production of a book that was beyond doubt 'a work of Incredible Pains as must be acknowledged by anyone who considers the uncommonness of the Subject never before so treated by anyone and the Scarcity and Obscurity of the Materials – these too not to be had but in several places and at vast distances'.[3] Nor could there be any question of the solidity of the scholarship which lay behind the production. *Anglia Sacra* was 'designed to exhibit a compleat Ecclesiastical History of England until the Reformation';[4] and it so nearly approached the fulfilment of its portentous purpose that all students of medieval antiquities were placed deeply in the debt of its compiler.[5] English scholarship in particular continued to find in *Anglia Sacra* a contribution of abiding value for the full comprehension of medieval chronicles.

The research embodied in these folios was prosecuted by Wharton at the same time as he was engaged in constructing one of the great catalogues of the seventeenth century. His catalogue of the MSS. in Lambeth Palace was conceived upon an elaborate scale. It was no bare list. A contemporary noted that Wharton besides giving a most exact catalogue of the MSS., under every book, transcribed all those treatises in them which are not yet published.[6] If this was an exaggeration, it at least expressed the spirit in which this work was undertaken and it indicated the measure of the achievement. Wharton's aim, as he himself described it, was to follow such a method, 'subjoining to every book those treatises, passages, or excerpts taken out of them which may tend to the public benefit'.[7] Wharton was never diffident in emphasizing the magnitude of his labours, and his catalogue will not compare with that which Wanley was soon to begin in the Harleian Library.

---

[1] *Anglia Sacra*, I, pp. xxxiv, xxxix-xlii. The Bollandists were to issue yet another version of the 'life' in 1707.

[2] STEWART: op. cit. Parts of the *Liber Eliensis* are, apparently, soon to be edited afresh under the auspices of the Royal Historical Society.

[3] Sermon Life.　　　　　　　　　　　　[4] NICOLSON: *Epist. Corr.*, p. 14.

[5] Cf. *Acta Eruditorum* (Leipsic, 1696), p. 425.

[6] Cf. D'OYLY: *Sancroft*, II, p. 162.　　　[7] Ibid.

But it was a notable performance which was later with advantage embodied in the printed catalogue of the Lambeth MSS. that Wilkins made in the early years of the next century. It formed moreover but a part of the large manuscript collections which Wharton left for the use of posterity, and which in the opinion of Stubbs were almost as valuable as his printed works.[1] It remains a continual marvel how these were amassed during the short years of Wharton's working life when he was engaged in a production so vast as *Anglia Sacra*.

Despite its obvious importance, *Anglia Sacra* met with severe criticism in certain quarters. The design was so ambitious, the subject so novel, and the execution so rapid that the young editor inevitably laid himself open to the charge of presumption. The speed with which the work was accomplished involved errors of detail that were quickly noted by the critics. William Nicolson, who greatly disliked Wharton for personal reasons, immediately drew attention to several mistakes, spoke of a progressive deterioration in the work, complained of the paucity of footnotes, and criticized the summaries with which Wharton had filled up the periods not traversed by his authorities. But even Nicolson could not refrain from faint praise. 'Upon the whole his industry is great and deserves encouragement,' he remarked, 'but his pertness and immodesty is as great and ought to be otherwise treated.' The most savage criticism came from Burnet. By 1691 that *'subodoratus episcopus'* was already attacking Wharton, and he professed later to have detected three capital errors in one line of *Anglia Sacra*.[2]

Such criticism contained an element of truth in so far as the rapidity of Wharton's work had involved many incidental mistakes. His selection of texts was, similarly, not always fortunate. The 'Life of Bregwin' ascribed to 'Osbern' was for instance nothing more than John of Tinmuth's abbreviation of Eadmer's biography, and Richard of Bardney's 'Life of Robert Grosseteste' is valueless.[3] Nor was Wharton more scrupulous than the majority of his contemporaries in the preparation of his editions, and his work is marred by much careless transcription. His method of summary led on occasion to grave abuse, and his design of 'leaving out miracles, fables and such like' severely detracted from the value of several of his textual discoveries. Thus Wharton made a notable contribution to medieval biography when he brought to light William of Malmesbury's Latin Life of Wulfstan which is in fact the sole extant version of Colman's vernacular life of the same prelate.

[1] STUBBS: *Registrum Sacrum Anglicanum* (1858), p. iv.
[2] NICOLSON: *Epist. Corr.*, pp. 18-20; *English Historical Library* (1736), p. 124; *Autobiography* (D'OYLY: II, p. 142); BURNET: op. cit.
[3] *Anglia Sacra*, II, pp. 75-77, 325-340.

But in his edition he omitted about two-fifths of the narrative, and though the excised portions deal largely with miracles, they also contain information of importance and are in any case essential to a proper understanding of the text as a whole.[1] For similar reasons, both Stubbs and Raine found it necessary to supplement Wharton's work in respect of Oswald and Dunstan.[2]

It would, however, be very easy in magnifying its defects to lose sight of the great positive achievements of this pioneer work. The criticisms of Burnet were embittered by personal animosity which can be explained if not excused by 'the pertness and immodesty' of which William Nicolson also complained. To one who had been chaplain to Sancroft the world of the Revolution was out of joint and Wharton at the age of twenty-eight was very ready to set it right. He offered therefore his condescending instruction to his seniors. When in 1693 under the assumed name of 'Anthony Harmer' he issued a pamphlet containing *A Specimen of some Errors and Defects in the History of the Reformation writ by Gilbert Burnet* it was hardly surprising that he goaded the prelate into a 'fury of rage'. For Wharton's admonishment was not couched in language likely to be agreeable to an important personage in the State, and to a man twenty-one years his senior. 'I thought it a duty owing to Posterity', wrote Wharton, 'not to permit it to be led into Mistakes in anything relating to the Reformation of the Church by errors contained in an History published with such seeming Authority . . . Nor can this great Historian justly take it ill if the title of Infallible which he with so great strength of Reason opposeth in others be denied to himself.' The criticism was nicely barbed. But Wharton should not have been surprised at the retaliation. Burnet, as a master of vituperation, was more than a match for the warped and sensitive youth who confronted him. His *Letter to the Bishop of Coventry and Litchfield* may have been 'prolix' but as invective it was highly competent.[3]

The controversy between Wharton and Burnet has more than the ephemeral interest of a quarrel between two distinguished writers of history. It displays the division which was beginning to appear in English public opinion regarding the study of medieval antiquities. Wharton's criticisms were on the whole moderate, and he confined himself to medieval questions about which he knew very much more

[1] *Anglia Sacra*, II, pp. 239-270; R. R. DARLINGTON: *Vita Wulfstani* (1928), pp. viii, ix.
[2] STUBBS: *Memorials of St. Dunstan*, pp. xlii-lii; RAINE: *Historians of the Church of York*, I, p. ix.
[3] WHARTON: *Specimen*, pp. iii, 150; *Autobiography* (D'OYLY, II, p. 150): 'Burnetus episcopus confestim furere debacchari usque ad rabiem irasci.'

than his eminent opponent. Burnet's replies on the other hand were couched in far more general terms. 'The barbarous Stile,' he writes, 'the mixture of so much Fable, the great want of Judgement that runs thro' the Writings of the Monks has so disgusted me at their Works that I confess I could never bring myself to read them with Pleasure. If any one that has more Patience than I, can think it worth the while to search into that Rubbish let him write volumes of Anglia Sacra and have the Glory of it for his Pains . . . To dig in Mines were not to me a more ungrateful imployment.' 'This is a very hard censure', justly retorts Wharton, 'to pass upon a whole order of Men who were once very honourable but always serviceable to the Church' and 'who set themselves with great Industry to restore learning'. Two ages of English scholarship seem here to meet, and Burnet, in commending ignorance of the writers he condemns, is speaking almost in the language of Bolingbroke. In the development of historical learning there can be little doubt which attitude was the more valuable. If the eighteenth century was to support the opinions of Burnet as to the proper limitations of historical scholarship, the more modern future was to give an emphatic verdict in favour of his opponent.[1]

Much of the criticism which Wharton had to face was undoubtedly inspired by political animus. The events of 1689 had placed this young man in an equivocal position which he was unable to sustain with dignity. He owed everything to Sancroft, and both by his opinions and by the ties of personal loyalty he was committed to the Archbishop who became the natural leader of the Non-juring schism against William III. But in the central political act of his life Wharton deserted his party and performed what to many seemed an act of apostasy. On the day when the new sovereigns were proclaimed, messengers appeared at Lambeth to demand their recognition, and Wharton, in the absence of definite instructions from Sancroft, publicly prayed in the chapel for William and Mary. The conduct of an emotionally unstable youth at a moment of crisis is not to be judged too harshly. But no Non-juror could ever hope to find a full forgiveness for such an act, and it caused the greatest anger in Sancroft himself. Usually the mildest of men, the Archbishop sent for his favourite chaplain, and – *vehementer excandescens* – upbraided him with ferocity. Later, Hearne kept alive the reproach.[2] 'Mr. Henry Wharton', he wrote, 'though a very learned man yet wanted that Integrity as Archbishop Sancroft and

[1] BURNET: op. cit., pp. 15, 16; *Specimen passim*. Cf. HEARNE in his edition of Leland's *Collectanea*, I, pp. xxiv-xxvi.
[2] *Autobiography* (D'OYLY: II, p. 152); *Sermon Life*.

many expected of him, and for that reason the suffering men esteemed him much less than they would otherwise have done; which, when he considered it, struck much upon his spirits.'[1]

Wharton was irrevocably committed to the Non-juring cause that he had betrayed. He was never happy under the new political regime which he did not hesitate to condemn, and it is probable that, as Hearne suggested, he suffered much remorse in later life for having abandoned his patron. At all events, it was from 'the suffering men' that he continued to receive kindness. Hickes, with his large charity, spoke up for him; and the relations between Sancroft and his former chaplain continued to be friendly. On his death-bed the Archbishop, who retained the highest regard for Wharton's intellectual abilities, gave the papers of Laud into his charge, and dismissed him with a tender benediction. But there were inevitable reserves, and at the very end Sancroft desired that only Non-jurors should be around him. Thus Wharton was pointedly forbidden to be present at the death of the man who had been largely responsible for his achievement in scholarship, and who always remained his inspiration and his pattern.[2]

The Revolution blasted Wharton's hopes of advancement in the Church. His taking the oaths in 1689 had been a special affront to the Non-jurors, but the connections of the former chaplain of Sancroft excluded him from favour, and the hostility of Nicolson and Burnet was shared by their supporters. To Wharton by temperament such neglect was unnecessarily painful, for he wholly lacked the courage that sent others for similar reasons undaunted into the paths of adversity. Wharton was always immoderately ambitious and covetous of applause. It was his self-confessed 'lust for praise' that led him to his early quarrel with Cave, and even if there was substance in his complaint that his work for the 'Literary History' never received proper commendation, the dignified rejoinder of the elder scholar was probably not unfair to the conduct of an overconfident and assertive young man. Wharton had no reserves of self-sufficient pride, and, with the doors of preferment firmly closed against him, with his self-respect outraged and his ambitions thwarted, he turned into a bitter and disappointed man.[3]

The transformation is easily explained from Wharton's character. But it would be unfair not to recognize that his resentment was due in part to the fact that he was hindered from pursuing research which had

[1] HEARNE: *Collections*, X, p. 112.
[2] *Autobiography* (D'OYLY: II, pp. 151, 152); OVERTON; *Non-Jurors*, p. 108; BIRCH: *Tillotson*, p. 143.
[3] D'OYLY: *Sancroft*, II, pp. 165–174; NICOLSON: *English Historical Library* (1736), p. 134.

already proved outstandingly brilliant. When men like Kennett were urging that a dignity in every cathedral church should be reserved for one who would study its antiquities, it was unfortunate that no place could be found for the greatest contemporary authority on ecclesiastical history, and the neglect may possibly have caused an irreparable loss to literature. Nicolson was quick to notice a degeneration in Wharton's work and thought it likely to continue 'til' some good preferment has sweetened his Humour',[1] and the last volume in the *Anglia Sacra* series was without doubt inferior to its predecessors. There was perhaps here a just ground for complaint, and Wharton who had once been the absentee Rector of Chartham and Minster keeping curates in each place that he might 'busy himself with the public concerns of learning', now loudly voiced the perennial grievance of all unendowed and unappreciated scholars. 'My circumstances', he exclaimed, 'are so much altered . . . that all my zeal for public service must be employed in teaching a few plough-jobbers who look upon what I say to concern them but little. Perhaps thirty years hence, if life and friends continue so long, when I shall become old and lazy, covetous and selfish, I may be removed to a station enabling me to do that service to the public which then I neither shall be able nor perhaps willing to do.'[2]

Life for Wharton was not, however, to continue for thirty more years, and the strange drama of his career moved swiftly to its end. The eccentricities, the odd frustrations, and the thwarted vanities, gradually became resolved into an harmony, and, at the last, the authentic Wharton is to be observed – a great scholar – standing at work in his study. 'He catched his Death', remarked Hearne, 'by making a Sermon one Saturday Night'; but this brief description needs to be supplemented from a more contemporary source. 'His too eager prosecution of his studies together with a weakness contracted in his stomach . . . so far broke the excellency of his constitution that no art nor the skill of the most experienced physicians could repair it. The summer before he died he went to Bath in hopes to have retrieved his decaying nature by the help of those excellent medicinal waters. Some benefit he had by them; but at his return from thence to Canterbury falling again to his studies immoderately and beyond what his strength could bear he quite undid all that they had done so that . . . he was brought at last to the utmost extremity of weakness.' He died on March 5th, 1695.[3]

[1] NICOLSON: *Epist. Corr.*, p. 20.
[2] *Autobiography* (D'OYLY, II, p. 162). Cf. *Gentleman's Magazine*, LXI (1791), p. 698.
[3] HEARNE: *Collections*, VII, p. 164; Sermon Life.

Wharton, always exceptional, was not however to make his final departure without especial ceremony. The scenes at his funeral were almost as remarkable as the circumstances of his birth. He became in death what he had never been in life, a popular figure; and nothing would now suffice but splendid obsequies in Westminster Abbey. High prelates gathered together in his honour, and the Bishop of Norwich conducted the service. The Dean and Prebendaries of Westminster attended, remitting their customary dues 'as the last the most proper testimony they could well give of the high esteem in which they held Mr. Wharton and his learned labours'. The King's scholars accompanied the body to the grave in the south aisle, and the choir sang anthems specially composed by 'that ingenious artist, Mr. Henry Purcell'. Such was the contemporary tribute paid to a young scholar in an age that was slow to recognize the claims of youth. There was little that was lovable in the personal character of Wharton, and it might seem that Purcell's anthems have echoed through the years with perhaps an exaggerated praise. But the achievement of this fine scholar remains as his abiding memorial. Every student of English chronicles, or of the history which is based upon them, owes something to his work, and it was the best qualified of his modern critics who passed the final verdict upon what he accomplished. 'This wonderful man', declared William Stubbs, 'died at the age of 30, having done for the elucidation of English Church History more than anyone before or since.'[1]

[1] STUBBS: *Registrum Sacrum Anglicanum* (1858), p. iv.

CHAPTER VIII

THE CHRONICLES OF ENGLAND

THE spectacular performance of Henry Wharton was so complete in its dramatic brevity that it might well serve as the symbol of the work which in the decades following the Restoration was being devoted to the chronicles of medieval England. It does not, however, stand in isolation since it bears a direct relation to a long series of publications which at this time enlarged the knowledge of the narrative sources of English history between the Norman Conquest and the end of the Middle Ages. The work of the men who produced these books was in one sense less original than any other of the antiquarian enterprises of the age since they were mainly concerned with carrying on an activity which was already old. But if the study of chronicles had since the sixteenth century taken a prominent place in English research, the men of the later generation had much to do not only in enlarging a great legacy but also in removing some of its defects. Their work advanced in two directions. The study of monastic bibliography which had begun in the fifteenth century moved forward until it culminated in the work of Thomas Tanner. And the still more important labour of editing the great medieval narratives was also continued so that the movement whose inception was marked in *Anglia Sacra* persisted in numerous other publications until it reached a fitting climax in the editions of Thomas Hearne.

The study of monastic bibliography was in England of long standing at the time of the Restoration. Men of that age could, for example, look back to the labours of John Boston who in the earlier half of the fifteenth century was monk, and perhaps librarian, at Bury St. Edmunds. This man, whose importance to monastic bibliography was properly emphasized by Dr. M. R. James,[1] travelled, according to Fuller, 'all over *England* and exactly perused the *Library* in all *Monasteries* whereby he was enabled to write a *Catalogue* of *Ecclesiastical Writers* as well *Forraign* as *English*'.[2] The statement was exaggerated but it is little wonder that such work was valued by later antiquaries or that it formed the starting point of subsequent studies. In particular, the

---

[1] M. R. JAMES: *On the Abbey of Bury St. Edmunds* (Cambridge Antiq. Soc., 1895) pp. 34 *sqq.*
[2] FULLER: *Worthies* (1662), pt. II, p. 166.

spoliation of the monasteries of England in the sixteenth century had
not only wrought havoc in the monastic libraries but had stimulated
among a minority of the Reformers a zeal to save and to catalogue the
MSS. which had thus been thrown on the mercy of an unkind world.
The most important result of this impetus had been the *Commentarii de
Scriptoribus* which John Leland had included in the remarkable *Collectanea* that he presented in 1546 as 'a newe yeares gyft' to Henry VIII.[1]
Leland's work was in fact to serve as the basis of every similar compilation for some three centuries, and though it was not itself to be published for over a hundred and fifty years, it provided very soon the
material for two vastly inferior books. One of these was the polemical
catalogue which John Bale, Protestant Bishop of Ossory, produced in
1548,[2] and the other was the equally polemical reply thereto of the
Catholic John Pits that was published posthumously in 1619.[3] The early
publication of these two treatises gave them an unjustified influence
upon later scholars. In truth both were inadequate. The former was
marred throughout by the uncritical partisanship of its 'bilious' author,
and the latter, though professedly based upon Leland (whose manuscript Pits in all probability had never seen), owed more to Bale himself than its compiler would ever have acknowledged. Even at the
time of the Restoration these remained the standard books of reference
for the subject with which they dealt, while the far more important
work of Leland remained unprinted.

These conditions demanded research of a special character. Not only
was it imperative that the collections of Leland should be published in
such a form that they should be properly utilized, but it was essential
that they should be supplemented in the light of the new knowledge
that had been laboriously acquired since his death. To this problem
therefore the scholars after the Restoration were to address themselves.
The publication of William Cave's *Historia Literaria*, to which Wharton had contributed, called the attention of the learned to much new
matter which had hitherto been neglected, and interest in Leland was
already becoming something of a fashion in Oxford. But all such
research was soon to be overshadowed by the work of a single scholar
who exactly envisaged the problem and devoted the greater part of his
life to its solution. It was Thomas Tanner who not only gave his
critical attention to the writings of both Boston and Leland but who

[1] Cf. *Laboryous Journey . . . of John Leylande* (*Lives of Leland, Wood and Hearne* – 1772 –
vol. 1).
[2] *Illustrium Majoris Britanniae Scriptorum Summarium* (1548). There were subsequent
editions.
[3] *Relationum Historicarnum de Rebus Anglicis Tomus I* (1619).

made his own most valuable contribution to the subject which they had studied. And though other scholars (especially at Oxford) were associated with the investigations which he made particularly his own, it was Tanner's *Bibliotheca Britannico-Hibernica sive De Scriptoribus*[1] which was in due course to prove the most constructive achievement of the age in this branch of learned inquiry.

Thomas Tanner lacked the colourful personality of many of his contemporaries, and his two great works were only to appear post-humously many years after the close of the period with which this work deals. But his career deserves some notice in this place because as a scholar he took a most prominent personal place among his contemporaries. He was born in 1674, the son of a Wiltshire vicar, and like so many of his fellows he developed his antiquarian interests as an undergraduate at Queen's College, Oxford, where he became the friend of Edmund Gibson who ever afterwards remained 'his intimate acquaintance'. His early promise was such that he attracted the attention of Arthur Charlett, the Master of University College, and also of Thomas Finch, the Warden of All Souls. Consequently, when he had taken his degree and it seemed as if he 'must have left this beloved place and his studies', he was made chaplain of All Souls. Later he came under the notice of John Moore, then Bishop of Norwich, who made him his chaplain, and collated him in 1701 to the chancellorship of that see. When Moore was translated to Ely he bestowed on Tanner a canonry in that cathedral. Afterwards promotions followed fast. Tanner became Archdeacon of Norfolk in 1721, and in 1724 he was made canon of Christ Church in Oxford. Such was the respect in which his character was held that the Lower House of Convocation in 1727 appointed him its Prolocutor, and in 1732 he became Bishop of St. Asaph's. He did not however long enjoy this dignity for in 1735 he returned to Christ Church to die.[2]

The influence of Tanner upon his generation was far more extensive than the smooth progress of his career would of itself suggest. This was primarily due to the immense industry which made him in due course one of the most erudite members of a learned Church. It must also, however, in part be attributed to a general benevolence which enabled him, though sincerely devoted to the Low Church party in the Establishment, to avoid the acrimonies of contemporary politics and to infuse a friendly forbearance into his relations with his fellows. His advice

[1] For the preparation of Tanner's *Bibliotheca*, see W. T. DAVIES in *Times Literary Supplement*, Dec. 14th, 1935.
[2] *Biographia Britt.*, sub. Tanner; *Dict. Nat. Biog.*, sub. Tanner.

was relied on: his weighty collaboration was eagerly sought. Both were freely given; and for this reason the importance of Thomas Tanner will probably best be appraised in connection with the corporate achievement made by the Anglican Church in his time in politics and scholarship. Few scholars, themselves distinguished, have ever had a larger anonymous share in the books of other men. Thus (for example) he took part in the compilation of Bernard's catalogue of the Bodleian manuscripts which appeared in 1697; he contributed to Gibson's edition of Camden's *Britannia*; he co-operated with Gibson, again, in the editing of Spelman's English works; and he was above all one of those most concerned in the preparation of the *Concilia* of 1737 which was perhaps the greatest single accomplishment in medieval scholarship made by the Anglican Church in this period.[1] Only a man of astonishing industry could have sustained such connections in the midst of his own laborious undertakings, and it was his personal character which continued to illuminate his correspondence with a kindly charity. This was the man who was to be found pleading on behalf of a poor scholar apprenticed to a working tailor,[2] and who also gave his assistance to 'a very meritorious young clergyman one Mr. Blomefield' who was even then contemplating his *History of Norfolk*.[3] Many others had cause to think well of one who was 'so extraordinarily a good Humoured person and so communicate that everybody admires him'.[4] Some contemporaries might dissent from Tanner's eulogy of the three wives who successively shared his bed, and augmented his fortune.[5] Comment might even be made of the 'gross body' which succumbed at last to a dose of Dr. Ward's pills. But the happy disposition of Dr. Tanner always went far towards disarming criticism.

It was indeed a reluctance to avoid offence which involved Tanner at the beginning of his career in a confused transaction which is of only incidental importance in estimating his position as a scholar. In 1695 when Anthony Wood lay a-dying his friends could think of no one better to inherit his unpublished papers than this 'careful true faithful and discreet' young man who might in particular be given the task of preparing for publication a third and concluding volume for the *Athenae Oxonienses*, and Wood on his death-bed apparently actually handed over to Tanner the necessary papers 'with great ceremony'. The terms under which the transference was made were afterwards

---

[1] See below, pp. 273-284.
[2] *Bodleian Letters*, I, p. 300.
[3] Ibid., II, p. 105.
[4] Cf. S. KNIGHT: *Life of Dr. John Colet* (1724), Preface.
[5] HEARNE: *Collections*, II, p. 9.

disputed, but it is certain that Tanner found the charge not only honourable but also embarrassing. Wood's pen had been notoriously sharp; it had already inspired prosecution; and the volume which thus blandly committed to the care of a young student with his career to make, contained caustic criticisms of many men who were still living. Tanner shrank from the task, and it is possible that had not others later intervened, Wood's additional volume might not have seen the light. As it was, when in 1721 the new edition of the *Athenae* appeared (perhaps under the editorship of Laurence Echard) many considered that either Tanner or his advisers had modified much that Wood had originally written; and since Tanner himself did not deposit the original papers in the Bodleian Library it is impossible to determine the truth of the accusation. Hearne and his friends did not shrink from calling this a 'spurious edition', and though it would be rash to interpose an incidental judgment upon a controversial transaction, it is hard to acquit Tanner completely of having in this matter committed a breach of trust.[1]

At all events, the attempt to make Tanner responsible for carrying on the work of Wood shows that before he was twenty-five he was considered as a scholar of the highest promise. He was actively engaged upon preparing an edition of Hegge's Legend of St. Cuthbert, and after consultation with John Aubrey he had begun to collect materials for a history of his native county of Wiltshire. He issued plans for this book in 1694 and in the course of years he was to amass collections which were commensurate with the magnitude of his design. The work however was never finished. It was suggested that 'as he happened to be preferred at some distance (from Wiltshire) he was by that means hindered from prosecuting and finishing that work'.[2] But an additional explantion may also be found in the numerous undertakings to which he became committed. The extent of his labours may, however, now be seen among the extensive manuscript collections which came into the Bodleian Library, some by the bequest of their compiler in 1736,[3] and some by the gift of Tanner's son in 1751. The Tanner manuscripts form to-day one of the most precious collections in the library of his beloved university, and apart from all else they suggest that his *Wiltshire* may have been one of the great unwritten county histories of England. Certainly, in the preparation which he made for this purpose, Tanner demonstrated in company with so many of his contemporaries

---

[1] Cf. WOOD: *Ath. Oxon.*, ed. Bliss, vol. I, Preface; *Biographia Britt.* sub. Tanner; HEARNE: *Collections*, x, p. 215.

[2] *Biographia Britt.*, loc. cit.

[3] Cf. MACRAY: *Annals of the Bodleian Library* (1868), p. 153.

the importance of local studies in giving actuality to investigations of the development of medieval England. In this he followed in the tradition established by Dugdale.

The same connection was also to be seen in another project upon which Tanner was already engaged by the time that he was twenty-two. In 1695, with the encouragement of Samuel Pepys, he produced a small volume with the title of *Notitia Monastica* which he dedicated to his friend and patron Thomas Finch of All Souls.[1] This attempted to supply 'a short History of the Foundation and chief Revolutions of all our religious Houses' and also 'a Catalogue of such Writers (noting the Places where we may find them) as will abundantly furnish us with further Particulars'.[2] William Nicolson, who had apparently contemplated such a book himself, was quick to appreciate its significance, and also its relation to the earlier work of Dodsworth and Dugdale. 'The Compilers of the *Monasticon Anglicanum*', he wrote, 'took care to make the like References; and to let the world know from whose Hands they had the perusal of the Records of this or the other Monastery. But, as many new Discoveries have been made since their Time so several of the Books they met with have changed their Owners; and therefore their Defects are not only here supply'd but the present Proprietors of what they mention much better ascertained.'[3] But the prime significance of Tanner's book of 1695 was that it served as the basis of his own later studies and those of his successors. He was always himself adding to it, and the results of his labours were seen in the vastly enlarged edition which was in 1744 to appear after his death, and in the still further augmented edition which James Nasmith produced in 1787. Tanner's original volume of 1695 was thus to develop into a standard work of reference, and in its final form was not only to contain brief accounts of the history of individual monasteries, but also to be especially replete with references to unprinted monastic literature. Its influence may best be traced in the countless footnotes in which it is quoted.

The *Notitia Monastica* of 1695 indicated Tanner's early preoccupation with the problems of monastic bibliography, and it may here be considered as a pendant to the larger undertaking to which Tanner was to devote his main energies for the remaining forty years of his life. As early as 1693 Tanner issued proposals for printing the works of Leland, and from the first his friend Gibson urged that no man could be better

[1] *Notitia Monastica, or A Short History of the Religious Houses in England and Wales* (1695); cf. HEARNE, *Collections*, I, p. 200.
[2] NICOLSON: *English Historical Library* (1736), p. 145.
[3] Ibid.

L

fitted to give effect to the widespread desire among scholars for a proper edition of the *De Scriptoribus* which was still only available in the perverted extracts of Bale and Pits. The new editor, it was considered, would be both 'cautious' and 'speedy', and the original plan was merely 'the bare printing of Leland and Boston of Bury and supplying what was wanted by wholesale out of Bale and Pits within a twelve month'. Tanner, however, was by temperament industrious rather than 'speedy', and it is to his lasting credit that from the first he resisted advice to do his work in a perfunctory way. He 'could not be perswaded to take characters of men and notices of books upon trust'. Leland, he discovered, 'had entirely omitted above 2000 British Writers' and 'of those he does mention he had given a very imperfect account'. Tanner's design was thus enlarged into an original undertaking of wide scope, and he came to the resolve not only to print Leland in full but also 'to add such new Authors and writings as later searches of Libraries have discovered, interweaving his Writers with my own'.[1]

An enterprise of this character was clearly one which, under the most favourable circumstances, would entail years of labour and the preparation of this book was for many reasons unduly protracted. Already in 1698 Tanner could declare that he had gathered most of the materials which could be found in Oxford, and two years later he was working in London. But his appointment to the Norwich chancellorship in 1701 imposed additional difficulties upon him, and the years rolled by without the book showing any appreciable signs of approaching publication. Even in 1709 there was little ground for his optimism that the book would be published 'by the end of the winter', and it was small wonder that such delay provoked widespread impatience. Charlett, for example, was continually urging haste, and Hearne, conscious of the persisting gap in England scholarship, was beginning to study Leland on his own account. But nothing could excuse the secret preparation of an independent edition of the *De Scriptobirus* by Anthony Hall which was made in 1709 with the connivance of a group of Fellows of Queen's College 'out of a design of prejudice to Mr. Tanner' who 'having had no letter to ask his leave' was naturally 'somewhat startled' when Hall's book appeared. Tanner had already devoted fifteen arduous years to the preparation of his own edition, and Hall's production, full of the grossest errors and showing all the marks of undue haste, was the outcome of one of the shabbiest tricks in the whole history of English scholarship. 'However Mr. Hall and the rest of Queen's College may brag of the performance,' wrote

[1] DAVIES: op. cit.

Hearne, 'they are and will be condemned by all men of Ingenuity and sincerity such as are guided by a publick spirit.'[1] It said much for Tanner's pertinacity that he refused to be unduly discouraged by such 'disingenuous and ill usage', but, though his labours were continued, the years still passed without the publication of the book for which all scholars were waiting. In 1722 the current number of the *Bibliotheca Literaria*[2] announced that the book was 'preparing for the press', but three years later it was still in manuscript, and Hearne found its author with 'about six Folios before him which he said were what he had done for his *Scriptores Britannici* which I understood from him he still prosecutes with as much Industry and Application as his Affairs will permit'. Ten more years of life were to be vouchsafed to him but even these were not to prove sufficient. Tanner died without ever seeing his greatest work in print. And the book which he had begun in 1694 was not published until more than half a century later when in 1748 David Wilkins at last successfully saw it through the press.[3]

The book was worth the labour which had been expended upon it, and its quality excused the long delays in its preparation. Tanner, as Nicolson declared, had 'diligently compared Leland's Original Manuscript with the scandalously false Copies given of it by Bale and Pits'; and this in itself was a work of the highest value. But the additions and corrections which Tanner had supplied were such that they justified him in regarding the book as 'intirely new and his own'.[4] Leland, it is true, remained properly the backbone of the work, and the influence of both Bale and Pits was to be discerned. But Tanner had himself examined the texts which he discussed in his catalogue, and his notes showed that he had read widely in them. He had striven successfully after both impartiality and accuracy, and for this reason it was the scholarly nature of the *Bibliotheca* as well as its scope which rendered it of permanent value. Modern scholars may note certain curious omissions and inclusions. The influence of Wood's collections was not always beneficial, and the text of Boston's catalogue which was appended to Wilkins's preface was most unfortunately defective.[5] But with all its limitations the book was of the first importance. As a standard work of reference it exercised a great influence both upon literary criticism and upon historical research, and it was long before it was superseded. As late as 1861, it could be justly remarked that 'on all questions connected with the early literature of our nation, Tanner's *Bibliotheca* notwith-

[1] HEARNE: *Collections*, II, p. 164; cf. II, p. 94.
[2] *Bibliotheca Literaria*, I, p. 46.   [3] DAVIES: op. cit.
[4] NICOLSON: *English Historical Library* (1736), p. 157.
[5] M. R. JAMES: op. cit., p. 34.

standing its many omissions defects and redundancies is still the highest authority to which the inquirer can refer' and that 'as a storehouse of historical materials it is invaluable'.[1] Tanner's book in short marked the climax of a long effort of research into medieval bibliography, and it summed up in itself the special contribution made during the period following the Restoration to our knowledge of the scope of monastic literature in medieval England.

Between 1660 and 1730 scholars in England were thus profitably at work in analysing the extent of the literary production of the English monasteries. Of all these writings the most important for the historian were the monastic chronicles, and in the actual publication of these the scholars at the end of the seventeenth century found themselves, again, not only with a legacy from their predecessors but also with a special task to perform. Even before the death of Elizabeth, Henry Savile succinctly stated what were to be the aims of all future editors of chronicles:

> Though some have undertaken portions of our history – he wrote in 1597 – no one hitherto appears to have attempted to write the whole with that fidelity and dignity which the magnitude of the work demanded ... I have sought a remedy for this evil attempting to bring to light the most ancient of our authors if not the most eloquent certainly the most faithful recorders of facts to the end that others possessing both leisure and genius for the task might have their authors ready to their hand from which to derive their materials.[2]

Such aspirations gave expression to the motives which animated a production which, stretching back to the sixteenth century, had by the time of the Restoration supplied an imposing mass of printed chronicle texts for later scholars to criticize and to augment.

The mainspring of this early movement in the publication of chronicles was undoubtedly Matthew Parker himself, who besides his edition of Asser sponsored the publication of the *Flores Historiarum* of the so-called 'Matthew of Westminster' in 1567, and followed this up with a text of the *Historia Major* of Matthew Paris in 1571 and with a composite version of Walsingham's chronicle three years later. Such a performance set an example to later students, who could imitate the zeal of the Archbishop without indulging in his editorial vices, and despite their intrinsic defects, the productions of Matthew Parker served as the stimulus to a long series of publications which before the Restoration had supplied scholars with a printed version of many of the most important narrative sources of English medieval history. In 1587,

[1] HARDY: *Catalogue of Materials*, I, p. xlii.
SAVILE: *Scriptores post Bedam*, Preface (trans.).

for example, Jerome Commelin issued from his press at Heidelberg a collection of English chronicles which included Geoffrey of Monmouth, Gildas, Bede's Ecclesiastical History and William of Newburgh. The book it is true contained nothing that had not been printed before save a portion of William of Malmesbury's *Gesta Regum* which the editor thought to be a continuation of Bede, and even in respect of its more important sections, it was soon to be superseded. But it was none the less a notable publication if only because of its wide scope, and it deserves therefore to be compared with the collection of chronicles which Camden produced in 1603, itself perhaps a more ambitious production but one similarly marred by faults. The larger part of Camden's book reproduced with modifications Parker's text of Asser and also the Archbishop's text of Thomas Walsingham with apparently a few minor emendations. But the originality of the editor was better expressed by the large amount of narrative which here made its first appearance in print. This included much of the writing of Gerald the Welshman and also an edition of the important Norman Chronicle of William of Jumièges.[1]

Such editing represented a constructive achievement of solid worth to which later generations of scholars were to be vastly indebted. It proved easy – it was for many reasons excusable – for some nineteenth-century scholars to wax righteously indignant over the shortcomings of these early editors,[2] but elementary piety ought also surely to recall the special difficulties under which their work was performed.[3] The textual criticism of medieval documents had yet to be elaborated as a science, and some of the later censures of these men have themselves been exaggerated. When, three centuries after Parker's death, H. T. Riley produced, under vastly easier conditions, an edition of Walsingham's *Historia Anglicana* for the 'Rolls Series', he not only permitted himself in his introduction to be 'too severe' upon the work of his sixteenth-century predecessor, but actually produced a text which in a few respects was inferior to that which he so savagely criticized; and the latest editor of the St. Albans Chronicle considers that Parker's version of this chronicle, though a conflated edition was none the less 'essentially sound'.[4]

[1] *Anglica, Hibernica, Normannica, Cambrica a veteribus scripta.* Ed. Camden – esp. pp. 604-898. The final establishment of the text of William of Jumièges was only achieved in 1914, when Jean Marx, on the instruction of Léopold Delisle, disentangled the text of this chronicle from that of its later interpolators.
[2] Cf. LUARD: *Flores Historiarum* (1890), I, p. xliv; *Chronica Majora* (Matthew Paris) (1872-1882), II, p. xii; IV, p. xvii.
W. H. STEVENSON: *Asser*, pp. xviii.
[4] GALBRAITH: *St. Albans Chronicle* (1937), pp. xi, xii, xxviii.

Nevertheless, while Parker rendered to posterity unparalleled services in rescuing so many priceless MSS., his treatment of his texts was in very many cases undoubtedly deplorable, and neither Commelin nor Camden displayed a sufficient regard for accuracy or a nice discrimination in their choice of materials. The former could place Geoffrey of Monmouth and a Latin abridgment of Froissart on the same level of historical credibility as Bede's Ecclesiastical History. And the latter not only allowed a modern forgery to be inserted into a ninth-century text, but also interlarded his work with unimportant derivative fragments. As editors they lacked the power of selection displayed by Henry Savile, who, seven years before the appearance of Camden's book, issued a far more important collection of English chronicles. It is true that this work included the chronicle of the pseudo-Ingulf as a genuine narrative, and it is true also that transcription is sometimes so inaccurate as to make it doubtful whether Savile himself ever revised his own proofs. But despite this, an editor who gave to the learned world the first complete edition of the three most important works of William of Malmesbury, who added to them the first printed text of the eight books of Henry of Huntingdon, and who published for the first time both parts of the chronicle of Roger Hoveden, abundantly earned the thanks of all students of twelfth-century history. The inclusion in this book of the chronicle of 'Fabius Ethelweard' was fortuitously to prove of great service to later critics of the Anglo-Saxon chronicle, since it was taken from a manuscript that was destroyed in 1731, and so with all its defects was itself to serve as the basis of subsequent editions.[1]

Later students of English chronicles were thus to find themselves under great obligations to the Elizabethans. But they were hardly less indebted to a group of editors of the succeeding generations. Thus in 1619 there had appeared, in Paris, Duchesne's great collection of Norman writers which contained much that was relative to England history, and in particular the first printed version of *Ordericus Vitalis*. And while such publications were being produced abroad scholars at home were not idle. In 1623 John Selden issued his admirable edition of Eadmer's *Historia Novorum* which included, in its introduction, the first critical essay on Domesday Book, and, in its appendices, a fine commentary on the main text and numerous documents related to it. Selden's *Eadmer* was, for the time when it appeared, a model of good editing, but it was not isolated even in its merits, and it must be placed alongside of the great edition of the *Historia Major* of Matthew Paris which appeared in 1640 at the hands of William Wats who had pre-

[1] HARDY: *Catalogue of Materials*, I, pp. xlv, 572.

viously assisted Spelman with his Glossary, and who was later to be chaplain to Prince Rupert. Wats's book had its faults which subsequent commentators have not been slow to point out. But in the great learning which it embodied, it was one of the most notable productions of its time, and it well deserved the praise which it received. Both for the quantity of additional matter which it contained and also for its quality, Wats's edition of Matthew Paris marked an important advance on the work previously done on the St. Albans chronicles by Parker and Camden. It was not to be superseded until the appearance of Luard's great edition of 1872-83, and it attempted for the first time and with considerable success to supply a critical apparatus to the most important single narrative source of the history of England in the later Middle Ages.

The editions of Selden and Wats exemplified the constructive interest displayed by so many of their contemporaries in English medieval chronicles. And the labours of this group resulted at last in a corporate undertaking which was only completed eight years before the Restoration itself. This was the *Historiae Anglicanae Scriptores Decem* which is often assigned solely to Roger Twysden but to which many other scholars including Selden and James Ussher also contributed. The book matured slowly and was at last seen through the press by Jennynge, a Cambridge graduate who collated with the original MSS. such portions of it as were derived from texts in the Library of Corpus Christi College. It included first editions of Simeon of Durham, of Ralph de Diceto, and of Henry Knighton;[1] it was embellished by a long introductory essay from the pen of Selden; and it concluded with a fine and influential glossary compiled by William Somner.[2] The *Decem Scriptores* of 1652 was in fact by far the best edited of the collections of English chroniclers which appeared before the Restoration, and it marked the climax of a continuous activity in the editing of such texts which had begun in the reign of Elizabeth and which persisted almost to the accession of Charles II.[3]

This production had been so large that English scholars after the Restoration, though they had a special contribution to make to chronicle study, were here inevitably concerned in the first instance to see that there was no interruption in an endeavour which was already old. For the Civil War here, as elsewhere, marked a break in the intellectual development of Stuart England, and even before the appearance

---

[1] Cf. TAIT: *English Historical Review*, XI, p. 568.
[2] Cf. MARSHAM: 'Propylaeum' to *Monasticon*.
[3] HARDY: *Catalogue of Materials*, I, p. xlv.

of Twysden's collection there were signs that the earlier zeal for the publication of chronicles was beginning to wane. Two decades were to pass after the Restoration before anything comparable in scale to the earlier productions was again attempted, and in consequence it was in some sense a new movement in the editing of English chronicles which began about 1680 though it was indebted at every turn to what had gone before. Of this new development the work of Henry Wharton was to be the fine flower. But its inception was marked rather by the appearance at Oxford between 1684 and 1691 of three massive folio volumes whose double columns of packed Latin to-day invite neglectful dust. Nevertheless the *Rerum Anglicarum Scriptores*, the *Historiae Anglicanae Scriptores Quinque*, and the *Historiae Britanniae Scriptores* were of considerable importance in the development of English historical knowledge. The books with their forbidding titles were issued anonymously. But the first was the work of William Fulman and the others were produced by Thomas Gale.[1]

William Fulman was born at Penshurst in 1623, and as 'the son of a sufficient carpenter', who came as a scholar to Oxford, materially advanced the study of English chronicles and, before his death in 1688, became 'a most excellent theologist admirably well versed in ecclesiastical and profane history', he surely attracts attention. But despite his loyalty to the Crown which entailed his expulsion from Oxford in 1648, and despite his friendship with the loquacious Anthony Wood, Fulman has lacked any adequate memorial. He was, indeed, the type of English scholar who, in any century, fails of his due appreciation. Too interested in his proper work to seek academic or ecclesiastical preferment, his labours brought him singularly little material benefit. As Fellow of Corpus, he issued anonymously his important edition of chronicles with the encouragement of William Fell, the famous Dean of Christ Church, and immediately saw his book generally attributed not to its author but to the patron. 'He also with great pains sought after and found out the Works of King Charles I and collected them into one large volume with intentions to write the life of that most religious prince and to set it before them; but he, being unexpectedly taken with the small pox, the bookseller employed Richard Perinchief D.D. to draw up a history of it. Which being so done, (not without the notes of Fulman) it was printed before the said collection, with the name of Perinchief to it, and so consequently the whole work was looked upon

---

[1] Fulman's book appeared in 1684 under the auspices of Fell. In 1687 'vol. II' of Gale's collection appeared. In 1691 Gale's 'vol. I' was issued. These conditions led some to treat Gale's 'first volume' as vol. III of a common collection made by Fulman and Gale. But the book of 1684 was probably distinct and the work of Fulman.

and esteemed as due to him which otherwise was to have been due to Fulman'.[1]

Here was a constant figure in English academic life, and it was natural that, when this scholar later revised by command a volume of Burnet's *History of the Reformation*, he immediately met with a similar reward for his disinterested and unostentatious labour. 'That I might take as much advantage from Mr. Fulman as was possible', wrote Burnet, 'I bore with an odd strain of sourness in his character. Bishop Fell had prepared me for that; and I took everything well at his hands.' The agreement between the Bishops was highly satisfactory as the one ecclesiastical magnate supplied the other with materials for the disparagement of the scholar who had added to the reputations of both. It only needed the comments of Anthony Wood to complete the sketch. William Fulman, he remarked, 'had a great insight into English history and antiquities, but being totally averse from making himself known, his great learning did in a manner dye with him'. 'He wrote much and was a great collector but published little.'[2]

He published, however, two large books which were of permanent value, for besides his *Scriptores* he produced in 1665 his *Academiae Oxoniensis Notitia* which was reissued ten years later with corrections and additions. Indeed, it was through his work on academic history that Fulman became connected with Wood, and it need hardly be added that it was Wood who reaped the benefit of the association. It was to Fulman that Wood owed permission to work among the archives of Corpus, and the permit in Fulman's beautiful handwriting still exists. It was Fulman, again, who wrote a preface for Wood's history of Oxford, and sent to its author numerous corrections which were embodied in that book. A whole volume of Wood's manuscript notes was labelled by him *Fulmanniana*, and after Fulman's death Wood found a very different reception in Corpus. But not all Fulman's collections were used by Wood, and opportunity was thus given to other academic historians in their turn to profit by them. The twenty-two volumes in which they were comprised were thus used by Philip Bliss when in 1820 he produced his own edition of the *Athenae Oxonienses*, so that once again it is in the reputation of another that must be sought evidence of the labour of William Fulman.[3]

The place occupied by Fulman among his literary contemporaries could in fact hardly be better illustrated than in the manner in which he

[1] WOOD: *Ath. Oxon.*, IV, col. 242.
[2] WOOD: op. cit., loc cit.; BURNET: *Letter to the Bishop of Coventry and Litchfield* (1693), p. 10.
[3] WOOD: *Life and Times*, II, pp. 116, 117, 403, 449, 468; III, pp. 139, 270.

became the cause of the remarkable association between Anthony
Wood and John Aubrey. Aubrey who was then considering his Wiltshire collections, and contemplating his entertaining 'Lives', came up to
Oxford in 1667, being 'in a sparkish humour', with his head full of
gossip and scandal. He found Fulman's *Notitia* lying on a bookseller's
stall, and was told of the 'report' that 'Mr. Anthony Wood of Merton
College was the author'. Whereupon Aubrey, that 'pretender to antiquities', 'thought he might be acquainted with A.W. himself'.[1] The
book of Fulman thus produced a relationship which was later to become notorious, but the author of it once more faded into obscurity.
There is surely an irony in the final summary by Wood who remarked
that Fulman 'had not in him a complaisant humour unless flattered and
admired'.[2] It was a persistent lack of bare recognition which produced
what Burnet quaintly called 'the odd streak of sourness' in a scholar
whose achievements contemporaries and posterity were slow to
acknowledge.

Fulman's greatest work was done in close connection with Thomas
Gale, and, in the circumstances, it was perhaps inevitable that Fulman's
collection of chronicles should often be attributed to Gale together with
the two volumes for which the latter scholar was actually responsible.
The relation between the two men was curious in that Gale loomed
very large in the ecclesiastical and religious life of his age, and he earned,
as a fine scholar, his full meed of well-merited recognition.[3] His studies
on English antiquities formed only a part of his learned interests, and
even in these his main concern was in pre-Conquest history. But it was
a fitting close to a long career of learned endeavour when he rounded
off his achievement in scholarship by editing a whole series of English
monastic annals.

Gale took as of right a leading place among the English medievalists
of his time. Nicolson gave him unstinted admiration; to Francis Drake,
the historian of York, he was 'that profound antiquary'; and Hearne
correctly described him as 'doctissimus'.[4] He became also a European
figure, and, in his lengthy correspondence with foreign scholars such
as Mabillon, he fitly represented the cosmopolitan character of much
of English contemporary learning. The very quality of his reputation
made it sometimes difficult for him to co-operate with men at home in
more localized studies, or at any rate to work under the direction of

[1] J. COLLIER: *Scandal and Credulities of John Aubrey* (1931), Preface.
[2] WOOD: *Ath. Oxon.*, IV, col. 240.
[3] See above, p. 59.
[4] NICOLSON: *English Historical Library* (1736), pp. 60, 61, 65; DRAKE: *Eboracum* (1736),
p. 565; HEARNE: 'Walter of Hemingford' (1731), I, p. xxiii.

others. It was a virtue to befriend consistently the worthy Thoresby, to send him letters of learned advice and to secure his election to the Royal Society, but the famous scholar appears to have felt no enthusiasm when Nicolson informed Gibson that for a new edition of the *Britannia*: 'I know of no one better qualified to assist you than Dr. Gale'. Gibson was then a young man at the outset of his career, and he was in any case thirty-four years the junior of the distinguished Dean of York. It was therefore not perhaps surprising that, when Awnsham Churchill, the bookseller, tried to advance the project, he had to report that 'Dr. Gale is out of humour', and Gibson lost his temper in words packed with unconscious humour:

> You refer us to Dr. Gale – he wrote – and add he is excellently qualified to help us; for my part I could heartily wish he were either less qualified or more ready to serve the world with his abilities. How it comes to pass, I know not, that these men be so wedded to their nostrums; and that learning, one of the most sociable best-natured things in the world should beget in their tempers a sort of morose reservedness.[1]

But if Gibson was partially denied the 'assistance' of Gale, the world at large had no reason to complain of any lack of industry in the Dean, or in particular of the zeal with which towards the close of his life he attacked the study of English chronicles.

Though the scholarship of Thomas Gale was wider than that of Fulman, their three volumes may be suitably considered as a single contribution to English scholarship which brought to light a large number of monastic annals, and demonstrated afresh their importance as historical evidence. In this the work of these men may be compared with that of Henry Wharton. But while Wharton directed his attention in the main to monasteries connected with the great English sees, Fulman and Gale investigated the chronicles of lesser houses such as Burton and Margam. They made available to students a class of narrative sources which they showed to be valuable not only for local history but also as throwing a new light on the general development of medieval England. What Dodsworth and Dugdale had done for the charters of English monasteries, Fulman and Gale began to do for their chronicles; and their work in consequence was inevitably productive of much future study so that the full value of their labour can only be seen in the later and better editions which it inspired.

These men had an eye for the significant, and subsequent scholars have in consequence, again and again, found it necessary to use their

[1] THORESBY: *Correspondence*, I, p. 157; cf. ibid., I, pp. 141, 298, 303, 304, 308.

improved technique on the texts which Fulman and Gale first discovered for the learned public. Looking back on the part played by the
investigation of monastic chronicles in the development of our medieval knowledge, it is astonishing to note the number of these which
made their first appearance in print owing to the initiative of Fulman
and Gale. The so-called 'Annals of St. Neot' have provided abundant
material for the constructive criticism of later scholars,[1] but it was
Thomas Gale who first published them. The Melrose chronicle whose
first edition was produced by Fulman is still recognized as one of the
most important original authorities for the history of northern England
in the twelfth century. The Burton annals, again, which Fulman introduced to scholars, are of particular value for the period 1211-1260,
while the research of Professor Powicke has shown that the chronicle
of Margam Abbey is essential to a proper understanding of the career
and character of King John.[2] The fine work of Luard was, in the nineteenth century, to perform a similar service to the minor monastic
chronicles as was done by Fulman and Gale two hundred years before,
and the bulk of his five volumes of *Annales Monastici* embodied improved texts of chronicles which had been discovered and for the first
time printed by his two great predecessors. The individual contribution
of Thomas Gale to this achievement is easy to isolate since it was in
these volumes that he printed those editions of Gildas, Nennius, and
Eddi, which did so much to the elucidation of pre-Conquest history.[3]
But as far as the editing of later monastic chronicles is concerned the
credit for the performance must be shared equally between the two
men. And more perhaps than any other scholars, Fulman and Gale
must be praised for helping to establish the individual chronicles of particular monastic houses as an essential part of the material from which
the detailed story of medieval England was in time to be constructed.

It was by emphasizing that the chronicle sources of English history
could only be appraised through attention to their monastic provenance, that the work of Fulman and Gale was original. In other respects
the character of their editorship marked no advance on the productions
of an earlier age. Thus Fulman, without critical scruple, reprinted once
again the history of the pseudo-Ingulf which had before disfigured
Savile's book. And it was perhaps the very fact of this reissue which
provoked the first adverse judgments on a text which had hitherto
been treated with such misplaced reverence. At all events, only a few

[1] Cf. W. H. Stevenson: *Asser*, pp. 97-145.
[2] F. M. Powicke: *King John and Arthur of Brittany* in *English Historical Review*, vol. xxiv,
pp. 659 *sqq.*
[3] See above, pp. 59-61.

years after Fulman had printed not only the alleged chronicle of Ingulf but also its continuation, doubts of its authenticity were expressed by Henry Wharton who pointed out that some of the charters contained therein were undoubtedly spurious.[1] Wanley and Hickes were also suspicious, and the charters were soon to be definitely rejected as forgeries. But the narrative continued to be accepted as genuine, and as late as 1883 De Gray Birch produced a new edition of Ingulf which was in many respects inferior to that of Fulman, and argued for its authenticity without any of the excuses to which Fulman could lay claim. For in 1824 Palgrave had given good reasons for regarding the whole compilation as spurious, and between 1862 and 1893 Riley and Liebermann proved finally that the work of 'Ingulf' and of his continuator 'Peter of Blois' were fabrications of the late fourteenth or early fifteenth century. The exposure of the forgery 'necessitated the revision of every standard book on early English history', and Fulman, though with considerable excuse, must be held responsible for fashioning a link in a chain or error which it needed all the resources of modern scholarship to break.

No such unfortunate inclusion is to be found in Gale's collection of chronicles, but here also the editor displayed a strange lack of critical discrimination in some of the narratives he chose to print. The sketch of 'the history of the Britons' purporting to be from the pen of Ralph de Diceto may be authentic but it is more probably the work of John Pike, and in any case it is but an inaccurate copy of Ralph's own abridgment of Geoffrey of Monmouth – a work with which Gale was familiar.[2] Similarly, Gale failed to realize that part of the annals of Waverley were translated from the Anglo-Saxon Chronicle, though Wheloc's edition of that chronicle was in his possession. It would probably be unfair to censure Gale for printing the English sections of Higden's *Polichronicon* from an inferior MS.,[3] but even with his predilection for pre-Conquest history, it was a grave fault to omit the later and more important section of Walter of Hemingburgh. Nor can these scholars be acquitted of gross carelessness in the presentation of their authors. John Loveday later asserted that in this matter Fulman was more accurate than Gale,[4] but neither of these editors here made an advance on the standards of Savile and their work was inferior to that of Twysden. They both employed amanuenses, and apparently failed to collate their transcripts with the originals from which they were derived. As a result, though Gale corrected many misreadings in a long

[1] WHARTON: *De Episcopis . . . Londoniensibus* (1695), pp. 19, 24-26.
[2] STUBBS: *Ralph Diceto: Opera Historica* (Rolls Series, 1876), I, p. lxxxviii.
[3] LUMBY in *Higden: Polichronicon* (Rolls Series, 1865), I, p. xliv.
[4] John Loveday quoted in WOOD: *Ath. Oxon.*, IV, col. 242.

list of *errata*, these three volumes are marred by omissions which are sometimes large, and by errors which are occasionally grotesque.

Nevertheless, for all their faults the editions of Fulman and Gale represented a great work performed under difficult conditions that were themselves ameliorated by the very fact of its accomplishment. If Fulman popularized afresh the Crowland forgeries, if Gale mishandled Walter of Hemingburgh, if both were guilty of carelessness in transcription, they nevertheless produced in great bulk texts which for all their defects served the learned world for several generations. In company with Henry Wharton, Fulman and Thomas Gale brought the annals of particular religious houses into their proper place among the sources of English history, and they provided a mass of new-printed material upon which successive scholars in the future were enabled profitably to work. For these reasons, if for no others, Fulman and Thomas Gale must take a prominent place among those who were chiefly responsible for concentrating attention upon the narrative sources of English medieval history.

Thomas Gale died in 1702; and Thoresby bewailed the death of his 'kind friend' 'which is a public loss both as he was a very religious and pious divine and as he was one of the most learned men in the Christian world'. 'The loss of this great man', added Francis Drake, in his history of York, 'would have been irreparable had not the father's genius subsisted in the son.' The statement was an exaggeration, but to Roger Gale the world of scholarship was none the less indebted for a careful patronage of learning exercised as the owner of a fine collection of manuscripts which he was not slow to lend.[1] This cultured country gentleman moved freely if with a certain stiffness among the scholars of the time. With a faint air of patronage, he was 'the very good and kind friend' of Hearne, ever ready to discuss Leland or to lend a text or to subscribe to the edition of a new chronicle. Similarly, he encouraged Ralph Thoresby, giving advice on the history of Leeds, or becoming discursive upon such themes as the fragment of a Roman aqueduct or the discovery of a bust of Jupiter.[2] With the strolling gait of a more leisured life he came down from Parliament to the Harleian Library, and accompanied by his amanuensis turned over MSS., chatted a little loftily with Humphrey Wanley at his work, and 'looked into some cartularies of Edmund Bury Abbey'.[3] It was perhaps inevitable that such a man should attain to greater distinction than he deserved. But

[1] THORESBY: *Diary*, I, pp. 360, 361; DRAKE: *Eboracum* (1736), p. 565.
[2] HEARNE: *Collections*, IX, p. 25; THORESBY: *Correspondence*, II, pp. 159, 253.
[3] Lansdowne MS. 771, fols. 36, 38b, 40b.

Roger Gale was to produce one notable book, and as if naturally he became the first Vice-President of the revived Society of Antiquaries, and Treasurer of the Royal Society, to whose *Philosophical Transactions* he contributed several papers of perhaps more pomp than value.

Roger Gale produced anonymously in 1722 a folio with the title of *Registrum Honoris de Richmond*. It was a curious book consisting mainly of documents which, according to Nicolson,[1] had before attracted the attention of Camden and Dugdale, but which had for the most part remained unprinted. It contained extracts from Domesday, a twelfth-century survey of the Richmond fee in Yorkshire and a long appendix of early charters relating to the house of Brittany and Richmond. Many of these charters were of the first importance and most of them had been omitted even from the extensive history of Brittany produced by Gui Alexis Lobineau in 1707. Their publication was thus of great service to all students of twelfth-century history. But Roger Gale's transcription was, like that of his father, often deplorable, and like many wealthy editors he was apparently content to leave the bulk of the labour of producing his book to other and nameless hands. Hare of the Heralds' Office had for example already contemplated a similar volume, and done some work towards its preparation, before Roger Gale at his death took over the task, and even the long Latin preface had been translated out of English by Michael Maittaire who protested that he never received either pay or proper acknowledgment for his work.[2] Indeed some (though not Thomas Hearne) had reason to think ill of Roger Gale. But until Mr. Clay in 1935 at last produced better versions of the Richmond charters,[3] Roger Gale's book remained an indispensable storehouse of twelfth-century material.

Roger Gale was no unworthy son of his greater father, but it is none the less impossible to escape the feeling that with him has passed away the atmosphere which made possible the work of editorship performed by men such as Fulman and Henry Wharton. Apart from an extraordinary figure which was already beginning to disturb the equanimity of Oxford, the early years of the eighteenth century in England produced no man who, in his work on monastic chronicles, could be compared with the great editors of the previous generation. Individual scholars were, however, busy, and none of these was more remarkable than Joseph Sparke of Peterborough who, after residence between 1699 and 1704 at St. John's College, Cambridge, had returned to be registrar of

---

[1] *English Historical Library* (1736), p. 27.

[2] Cf. HEARNE: *Collections*, VIII, p. 112; IX, p. 25; *Bibliotheca Literaria*, No. VI, pp. 15-28.

[3] *Early Yorkshire Charters* (Yorkshire Archaeological Society), vols. I to III, edited by W. Farrer, vols. IV and V concerning the Richmond Fee, edited by C. T. Clay.

the cathedral of his native city. He set himself to investigate its annals, and his character was as noteworthy as his industry. 'An excellent scholar of great memory', he was in the habit of being 'mad a quarter of a year together in every year'. But despite this peculiarity, and the additional eccentricity of 'being very sober having never drunk a glass wine or ale in his life', he was apparently popular since he had 'a great acquaintance with the nobility'. 'Of very good literature', 'admirably well versed in the editions of books', he arranged Lord Cardigan's fine library according to a new plan, and was afterwards entrusted with the charge of the valuable collections of White Kennett, his Bishop. 'Very rich, a married man, and about 36 years old', he began to prepare two volumes which in 1723 appeared under the title: *Historiae Anglicanae Scriptores Varii*.[1]

This notable book was almost entirely confined to chronicles connected with Peterborough, and its principles of arrangement and selection were perhaps derived from Wharton's *Anglia Sacra*. But the work was none the less original for the texts were nearly all here edited for the first time. The *Chronicon Angliae Petroburgense* was, for example, a notable discovery and so was Fitz-Stephen's Life of Becket even though it was printed from a defective manuscript. Moreover the chronicle of *Hugh Candidus* which is here printed is valuable not only for the occasional light it throws upon the twelfth century but also for its use of the Anglo-Saxon Chronicle from which it is in part derived.[2] The See of Peterborough had been omitted from the first volume of *Anglia Sacra*, and Sparke's book must therefore be regarded as filling a gap in English ecclesiastical history.

There was a quality in Joseph Sparke which would make it pleasant to linger with him as (when both sane and sober) he presided over the 'Gentlemen's Society' at Peterborough, or discoursed with his friend Maurice Johnson in the more famous club at Spalding. But as an editor Sparke laboured in some isolation, and few of his immediate associates produced similar work. There were, however, two other men, also educated at Cambridge, who about this time were engaged upon a task of similar importance. They were Thomas Bedford, a member of a famous Non-juring family, and Thomas Rud of Stockton, who had entered Trinity College in 1683. Both these men had, like John Smith, the editor of Bede, migrated from Cambridge to Durham where Rud had set himself to catalogue the cathedral manuscripts in a manner

---

[1] HEARNE: *Collections*, VIII, p. 382.

[2] SPARKE: op. cit.; *History, Ancient English and French exemplified in a regular dissection o, the Anglo-Saxon Chronicle* (1830); *The Chronicle of Hugh Candidus*, ed. W. T. Mellows (1948); STENTON: *Types of Manorial Structure in the Northern Danelaw* (1910), p. 6.

which won the admiration of later investigators.[1] Their new residence inspired a fertile collaboration between them, and in 1732 there appeared at their hands an admirable edition of the *Historia Dunelmensis Ecclesiae* of Simeon of Durham, itself one of the cardinal sources of English medieval history. Since this edition was based upon what is perhaps the author's autograph manuscript, it superseded the version which had already appeared in the collection of Twysden. And in a preface of considerable critical power Rud demonstrated, as against the previous opinions of Bale and Selden, the extreme probability that the chronicle was in fact the work of Simeon and not, as had hitherto been supposed, of Turgot.[2]

The centre of activity in chronicle study was however shifting once more to Oxford, where antiquarian interests of this kind were beginning to take hold of a considerable section of academic opinion. A large number of dons were, for instance, devoting a disproportionate amount of attention to the labours of Anthony Hall of Queen's College, and heavily subscribing to the grossly inaccurate editions of Nicolas Trivet and Adam of Murimuth which that 'dull sleepy fellow' produced in the intervals of his potations between 1719 and 1722.[3] Such concern with monastic annals at the University was certainly admirable, but it needed a more trustworthy editor to give it expression. Already there was to be seen moving about the Oxford streets a soured, untidy, little man who with an observant eye was eagerly jotting down all he saw to the detriment of his enemies. The dust of controversy covered his progress, but he would regularly slip away into the strict privacy of a locked room to perform work which was to revolutionize the editing of English chronicles. Hitherto, the scholars subsequent to the Restoration had in this matter continued, but scarcely modified, the tradition of an earlier age. The work of Fulman, Gale, and Sparke made little advance in accuracy upon that of their predecessors, and it was in some respects inferior to that of Twysden and Wats. No production of a later chronicle made at this time could be compared with Smith's edition of Bede. But now this Oxford eccentric was in his own editions of chronicles to apply new standards of accuracy if not of criticism. His coming therefore marked an epoch; and his name was Thomas Hearne.

[1] *Codicum Manuscriptorum Ecclesiae Cathedralis Dunelmensis Catalogus*, ed. James Raine (1825).

[2] *De Excidio atque procursu Dunhelmensis Ecclesiae* (1732). Selden in Preface to Twysden *Scriptores*; HARDY: *Catalogue of Materials*, II, p. 72.

[3] *Nicolai Triveti Annales* (1719); *Nicolai Triveti Annalium Continuatio* (1722); HEARNE: *Collections*, VII, pp. 71, 317.

M

CHAPTER IX

PORTRAIT OF HEARNE

THOMAS HEARNE was born in 1678, and when he died fifty-seven years later he had won for himself a unique position among English scholars. He took his special position in the learned movement of his age, but by reason of his forceful and combative personality he stood to some extent outside it. Though, like Wharton and Gale, he was pre-eminently an editor of medieval texts he differed both in his aims and methods from both these men, and though he was rigorously secluded in his private life he yet suffered more persecution than either the Catholic Pits or the proscribed Dugdale. As a student of academic life he trod afresh the thorny path of Twine and Wood, but whilst his autobiographical collections will bear comparison with those of his predecessors, they were individual even in their malice. Finally, Hearne must be included among the great Non-juring scholars. He owed an allegiance to Hickes; he broke a lance with White Kennett; and he held his political convictions with a sustained enthusiasm that scorned discretion. But even within that embittered group of learned partisans Hearne once again escapes classification. Though Francis Cherry was his patron, and Dodwell his friend, he remains posthumously, as in life, a lonely and an isolated figure. He was the catalytic agent among contemporary groups of scholars, but, like a true catalytic, he was himself unabsorbed.[1]

Two dominating passions drove this extraordinary man through his tempestuous career: his love of antiquity and his hatred of the political system under which he lived. They transformed a child labourer in the fields of West Waltham into the central figure in the politics of a great University, and into a most prolific man of letters. Hearne was the son of a parish clerk, and as a boy he knew intimately a penury from which his family never wholly escaped. In later days it was easy to say of him that 'he lived in a slovenly manner and died possessed of what he had not the heart to enjoy',[2] but his youth had taught him hard lessons, and

---

[1] No full biography of Hearne exists though the completed edition of his Collections by the Oxford Historical Society forms a precious source for his life and for illustrating every aspect of contemporary scholarship. Dr. Salter's short introductions to vols. IX, X, and XI are extremely valuable. A list of Hearne's works is given as an appendix to Hearne's autobiographical sketch edited and extended by William Huddesford in his *Lives of Leland, Wood and Hearne* (1772). Another list is in T. D. HARDY: *Catalogue of Materials*, I, pp. 807-810.

[2] *Impartial Memorials of Thomas Hearne* (1736), p. 60.

his letters to his father written at a time when he had won fame for himself, together with the assistance they enclosed, take an honourable place in his correspondence among the learned missives by which they are surrounded.[1] For such a boy a patron was a necessity, and he was found in Francis Cherry, the neighbouring Non-juring squire of Shottesbrook. Cherry recognized young Hearne's precocity and had him educated at Bray School. And in 1695 he sent him to Oxford where he entered St. Edmund's Hall. There Hearne was to remain throughout his stormy academic career.[2]

His natural home was the Bodleian, and he was fortunate to become *architypographus*, and then Under-Keeper in that Library. But in 1715 he refused to take the oaths, and was in consequence deprived of all his academic offices.[3] In view of his own poverty the act commands admiration, and henceforth he was dependent upon what he could privately earn. He never lacked fortitude, and though he was mocked by his enemies, he faced them consistently without ever making the easy sacrifice of his convictions. 'By means of this Industry and of a good Disposition he raised himself from the lowest state of Dependence to a Station of Ease and Honour. When his worth was in some sort acknowledged by the offer of the best Offices the University had to bestow, he manifested uncommon Integrity in declining those Offers because the Acceptance of them appeared to him inconsistent with the Principles which he had adopted.'[4] In the same spirit, early in his career he rejected the advice of influential friends to seek advancement in Maryland on the ground that to do so would debar him from those studies to which he had resolved to give his life. He paid dearly for his resolution, but he had his reward, and now it is possible to penetrate to his baffling personality through his own voluminous writings. As his political principles received support from one party in the University, and provoked an ever fiercer opposition from the other, the scholar himself, his indefatigable pen in his hands, would retire with increasing frequency into the locked privacy of his study, his mind full of ancient texts and modern politics, and above all of personal insults which for the present must doubtless be borne, but which surely posterity might be made to understand and to avenge. He himself composed the best summary of his life when he wrote his own epitaph: 'Thomas Hearne who studied and preserved antiquities.' But

---

[1] *Letters addressed to Thomas Hearne* (ed. Ouvry 1874 – privately printed), pp. 46, 59, 63, 69.
[2] *Autobiography* (Huddesford), pp. 1-4.
[3] Ibid., pp. 16-21.
[4] Huddesford's continuation of autobiography (ibid., p. 34).

even this seems an inadequate description of a career which left to the
future over forty volumes of learned print and a hundred and forty-
five manuscript note-books.

It is only among the diminishing echoes of outworn controversies
that can now be heard the authentic voice of Thomas Hearne. He
claims attention as the most industrious of learned editors. But it was as
a Non-juror vociferously refusing to take the oaths to the new dynasty,
and violently denouncing those who did, that he adorned and vexed the
society in which he lived. No don has ever been more hated by his
opponents and few have struck more savagely at uncongenial colleagues. He is thus to be discovered going about his business, irrevocably devoted to assiduous scholarship, but noting down, for the benefit
of those who might come after, every fancied slight, credulous of
every infamy which has a Whig source, believing little evil of political
friends, and nothing good of political foes. An air of splenetic repres-
sion surrounds him, and he stands a strange figure in the forefront of
his Oxford: a little man in unkempt dress who peers out of Vertue's
print[1] with an odd expression blended of obstinacy and inquiry, a true
scholar in his tastes and industry, but a problem alike to the friends who
strove to help him and to the enemies whom he wished to confound.
It is a composite portrait since the devout Non-juror merges into the
retailer of malicious gossip, and the glowing controversialist into the
meticulous editor. But in spite of the confusion the secret is perhaps
not so recondite after all. For the tireless note-taker has preserved even
his private prayers:

> I continually meet with most signal instances of this Thy Providence, and
> one act yesterday when I unexpectedly met with three old MSS for which in
> a particular manner I return my thanks.[2]

It is surely a child-like simplicity that sustains this squat dynamic
student who, in his shabby suit, confronts a hostile world with the
sheets of an *editio princeps* in one pocket and a note-book crammed
with scandal in the other.

These note-books reflect, as in a glass which is coloured, but not
distorted, a critical phase in the development of English academic
scholarship. Hearne could write with force if not with elegance, and
though he was justifiably fearful lest his daily notes might be read by
contemporaries, he prepared them of intent for the eye of posterity; and

---

[1] The portrait was made 'without the Consent or Privity of Mr. Hearne' *Autobiography*
(Huddesford), p. 25, cf. Salter in HEARNE: *Collections*, XI, p. xi.
[2] *Bodleian Letters*, I, p. 118

if his own reputation has suffered somewhat thereby, he has enjoyed, as few others have done, a posthumous revenge over his enemies. Hearne's phrases have a robust vitality as they describe, for example, the Head who 'was never noted for learning or for anything else', or the scholar whose 'work had no manner of likeness to his originals'. Here is a picture, in which there are no half tones, sketched with a pen that has been dipped in gall. But it is a picture that is authentic of an Oxford rent with political strife. Already in the other interest there were dropping from the press the sheets of Amherst's *Terrae Filius* to testify similarly to a habit of mind conducive neither to dignity nor to sound learning. But the savage persecution of Hearne by his academic contemporaries may perhaps prompt the question whether Oxford at this time was as uniformly Jacobite in its sympathies as is sometimes supposed.[1]

Hearne's beliefs were, without doubt, sincere. As a very young man, it is true, he had written a Vindication of the Oaths of Allegiance for the private perusal of Francis Cherry, and when in 1729 Cherry's manuscripts came into the Bodleian, the existence of this essay gave an opportunity to Hearne's enemies for an exhibition of truly subtle cruelty. The tract was printed with the object of making Hearne appear ridiculous, and John Bilston of All Souls added a savage preface.[2] Hearne was, of course, grievously wounded, and proclaimed that he retracted every word of his 'Juvenile or Puerile exercise'. 'I know no hurt', he added, 'in changing any opinion for the better, especially when secular interest is not the motive for it.'[3] It was a fair retort, and in his maturity Hearne never flinched from the most severe consistency.

As no favour or kindnesses – he wrote – have moved me hitherto to write anything contrary to justice truth and conscience, so I am resolved for the future (and I hope God will bless the resolution) to keep strictly to the same principles and to be drawn from them by no secular consideration whatsoever.[4]

The resolve was bravely kept, and despite his lack of restraint, Hearne acquired thereby the dignity which informs every career that welcomes sacrifice for the sake of a cause. It was one thing for a wealthy squire like Francis Cherry to stand up in his own parish church and

---

[1] HEARNE: *Collections*, II, p. 395; VII, p. 276; JACOB: *R. Hist. Soc. Trans.*, 4th Series, XV, p. 91; AMHERST: *Terrae Filius* (1726), No. X.

[2] *Autobiography* (Huddesford), pp. 29-33; *Reliquiae Hearnianae* (ed. Bliss, III), pp. 209-217; Bilston's Preface became the substance of the *Impartial Memorials* of 1736.

[2] Hearne to Richard Rawlinson, March 9th, 1729-30 (*Collections*, X, p. 252).

[4] *Bodleian Letters*, I, p. 226.

face the congregation when the royal prayers were read, but it was quite a different matter for a poor scholar, anxious to keep his father 'off the parish', to rule himself out from such posts as the Camden Chair which otherwise might have been his. The passionate student underwent real hardship when, while still under-librarian, he found the doors of the Bodleian locked against him in 1715, and for the rest of his life he was denied access to its shelves. Here, probably, is a sufficient explanation of the sullen temper which grew upon him in his later years as he wrote behind the locked doors of his study, and imagined with a semblance of justice that the hand of every man was turned against him.

> I who live in Oxford – he bitterly remarked – seldom see or use other books than what my own poor library affords, or what are transmitted to me by particular friends which I hope (and do not doubt) that God will reward.[1]

Hearne suffered much injustice. But it would be false to deny that he invited the persecution which was inflicted upon him. His political principles, advocated with unnecessary violence, exposed him to inevitable attack, but he was beset by an enmity which even the politics of the day could not of themselves have aroused. A hypersensitive and even morbid nature led him to suspect an enemy in every meeting, and he could never forgive insults even when they had not been offered. His pen was steeped in venom and wrote unforgivable words. Savagely avenging affronts, imaginary as well as real, he compassed himself about with outraged hostility: esurient of antiquity, he became a whetstone of cheap wit. He lacked urbanity. But outside the febrile atmosphere of university politics, disinterested observers could discount the pettiness of Common Room animosities, and deplore the endless persecution of a 'poor suffering conscientious man' which 'appears to most here in town as the malice of a few persons who, being unable to outdo and rival his industry, lay hold of some little exceptions (at the worst heedless and which I grant by a more wary man might have been left out) to bring about his ruin'.[2]

It is now possible after two centuries to discount the vituperation of the diaries, and to welcome in them a unique description of an academic atmosphere that has passed away. To the Oxford of Anthony Wood succeeds as if inevitably the Oxford of Thomas Hearne: and it is surely remarkable that the two most illuminating pictures which we possess of past Oxford should thus have been drawn by men who lived isolated

---

[1] Cf. Salter in HEARNE: *Collections*, IX, p. ix.
[2] M. Maittaire to Charlett (*Bodleian Letters*, II, p. 38).

lives within her midst. Like Wood, Hearne began by being a welcome
member of this community, for if Wood's music parties were famous,
Hearne's conversation had once been lively and sought after. It was
only in later life that both men became solitary figures, widely disliked
and deeply suspicious. There was little in Hearne's writing to compare
with the gracious charm that is sometimes to be found in Wood's, but
Hearne was perhaps the better scholar, and he was imbued fully as
deeply with the conviction that the University was a living organism,
whose past should be the subject of loving study, and whose present
condition in all its multifarious manifestations should be the object of
an endless interest. Hearne's sympathies were exclusive rather than
preferential. But he left behind him a description of his own Oxford
more detailed than Wood's if less polished, more intimate if less
charitable, and in his daily notes the contrasted figures in that strange
microcosm of England move with a vitality which even the lapse of
years cannot impair.[1]

From day to day he makes an autobiographical excursion which
seems to traverse the whole field of academic life. He observes the
Master of University College at his correspondence, and 'Sly-Boots',
'the Northern Bear', vigorously presiding over Queen's and planning
to rebuild it. Descending from these august heights, he listens to the
conversation of scholars at 'Antiquity Hall', or deals with the letters
which have just arrived from Ralph Thoresby or Edmund Gibson,
from White Kennett or Roger Gale. There are always momentous
questions to be considered: Has Bentley at last got the better of Christ
Church in the matter of *Phalaris*, and can Hickes get his *Thesaurus*
published? Is Tanner a trustworthy editor, and is Rymer's *Foedera* anything more than a 'rhapsody' of 'trash'? Nor is this all. It is necessary
also to watch the 'learned imps' at the Coffee Houses, and to contemplate the behaviour of gentlemen commoners in their clubs and with
their 'toasts'. Alcoholic loyalty to Church or King is always worth a
note even when it meets with proctorial reproof: 'Gentlemen,' was
the admonition, 'we are to *pray* for the Church and to *fight* for the
Church but not to *drink* for the Church.' It is to be recorded with joy
that on Accession Day in 1715 'the bells only jambled being pulled by a
parcel of children and silly people so that there was not so much as one
good peel rung in Oxford'. But even this need not exhaust the attention. There is also that scandalous scene in All Souls' buttery to be
described, and the woman who came to life after being buried fourteen

[1] *Bodleian Letters*, ii, p. 15; WOOD: *Ath. Oxon.*, i, p. xxv; MALLET: *Oxford University*, iii,
p. 23.

days in the snow, and the plethora of learned tailors. From day to day he proceeds at his task, now the weighty commentator, now the astute critic, now the sprightly anecdotist, and now the picker up of unconsidered scraps. If Hearne is not in the first rank of diarists he can still claim an honoured place in a select company. Surveying the teeming life of a great university with unwearied observation, he left behind him an account in which no event was too small to be recorded, and no topic too exalted to be discussed.[1]

It was not as a diarist, however, that Hearne took his special place in the history of English scholarship. His true memorial is to be found in whole shelves of medieval writers whom he accurately edited with notes and prefaces of his own. This stupendous production represented the climax of a long effort in editorship, and it marked an epoch in these studies. Hearne's editions filled the gap which separates the work of Fulman and Gale from the appearance of the Rolls Series. Working on his own initiative, and at his private financial risk, he undertook and successfully prosecuted a work of national importance, and it was the mark of his own intrepid determination that he was 'forced to publish a few copies at an extravagant subscription of books important to national history, and of course interesting to all'.[2] Until the latter half of the nineteenth century many of the most important sources of English medieval history were to be found in Hearne's editions and there alone, and even to-day the student needs constantly to refer directly to his work. The best edition of the Black Book of the Exchequer is still possibly to be found in Hearne's text,[3] 'Heming's cartulary' is only printed in his volume, and the edition of the Textus Roffensis which he produced in 1720 is, despite its defects, still indispensable. The publication of over forty such volumes by a single editor represents the achievement of a dedicated energy which succeeded only by means of work which seems to-day incredibly rapid. In 1723 a journal announced that 'Heming's Cartulary' was 'just published', and added that 'Mr Hearne has now also in the press Robert of Gloucester's Chronicle which is to be printed in two volumes'.[4] And within eighteen months of July 1727, in addition to voluminous note taking and the conduct of a large correspondence, Hearne found time to produce the five volumes which comprise Adam of Domerham, Thomas of Elmham, and the Black

[1] HEARNE: Collections, II, pp. 290, 348; III, pp. 76, 77, 154; V, p. 83; VI, p. 37; X, p. 215; Bodleian Letters, I, pp. 224, 238; THORESBY:Correspondence,II, pp. 28, 88, 135,369;NICHOLS: Literary Anecdotes, I, pp. 383-400.
[2] GIBBON: Address recommending Mr. Pinkerton (Appendix) (Misc. Works, III, p. 596).
[3] Despite the text contained in the edition of the Red Book of the Exchequer contained in the Rolls Series in 1896.
[4] Bibliotheca Literaria, No. VIII, p. 45.

Book of the Exchequer. It was no exaggeration for a contemporary to say that Thomas Hearne 'ran away with burdens upon his shoulders which would have crushed others to atoms'.[1]

This extraordinary energy entailed its own defects. Gibbon declared that, intellectually, Hearne suffered from 'a voracious and undistinguishing appetite',[2] and in truth he seized indiscriminately upon 'morsels of antiquity' with which to sate it. The miscellaneous character of the appendices with which he overloaded his books might in part be explained by the demands of the varied subscribers to his editions. But even the texts which he selected for publication were not always chosen with wisdom. The chronicle of *Alured of Beverley* which he produced early in his career is in reality a feeble compilation taken mainly from Geoffrey of Monmouth and Simeon of Durham, and the narrative which he attributed erroneously to Thomas Sprott, and printed in 1719, was of little value. When he reissued William of Malmesbury's *Antiquitates Glastoniae* that had been published by Thomas Gale in 1691, he did so on the ground that Gale had omitted much of the narrative: but though Gale's edition was inaccurate, the passages which had been excised were mostly interpolations in the original text. Hearne's treatment of the St. Albans chronicles, too, was unfortunate. He could hardly be expected to discover that the history attributed to Thomas Otterburne was itself derivative, but his belief (shared by Tanner) that there were two authors of that name was probably wide of the mark.[3] Nor is there any evidence that Hearne became more discriminating as he grew older, for just before his death he issued proposals for an edition of the chronicle then attributed to 'John Bevere' which is contained in Harl. MS. 641, and this is nothing but a copy of the *Flores Historiarum* which had already passed through several editions, one of which at least was in his own library. Hearne was no critic. A hasty and ill-natured judgment might conclude that it sufficed for a document to appear old for him to wish to print it.

The influence of an uncritical temper detracted also from the value of Hearne's judgments on his fellow scholars and on the work they produced. The invective which supplies the malice, and much of the attraction, of the diaries impairs their comments on contemporary scholarship. In dealing with the men of a past generation his judgment was usually good, if perhaps eulogistic, but with regard to his own contemporaries he often applied criteria which had little to do with

[1] See Salter in HEARNE: *Collections*, IX, p. vi.
[2] GIBBON, op. cit., III, p. 567.
[3] GALBRAITH: *St. Albans Chronicle* (1937), pp. xvi, xvii, xxiii.

learning. To Hearne an 'honest' scholar meant one who held Non-juring opinions. His Jacobite geese were swans, and the title of 'most learned man' he sometimes bestowed for no other reason than political constancy. Nevertheless, not many of Hearne's judgments erred on the side of charity, for no man ever found it harder to be fair to work done by those who held different opinions from his own. It was probably too much to hope that the man who had suffered for his loyalty to the old dynasty should appreciate the book which celebrated the triumph of its enemies, and no surprise need be felt at the comment that 'learning is sunk so very low that nothing is now hardly read but Burnet's romance or Libel'.[1] But a scholar of Hearne's distinction ought to have recognized more fully the scholarship of such as White Kennett, and it is impossible not to be sceptical of criticism when it penetrates into the domestic privacy of Whig historians. Was it really true that Tanner's first wife was 'remarkable for the drinking of brandy', or that the wife of the Bishop of Peterborough 'wore the breeches and managed him as his haughty insolent temper deserved'?[2]

Hearne's own labours had been disparaged with such ungenerous ferocity that the malice of some of his notes may be understood if not excused. His sense of outrage, however, led him frequently to be fully as unscrupulous as his detractors, and prevented him from sharing in many of the learned achievements of his time. Wanley, for example, was a far greater scholar than Hearne, but Hearne was always blind to his merits, and finally recorded his death in one of the most inexcusable accounts of a great man ever written by one who ought to have been able to appreciate his work; and it is hard to respect the discrimination of a scholar who summed up the career of the greatest manuscript critic of his age with the remark: 'He might have been considerable had he stuck to any one Thing but he very much wanted Steddiness and Judgement.'[3] Hearne's diaries were written for posthumous publication, whilst his prefaces were designed for the contemporary public. Consequently, the greater charity which pervaded the latter is illuminating, though scarcely creditable. Nicolson whose *Historical Libraries* are described in the notebooks as being 'full of gross mistakes' becomes *vir doctissimus* in the preface to *Alured of Beverley*, and Roger Gale is there also praised after being privately castigated as 'but a poor stingy man'.[4] No one, however, could accuse Hearne of lack of courage, and the candid reader of his preface to Dodwell's work must

[1] HEARNE: *Collections*, XI, p. 317.
[2] Ibid., II, p. 9.
[3] Ibid., IX, p. 161.
[4] Ibid., pp. 25, 282; cf. *Bodleian Letters*, I, p. 257.

admit that, on the grounds of gratuitous slander, the university authorities were justified in ordering its suppression.

Thomas Warton later remarked uncharitably that while all antiquaries must be indebted to the diligence of Hearne, his conjectures were none the less 'generally wrong', and with a smug complacency another eighteenth-century scholar added: 'we are forced to despise the man to whose labours we are obliged'.[1] Certainly the weakness latent in much of Hearne's work, and the strength of his unreasoning prejudices, could not be better illustrated than in his treatment of those problems of early academic history in which he was permanently interested. He reverently edited the futile sixteenth-century controversy between John and Thomas Caius on the respective antiquity of Oxford and Cambridge, and he sedulously propagated a legend of the origins of Oxford which he might well have been able to expose in the interests of historical truth. Despite the fact that Francis Wise in his edition of Asser stated in 1722 that the passage describing King Alfred as a benefactor of Oxford University did not occur in the oldest MS., and despite the further fact that this MS. was available for Hearne's inspection until its destruction in 1731, Hearne continued to assert his complete belief in the legend, and only once seemed about to approach the matter in a critical spirit when he wrote to Ralph Thoresby asking him to test the authenticity of the disputed passage by reference to the Saviles of Banke.[2] In general, Hearne pursued this subject with an uncritical impetuosity that shows him to great disadvantage, and he refused even to consider the truth when it was thrust upon him. When Wanley remarked that 'he did not take the University of Oxford to be older than Henry I', Hearne retorted 'this is so ridiculous a notion that it needs no confutation'.[3] It was, indeed, partly owing to Hearne that the myth of Oxford's primitive origins, founded on forgery, and repeated with only a shadow of suspicion in the *Britannia* of 1772, enjoyed a wide currency, even among the learned, until its exhaustive exposure by James Parker in 1885. With some truth if with scant justice, Hearne has for this reason been described as 'a second Twine as regards credulity but without his learning'.[4]

The peculiarities of Hearne's temperament might be held to explain why he took no active part in the movement in Old English studies which was sweeping through Oxford during his lifetime, although its

---

[1] T. WARTON: *History of English Poetry* (1824), I, p. 91; GIBBON: *Misc. Works*, III, p. 595.
[2] W. H. STEVENSON: *Asser*, p. xxviii; PARKER: *Early History of Oxford*, chap. 1; THORESBY: *Correspondence*, II, p. 109.
[3] HEARNE: *Collections*, VII p. 287.   [4] Cf. PARKER, op. cit.

leader was a Non-juring 'bishop' whose sufferings had won his admiration. Hearne never became a 'Saxonist' either in competence or in appreciation. Elizabeth Elstob's work he greeted in 1709 as a 'farrago of vanity', and when Fortescue-Aland's fine preface in defence of Saxon studies appeared in 1714 it failed to arouse in him the least enthusiasm. He made his own contribution, however, to the development of such studies. With his editions of the *Textus Roffensis* and of *Heming's Cartulary* he placed all subsequent students of late Anglo-Saxon history in his debt, and he demonstrated in two long and emphatic prefaces the importance of charter material for their research. Though himself ignorant of Anglo-Saxon he possessed an enthusiasm for the history of the English tongue. In his *Robert of Gloucester* he produced the first workmanlike edition of a Middle-English text, and his preface to *Peter Langtoft* contributed substantially to the realization by modern scholars of the 'unbroken development of the English language'.[1]

The impetuosities of Hearne, and his variegated eccentricity, rendered him peculiarly vulnerable to attack, and they still make it easy to subject him to a criticism which is as plausible as it is fundamentally unsound. When everything possible has been said in his detraction, when his crudities have been laid bare, his prejudices exposed, and his credulities mocked, the essential scholar in him yet remains unscathed. As a critical antiquary he will not bear comparison with men like Wanley or Madox, but his enthusiasm, his accuracy as a transcriber, and his immense productivity enabled him to perform a service to English learning which is not unworthy to be ranked even by the side of theirs. He was a notable editor of medieval texts, and by reason of a lifetime of unflagging industry it was thus vouchsafed to him to transform in this respect the condition of English scholarship, and to leave behind him a legacy of print which was to serve his successors as an example and a stimulus. He marks the end of the long succession of seventeenth-century scholars whose business it had been to supply the learned world with editions of the cardinal sources of English history in the period following the Norman Conquest. Even when he was engaged merely in supplementing work which had already been done he usually succeeded in making an advance which has since proved of permanent value. His editions set up new standards of accuracy in the editorship of such texts. And his supreme achievement lay in his special contribution to making properly available to scholars, as the basis of English medieval history, the great chronicles of England.

[1] HEARNE: *Collections*, II, p. 209; *Bodleian Letters*, I, p. 292; D. N. SMITH: *Warton's History of English Poetry*, p. 9.

His methods and the value of his work could not be better illustrated than from his work on the chronicle generally, though wrongly, attributed to Benedict of Peterborough, whereby he supplied scholars with the most important narrative source for the reign of Henry II. This chronicle derives from three manuscripts. The first of these, *Cott. Julius A xi*, is not the original but an early copy; the second, *Cott. Vitellius E xvii*, which was once possessed by Camden who thought it a text of Simeon of Durham, was terribly damaged in the fire at the Cotton Library in 1731 and is now scarcely usable; the third, which was known to Thomas Gale and inspected by Henry Wharton, is now lost. Robert Brady knew only the Julius MS. as Benedict of Peterborough, but Gale discovered that all three MSS. represented the same chronicle. Then came Humphrey Wanley, who made an elaborate transcript and worked out the relationship between the two most important manuscripts. Within a month of the fire, Hearne applied for this transcript and from it he made his own admirable edition. In conjunction with Wanley he thus saved most of this fundamental text from being lost in the disaster which followed, and when Stubbs came in 1867 to prepare a modern edition of the chronicle he was constrained to speak in the highest terms of the value of the achievement. 'It seldom falls to the lot of an editor', he wrote, 'to be able to bestow on the labours of his predecessors in the same task the unqualified praise that I can give to this edition. Doubtless the greatest part of the credit is due to Wanley, as his transcript alone was used, and Hearne does not seem to have ever looked at the Cotton MS. But Wanley's recension has been most carefully followed, and Hearne's text is accordingly a very sound reproduction of the manuscripts.'[1]

The edition of *Benedict of Peterborough* was characteristic of Hearne's successful treatment of very many other English chronicles. When for example he edited *William of Newburgh* he gave for the first time a reliable presentation in print of what has been termed 'the finest historical work left us by an Englishman of the twelfth century', and if here, too, he had his predecessors, his edition completely superseded all that had gone before. Despite the issue of two modern editions of this chronicle, the only complete collection of all the extant works of the man whom Freeman described as 'the father of English historical criticism' is to be found in Hearne's book.[2] It would in fact be easy to multiply such illustrations of Hearne's services to English scholarship

[1] STUBBS: *Benedict of Peterborough* (Rolls Series), I, pp. xxi–xl.
[2] KATE NORGATE in *Dict. Nat. Biog.*, sub. William of Newburgh; FREEMAN: *Contemporary Review*, xxxiii, p. 216.

but one more must suffice. His edition of *Walter of Hemingford* was a notable performance which brought to a successful conclusion the work that had been done on this chronicler in an earlier generation. This chronicle is divided into two parts: the former dealing with the years 1066-1273 is largely derived from *Henry of Huntingdon* and *William of Newburgh*: the latter, containing an interrupted account of the ensuing period down to 1346, is a most important original source.[1] Thomas Gale in 1687 had printed only the earlier and less valuable section of this work, and it was thus left to Hearne to issue the first edition of what has come to be recognized as one of the essential sources of English history in the early fourteenth century.

Hearne's editions were not only very numerous: they were honest and reliable; and the credit to which he is entitled for his great production is enhanced by the difficulties under which he worked. From the time when he rejected the Maryland project he appears to have made it a rule never to leave Oxford; and in consequence he found it extremely difficult to obtain a sight of the manuscripts he needed, and impossible to make any extensive comparative study of them. The Bodleian was closed against him, he was allowed no general access to College Libraries, and he was cut off from the records in the Tower and from the manuscripts in the Cotton and Harley collections. He was thus dependent for his texts upon what he could borrow from private friends, and it was fortunate that he found so many who were willing to lend. Richard Graves supplied the MS. for *Heming's Cartulary* and for the *Black Book of the Exchequer*; Sir Edward Dering furnished the text of Sprott and the transcripts of the *Textus Roffensis*; whilst Sir Thomas Sebright provided the manuscript of *William of Newburgh*. Such conditions may explain the greatest defect in Hearne's editions: that they were so often made not from the original manuscripts themselves but from transcripts. But his conduct in respect of his production might well be held to mitigate the familiar strictures on his intractable temper. He had to borrow his materials, and he had to sell his works by subscription. Both these transactions demanded tact and patience. Hearne, perhaps, indeed, deserves remembrance in having been one of the very few Englishmen who, prior to the financing of the Rolls Series or since that time, have ever made money out of the preparations of learned editions.[2]

---

[1] There is a gap between 1316 and 1336. It has been suggested that the actual work of Walter stops at 1313 or at 1297. Hearne was unaware of this possibility. Mr. H. Rothwell is preparing a new edition which will doubtless elucidate these points.

[2] *Autobiography* (Huddesford), pp. 16-29; SALTER: op. cit.; HEARNE: *Collections*, IV, pp. 335, 336.

His service to scholarship cannot, however, be assessed in terms of money. Though deficient in historical imagination, he had no equal among his contemporaries in his presentation of medieval chronicles, and it was the quality of his editions even more than their number which caused them to mark an epoch in these studies. The meticulous accuracy which was his chief merit was made a reproach to him after his death:

> One rule which he generally speaking closely observed, was always to follow his Authors religiously. Their mistakes by this means were punctually copied and sacredly preserved ... *Sic MS* he has noted perhaps in the Margin to show he was not ignorant of the Error ... still amidst all these Regulations the text is generally kept purely corrupt, and scarce a blunder thro' the whole but what is very industriously preserved.[1]

It was a 'fault' for which generations of scholars have had cause to be abundantly grateful. Hearne had a respect for the sanctity of an original authority which had been shared by none of his predecessors among the editors of medieval chronicles – certainly not by Parker or Savile, Fulman or Gale. His accuracy, judged by the most rigid modern standards, was as extraordinary as his memory was excellent. His texts have never been thoroughly checked by means of a complete collation, but his claim that his reproductions of his manuscripts were letter perfect was well sustained. It was his constant concern for exactitude that gave an enduring value to the zeal with which he sought materials to print.

These qualities enabled Hearne to be one of the agents whereby there was preserved for England a glory of her early literature. In 1726 he printed as an appendix to his edition of *John of Glastonbury* the text of the Old English epic which describes the defeat of the Essex levies under Byrhtnoth at Maldon about 991.[2] The Maldon Poem had been alluded to by Wanley in his catalogue of 1705, but it was Hearne who first printed an epic which has since inspired the enthusiasm of a long succession of critics. 'There is no stronger composition in English', exclaimed W. P. Ker, 'till the work of Chaucer: there is nothing equally heroic before *Samson Agonistes*.' To have prepared the first edition of such a text was a sufficient distinction but circumstances gave here to Hearne's work an especial value. For the fire in the Cottonian Library only five years later destroyed the manuscript from which the poem was derived, and subsequent scholars were thus compelled to turn to Hearne's edition as if to the original. They found it worthy.

[1] *Impartial Memorials*, pp. 25, 26.
[2] *Iohannis Glastoniensis Chronica*, ed. Hearne (1726), II, pp. 570-577.

Only very recently has Mr. N. R. Ker discovered among the Bodleian MSS. the transcript made by Elphinstone from which Hearne worked, and as a result in 1937 a modern editor has at last been able to get in some measure behind Hearne's print.[1] It is a striking commentary on Hearne's accuracy that the consequent emendations have not been important. Hearne was not well acquainted with Anglo-Saxon; he did not realize that what he was editing was poetry, and printed it as prose. But such was his care that the numerous scholars who gave their attention to the Maldon poem were able to criticize it adequately from his text. For two centuries every word of this epic was subjected to minute scrutiny in an edition made by a man unaware of its full importance and partially ignorant of its language. Editorial accuracy could hardly have received a severer test, or have emerged therefrom with greater credit.

Hearne's editions were not only accurate. They were also free from affectations, and his rules of editing might well be taken to heart by many modern editors of medieval texts.

> The business of publishing [he wrote] is to make as clear as can be; that is to give the words at length and the abbreviations only at such times when such abbreviations may bear several significations and even then sometimes a note will be necessary . . . Let an able faithfull man (that is skilled in abbreviations and hath honesty) undertake the Work and give the Words at large in common Characters (unless it be where the signification is dubious) and he will deserve well of the learned World.[2]

The admirable advice is even to-day of immediate importance. For Hearne's instructions are in strict harmony with the reaction now supported by most competent scholars against the employment of such devices as 'record type' in the editing of medieval documents. Print and handwriting are distinct vehicles of expression, and the reproduction of the latter through the medium of the former must take cognizance of this fact even though to do so imposes heavy (but legitimate) responsibilities upon the 'skill' and 'honesty' of the editor. Accurate lucidity, and not an illusory impression of attention to detail ought to be the aim in the presentation of manuscripts in print. And common sense rather than pedantry will be found to be the best guarantee of clearness.

> General rules [remarked Hearne] may be laid down about abbreviations and the different ways of writing; but such rules will be found to fail very

---

[1] WÜLKER: *Grundgriss zur Geschichte der Angelsächsischen Litteratur*, pp. 334-338; KER: *Dark Ages*, p. 254; E. D. LABORDE: *Byrhtnoth and Maldon* (1936); E. V. GORDON: *The Battle of Maldon* (1937).
[2] HEARNE: *Collections*, x, p. 101.

THOMAS HEARNE M.A. of Edmund-Hall Oxon.
Obiit 10 Junii. 1735. Ætat. 57.

Vertue Sculp.

THOMAS HEARNE, 1735
Engraved by George Vertue

often, and experience and practice must be the best helps in explaining the most difficult remains of antiquity without a slavish regard to set rules laid down by even the best masters.[1]

At the beginning of the eighteenth century the crying need of English historical scholarship was the production of good, reliable and clearly edited texts. These Hearne supplied in such a way and to such an extent that all subsequent study of the chronicles of England has been directly or indirectly indebted to him at almost every point.

Hearne died on June 10th, 1735; and in death, as in life, he was surrounded by a rancorous clamour of conflicting voices. At his funeral in the Oxford church of St. Peter's in the East, there were present 'about forty gentlemen who all had gloves and wine' while 'those who carried had silk hat-bands and shammy gloves.'[2] But the pomp of facile eulogy seemed somehow here to miss its mark, and within six months of the ceremony a scurrilous biography appeared, in which venom sought to compensate for the lapse in taste.

> Hearnius behold in Closet close ypent
> Of sober Face with learned Dust besprent
> To future Ages will his Dullness last
> Who hath preserved the Dullness of the past.[3]

If Pope's lines did little credit to their author, the spirit which animated them none the less explains the campaign of disparagement which pursued Hearne beyond the grave. For the interests and the methods of this exact editor of medieval narratives were (speaking generally) alien to the rising literary fashion, and doubtless there was in him 'a singularity in his exterior Behaviour or Manner which was the Jest of the Man of Wit and polite Life'. Hearne himself had been told that 'good manners were hardly to be expected of a mere Scholar and Pedant',[4] and the worthy bookseller who sold his magnificent library 'very cheap' in 1736 saw fit to advertise his wares with a facetious condescension exactly adapted to the prejudices of the polite world:

> 'Pox on't', quoth Time to Thomas Hearne,
> 'Whatever I forget you learn.'[5]

---

[1] HEARNE: *Curious Discourses*, I, p. ii. It is interesting to observe the essential modernity of Hearne's advice by comparing it with the instructions given by Galbraith in *Public Record Office* (1934), pp. 77, 78.
[2] MS. Letter to Ballard from Lake Reeve pasted in the cover of the British Museum's copy of *Impartial Memorials* (ref. C.45 e 17).
[3] *Impartial Memorials* paraphrasing *Dunciad*.
[4] HUDDESFORD in *Autobiography*, p. 34; *Impartial Memorials*.
[5] *A Catalogue of the Valuable Library of* T. Hearne (1736).

Nevertheless some of his detractors might perhaps have listened with
profit to a conversation which Hearne once held with a famous Master
of University College:

> 'As for Dr. Aldritch', said the Master, 'he was a Despiser of Antiquities. I
> told him that the Dean was a truly learned man . . . 'He was only for polite
> learning', said the Master. 'Why', said I, 'that is Antiquity'.[1]

It was doubtless the sweeping statement of an enthusiast who rises
eagerly to a bait. But it revealed the man himself.

If Hearne belonged in spirit to the century preceding that in which he
died, he was also related by a proleptic affinity to a distant future which
was to share his interests and to revive the accuracy of his methods. He
left it on record that when Lord Kingsale suggested that he should
write a general history, he refused to do so, but added: 'If I had done
it . . . I would have taken care to have given originals.'[2] There spoke a
man who with all his credulous eccentricities would have felt no alien
among the founders of a later school of 'scientific' history. 'His editions', remarked Gibbon, 'will be always recommended by their
accuracy and use.'[3] And a generation which has made it a boast to base
its historical judgment on original authorities may well reflect gratefully on the career of a man who gave his life to the publication of
sources, and here improved on the accuracy of all his predecessors. It
may be said of Hearne as of very few scholars that time has been
friendly to his reputation. Less than a century elapsed before it was
observed that 'the ridicule and satire which once pursued the person
and the publications of this author are now forgotten, and Hearne
stands upon a pedestal which may be said to have truth and honour for
its basis'.[4] Posterity whom he took so ingenuously into his confidence
has thus found occasion to endorse the early judgment of one who survived him: 'Succeeding times have given Testimony to his Abilities.
It is at least not flattery to consider him as a pattern to all whose Duty
it is as well as Inclination to unite much Learning and Erudition with
the greatest Plainness and Simplicity of Manners.'[5]

---

[1] HEARNE: *Collections*, VI, p. 47.
[2] Ibid., VIII, p. 268.
[3] GIBBON: *Address recommending Mr. Pinkerton* (*Misc. Works*, III, p. 567).
[4] Quoted BLISS: *Reliquaie Hearnianae*, III, p. 274.
[5] HEARNE: *Autobiography*, p. 35 (Huddesford, *Lives*).

CHAPTER X

CLERICS IN CONTROVERSY

THE strange endeavour of Thomas Hearne formed the fitting close of the corporate effort whereby in the space of little more than half a century the sources of English history in the later Middle Ages had been elucidated. This research which had invested the arguments of constitutional debate with a permanent importance also reacted upon other departments of the national life. In particular, the churchmen who had led the way in these studies were quick to perceive their ecclesiastical implications, and were led thereby to approach the special problems of the contemporary Establishment from the point of view of its recently discovered antiquities. No student of the Middle Ages could afford to distinguish too rigidly between secular and religious history, and just as the investigation of medieval materials had produced both the *Monasticon* and *Anglia Sacra*, so also did the editing of chronicles illuminate the past of the English Church as surely as it made clear the development of the English State. The appeal to precedent which had been so consistently made in the political controversies of the age thus became characteristic also of its ecclesiastical contentions.

To divines trained to turn to historical study for the solution of the problems of present politics, few periods in the whole history of Anglicanism have been more stimulating than that which elapsed between 1660 and 1730. The restoration of the Church in 1660 inevitably prompted a vindication of the 'dignity of the episcopal order' against Presbyterian pretensions, and on the other hand no churchman zealous for the maintenance of the traditional alliance of Church and King could between 1669 and 1688 neglect the history of Papal jurisdiction. Even the Revolution of 1688 offered to such men no solution of their difficulties, but rather created an unparalleled situation in which the Anglican Church, which had preached passive obedience for nearly a century, had to adapt itself uneasily to the demands of equivocal circumstance. The Non-jurors were every whit as great a problem to the Church as they were in the State, and their writings proved a new and most effective stimulus to the study of ecclesiastical history. It was impossible to brush aside as of no account men such as Sancroft and Hickes, but to meet them on the field of scholarship demanded from

their opponents a comparable erudition; and with the regrouping of
ecclesiastical parties under William III and Anne a yet further incentive
was supplied to historical research.

Thus to the age of Stillingfleet succeeded that of Wake, and while
across a flood of erudition a new high church party was led to attack an
episcopate which had once been presided over by Laud, the Bench of
Bishops now supporting the changes of 1688 and 1714 was forced in its
own defence to essay yet another exposition of ecclesiastical history.
Faction has seldom played a greater part in Anglican politics than
during these years. The two canons who fell to fisticuffs in the Carlisle
Chapter might have found their spiritual peers not only in the mob
which shouted round Sacheverell's chariot, but also in that committee
of Convocation which (as was acidly remarked) could be watched
'lowering the price of claret at the Vine in Long Acre'. But though
these disputes produced an ephemeral literature remarkable for its
immense bulk, they were at the same time provocative of a scholarship
whose positive value has far outlasted the heats which gave it birth. In
respect of the development of medieval learning, the true successors
of the Non-jurors were the great prelates of the reign of George I who
resisted their doctrine. It was owing to these men that an age of ecclesiastical disorder saw an efflorescence in the historical study of English
church law, and it was due to their scholarship that the febrile decline
of Convocation was accompanied by the appearance of volumes which
are still indispensable to all students of medieval councils.[1]

English ecclesiastics in 1660 inherited the tradition of Anglican history which had been expressed, for example, in the very different
works of Thomas Fuller and James Ussher. The lively style of Fuller's
Church History was already beginning to ensure its subsequent popularity, but it scandalized critics who, considering 'puns', 'quibbles' and
'trencher jests' unsuited to a lofty theme, were unable to appreciate the
solid merits of the author's scholarship. On the other hand, the massive
erudition of James Ussher[2] compelled attention. This man 'learned to a
miracle' was born in 1581. He belonged to an earlier generation, and
died in 1656. But his greatest work on the antiquities of the British
Church, originally published in 1639, was reissued in an enlarged form
seventeen years after the accession of Charles II. It was fitting that it
should be so, for Ussher's views of Anglican origins were exactly calculated to appeal to the leaders of the Restoration Church. In his

[1] NICOLSON: *Diary* (Cumberland and Westmorland Antiq. Soc., II, p. 216); SYKES:
Gibson, p. 47; ABBEY and OVERTON: *English Church in the Eighteenth Century*, I, p. 29.
[2] PARR: *Life of Ussher* (1686), especially the appendix of three hundred wonderful letters;
C. E. ELRINGTON: *Life of the Most Rev. James Ussher* (1848).

Discourse of the Religion anciently practised by the Irish he had, for example, insisted in 1623 on the independence of the Keltic Church from the authority of the Papacy, and in his *Treatise on the Originall of Bishops* (1641) he had claimed that episcopacy was an institution derived from Apostolic times. Ussher's attempt to discover in England a primitive Protestantism, and in particular his effort to find the spiritual ancestry of Anglicanism in heretical movements such as those of the Pelagians and Waldenses was in the hands of his successors to give an unfortunate twist to much of the study of early Church history in this country.[1] But when Restoration prelates such as William Lloyd and Edward Stillingfleet continued the studies which he had inaugurated, they came under the influence not only of historical theories which later scholars were to correct, but also of an exact scholarship which in its range and accuracy has been the wonder of subsequent critics. A man who collated eleven manuscripts of Nennius had no need to be taught the merits of an exhaustive examination of material, and there is little doubt that in this branch of historical criticism this great scholar was immeasurably superior to most of his contemporaries and successors. 'Passing from Parker, Camden, Anthony Wood, Hearne, and Wise, to Ussher', remarked W. H. Stevenson, 'gives one the impression of being suddenly transferred from the critical atmosphere of the later Middle Ages to that of modern times.'[2]

The majestic shadow of James Ussher thus loomed heavily over those who during the reign of Charles II sought, in the interests of restored Anglicanism, to discover in the past a church similarly independent of Rome and equally subjected to Bishops. Challenged like their greater predecessor by diverse opponents they strove to use all the weapons of scholarship in defence of the ecclesiastical system which they had been called to administer; and like him they had no difficulty in finding adversaries. In 1668, for example, the publication of the *Church History* of Hugh Cressy had clearly restated the Catholic case in historical terms, and brought the massive collections made at an earlier date by the Jesuit, Michael Alford, into the sphere of public discussion;[3] and on the other hand the researches of Scottish antiquaries had for some time past taken an uncomfortably nationalist and anti-episcopal turn. Consequently, when, in 1677, William Lloyd, later to be one of the seven Bishops, and successively to occupy the sees of St. Asaph, Lichfield, and Worcester, published his *Historical Account of Church*

---

[1] E. W. WATSON: *Ussher* in *Typical English Churchmen from Parker to Maurice*, p. 64.
[2] W. H. STEVENSON: *Asser*, p. xli.
[3] Cf. WOOD: *Ath. Oxon.*, III, cols. 1011, 1012.

Government, he did so avowedly to combat 'the arguments that have
been used of late times against episcopal government' and in particular
those 'which have been drawn from the example of the ancient Scottish
Church'. Lloyd's book was acute, and its immediate result was to revive
an old controversy in a furious form. His main object had been the
historical vindication of episcopacy, but he thought it necessary to his
design to give a short history of the first planting of the Scots in Great
Britain which 'thwarted the common Road of their Historians since
the Days of Hector Boethius and bereaved them of about Forty of their
first Monarchs'. *Nemo me impune lacessit*; and this monograph immediately became the centre of a dispute which was almost national in its
scope. Sir George Mackenzie, 'so set on fire that 'twas not safe for the
Bishop to approach him', wrote a series of books repudiating what he
considered as a slur on his race; and Robert Sibbald composed in manuscript a detailed refutation. The Scots, it seemed, were 'reformed from
Popery not from Hector Boethius', and the controversy to which even
Walter Scott later contributed is hardly ended to-day.[1]

The solid erudition produced by this spate of argument in the latter
half of the seventeenth century could perhaps best be appreciated by
means of a reference to the most important single work which it
evoked. For the controversy early drew into its orbit Edward Stillingfleet,[2] and his *Origines Britannicae* which appeared in 1685 was concerned to vindicate Lloyd and was prefaced by a long introduction
directly devoted to his defence. Stillingfleet moreover was a worthy
champion, though men may have felt some surprise when this familiar
of kings, moving in 'the beauty of holiness' about the world of Restoration fashion, turned aside to the drudgery of learned controversy.
Pepys could find no standing room among the distinguished audience
which crowded to hear 'the ablest young man to preach the gospel
since the days of the apostles',[3] and Stillingfleet, who in 1689 at the age
of fifty-four was to become Bishop of Worcester, certainly received
sufficient adulation to turn his head. But if time, despite the later admiration of S. T. Coleridge, has done much to tarnish the laurels which
Stillingfleet once wore with complacent grace, there must have been
in him some really remarkable qualities to make Bentley write a

[1] Lloyd's treatise was reprinted by T. P. Pantin in vol. II of his edition of Stillingfleet's
Origines Britannicae, cf. NICOLSON: *English Historical Library* (1736), pp. 93, 94. Modern
controversy on the theme may be illustrated from M. V. HAY: *Chain of Error in Scottish
History* (1927).
[2] *Life and Character of Edward Stillingfleet* (1710), apparently written by Richard Bentley
and not, as Hearne surmised, by Timothy Godwin, 'now the snivelling sneaking archdeacon of Oxford' (HEARNE: *Collections,* I, p. 373; X, p. 429).
[3] PEPYS: *Diary,* April 23rd, 1665; May 9th, 1669.

scholarly eulogy of his life, and to impel John Hough, whose struggles
with James II at Magdalen had made him no respecter of persons, to
pronounce him 'the ablest man of his time'. The chorus of praise which
followed Stillingfleet through his career must now appear excessive,
but it may in some measure be explained by the perusal, not of the
faded conceits of antiquated sermons, but of the pages of an historical
work which for all its defects has even yet not wholly lost its value.[1]

The *Origines Britannicae* attempted to 'give as clear and distinct a
view of the state and condition of the British churches from their first
plantation to the conversion of the Saxons as could be had at so great a
distance', and its author 'resolved to attempt something towards the
rescuing this part of church history . . . from the fabulous antiquities
which have so much debased the value and eclipsed the glory of it'.[2]
It is true that this was yet another of the attempts to demonstrate the
independence of the British Church from Rome and its acceptance of
episcopacy; and as such the book had immediately to face the onslaught
of Lloyd's critics while later scholars have not been slow to point out
how sectarian bias could lead its author into occasional mistranslations
and even into distortions of fact. But on the whole the erudition which
lay behind this book, and the manner in which it was presented, raised
it far above the level of a party statement. There was a real originality
in the work. 'I have neither neglected', remarked Stillingfleet, 'nor
transcribed those who have written before me; and if in some things I
differ from them it was not out of the humour of opposing any great
names, but because I intended not to deliver other men's judgements
but my own.'[3] No author writing on ecclesiastical antiquities within a
century of Ussher could escape being profoundly indebted to him, and
Stillingfleet's book could never have been produced apart from the
labours of the earlier scholar. But here there was undoubtedly a fresh-
ness of treatment, and Stillingfleet had the courage to dissent from his
great authority on such points as the position of London in Roman
Britain or the presence of the British Bishops at the Council of
Arles in 341.[4] Similarly Stillingfleet was politely sceptical about the
interpolations which were to be found in Camden's edition of Asser,[5]
and when he dealt with Arthur he could state his case with a truly
modern caution: 'I think both sorts are to blame about him; I mean
those who tell incredible tales of him such as are utterly inconsistent
with the circumstances of the British affairs at that time; and those who

---

[1] JOHN HOUGH in a letter prefixed to Stillingfleet's *Miscellaneous Discourses* (1735);
S. T. COLERIDGE: *Notes on Stillingfleet* (privately printed – 1875).
[2] *Origines Brit.* (1685), pp. i, ii.   [3] Ibid., p. lxxiii.
[4] Ibid., pp. 75, 76.   [5] Ibid., p. 208.

deny there was any such person.'[1] Hearne might grow restive under
the restraint of such scepticism and complain that this 'running down
much of our old history proceeds upon indifferent Grounds', but
Nicolson's eulogy of the 'Accuracy of Judgement' and 'the Purity of
Stile' contained in the book was better deserved.[2] Despite its faults, the
Origines Britannicae of Edward Stillingfleet must be considered as one
of the most important works on the first age of English Church history
written between the time of Ussher and the nineteenth century.

Stillingfleet's book ended with the Teutonic invasions of the fifth
century, and its character invited a continuation by a lesser man who
might fairly easily reproduce the polemic without displaying the
erudition which had given it value. This was in fact the defect of the
Origines Anglicanae which John Inett, precentor at Lincoln, produced
between 1704 and 1710 in an attempt to bridge the gap between
Stillingfleet's treatise and Burnet's *History of the Reformation*. The work
was vigorously written, but in so far as medieval history was concerned, it was little more than a record of Papal aggression, and subsequent criticism has shown that its author, depending too much upon
secondary authorities, had been led by his preconceptions into numerous mistakes. In truth, the controversial character of so much of the
earlier work on Church history was now becoming exaggerated, and
the attempt to illustrate a primitive independence from the Papacy was
leading to the application to the Middle Ages of Erastian ideas which
were alien to them. High Church divines had often protested against
such theories as unhistorical and damaging to their notions of the
Church as *societas perfecta*; and after the Revolution the whole trend of
Non-juring studies was to move away from the notions which had
been advocated with moderation by Stillingfleet and with violence by
Prynne. These men were now ready 'to prove beyond all Contradic-
tion that the Church from the beginning had its peculiar Rights and
Privileges immediately from Christ Himself wholly independent of the
Civil Magistrates or any Temporal Authority whatsoever'.[3] In consequence when the work of Inett on the medieval Church was, in 1708,
superseded by that of Jeremy Collier, it was by a book that was not
only its superior in knowledge but one which was written from a
wholly different point of view.

It was to be expected that the man who was to succeed Hickes as the

---

[1] *Origines Brit.*, p. 334.
[2] HEARNE: *Collections*, VIII, pp. 309, 310; NICOLSON: *English Historical Library* (1736),
p. 94.
[3] T. BRETT: *Church Government* (1710), Preface; cf. S. LOWTH: *Subject of Church Power*
1685).

leader of the Non-juring communion would have strong principles and sound learning; and Collier who had been one of the first to denounce the oaths in print, and who had since waged a pamphlet war on stage corruption, could wield a lively pen. Hearne and others might fear that he would not submit himself to the labour of research, but when his book appeared their doubts were dispelled. The *Ecclesiastical History* of Jeremy Collier based upon an extensive reading of original authorities was a highly remarkable production, and its first volume at once took its place as the most comprehensive account of the medieval English Church that had appeared since the days of Fuller. Moreover, it marked a break in tradition, for it discovered the essential feature of our early ecclesiastical history, not in the pristine independence of the Church in Britain but rather in the harmony of a primitive Catholicity that held together the British and Roman Churches until it was dissolved by the later growth of abuses. Though Collier laid full stress upon the functions of episcopacy on the primitive Church his work was therefore highly distasteful to men such as Nicolson and Burnet who saw therein an attempt to discount the rights of the State over the Church as established in England by the Reformation.[1] But it was a refreshing change to find in England a clerical writer upon the medieval Church engaged in stating the case for Anselm against Rufus, or for Becket against Henry II. Collier's work, if perhaps no less coloured by partisan feeling than that of his opponents, probably approached nearer to an understanding of the motives which underlay medieval politics.

The immediate resentment caused by his book was inevitable. Collier was suspect to the government; he was under sentence of outlawry; his connections with the literary world of London had made him a notorious figure; he had long been the outspoken champion of unpopular causes. Now he was stating an historical theory at variance with those held both by Anglicans and by their opponents. Here, however, he could well afford to await the judgment of posterity which perforce had to recognize his history as of high importance. An eighteenth-century bishop could ruefully exclaim: 'We have only two historians of our national church worthy of the title: Collier the Nonjuror and Fuller the jester.' As late as 1840 Collier's work could be described as 'emphatically *the* Ecclesiastical History of Britain to which all similar works must be referred as to their legitimate centre',[2] and even to-day, despite the inevitable corrections which have been made thereto by later scholars, the book remains of substantial value alike

[1] Cf. NICOLSON: *English Historical Library* (1736), pp. 117, 118.
Preface to 1840 edition of COLLIER: *Ecclesiastical History*, by F. Barham, 'the Alist'.

because of its wide scope and for the sake of the copious and minute references to authorities which it contains.

The approach of Collier to his subject was indicative of an old cleavage which had subsisted in Anglican opinion with regard to the problems of medieval Church history. The theory that a catholic Christianity was the foundation of both the Roman and British Churches had coloured much of Anglican historiography in earlier days. It had, for example, been elaborated in 1627 when, in an illuminating controversy, Peter Heylin, then a young Oxford graduate, had contended against the Regius Professor of Divinity in his University that the visible Church of England derived more directly from Rome than from such sects as the Wycliffites.[1] This interpretation of Anglican origins, smothered for a time under the superior learning of Ussher, had never been allowed to die, and it now found expression in the copious writings of Non-jurors who coupled their scepticism of a primitive British Protestantism with an implacable hostility to those abuses which, as they conceived, had later disfigured the Roman system. To these men apostolical succession was an article of faith, and one which they considered capable of historical proof not only in respect of Bishops, but also with regard to those monarchies, which *jure divino* constituted an essential link in the chain of interdependent powers that were all alike, in their proper relationship, directly delegated by God for the governance of man. These scholars thus became increasingly intolerant of any historical theory which ascribed to the English medieval kings an absolute supremacy in matters both ecclesiastical and civil. And they could find no sufficient evidence in the past history of their country to justify the view that a king should be reverenced for the mere possession of *de facto* authority. After the Revolution, the Non-juring Schism concentrated such opinion outside the Church where it was developed with a wealth of antiquarian learning. But in opposition thereto there grew up within the orthodox fold a new school of history led by men who were concerned to justify by reference to precedent a theory of monarchy and of the constitution radically different from that which had previously been held by the majority of Anglican divines. 'Whenever', exclaimed one of them in 1708,

> a Sovereign *de facto* is unanimously submitted to and recognized by all the Three Estates in several successive free Parliaments, I must believe that person to be lawful and rightful Monarch of this Kingdom; who alone has a just title to my allegiance.[2]

[1] M. CREIGHTON in *Dict. Nat. Biog.*, sub. Peter Heylin.
[2] Nicolson to Salkeld, July 24th, 1708 (*Epist. Corr.*, p. 387).

The events of 1688 inevitably brought to the forefront of Anglican politics those who were ready to subscribe to a theory of monarchical authority compatible with the principles of the Revolution. But the policy of the Whig Bishops was opposed not only by the Non-jurors but by a strong party within the Church composed of men who, while they accepted with reluctance the change of dynasty, were by no means content to see the direction of Anglican affairs given over without protest to a 'Low Church' episcopate whose political theories they abhorred. The whole question of the constitution of the Church thus came under discussion; and it could hardly be debated without reference to ecclesiastical history. The acrimonious controversy concerning the rights of Convocations, which echoed through England between 1697 and 1717, not only formed an important part of the struggle of English political parties, but also provided the occasion for a notable advance in English medieval studies. The stage for the later conflict had in truth been set as early as 1664 when Archbishop Sheldon and Clarendon had made their private arrangement whereby the clergy waived the privilege of taxing themselves and submitted to inclusion in the money bills of the Commons. For the Crown, liberated from the necessity of using Convocation for the raising of taxes, found itself without any compelling motive for summoning Convocation at all. In consequence, with the exception of one transitory session in 1689, Convocation did not meet for more than thirty years, and there thus took place what Gibson described as 'the greatest alteration in the constitution ever made without an express law'. When therefore in 1697, Francis Atterbury anonymously advanced to the defence of ecclesiastical synods in his famous *Letter to a Convocation Man*, he had a real grievance to redress; and the sting of his attack came from its being directed not only against the authority of a Whig Bench of Bishops but also against a constitutional abuse which they had been content to condone.[1]

Atterbury's tract was couched in historical terms and was predominantly anti-Erastian. It demanded the restoration of a sitting convocation not as a matter of grace from the King but as a matter of right, since the Crown (as was urged) had no more authority to prevent its meeting than it had to refuse to summon Parliament. Atterbury in fact claimed for Convocation 'a power to debate, draft and pass decrees upon spiritual subjects equal to that of Parliament in temporal affairs'; and it was small wonder that the book made 'a considerable Noise and Pother in the Kingdom'. In particular, it provoked in the same year an

[1] SYKES: *Gibson*, pp. 25-28; BEECHING: *Atterbury*, p. 53; CARDWELL: *Synodalia*, p. 694.

elaborate reply from William Wake who as Canon of Christ Church undertook to vindicate the *Authority of Christian Princes* over their Ecclesiastical Synods, and he asserted his case in such an extreme form as to disturb some even of his own supporters. Atterbury, not perturbed, immediately set about compiling in reply his *Rights, Powers and Privileges of an English Convocation* which appeared in 1700, and three years later this was in turn answered by Wake with a large folio on the *State of the Church and Clergy of England*. Less emphatic, perhaps, than its predecessor in its assertion of the rights of the Crown, it none the less triumphantly illustrated by reference to history his original contention that the final authority rested in the sovereign alike to decide whether convocations should be allowed to sit, and also to determine what business if any should be submitted to their discussion.[1]

By the time that Wake's *State of the Church* appeared, Atterbury had already attained the first of his objectives, for in 1700 the new Ministry of William III insisted that Convocation should be allowed to sit concurrently with the newly elected Parliament. The aim of the High Church politician had now therefore to be directed not so much towards magnifying the privileges of its Lower House in opposition to the authority of a Whig episcopate, and in particular to that of its presiding Archbishop. Atterbury therefore, still arguing in historical terms, drew a strict parallel between the Lower House of Convocation and the Commons in Parliament, and claimed for it the right not only to separate debates, and to disagreement from the decision of the Upper House, but also to the privilege of rising and sitting at its own pleasure. Here was something which very directly challenged the whole Bench of Bishops, and from this time forward the spate of books, pamphlets, and tracts increased so prodigiously as almost to overwhelm the author of the dispute. 'When you come to town', wrote Atterbury to a friend in January 1701,

> you will be entertained with answers of all sorts to my book. Dr. Hody has one just coming out in two thick octavo volumes . . . which he calls an 'History of Convocations'. Another gentleman has by order wrote and printed a good part of another. It is to be of about two or three hundred pages; and is to be a first part only, two more being to follow. And this gentleman is ordered to use me rudely, and to put as much gall as he can into his ink. Dr. Hody is to be in the meek way . . . After all Dr. Wake is to come with a mighty folio.[2]

[1] SYKES: *Gibson*, pp. 29-53; *Church and State*, pp. 300-310; LATHBURY: *Convocation* (1853) pp. 392-394; Nicolson to Wake (NICOLSON: *Epist. Corr.*, p. 64).
[2] Atterbury to Newey, Jan. 18th, 1700-1 (NICOLSON: *Epist. Corr.*, pp. 215, 216).

'Under all this threatening news', he added, 'I am in heart', and it is possible to feel some sympathy with him as he struggled to keep afloat on the torrent of ink. But the practical issues of the controversy were steadily going against him. On the one hand the fundamental weakness of the Convocations was illustrated by the quiescence of the northern assembly, and on the other hand the position of the lower clergy was never sufficiently strong for them to impose their will upon the exceedingly able members of the Upper House. The debates in the Lower House of the Canterbury Convocation became more and more factious, and its energy was wasted in futile bickering. Progressively losing the respect of the community, Convocation, distrusted by all its most distinguished members, rapidly declined in prestige as it found ever less business of real importance to discuss. And the real cause of the final collapse of Convocation in 1717, and of its long suspension until 1855, was to be found not so much in the action of Whig politicians anxious to seize the occasion of the attack on Hoadly's sermon to effect a change in the constitution of the Church, as in the fact that already the Canterbury assembly had forfeited the good will of the nation by the open scandal of its own proceedings.[1]

For a score of years in fact the Church of England was harassed by a factious controversy which as Gibson remarked might well have been 'managed in a more calm and Christian way', and yet out of the prolific verbiage of the dispute there emerged works of fine scholarship. In a sense, Atterbury himself must be regarded as having contributed to this end for he directed opinion to matters which might otherwise have never commanded attention, and, dealing lightly with the problems of medieval Church history, he forced his opponents to investigate them with a thoroughness of which he was himself incapable. His confident superficiality seemed to excite research in others, and the man who had once brought the full scholarship of Bentley in a torrent on his unworthy head might have been expected in the future to avoid similar adventures. But Atterbury could write. He was prone to mistake felicity of expression for learning, and he had learnt too well at Oxford a 'humanity' which could affect to despise the learning it had been unable to master. Atterbury deserved his place as a member of the literary group adorned by his friends, Swift and Prior. But when parading as an erudite controversialist, his personal failure was egregious. His chief service to learning lay in eliciting the rejoinders of scholars with whom he was unworthy to cross swords.[2]

---

[1] SYKES: *Gibson*, pp. 29-53; *Church and State*, loc. cit.; LATHBURY: op. cit., pp. 359-460.
[2] F. WILLIAMS: *Memoirs and Correspondence o Atterbury*; BEECHING: op. cit.

Though he wrote voluminously on points of medieval history, Atterbury was an indifferent medievalist. He professed to have come to prefer the study of records to that of classical texts, and he sometimes investigated them himself. Once, apparently, he went so far as to invite the collaboration of Hearne. But in the main, Atterbury's acquaintance with medieval learning was superficial and derivative. He relied largely on the collections of others, and in his pretentious *Rights of Convocation* 'the Historical Part of the Argument' was correctly stigmatized as 'very falsely Represented'.[1] Even those who were sympathetic to Atterbury's politics distrusted his scholarship, and Hearne who considered himself a friend was constrained to remark:

> I do not look on him to be a Man of extraordinary Depth. He has not a true Genius to the Study of Antiquity; nor has he taken much Pains to make himself a Master of our English History. He may be cry'd up for a Master of Style . . . yet . . . Affectation of Wit and Satyr does not become a grave Subject.[2]

Ten years before, another observer wrote of Atterbury with less charity:

> A lucky turn of Words and Thoughts and a Talent at expressing Malice and Envy successfully may give vent to a Book . . . though it may prove upon examination to have not one jot of Truth in it.[3]

Atterbury was not given to modesty; but he once succinctly passed judgment on his own work. 'I sometimes know', he said, 'where learning is and how to make use of it when I want it.'[4] It is the description of a dilettante; and it represents Atterbury's position in the contemporary world of historical scholarship.

Atterbury's apologists have claimed that he appealed from precedents to principle, but it must be added that he usually mistook principle for passion. In making enemies he could challenge comparison with Hearne himself, and he carried the dust of conflict with him into every public office which he held. He was a man wedded to strife and prone to impart into learned argument all the spleen which personal animosity could excite. The Convocation Controversy was in its theoretical aspects undoubtedly dull, and he took it upon himself, by means of personal invective and bright superficiality, 'to inspirit a dry

---

[1] KENNETT: *Ecclesiastical Synods*, p. 11.
[2] HEARNE: *Collections*, III, p. 108.
[3] Cf. BEECHING: *Atterbury*, p. 23.
[4] NICHOLS: *Literary Anecdotes*, IV, p. 456.

subject'. Such devices were peculiarly galling to a company of exact and learned scholars whose ponderous erudition was an easy target for light wit. And it is easier to explain than to excuse the extraordinary venom which came to inform this discussion of medieval politics, as with an outraged rectitude the opponents of Atterbury reproved the methods of their nimble assailant. 'A thread of ignorance', exclaimed Burnet, 'ran through his work.'[1] 'He was', added another, 'a Man of Pride and Arrogance, Full of Himself and a Despiser of all others.'[2] And Nicolson, corrected on insufficient grounds by this 'insolent bungling and illogical compiler', found it 'a Discouraging Prospect to see so many Men of Gravity and Good Learning caressing an Empty Misrepresenter of our Antiquities'.[3] Therein lay the chief grievance. It was hard for meticulous scholars to forgive Atterbury for his confident mistakes; but the burden was made heavier to bear when his books by their lively style attracted the attention of a wider public than that which they themselves could command. The correction of Atterbury thus became almost a moral duty to be undertaken with fierce energy by the foremost medievalists of the day.

Atterbury supplied the stimulus to much of the production, and to most of the acerbity, of the Convocation Controversy. But the positive achievements in scholarship which resulted therefrom were the work of a group of men whose prominence in the Anglican Church in the closing years of the seventeenth century was a social phenomenon as significant as it was important. After 1688 it was inevitable that compliance with the Revolution settlement should have been regarded as essential to ecclesiastical advancement. But what was more remarkable was that the most prominent champions of the new political order within the Church were men who owed their rise to power very largely to the distinctions which they had won in the field of medieval scholarship. Once established, these men were ready to justify the changes of Revolution not by appealing to expediency but by making an exhaustive examination of past history. As the years elapsed it began almost to appear as if historical erudition was coming to be held as an indispensable qualification for elevation to the new episcopate, until at last within two years of the accession of George I, Anglican policy was largely directed by a group of men who, closely knit together by their political opinions, were further united by the fact that their special achievements had been in the sphere of historical scholarship. Never

[1] BURNET: *Own Times* (1734), II, p. 281.
[2] WAKE: *State of the Church*, Preface, p. iii.
[3] *A Letter to Dr. White Kennett*, p. 18 (added to NICOLSON: *English Historical Library*, 1736).

before or since has proficiency in medieval studies been a more characteristic quality among Anglican Bishops.

By the last decade of the seventeenth century this most remarkable group was already giving signs alike of its importance, and of the character of its influence. William Nicolson, for example, its senior member, before he became Bishop of Carlisle in 1702, had been a leader among the Oxford Saxonists, and after his elevation, his abundant energy was almost equally divided between the politics of the Church and his valuable 'Historical Libraries'. At the same time his extensive correspondence canvassed the learned world insistently on questions relating both to Teutonic philology and ecclesiastical affairs. White Kennett, his junior by five years, who was destined to occupy the See of Peterborough in 1716, had achieved notoriety in 1689 by renouncing his high-church principles and openly supporting the Revolution. Such profitable changes of opinion were not, however, uncommon, and a further claim to be singled out for promotion was discovered in his having, as an antiquary, issued in 1695 a pioneer work on parish history. Edmund Gibson who, in his turn, was made Bishop of Lincoln in 1716 and Bishop of London in 1723, was an adept at politics, but his advancement in the Church seemed assured even before the death of Queen Anne by his having edited a text of the Anglo-Saxon Chronicle in 1692, and a revised version of Camden's *Britannia* in 1695. Finally, William Wake had already before the end of the seventeenth century established for himself by historical research his claim to that career of success which was later to lead him to the Primacy of England.

Wake was pre-eminent among those men who all in their several ways owed their promotion in the Church to an early proficiency in medieval study. He rose to higher ecclesiastical rank than any of them, and he made a more enduring mark upon the development of English scholarship. The honours which fell so thickly upon him were throughout intermingled with the continuous production of works dealing with ecclesiastical history, and these in their turn carried his influence far beyond the limits of the Church he ruled. His learned correspondence with French scholars which had begun as early as 1682, developed between 1717 and 1720 into negotiations with the French ecclesiastical historian Du Pin for a union between the Anglican and Gallican Churches. The project was perhaps doomed to failure, but Wake's share in this illuminating correspondence is none the less interesting. He combined learning with conciliation, but he was mindful of his own dignity, and claimed the right to negotiate at least upon equal terms

WILLIAM WAKE
From the original portrait, possibly by Thomas Gibson

with the Cardinal Archbishop of Paris. 'As Archbishop of Canterbury', he wrote to Du Pin, 'I have more power, larger privileges and a greater authority than any of their Archbishops; from which by the grace of God I will not depart, no not for the sake of union with them.'[1] It was with some justice that in 1716 an English observer had noted: 'We have now an Archbishop who is priest enough.'[2]

Wake's foreign connections were formed by his learned interests, and they provoked congratulations from places as far apart as Poland and Geneva. But it was more specifically towards the medieval history of his own Church that he was drawn, and here too he achieved a reputation that transcended the bounds of party. It was perhaps natural that Burnet who was his political friend should praise him as 'eminently learned, an excellent writer . . . and a Man of exemplary life'.[3] But Hickes the Non-juror could add his own tribute to Wake's scholarship, and Hearne whose prejudices seldom allowed him to commend a political opponent applauded his learned interests.[4] When he was forty-six Wake was still without major preferment. But he had made himself a recognized authority on English ecclesiastical history, and in these years this might almost have been held a guarantee of the rapid advancement which followed. Dean of Exeter in 1703, Wake was Bishop of Lincoln three years later, and by 1716 he was Primate of England. The career reflected the man; and also the temper of the Church. Himself a great scholar, and always the promoter of scholarship in others, Wake, with his 'study well furnished with all Books of our English History and Antiquities', was exactly fitted to preside over a group of prelates whose dominant interest in historical research had been signally demonstrated in the learned literature of the past decades.

It was characteristic of the English Revolution – it was also symptomatic of a permanent quality in the English mind – that an age of change should thus have conferred authority on men zealous for precedent and learned in its exposition. And it deserves emphasis that the Anglican Church when convulsed by the greatest threat to its historic continuity since the Reformation should at such a time have accepted the control of men who were before all else students of history. These prelates were intimates one with another, and they came to form within the Anglican Church a compact party whose common policy it was almost impossible to withstand. They might differ on individual ques-

---

[1] J. H. LUPTON: *Archbishop Wake and the Project of Union between the Anglican and Gallican Churches* (1896), p. 58.
[2] Samuel Clarke quoted in NICHOLS: *Literary Anecdotes*, IV, p. 720.
[3] BURNET: *Own Times* (1734), II, p. 407.
[4] HEARNE: *Collections*, I, p. 162; III, pp. 35-36; VI, p. 256; IX, p. 395; X, pp. 64, 425.

tions as in the matter of the repeal of the Occasional Conformity Act in 1718 when Gibson and Kennett supported the cause of toleration against Nicolson and Wake.[1] But at a hint of opposition from outside they came, as if inevitably, together. For they were united not only in their attitude to the events of 1688 and 1714, but also, and perhaps more fundamentally, in the harmony of their intellectual interests. They had all derived their mental training through distinguished and arduous historical study, and when at last they had themselves to deal with a crisis in ecclesiastical affairs it was natural to them to apply here also the same methods of research into precedent which they had used with such success in their antiquarian pursuits. When Francis Atterbury led his revolt against them, they replied by means of an achievement in scholarship whose excellence remains their enduring memorial.

It was the good fortune of English learning that the Convocation Controversy occurred at a time when these men were so placed in the Church. They came into the conflict as lively partisans, but they played their part therein as scholars whose exploration of the past was so un- tiring as to overwhelm the polemical impulse which inspired it. 'The very dust of their writings is gold,' remarked William Stubbs,[2] and if, like the Convocation Controversy itself, the learning which it invoked was largely concerned with the development of the Church of England after the Reformation, nevertheless the bearing of these studies on medieval history was also extremely extensive. William Nicolson, for example, who compiled perhaps the best contemporary bibliography of this extensive literature, and contributed anonymously to the works of many of his friends, was in this matter primarily interested in medieval precedent; and White Kennett's book of 1701 which sought with success to make a proper distinction between ecclesiastical synods and Parliamentary conventions, dealt largely with medieval antiqui- ties.[3] When Humphrey Hody in the same year produced his remark- able *History of English Councils and Convocations* he confined his atten- tion almost exclusively to the period before the reign of Henry VII.

Hody was 'one of the ablest members of a very remarkable group of historians'.[4] Born in 1659 he spent most of his learned life at Wadham College, Oxford, of which he was the sub-warden and benefactor, and before he entered the Convocation Controversy he had successfully opposed Isaac Vossius in his criticisms of 'Aristeas' and combated the

---

[1] Wilkins to Nicolson, Dec. 20th, 1718 (NICOLSON: *Epist. Corr.*, p. 484).
[2] STUBBS: *Seventeen Lectures* (1900), p. 381.
[3] NICOLSON: *English Historical Library* (1736), pp. 161-164; *Epist. Corr.*, pp. 66, 133, 173, 185, 194; KENNETT: *Ecclesiastical Synods and Parliamentary Convocations* (1701).
[4] STENTON: *English Feudalism* (1932), p. 86.

Non-jurors in their exposition of Byzantine antiquities.[1] He now turned his attention to the problems of English Church history, and endeavoured to approach them with a proper detachment:

> I am an Adversary to no one – he wrote. I go not out of my way to find Faults in other Men 'sWritings. If I take notice of any, 'tis because they lay directly in my way . . . I cannot say I have endeavoured to avoid, for (thank God) I have no Inclination to, those Modish *Figures* of Writing *Raillery* and *Contempt* . . . I am too often guilty of Mistakes myself to insult over others on that Account. And I know Human Nature too well to despise or think meanly of any because I find 'em sometimes mistaken.[2]

It was exactly the spirit which was needed to turn to good account an acrimonious wrangle, and Hody was fully conscious of the fact.

> The Controversie about the Powers and Privileges of an *English Synod* or *Convocation*, and the Clergy's ancient Right of Sitting in *Parliament* growing warm and earnest, I thought if a Bystander should interpose so far as to give a faithful and Impartial History both of the one and the other, it could not but be a Work very acceptable to the Publick . . . For I never found in myself any great Inclination to be led about blindfold by any Party; on the contrary a very great one to search diligently after Truth.'[3]

The boast was justified by the book. And though Hody distinguished in the same sense as did Kennett between Parliament and Convocation, the manner in which his work was planned and executed gave it an individual importance. Samuel Jebb in his Latin life of Hody declared that the book was written in the space of a few months. But the assertion is difficult to believe in that the treatise was based upon an elaborate reading of medieval authorities. Hody examined the Old English Laws; he used both charters and chronicles; he interpreted his subject widely; and his incidental remarks on diverse topics are often illuminating. As an exposition of the early constitutional history of the English Church, and even of the early development of Parliament, Hody's book has influenced the writings of many that came after him, and despite the inevitable corrections which can now be supplied to points of detail, it still, by reason of its copious citations from authorities, remains of substantial value.

A similar objectivity was to be found in the work which the Convocation Controversy produced from the pen of Edmund Gibson. As

---

[1] JEBB: *De Vita Hodii* prefixed to Hody, *De Graecis Illustribus* (1724); HODY: *The Unreasonableness of a separation from the New Bishops* (1691).
[2] HODY: *History of English Councils and Convocations* (1701), Preface.
[3] Ibid.

Librarian and Chaplain to Archbishop Tenison, Gibson had special facilities for consulting ecclesiastical records, and he used his opportunities to refute the assertions of Atterbury by exact reference to the documents themselves. 'Points of power, privilege and jurisdiction', he observed, 'were determined by usage and precedent, not by uncertain inferences from the nature of things.' By pinning his adversary down to the chapter and verse of his authorities, he set up a defence which was impervious to attack. His vindication of the *Right of the Archbishop to Continue or Prorogue the whole Convocation* made, for instance, such short work of Atterbury's constitutional theories that these by 1703 began to show all the *Marks of a Defenceless Cause*. Gibson's controversial methods endowed his tracts with a positive value as investigations of history, and his study of records led him from rebutting the assertions of an ill-informed adversary to setting his own historical theory based upon documentary evidence. His *Synodus Anglicana* (1702) was a comprehensive view of 'the Constitution and Proceedings of an English Convocation', and few books of the period in which it was written give such an impression of modernity as this cool and lucid statement of procedure which was based upon a careful examination of the written records. It led irresistibly to its final conclusion:

> that an English Convocation, though laid under some restraints from the civil constitution, was far from being so much transformed into a civil meeting as had been pleaded of late; that in the summoning, opening and acting, it appears what it is, an Ecclesiastical Synod of bishops with their presbyters, and neither a parliamentary body on the one hand nor an assembly of presbyters on the other; and that it was evident that as to the nature of our Synods the English Reformation left them in the same ecclesiastical state as it found them.

The *Synodus Anglicana* was not directly concerned with the medieval constitution though it made plentiful reference thereto. It was an authoritative statement of ecclesiastical law and as such it has remained. When Convocation was once more summoned in 1861 the book was reprinted as 'the most accurate and trustworthy authority on the subject with which it deals'.[1]

Gibson, as one of the Queen's College 'Saxonists', was a scholar before ever he was a controversialist, and the legal antiquities of the Church interested him more than his argument with Atterbury. Seven years after the publication of *Synodus Anglicana* he was still brooding on the development of English Church law as the subject 'which had

[1] SYKES: *Gibson*, pp. 31-52.

been for many years the employment of his spare hours'. His leisure must have been arduously as well as profitably spent for in 1713 he was able to issue in two large folio volumes his *Codex Juris Ecclesiastici Anglicani*. The book which was later to be the subject of a new controversy at once took rank as an indispensable work of reference and it was seemly that the Lower House of Convocation should offer thanks to its compiler for the 'usefull pains' which he had taken. Dealing mainly with materials derived from the post-Reformation period, the book none the less deserves a respectful reference even in this place, not only because it contained the text of certain medieval documents never before published, but because it was the chief achievement of one who elsewhere made his own special contribution to English medieval studies. Gibson henceforth inevitably became 'Dr. Codex' to the facetious, and it was for him a title of honour.[1] 'He stands out', remarks Stubbs, 'as a great canonist, and his Codex or Collection of English Church Statutes is still the standard work and treasury of all such sorts of law.'[2]

The chief benefits which the Convocation Controversy conferred upon English medieval scholarship came, however, not from the work of Hody, nor yet from the legal studies of Gibson, but from the fact that the rash assertions of Atterbury stimulated in the first instance the wonderful researches of William Wake himself. And the most remarkable work which was produced in the course of the dispute was the *State of the Church and Clergy of England . . . Historically deduced from the Conversion of the Saxons to the Present Times*. The primary purpose of this great work, which appeared in 1703, was to answer Atterbury's *Rights of Convocation*, and as a reply it was final. The view of English ecclesiastical constitution, first taken up by Wake in his *Authority of Christian Princes*, was here so completely established by means of an elaborate citation of authorities that 'no one has since been able to shake it'. At the same time from an exhaustive enumeration of instances, Wake showed that there was in the Middle Ages no close interrelation between Convocation and Parliament, and his conclusions on the significance of the *praemunientes* clause in the summons of Bishops to Parliament have been accepted by all modern critics. But Wake's book, with its eight hundred pages of packed erudition, was far more than a party statement, and like Bentley's *Phalaris*, with which it may aptly be compared, it did much more than confound an opponent. It embodied all the most productive research that a prolific dispute had

[1] SYKES: op. cit., pp. 65-67.
[2] STUBBS: *Seventeen Lectures*, p. 380.

called forth. It expressed and illustrated the considered views on this subject of scholars like Nicolson and Hody, Gibson and Tanner who all contributed to its successful completion. And it established once and for all the claims of its author to a place in the very front rank of English medievalists.[1]

The book was nothing less than an elaborate history of synodical proceedings in England from the fifth century to the seventeenth. But it was naturally coloured by the circumstances under which it was written. During the five years when Wake was engaged in its composition he was suffering under a sense of outrage, and was justifiably a very angry man. He considered it necessary therefore to make many digressions to refute his opponent on points of detail by means of the cumulative testimony of massed authorities. On the other hand, moved by the issues which the controversy had raised, he may have accepted too easily some of the theories of English ecclesiastical development which had been put forward by the successors of Ussher. Wake considered the Old English period as one in which the rights exercised by the Crown over the Church were essentially similar to those reasserted by the English monarchy after the Submission of the Clergy in 1532, while in the intervening period he postulated those same rights as having been usurped by the Papacy. It was perhaps well that he did not push this interpretation of English ecclesiastical history too far, and it would obviously be unfair to criticize him for not having anticipated the work of Maitland and Z. N. Brooke in elucidating the application of Canon Law to English ecclesiastical courts in the Middle Ages. But Wake's Erastian theories prevented him from appreciating the true significance in English history of the careers of men such as Anselm and Thomas Becket, and there was a danger that he might mar his great book by citing the extreme claims made by Rufus or Henry I at the time of the Investitures Contest as establishing the constitutional prerogatives of their successors.

The special merit of Wake's work was that it subordinated controversy to constructive learning.

> Having thus determined to proceed in my Own just Defence – he wrote – the next thing was to resolve after what Manner I should proceed in it. And here I needed not any long Deliberation: The Controversial way was not only the least Instructive, but of all others the least Agreeable to my own Nature and Disposition. I determined therefore to pursue my Subject in an

---

[1] LATHBURY: *Convocation*, pp. 392–394; SYKES: *Church and State*, p. 302; STUBBS: *Const. History*, II (4th ed.), p. 210; III (5th ed.), pp. 330–338; *Select Charters* (1913), p. 480; cf. A. F. POLLARD, *The Times*, Aug. 5th, 1937.

Historical manner; and to meddle no farther with my angry Adversary than as he should necessarily fall in my way.[1]

The resolution was so well kept that Wake's exhaustive research produced what is still the most comprehensive account of English ecclesiastical synods in the Middle Ages. He undertook the stupendous task of describing all the church assemblies which had ever been held in this country. He brought to light the activities of many synods whose very existence had never been suspected before. And the range of his vast reading was such that his book still remains an abundant storehouse of documentary material. The long and elaborate chapters which here deal with the period between the Norman Conquest and the death of Richard II were particularly valuable,[2] and to the whole work there was added a long appendix 'wherein are Copies of the choicest authentick Instruments, Vouchers of the whole'. Nicolson was right when he remarked that the Subject Matter of the Controversy was here wholly exhausted, 'all the Stores of our MS Histories and Chronicles as well as Registries of the Sees of both Provinces being brought into this common Treasury'.[3] To-day it may merely be added that if and when Wake's book is superseded it will be only through the collaboration of a number of scholars each of whom may be able to revise some part of the gigantic undertaking of William Wake.

'Archbishop Wake's folio book of the *State of the Church*', wrote Hearne in 1733, 'cost him prodigious pains and probably broke his constitution which is now very much shattered.' 'It was then', he added, 'he made his collection towards the Councills now in Dr Wilkins' hands.'[4] With this remark Hearne indicated the fundamental character of Wake's research and the full extent to which historical scholarship was to benefit thereby. For the *Concilia* which was published by David Wilkins in four folio volumes in 1737 was itself an indirect outcome of the Convocation Controversy. The story of the prolonged compilation of this fundamental book has recently been told afresh by Professor Powicke and Professor Jacob.[5] The more the magnitude of that great undertaking is contemplated, the greater does Wake's share therein appear, and the closer does the connection seem between the

---

[1] WAKE: *State of the Church*, Preface, pp. iv, v.
[2] Ibid., esp. pp. i-xvii and chaps. VI and VII; NICOLSON: *English Historical Library* (1736), p. 161.
[3] Ibid.
[4] HEARNE: *Collections*, XI, p. 144.
[5] F. M. POWICKE: *Sir Henry Spelman and the Concilia* (Raleigh Lecture to the British Academy, 1930); E. F. JACOB: *Wilkins's Concilia and the Fifteenth Century* (R. Hist. Soc. Trans., 4th series, vol. XV, pp. 91-131).

Concilia of 1737 and the massive treatise which Wake wrote against Atterbury more than thirty years before.

Wake's investigation of medieval convocations brought him into contact with a stream of European learning whose significance and purport he was well able to appreciate. Even before the end of the sixteenth century important work on the councils of the medieval Church had been published by scholars such as Jacques Merlin, Peter Crabbe, Surius and Nicolini; the *Generalia Concilia* of Severini Bini had followed in 1606; and Sirmond's work on the French Councils conceived and executed in a manner fuller than its predecessors had appeared in 1629. When, therefore, ten years later, the first volume of Henry Spelman's wonderful book on the English Councils appeared, it took its place in a European sequence, and it could challenge comparison with any of its fellows. But the work was never finished, and when the Convocation Controversy revived interest in medieval synods and called attention to the growing acquaintance with the manuscript materials relating to them, it seemed that the time had come for it to be revised and augmented. Already, on the continent, the books of Labbe and Cossart (1671-2), of Baluze (1682) and of Hardouin (1685) had successively set a higher standard of criticism of the texts with which they dealt. And it was seemly that once again English scholars should take their share in a research which was becoming so productive. Wake was well fitted to take the lead in this matter. His investigations had placed him in possession of knowledge such as no other English scholar enjoyed, while his intimate connection with French ecclesiastical thought had brought him into contact with the intense interest in the Conciliar Movement aroused by Gallican inquiries. Though the need for a new and an enlarged edition of Spelman was generally felt in learned English circles at the close of the seventeenth century, this would probably never have been met, had not Wake given his personal stimulus to a co-operative endeavour, and the collections which he had made for his *State of the Church* supplies abundant material which in the years that followed could be criticized and augmented.[1]

The affairs of the English Church might incite in Wake an ever increasing interest in ecclesiastical councils, while his correspondence with such as Du Pin might make him ever more conscious of the similar research which was being devoted to them abroad; but the consistent application of a busy Archbishop to this task over a period of

---

[1] POWICKE: op. cit., p. 14; HEFELE (Leclerc): *Histoire de Conciles*, I, pp. 107-110; LUPTON: op. cit.; JACOB: op. cit.

'near thirty years' was none the less remarkable. Even if the under-taking had not of itself been so large as to demand wide collaboration, the multifarious duties of Wake's high office would have compelled him to delegate some of the responsibility for the book to other hands. To do this was not, however, easy. 'Dr. Wake', remarked Hearne, 'would have had Zachary Pearce to have undertaken the Councils, but he declined it as did likewise Dr. Walker, the latter as I hear because of his being ingaged in Classicks.'[1] But another venture was much more fortunate. About 1709, before ever he was archbishop, Wake had started experimenting with the services of a young man still in his twenties who was being 'mightily caressed' in London.[2] His name was David Wilkins. And to him, after the Archbishop, the eventual com-pletion and the success of the *Concilia* were primarily due.

'It must be something of a shock', remarks Professor Powicke, 'to those who are wont to consider Wilkins's *Concilia* as one of the glories of English learning to find that the editor was a Prussian, who settled in this country after studying in Berlin, Rome, Vienna, Paris and Amsterdam. Consolation may perhaps be sought in the reflection that Herr Wilke found livelihood and opportunity in England. He ended his laborious life as a doctor of the University of Cambridge, a former librarian of Lambeth, an archdeacon in the Anglican Church, and the son-in-law of an English peer.'[3] The reflection becomes even more satisfactory when it is remembered that the greatest work that bears the name of Wilkins owed more to an English archbishop than to any other man. And the career of the Prussian in England was hardly smooth. Born in 1685 he had long wandered in Europe as a student, and after his arrival in England he identified himself so completely with the Whigs that he often found himself the object of intense dislike. He was loud in his complaints of the treatment that was meted out to him at Oxford where he was refused a degree. In 1716, he complained that he 'suffered throwing of stones and dirt before the soldiers came'.[4] Perhaps it was not surprising that an alien of such pronounced views on the politics of the country of his adoption should have been regarded by the Non-jurors as 'very perfidious and false and a very great enemy of the Church of England';[5] but William Stratford, who as Canon of Christ Church was a bitter opponent of Atterbury, painted an equally unfavourable picture of Wilkins. 'This man,' he remarked:

[1] HEARNE: *Collections*, XI, p. 119.
[2] JACOB: op. cit., p. 93.
[3] POWICKE: op. cit., p. 25.
[4] Wilkins to Nicolson, Jan. 31st, 1716 (NICOLSON: *Epist. Corr.*, p. 438).
[5] JACOB: op. cit., p. 91.

had been recommended by poor Grabe to me and others . . . When his great benefactor, Grabe, was dead, he gave out that he died a Papist and of the pox. He was a spy here whilst he was living in a great measure on the kindness of the place.[1]

Even the rewards of his industry were not always as satisfactory as a summary would suggest. It was, doubtless, gratifying to marry into the English aristocracy, the more so when the dowry was £4000. But the circumstances were none the less somewhat unusual. 'He married lately', wrote Stratford, 'a daughter of Lord Fairfax, a natural, that lived in Canterbury with one to feed and nurse her.'[2] 'Twas thought formerly', added another commentator, 'that he would marry one, Betty Crowder, a pretty forward girl, who was his Laundress in Holywell where she lives poorly with her Mother. When Wilkins lodg'd in Holywell he was frequently seen to go in there, and tis reported that there were many free Actions between them, but Money will buy all off.'[3] The arrangements were apparently completed without mishap, but the resulting marriage hardly supplied cause for congratulation. 'Dr. Wilkins' Lady', it was observed, 'is half witted. The Dr. is ashamed to carry her with him. She is for that and other reasons angry with him.'[4]

'Wilkins will do anything for a penny.'[5] The taunt was unfair to a man who gave his life to the production of works of learning, and, in 1744, refused a payment of £50 under Tanner's will for the work which he was contributing to the *Bibliotheca Britannica*. But in the earlier days of his career Wilkins was a professional transcriber willing to hire his services to any scholars able to pay for them. In 1715 he told Nicolson and 'the rest of his friends and patrons . . . that if they continue in their kind resolutions of recommending him either to the King or the Archbishop, he will be a mere *tabula rasa* susceptible of any impressions they please to stamp upon him'.[6] Here was an instrument ready to Wake's hand, and it seems probable that as early as 'Queen Anne's time', Wilkins had started work upon the *Concilia* but 'was then hindered not being thought a proper person'.[7] The years which followed were to place his qualifications beyond doubt. In 1716 he published the first of his books on the Coptic gospels; in 1721 under the guidance of Nicolson he produced his edition of the Anglo-Saxon

[1] W. Stratford to Edward Harley, May 2nd, 1726 (*Portland MSS. Rep.*, VII, p. 435).
[2] *Portland MSS. Rep.*, VII, p. 435.
[3] HEARNE: *Collections*, IX, p. 127.
[4] Ibid., IX, p. 134.
[5] Ibid., VII, p. 380; JACOB. op. cit., p. 91.
[6] Chamberlayne to Nicolson, July 6th, 1715 (NICOLSON: *Epist. Corr.*, p. 431); cf. JACOB, op. cit., p. 94.
[7] HEARNE: *Collections*, XI, p. 285; cf. JACOB: op. cit. p. 93.

laws; and the edition of Selden's works which he issued in 1726 is still, for all its defects, the best collection of the writings of that scholar. If to this total there be added the 'very curious catalogue of all the MSS and printed books' in the Lambeth Library 'in which was incorporated the earlier catalogue of Mr. Henry Wharton', and also the final edition of Tanner's *Bibliotheca* which was published after the death of both its author and editor, some impression may be gathered of the informed and untiring energy which made Wilkins the ideal collaborator for Wake.

The compilation of the *Concilia*, under Wake's direction, became the major interest in Wilkins's life. As time went on he was able more and more to introduce his own ideas into the work, and he must be held primarily responsible for the form finally taken by the great book which Wake had planned. Before long Wilkins became recognized indeed as the official editor, and as such he entered into relations with all those scholars who might be willing to help him. Gibson at London gave him access to the muniments of his see and 'full authority to make excerpts'. Wanley became his friend; other scholars sent him transcripts from the public records; and the Bishops of Durham, Lincoln and Exeter offered him assistance.[1] Wilkins's industry was commanding a wide respect, and with the lapse of years he assumed much of the initiative in the selection and in the arrangement of the material. Consequently, when at last there appeared this monument of labour and learning, the great book bore the name of David Wilkins as its editor. It is to-day generally studied and praised as *Wilkins's Concilia*.

The *Concilia* of 1737 was a work of such magnitude, and it has proved of such service to English scholarship that it would be ungenerous to minimize the achievement of any man who took a large share in its preparation. Nevertheless the attribution of the work solely to David Wilkins has committed an injustice to many scholars whose labours contributed to its final success. The book embodied the earlier work of Spelman, and without the research of that great scholar it would never have appeared. Moreover the transmission of Spelman's legacy of ecclesiastical learning would of itself have been far less productive had it not been for the labours of Tanner to whom Wilkins was indebted not only for the many important additions which had been made to Spelman by other scholars but also for much material which Tanner had collected with his own hands. The research of Tanner had even embellished Wake's *State of the Church*, since numerous transcripts by Tanner were printed in that book without alteration and

[1] JACOB: op. cit., p. 94.

with the gaps originally left in them by their compiler. And as the material contained in the *State of the Church* was gradually augmented to become the basis of the larger work, Tanner's advice and erudition was always available. Wake's own share in the undertaking though diminishing with the years always remained very large. As late as 1732, Hearne remained of the opinion the *Concilia* would contain only 'the Archbishop of Canterbury's own collections' and he added 'what they are may I suppose in some measure be learned from the Archbishop's large book of Convocations'.[1] Professor Jacob's investigations have shown that many of the texts which in the *Concilia* Wilkins denoted as of 'our own' collecting came from Wake's transcripts. In short, it seems that in this respect there is a close comparison to be made between the *Monasticon* and the *Concilia*. Both were great co-operative works of scholarship; and both have been attributed too exclusively to the man who (in Dugdale's phrase) 'methodized them for the Press'. The greatest single work which has ever been produced on the medieval English Church derived from the labours of scholars scattered over England. It was originally planned and largely developed by an English archbishop. It was completed 'by an Archdeacon who began life as a Prussian stranger working for pay'.[2]

Wilkins's 'methodizing', and his general editorship, have themselves not escaped criticism. When Haddan and Stubbs in 1869 aimed, as far as the pre-Conquest period was concerned, at a reproduction of the *Concilia* 'in accordance with the present state of our knowledge and materials', they freely admitted that the eighteenth-century book 'alone rendered' their own work 'possible at all'. But they discovered that, judged by modern standards, Wilkins's editing was often 'exceedingly defective and incomplete and, especially in its earlier portions, uncritical'.[3] Wilkins was not impeccable in his Anglo-Saxon readings and translations; with regard to the *Origines* of the British Church, he merely reproduced speculations by Spelman which had already become obsolete; and in the Old English period he followed no very sure method in his choice of materials. His shortcomings in the latter portion of the work have also been noted. He was wont to work from inferior MSS., and he sometimes paraphrased in his own words documents which he purported to give in the exact terms of the originals. His book vastly improved the reports of convocation proceedings as given in Dugdale's continuation of Spelman, but he con-

---

[1] HEARNE: *Collections*, XI, p. 119.
[2] JACOB: op. cit.; POWICKE, op. cit., pp. 35-37.
[3] HADDAN and STUBBS: *Councils*, I, pp. vii-xx.

cerned himself too exclusively with questions of ecclesiastical finance, and he neglected the part played by the English delegations in the great European Councils of the fifteenth century. For all these reasons Wilkins has been adjudged to have possessed 'a mind unquickened by the finer questionings of historical investigation'. But when all has been said in his dispraise, the *Concilia* itself must be regarded as an indispensable treasury of materials, and it still remains a standard work of reference. Perhaps the best measure of its worth may be obtained in the reflection that now, when, after two hundred years, schemes are once again afoot to prepare a new *Concilia*, the promoters of the undertaking have realized that their work, like its predecessor, must be a co-operative enterprise and must itself be based upon the earlier book of Wake and Wilkins. Those engaged in this fine task, even as they became conscious of mistakes to be corrected, none the less in facing the same difficulties which confronted their great fore-runners, tend to rank ever higher the magnitude of the achievement which they are striving to supersede.[1]

The *Concilia* of 1737 was the climax of a prolific movement in English ecclesiastical scholarship. During the eighty years which followed the Restoration, Anglican divines spurred to their task by particular problems in the Church conducted an arduous and comprehensive investigation of its past history. The fierce arguments which attended the writings of William Lloyd and Stillingfleet, the attempts at synthesis made by Inett and Collier, the Non-juring protest and the Convocation Controversy, resulted in a learned production of which the Anglican Church might well be proud. It culminated in a work which might justly be described as the crowning glory of a great age of ecclesiastical erudition. The febrile bickerings of a factious epoch, the spleen of Atterbury, the vapourings of convocation men, may well pale into insignificance before an achievement which could only have been made possible at last by a disinterested search for historic truth. English scholars have had greater cause than ever had contemporary politicians to be grateful to the labours of men like Nicolson and Gibson, Kennett and Hody. Above them towered the figure of William Wake. The *Concilia* is his abiding memorial. It displays an archbishop great in his erudition, the fit ruler of a learned Church, whose members, while often contending together, so contrived to master the happy discipline of research as to leave all their fortunate successors in scholarship immeasurably in their debt.

[1] JACOB: op. cit., pp. 104-131; POWICKE: op. cit., pp. 26-29.

CHAPTER XI

RYMER AND MADOX

IN the long succession of the scholars there were two whose work may be regarded as a unity and whose contributions to learning symbolized in some sense the conclusion of these seventy years of corporate endeavour. The labours of Thomas Rymer[1] and Thomas Madox stretched, it is true, across a considerable section of this period, but the first volume of Rymer's *Foedera* did not appear until 1704, and Madox, his junior by twenty-five years, had, two years earlier, made his own entrance into the learned world. From that time forward, however, both these men maintained a constant output of works of erudition. When Rymer died in 1713, no less than fifteen volumes of his *Foedera* had been published, and Madox, after issuing in 1711 his great treatise on the Exchequer, continued to add to the mass of his production until his own death in 1727. Nor is it merely an accident of time which connects the work of these two men or relates it to the concluding years of this epoch of English scholarship. Secular in their interests, specialized in their research, Rymer and Madox were the first two men to grace the office of Historiographer Royal with the attributes of historical scholarship. Sharing the interests of many of their predecessors, even at times actively concerned with developing their work, these scholars none the less seemed to move in an atmosphere strangely unlike that which surrounded Spelman and Gale, or even Baker and Thomas Hearne. Their habit of mind derived from a society in which William Somner would have felt a stranger, and in which, among their contemporaries in historical scholarship, only Wanley perhaps would have felt at home. It would of course be easy to exaggerate a contrast, which if over-emphasized might distort chronology, but it comes almost as a shock to remember that Rymer started to write before the death of Fabian Philipps and that Madox bandied learned argument with Hickes.[2]

The scholarly achievement of Thomas Rymer was hatched out of adversity. His father, Ralph Rymer, had been a country gentleman of substance and lord of the manor of Brafferton in Yorkshire. 'Of the

[1] Sir Thomas Duffus Hardy prefaced the first two volumes of his *Syllabus . . . of Rymer's Foedera* (1869-1885) with an admirable biographical essay on Rymer and his work.
[2] HICKES: *Thesaurus*, Preface to Ottley, pp. xxix, xxx; *Diss. Ep.*, p. 63; MADOX: *Exchequer* (1711), pp. ix-xvii.

better sort of grand-jury man' he was, according to Clarendon, generally 'esteemed a wise man'. But his wisdom did not extend into his
intervention in politics. A zealous opponent of the monarchy, he had
prospered in the time of the Commonwealth, and as treasurer of his
district he had used his position to obtain the estate of one of his royalist
neighbours. When the Restoration came and such booty had to be
returned, he indulged in rebellion. One of the leaders of the Presbyterian rising in 1663, he was arrested in October of that year and was
hanged at York leaving his son to face a bleak personal future.[1] Thomas
Rymer, born in 1641 and bred to affluence, had been a fellow pupil
with Hickes at school in Northallerton. Later he had studied at Cambridge in Sidney Sussex College. At the age of twenty-two he was
left destitute and for many years his father's head was exposed rotting
at Doncaster to bear witness to the family disgrace.[2] In these circumstances the path to success could be no easy one, and in 1668 it was as
a literary hack that Thomas Rymer made his first appearance in print,
issuing a volume of Latin translations and dedicating his work inauspi-
ciously to the Duke of Monmouth.

The prospects of the young man were hardly encouraging, and
neither the quality of his book nor its dedication suggested that Rymer
would ever emerge from the shadows which surrounded him. Perhaps,
however, as if the case of Hickes, the alcoholic loyalism of Thomas
Smelt, their former schoolmaster,[3] had somewhat modified the republican principles of Rymer's inheritance. At all events, the next production of his pen was an 'Heroick Tragedy' which, in epic verse, 'chiefly
sought occasions to extoll the English Monarchy'. '*Edgar*': *or the
English Monarch* was a highly correct composition which had all the
qualities of a typical failure, and the modern reader finds no difficulty
in sharing the boredom it induced in those who first perused it. Rymer
might move on terms of familiarity with Hobbes and Waller, but he
could write neither the prose of the one nor the verse of the other; and
by 1677 it had become clear that only by cultivating some fresh field
of literature could he obtain a bare subsistence. Tradition pointed out
the path later to be trodden hard; and the unsuccessful playwright
forthwith became dramatic critic.[4]

Rymer's criticism, written as it was by a man who was later to make
a permanent mark on English scholarship, constitutes a literary curiosity. The young man whose play had met with no success, did not lose

[1] SYDNEY LEE in *Dict. Nat. Biog.*, sub. Thomas Rymer.
[2] NICOLSON: *Diary* (Cumberland and Westmorland Arch. Soc.), Dec. 1st, 1702.
[3] KETTLEWELL: *Works* (1719), I, pp. 10-14.
[4] *Syllabus*, I, pp. xv-xxiv.

confidence. He turned his indignant attention to 'the tragedies of the last age' and 'examined them by the practice of the ancients and by the common sense of all ages'. He also attempted 'A Short View of Tragedy; its original Excellency and Corruption; with some reflections on Shakespeare and other practitioners for the Stage'. Fresh from a reading of the *Poetics* Rymer thus came forward as the champion of Aristotelian principles of drama, and he was delighted to show how these had been violated by Shakespeare, Fletcher and Milton. *Paradise Lost* which 'some are pleased to call a poem' took its place beside *Othello* 'a bloody farce without salt or savour';[1] and there was some excuse for Macaulay when, with an assurance equal to that of his victim, he called Rymer 'the worst critic that ever lived'.[2] But several men more distinguished than Macaulay pronounced a very different judgment. It was doubtless strange to find the creator of *Edgar* exposing the deficiencies in the author of *Lear*, but Dryden thought well of the essay, and Pope described Rymer as a 'learned and strict critic'. The truth was that Rymer with considerable erudition here exaggerated all the worst prejudices of the age in which he lived, and it would be unhistorical to judge his criticism out of relation to contemporary opinion. A more modern commentator than Macaulay has judged Rymer as 'a learned fanatic from whose extravagances any level-headed student of the drama may derive much amusement and some profit'.[3] Charity can go no further. As *Edgar* had shown that 'it was possible for Drama to be extremely regular and at the same time intolerably dull', so did Rymer's criticism indicate how far learned comment could proceed without displaying critical skill.

An historical play, some fantastic criticism, and a few party pamphlets did not suffice to relieve even the more pressing needs of Rymer's everyday life, and although he had published in 1684 an indifferent tract on 'the antiquity power and decay of parliaments', it is surprising that this crescendo of failure should have culminated in his appointment in 1693 as Historiographer Royal. A specialized qualification was not, it is true, yet required for this exalted office. James Howell, William Davenant and John Dryden, who had before held the post, were all men of outstanding ability, but their interests had not lain in the direction of historical research, and Thomas Shadwell who became Laureate as well as Historiographer was neither a poet nor an historian. Even Rymer himself in his early days appears to have had few illusions

[1] *Syllabus*, I, pp. xx–xxv.
[2] MACAULAY: *Boswell's Life of Johnson.*
[3] LEE: op. cit.

about the office which he was later to adorn. 'You are not to expect truth from an historiographer royal,' he wrote, 'it may drop from their pen by chance, but the general herd understano not their business; they fill us with story, accidental, incoherent, without end or side, and never know the *government* or *policy* of what they write. Even the Records themselves are not always accurately worded.'[1] Even the Records! The opinion is surely interesting since it was the peculiar function of Rymer to remove precisely this stigma from the office of Historiographer Royal, and by his labours abundantly to justify its establishment.

The achievement of Thomas Rymer was due in the first instance to that group of noble patrons of learning whose zeal at the beginning of the eighteenth century was so notable a mark of the culture of the age. With these men the project had for some time been forming of preparing an authoritative collection of all the transactions into which England had ever entered with foreign powers. It was an undertaking that was in some respects revolutionary. Arthur Agarde, Deputy-Chamberlain at the Exchequer in 1570, had formed a small collection of this nature, and Sir Julius Caesar, his younger contemporary, had at the instance of Lord Burleigh made a treaty book for his own use. But despite the fact that James I published with authority the texts of his treaties with Spain in 1604 and with France in 1606, all State documents of this kind were in general preserved with the strictest secrecy. Only during the Civil War when both parties had been forced to appeal to public opinion did a change occur in the official attitude, and after the Restoration the rise of the new journalism gave an added impulse to this tendency towards publicity. In 1669, Sir Joseph Williamson used his political and literary connections to obtain permission 'to peruse and copy all such treaties leagues and public acts which he should deem fit for the King's service', and between 1660 and 1688 all the public treaties to which England was a party were published by authority. The tradition of secrecy however died very hard, and before the Revolution no collection of ancient documents of this type seems to have been contemplated in England.[2]

Continental scholars had been more active. The compilations which Melchoir Goldast made between 1607 and 1614 contained several of the ancient diplomatic documents of Germany, and his example was imitated both in the *Theatrum Pacis* in 1685, and in the catalogue which

---

[1] *Syllabus*, I, p. xxii.
[2] Ibid., pp. i–iii; cf. *Second General Report on the Public Records* (1819), Appendix N (p. 477).

P

Nessel published in Vienna in 1690. With respect to France the development was still more notable. In 1644 Jean Jacques Chifflet, who had been physician to Philip IV of Spain, published a collection of Franco-Spanish treaties; this was followed six years later by another small collection of Franch treaties; and between 1683 and 1697 Frederic Léonard published in seven large folio volumes no less than three hundred treaties made between France and foreign powers in the fifteenth and sixteenth centuries. But none of these publications were so intrinsically important, and none exercised so much influence on England, as did the *Codex Juris Gentium Diplomaticus* of Leibnitz which was issued in March 1693 only a few months before the *Foedera* was projected in England. Its object was to supply documentary materials for practical statesmen, and at the same time to place on a securer basis the scientific study of the 'Law of Nations', but in a supplementary volume its editor stressed the fact that his careful and elaborate collections could also be made of service to students of history. Leibnitz's book may in fact be regarded as the prototype of Rymer's *Foedera*. England with her vast stores of documentary material, and with the historical enthusiasm which informed her most influential classes, could hardly lag behind the activity of other countries in this matter. By 1693 the plan for the *Foedera* had been definitely formed, and it is significant that throughout the long process of its compilation Rymer, who was formally introduced to Leibnitz in 1694, maintained a constant and a friendly intercourse with his predecessor in Hanover.[1]

A tradition dating from the later years of the eighteenth century ascribed the original scheme of the *Foedera* to Robert Harley[2] but there is little justification for assigning to that great benefactor of scholarship this further service to letters. Edmund Calamy and Leibnitz himself both gave the credit of the original notion to Halifax, and other circumstances also indicate that he had the greatest share in putting the plan into execution; Madox, White Kennett, and others asserted with reason that Lord Somers, too, played a most important part in the early days of the enterprise.[3] Through the efforts of these men, the Government in 1693 determined to print under public auspices the conventions of Great Britain with foreign powers, and on August 20th of that year a royal warrant appointed Rymer as editor and directed him 'to transcribe and publish all the leagues treaties alliances capitulations and confederacies which have at any time been made between the Crown

[1] *Syllabus*, I, pp. iii-vii; xxxi-xxxviii.
[2] AYLOFFE: *Calendars* (1774), p. xxxvii.
[3] *Syllabus*, I, pp. vii-xiii.

of England and any other kingdoms princes and states as a work highly conducing to our service and the honour of this our realm'.[1] The authors of the scheme seem to have been conscious of the vast burden that they were imposing upon the shoulders of the editor, and they therefore gave him special privileges. 'He is empowered', the warrant ran,

> to have free liberty and access from time to time to search into the records in our Tower of London, in the Rolls, in the Augmentation Office, our Exchequer, the Journals of both Houses of Parliament, or any other places where records are kept, for such records as we have or shall direct, and the same to transcribe: And that he also have access from time to time to our library at St. James's and our Paper Office, upon such matters as we have or shall appoint for our service without paying any fees; whereof the respective officers and all other persons whom it may concern are to take notice and yield due obedience to our pleasure herein declared.[2]

It was a new departure in public policy, and it remained to be seen whether the State in its patronage would be as careful of its scholarly protégés as were the private benefactors of an earlier generation. There could at least be no doubt that a national enterprise in erudition had now been publicly sponsored. And the editor lost no time in getting to work. When eighteen months later Ralph Thoresby visited the Westminster treasury he found there 'the industrious antiquary and ingenious poet Mr. Rymer . . . amongst the musty record supervising his Amanuensis transcribing'.[3]

Up to this time Rymer could himself claim little share in the credit of the undertaking. He had been appointed to the office of Historiographer in preference to several other men much better qualified to fill it, and he was at the very beginning of his labours to display his inexperience by selecting for publication an instrument which was obviously spurious.[4] But through long years of amazing industry he was abundantly to justify his editorship, and that the *Foedera* ever reached completion at all was due to his devotion and to his determination. Not the least of his services was, at the start, successfully to delimit the scope of the undertaking by confining his attention to two objects: 'first to publish all records of alliances and other transactions in which England was concerned with foreign powers from the year 1101 down to his own times; and secondly to limit his collection to the originals

---

[1] *Syllabus*, I, p. xxvi.   [2] Ibid., p. xxvii.
[3] THORESBY: *Diary*, I, p. 296.
[4] *Syllabus*, I, pp. xxxix-xli; G. RIDPATH: *Scotland's Sovereignty Asserted* (1695) Preface; HICKES: *Thesaurus*, Preface to Ottley, p. xxv.

preserved in the Royal archives adding thereto such documents from
the Cottonian, Lambeth and the Universities' Libraries as might serve
to supply the links required in the chain of evidence'.[1] Only by some
such limitation was it possible to reduce the scheme of the *Foedera* to
manageable proportions, and though Thomas Smith, the Librarian of
the Cottons, might grumble to Wanley that the plan had been unnecessarily curtailed,[2] there can be no doubt that Rymer was fully
justified in his method, and neither he nor any of his successors ever
deviated from his original intention with profit.

The greatest debt under which Thomas Rymer placed posterity was
undoubtedly in respect of the dogged courage which alone made possible the completion of the task that he had undertaken. The labour was
in any case immense as the long series of large folios which resulted
therefrom may testify. Documents had to be discovered; reluctant
officials had to be cajoled or compelled to produce them; and the long
process of proof correcting had laboriously to be gone through.
Twenty years of unremitting toil was insufficient to bring the publication to its close but when Rymer died there could be no doubt that the
fifteen great volumes which he had issued would form a fitting
memorial to the editor and supply the incentive to any further continuation that might seem necessary. This was of itself enough. But it
remains the great distinction of Rymer that this vast work was carried
out despite difficulties and adversities which would have overwhelmed
any ordinary man. For though the office of Historiographer with its
salary of £200 a year might perhaps have been expected to serve as
the means by which the untiring scholar might live, the stipend thereof
was speedily allowed to fall into arrears, and money was not even forth-
coming to defray the expenses which Rymer was willingly obliged to
undergo in the public service. Five years after the beginning of the
work he was compelled to 'crave leave to repeat . . . that no provision
being made to defray the charges, it lay upon me to provide the money,
and I gave account from time to time to the Lords of the Treasury in
order to be reimbursed, and from them had several sums but in such
proportion that by an account I stated this last midsummer there
appeared to be laid out by me more than received £563'.[3] Three years
later a more urgent note appeared in his remonstrance: 'By this means',
he wrote, 'a debt is brought and grows upon me which of necessity I
must sink under . . . which I may the rather expect in regard that

[1] *Syllabus*, I, p. xxix.
[2] Smith to Wanley, July 3rd, 1697 (Ellis, *Letters of Eminent Literary Men*, p. 251).
[3] *Syllabus*, I, p. xlv; cf. p. lxxv.

hitherto no manner of consideration hath been had of my almost ten
years constant attendance in that service. Let me also remind you that
old age comes so fast upon me that I cannot expect to be much longer
in a condition to do anything.'[1]

This treatment of devoted industry, which alone was making possible a great national undertaking, would have been shameful had it
been meted out to a man of affluence. When it was applied to a person
subsisting on the edge of complete destitution, it places a deep blot on
the reputation of an age deservedly famous for its enlightened patronage. A sentimental portrait might be drawn by Thoresby of 'good old
Mr. Rymer' at work amongst the musty records;[2] but it dissolves into
something far less pleasant at the touch of reality. After 1703, it is true,
Rymer's circumstances, for a little, became somewhat more easy. But
in 1711 when men like William Nicolson were beginning to praise
his work as 'one of the many glories of perhaps the brightest period of
English history', this scholar of seventy-one was forced to sell his
books for bread, and when two years later he died, some of his effects
had hastily to be hawked to provide the expenses of his funeral.[3]

The reek of the garret hangs over Rymer's work, and it surely in-
creases the obligation of the generations of scholars who have profited
by the Foedera. The first volume of the collection – a folio of nine
hundred pages – dealing with the period 1101 to 1273 appeared in
1702, and from that time until his death Rymer worked incessantly,
and in nine years produced fourteen more volumes of a similar scope
carrying the compilation down to the year 1543. From the start there
could be no doubt about the value of the book which was the most
elaborate work of its kind that had hitherto appeared in Europe, and
it immediately won praise from competent critics both in England and
abroad. William Nicolson, for example, commented on the fact that
it had been produced with the assistance of the Queen, and added that
it was one of the glories of her reign; Rapin, who examined the first
volume with meticulous care and was thereby enabled to continue and
enlarge his own history, was loud in his praise; and White Kennett
gave it as his opinion that 'these fifteen volumes of public acts are the
best monument of the past glories of a nation that ever yet appeared
since the beginning of nations'. The book was obviously indispensable
for all future students of English medieval history, and there was an
immediate demand for copies. But since only two hundred and fifty

[1] Syllabus, I, p. xlvi.
[2] THORESBY: Diary, I, p. 296; II, p. 24.
[3] Syllabus, I, p. lxxvii.

of these had been printed and none for public sale these were extremely difficult to obtain. Even keen collectors were unable to procure copies of their own, and the price of a work, at once so scarce and so much in demand, immediately rose to a fantastic height.[1]

The best test of the immediate effect of Rymer's *Foedera* is perhaps to be found in the treatment of his work by subsequent editors From 1696 Rymer had intermittently employed as his assistant, Robert Sanderson, who had been at St. John's College, Cambridge, with Matthew Prior, and who had later become Clerk of the Rolls in the Rolls Chapel. After Rymer's death this man continued the *Foedera*. He showed himself unequal to the task, seldom pursuing his researches beyond documents which came easily to his hand, and making no proper distinction between texts proper to the undertaking, and those which were not germane to it. In consequence, he went far, in the volumes for which he was responsible, towards transforming the *Foedera* into a collection of materials for domestic history in which documents relating to foreign affairs were but sparsely intermingled. None the less, he issued between 1715 and 1717 two additional volumes which with Rymer's own production (seventeen volumes in all) are usually considered to comprise the first edition of the *Foedera* as published by Awnsham Churchill the bookseller and his brother John.[2]

Even so the work was not regarded as being complete. Starting in 1716 Jacob Tonson the publisher who was described by Wycherley as 'gentleman-usher to the Muses', issued under the direction of Sanderson three additional volumes (xviii-xx) to carry the collection down to 1654, and then obtained permission to reprint the first seventeen volumes thus creating in all a complete and enlarged new edition. This edition viewed in its totality was little more than a reprint of Rymer's original collection with Sanderson's inferior continuations, but it did also contain some valuable emendations which were made by George Holmes, then Deputy Keeper of the records at the Tower. The demand for the *Foedera* however continued to be so great that it was not satisfied even thus, and between 1737 and 1745 there was published at the Hague, in an inconvenient format, a third edition which added a few documents relating to Mary's reign, an English translation of Thomas Smith's *De Republica Anglorum*, and a French synopsis of the whole work. By the middle of the eighteenth century therefore there

[1] *Syllabus*, I, pp. lii, liii, lxxxi, xciii; KENNETT: *Second Letter to the Bp. of Carlisle*, p. 32.
[2] *Syllabus*, I, pp. xcvi-xcix, cv; II, p. viii; *Second General Report on the Public Records* (1819), Appendix N. Awnsham Churchill became possessed at one time of Rymer's manuscript collections (now B.M. Add. MSS. 4573-4630), and came badly out of the examination concerning them.

were in existence three separate editions of the *Foedera* but the changes made since Rymer's death were confined to the continuations made by Sanderson which were of poor quality, to the emendations by Holmes which were valuable but not numerous, and to a few unimportant additions and a greater typographical accuracy in the Dutch edition.[1]

With such material at its disposal the 'Record Commission' at the beginning of the nineteenth century turned its attention to the *Foedera*, and conceived the plan of continuing the collection down to the Revolution or even to the accession of George I, and, for reasons which have never been fully explained, they selected as their editor Dr. Adam Clarke, who had previously had a successful career as a Wesleyan preacher and as a writer upon theology. Clarke, fresh to his task, persuaded the Commission that a wholly new edition of the *Foedera* was necessary, partly owing to the scarcity of the former editions, but still more (as he asserted) because of the defects in the work of Rymer, Holmes and their collaborators. His censures of these men were ill conceived, and very often unfounded, but his advice was allowed to prevail with the result that he was responsible for a new edition of the *Foedera* which, when it appeared between 1816 and 1833, was found not only to repeat with far less excuse the mistakes of its predecessor, but to add fresh defects of its own. Clarke and his coadjutors relied very frequently on printed texts even when the originals were available; the new pieces which they introduced were very seldom of sufficient importance or relevance to justify their inclusion; they abandoned the wise restrictions made by Rymer at the beginning of his work; and in the selection of their documents they displayed a lack of discrimination equal to that of Sanderson. In consequence they went far towards denaturalizing a great work whose merits they had failed to appreciate.[2]

In truth, the new editors relied uncritically upon the earlier work of men whose reputations they were concerned to disparage, and the Record Commission's edition of the *Foedera* bears the same relation to the production of Rymer as does the nineteenth century edition of the *Monasticon* to the work of Dodsworth and Dugdale. Thomas Duffus Hardy, from 1861 to 1878 Deputy Keeper of the Public Records, and himself a great student of the sources of English history, gave more attention to the various editions of the *Foedera* than has any man before or since, and he was unable to discover in the last edition of that work

[1] *Syllabus*, I, pp. xcvi-xcix.
[2] Ibid., pp. ciii-cviii; II, pp. i-xxxiv.

'any emendation of importance' beyond those which had been made
by Holmes. In consequence he rightly concluded that such occasional
improvements as might be found were not sufficient to justify the
appearance of a publication in which the design and nature of the
Foedera were mistaken.[1] Once again the facile disparagement of an
earlier scholar failed to find any excuse in the work of his more modern
critics. Even to-day the *Foedera* which remains an indispensable work
of reference, must, despite three editions issued with 'improvements'
since his death, still be judged and criticized as essentially the work of
Thomas Rymer.

A pioneer collection of this vast scope inevitably contained faults.
The most severe criticism which can be brought against it, derives
from the fact that as the work progressed the editor was led increasingly
to depart from the rule which at the beginning he himself had laid down
as proper to the undertaking. It was always difficult for Rymer to isolate
the texts which related primarily to foreign affairs, and in his later
volumes he was progressively less successful in so doing. While his
shortcomings in this respect were as nothing by comparison with those
of his successors, it would be idle to deny that many irrelevant documents were inserted into the *Foedera* by Rymer himself, or that many
texts which he ought to have included were omitted. He neglected
foreign sources, and he was sometimes deceived by a forgery. With
more excuse than had later editors of the *Foedera*, he was also, like
them, careless of the versions which he printed. Thus, without proper
notice, he often culled his texts not from records at all but from the
writings of chroniclers, and sometimes from printed sources which
had not been checked with their originals. Finally, he was occasionally
most unfortunate in the dating and in the arrangement of his documents. He placed, for instance, a charter of 1236 under the year 1174,
and under the year 1101 he printed three deeds belonging respectively
to the years 1239, 1177 and 1174. His work in this respect stood in need
of the checking and revision which it did not receive until Hardy supplied it in his admirable *Syllabus* of 1869.[2]

Rymer was an assiduous collector, but he was never a great critical
scholar. A contemporary commentator considered that 'Mr. Rymer
was qualified with sufficiency as a Critick and Antiquary (till his later
years) to have obliged the world with learned notes on his instruments',
but he was compelled to add: 'he never did anything of that nature

[1] *Syllabus*, II, pp. xxii-xxiv.
[2] Ibid., I, pp. lxxxiii, lxxxiv, lxxxviii, cix; II, pp. vii, xxxiv; HICKES: *Thesaurus*,
Preface to Ottley, pp. xxv, xxvi.

though I frequently desired him to do it upon each instrument while the matter was fresh in his memory'.[1] It was probably fortunate that the attempt was never made, for on the occasions when Rymer did enlarge on his documents the results were seldom happy, and the turgid introductions which he added to his volumes do not enhance his reputation. 'They do not exhibit any critical skill or show that he appreciated the value of the important materials upon which he was engaged. He seems to have had little or no other object beyond eulogizing his royal patron.'[2]

Merely to enumerate the shortcomings of Thomas Rymer is, however, wholly to misconceive the character of his achievement. If to-day the *Foedera* remains a fundamental source of English medieval history, the credit is due to the laborious years of labour expended upon it by a poverty-stricken scholar, and the merits of the book so far outweigh its defects that it has become almost a truism to emphasize its importance. The measure of the value of the *Foedera* is, in short, the extent to which it has been profitably used, and the test of Rymer's personal share in this achievement is to be found in the failure of later editors to supersede his work. Its influence has not waned. When in 1937 a new Professor of Medieval History at Cambridge inaugurated the tenure of his Chair he paid a proper tribute to one who had also for a short space been a Cambridge man. 'It is superfluous', he remarked, 'to insist on the merits of the monumental *Foedera*; that collection of documents meets one in countless notes of countless books. If (Rymer) was not strictly speaking a pioneer he brought to light and made usable a whole department of one of the richest archives in Europe. No doubt his texts are not free from errors; fortunately for his successors he did not sweep the archives clean of the class of documents he published. But with the *Foedera* as with the *Concilia* the medievalist obtained one of the most useful tools in the second division of his sources, the documentary, perhaps now the most fruitful material for new work and new discoveries.'[3] Particular criticisms, however justified in detail, fail altogether to detract from an achievement of this character. The modern scholar who was best qualified to pass judgment on Thomas Rymer was right when he asserted that the *Foedera* has 'no rival in its class'; and (it may be added) 'few men could have executed a design with so much accuracy at once as difficult and complex as it was important and useful'.[4]

[1] Anstis to Hearne, July 13th, 1714 (HEARNE: *Collections*, IV, p. 377).
[2] *Syllabus*, I, p. lxxv.
[3] PREVITÉ-ORTON: *The Study o Medieval History* (1937), pp. 9-10.
[4] *Syllabus*, II, p. xxxvi.

After Rymer's death, there was appointed to the office of Historiographer Royal a man of forty-eight who had already shown himself by the publication of two remarkable books to be abundantly qualified to discharge the new duties he undertook, and to carry on the tradition laid down by the editor of the *Foedera*. Thomas Madox was, like Rymer himself, first and foremost, a student of records, and, if his production was less extensive in bulk than that of his predecessor, it was of even greater intrinsic value. This man was not only a tireless collector, familiar with all categories of English medieval documents, but he was also a fine critic of manuscripts whose work, as Hickes was concerned to point out, was informed by 'great diligence and not less judgement'.[1] Madox shared in the abundant zeal of the scholars with whom he moved; he possessed 'a Herculean industry and a generous thirst;'[2] he was closely connected with Rymer not only as his successor in office but also by kindred adventures in erudition. But none the less he was in many ways an isolated figure. The special quality of this fine intelligence coupled with the secular objectivity of his studies related his aims to a future which was still far removed, and until the latter half of the nineteenth century it would be hard to discover any English medievalist whose methods were more strictly scientific than his.

Something of this objectivity, and something also of this isolation, may perhaps be discerned in the lack of biographical information which exists concerning Madox. Unlike most of his fellow scholars he seems to have impinged on the consciousness of his contemporaries almost exclusively through the medium of the books which he wrote. Madox was distantly related to Thoresby who knew him; he visited Oxford in the course of his researches and conversed with Hearne; he frequented the Harleian Library and consulted Wanley. It is therefore remarkable that he yet remains one of the very few personages who do not come to life in the pages of those vivid and contrasted commentators. Thoresby alludes to his mother as to a pious dissenter with connections at Konigsberg, and Hearne remarks unnecessarily that he was 'well versed in Affairs belonging to the Exchequer'. He is known vaguely as a man who never took a university degree, and as a member of the Middle Temple who was never called to the Bar. He became a clerk in the Augmentations Office after service in the Office of the Lord Treasurer's Remembrancer, and in this capacity he assisted the Lords' Committee in their work on the Public Records. He was a Fellow of the Society of Antiquaries to which he was proposed by

[1] HICKES: *Thesaurus*, Preface to Ottley, p. xxx (trans.).
[2] Marmaduke Fothergill to Hearne, Aug. 22nd, 1715 (HEARNE: *Collections*. v, p. 102).

George Holmes.[1] But beyond this it is strangely hard to discover any information regarding the private life of this man who was not only a great scholar but one of influence. The explanation may most probably be found in odd phrases in his books which suggest something of the pride, and much of the sensitive diffidence, of the isolated scholar who is sure of his own standards but by no means convinced that they will be generally accepted. He certainly discouraged intimacy, and cultivated a seclusion which posterity must perforce respect. He must make himself known to-day, as he did to his fellows, almost entirely through his learned works. And the strongest personal connection which he formed may perhaps have been that with Lord Somers whose patronage made possible his books.

'Your Lordship's Approbation', wrote Madox in the preface to the first of his great books, 'was the Principal Encouragement I had in the Beginning and Progress of this Undertaking.' This book which appeared in 1702 had the somewhat forbidding title of *Formulare Anglicanum*, and it was 'a collection of ancient Charters and Instruments of Divers Kinds taken from the Originals, placed under several Heads, and deduced (in a Series according to Order of Time) from the Norman Conquest to the end of the Reign of King Henry the VIII'. The purpose of the work was in fact simple in its originality. 'When I considered', wrote Madox, 'that there is not extant any Methodical History or Systeme of Ancient Charters and Instruments of this Nation: I thought it might probably be Acceptable to Curious persons and Usefull to the Publique if something were done toward supplying that Defect. And having found in the Repository of the Late Court of *Augmentations* a Vast collection of Ancient Original Charters, I conceived one might be furnish'd from Thence with Materials for Such an Undertaking.' Conception was, however, one thing and production another; and the labour involved was long and arduous. 'It would ill become me', concluded the weary scholar, 'to boast of having used great industry . . . yet I must beg leave to say that in compiling the Collection as it is I have perused an incredible number of Ancient Charters and Writings.'[2]

The appearance of the *Formulare Anglicanum* marked a definite stage in the development of an important branch of medieval learning. Hearne remarked that the work had been performed with 'much judgement and industry',[3] and Nicolson added that it would prove 'of unspeakable Service to our Students in Law and Antiquities'.[4] But it

---

[1] THORESBY: *Diary*, I, p. 456; II, p. 24; HEARNE: *Collections*, IX, p. 262; ELLIS: *Letters of Eminent Literary Men*, p. 101; NICOLSON: *Epist. Corr.*, p. 310; *Bodleian Letters*, I, p. 214.
[2] *Formulare Anglicanum*, Dedication and Preface, Sects. i and ii.
[3] HEARNE: *Collections*, I, p. 46.   [4] NICOLSON: *English Historical Library* (1736), p. 240.

may be doubted whether either of these men fully understood the real importance of the work they were concerned to praise. For in truth the *Formulare* was the first attempt to base the study of the post-Conquest charters of medieval England upon a scientific base such as a later age would especially appreciate. As time went on, scholars were to become increasingly aware that the study of the social history of England in the Middle Ages was dependent upon just the type of evidence which Madox set himself to sift, and his collection was thus in the future to prove of inestimable value both for itself and as a pattern for future work. The main body of the book contained nearly eight hundred documents edited with a critical accuracy that had never before been applied to such texts. And the long 'dissertation' which preceded them was itself the first comprehensive work on the form and structure of English medieval charters in the post-Conquest period. It applied the continental labours of Mabillon to the practical problems of English feudal history, and in this respect it has never been superseded. Perhaps, indeed, the best summary of the importance of this pioneer work is to be found in the fact that the only general treatment of English feudal Charters which even to-day can be compared with that of Madox was written in 1922, and is still most unfortunately only to be discovered in the transactions of a local society.[1]

Madox worked from originals: therein is to be found the importance of this his first book. Charter evidence is difficult to interpret, and its correct elucidation depends directly upon a close attention to the minutiae of handwriting and formulae. This in its turn could not be undertaken in even the transcripts made in the great medieval cartularies. When therefore Madox declared in his preface that 'the Formulas here exhibited are all taken from Original Charters . . . except in those instances (which comparatively are not many) wherein it evidently appears from the Notes subjoined',[2] he was enunciating a new and an important principle in the editorship of such texts. Here too is to be found the measure of his advance on the work of Dodsworth and Dugdale who made no such distinctions, and who in consequence produced versions which, for all their value, could not be used by subsequent students for technical charter study. Madox, unlike some more recent editors of charters, did not need to be told that every word of a twelfth-century charter may be of importance, and he had thus a wholesome fear of suppressing any part of the deeds he printed and

---

[1] STENTON: *Transcripts of Gilbertine Charters*, Introduction (Lincoln Record Society, vol. 18).
[2] *Formulare Anglicanum*, Preface, Sect. vi.

particularly of abbreviating the lists of their witnesses. He handled his sources with a care which was shared perhaps by none of his contemporaries except Wanley, and this, connected with great critical power, enabled him to set the study of English charters moving on new and more profitable lines.

Like all the greatest students of diplomatic, Madox was convinced that this was an ancillary science, and his primary object was to demonstrate how this technical study could be made to subserve the larger ends of history. It is in the fine preface to the *Formulare*, for example, that most notably appears the plea that in the charter is to be found the fundamental source of feudal history. 'One may justly wonder', he exclaimed, 'that *Feudal* Learning (if I may so call it) should be so little known or regarded as it seems to be by the Students (I ask their pardon) of the Common Law of *England*.'[1] Even parentheses could not diminish the force of the innuendo, and the remedy was plainly indicated. 'In Ancient Charters', he added, 'we may discern much of the Genius of our Ancestours; and much concerning their Manners and Customs . . . By These Monuments we may see in what manner our Ancestours transferr'd their Possession to one another and transacted several other Weighty affairs. Considerable use may I conceive be made of Them in History; and some in Chronology. In them the student of Law may observe several Rudiments of our Common Law appearing in a Plainness and Simplicity agreable to the Ancient Times.'[2] In the technical study of the feudal charter Madox had scarcely any successor in England until the advent of W. H. Stevenson.[3] And the importance of charter testimony as the basis of our knowledge of Feudal England is more strongly felt to-day than at any time since his death.[4]

The *Formulare Anglicanum* appeared in 1702 but already Madox had been at work for some five years upon a book of even greater importance, since in 1697 he had begun to collect materials for a comprehensive and definitive history of the medieval English Exchequer. It was an enterprise as original as was its predecessor. For though the Exchequer records as deposited in the Treasuries of Westminster had long been well known and reasonably accessible, they had, despite Agarde's sixteenth-century catalogue, been largely neglected, and the great scholars of the seventeenth century had worked in the main either from chronicles and cartularies or from the records of the Chancery. Robert Brady, for example, scarcely concerned himself with records outside the

---

[1] *Formulare Anglicanum*, Preface, Sect. viii. [2] Ibid.
[3] STEVENSON: *English Historical Review*, XI, p. 731; XXI, p. 1.
[4] STENTON: *English Feudalism*, pp. 88, 151, 152, 161, 203.

Chancery except when he cited Domesday Book, and Cotton's treatise on records as later enlarged by Prynne dealt with the Chancery documents in the Tower. At the beginning of the eighteenth century almost the only works directly related to the Exchequer or to its records were Prynne's *Aurum Reginae* of 1688, and the slight but lucid essay on *Sheriff's Accompts* by Matthew Hale which was published in 1683.[1] Here was certainly a gap in English historical erudition which it was imperative to fill. And it was clear that if a single man could be found competent to carry out a task of such magnitude, he would not only expose for the first time the essential workings of English medieval administration, but also make available a wholly new range of historical material. In the words of Madox himself, such a work would not be merely a History of the Exchequer; it would also comprise 'an *Apparatus* towards a History of the Ancient Law of England'.[2]

The subsequent success of this famous book was due not only to its subject but even more to the manner in which it was created. And we are very fortunate in having, from the pen of Madox himself, a detailed description of the methods he employed in constructing a work which was to mark an epoch in the study of English administrative history, and which has remained an indispensable source of reference for generations of scholars.

> The first part of my business – wrote Madox – was to make as full a collection from Records as I could of Materials relating to the Subject. Those materials being ranged in a certain order in several books of *Collectanea*, I reviewed them, and weighing what they imported, and how they might be applied, drew from thence a general scheme of the projected Design. When I had pitched upon Chapters or heads of Discourse, I took the Materials out of the stock provided, and digested them in proper places under the chapters or heads assumed. In doing this, I used for the most part to write down in the draught of this Book the respective Records or testimonies. First of all (that is before I wrote my own text or composition); . . . connecting and applying them afterwards as the case would admitt. For I thought I should by That means be held more steadily to the Rule I desired to observe which was, To give such an account of things as might be elicited and drawn out of the memorials cited from time to time; and not to cite memorials and vouchers for establishing of any private opinions preconceived in my own mind.[3]

The procedure would surely satisfy the most exigent demands of the most scientific methodologist, and its successful application explains the fundamental importance of the book which resulted therefrom.

---

[1] R. L. POOLE: *Exchequer in the Twelfth Century* (1912), pp. 15-16.
[2] *Exchequer* (1711), p. iii.   [3] Ibid., p. iv.

At the same time the last sentence of the description indicates more clearly than could pages of commentary the advance made by Madox on the whole series of constitutional historians who preceded him.

According to Hearne, Madox began work on his *Exchequer* at the age of thirty-one;[1] and he devoted the best years of his strenuous life to the completion of his task. 'The labour', he wrote, 'besides the expense of resorting often and often to Respositories of Records in distant places, Of enoteing and copying Memorials from thence, And of perusing a vast number of things for a Few comparatively that one actually Collects: I say the labour of this cannot easily be estimated by any man who has not had some experience of it.' He was right; and the fourteen years which elapsed between the beginning and the completion of the design must have been very arduously spent. But at length 'the materials were dug out of deep and hidden mines, the model of the Building was framed, the columns adjusted, the stones squared weighed and disposed, and in summ the whole Fabrick raised and perfected in such manner as it is'.[2] By such means there was finally given to the world in May 1711 *The History and Antiquities of the Exchequer of the Kings of England in two periods, to wit, From the Norman Conquest to the End of the Reign of King John, and From the End of the Reign of King John to the End of the Reign of King Edward II.*[3]

The value of this great book derives from the critical methods of its production, and like its predecessor its supreme virtue was that it was wholly based upon original sources. Here, for perhaps the first time in English scholarship, an attempt was made for the period with which the treatise deals, not only to adhere strictly to the very meaning of primary authorities, but to distinguish between them in a manner which has only really become familiar to students since the publication of T. F. Tout's volumes in the present century. The emphasis which Madox deliberately gave to such distinctions has in fact an extraordinarily modern ring:

> The Memorials or Vouchers contained in this Work are taken from Records of the Highest Nature; to wit from the *Great Rolls* of the *Pipe*, the *Memoranda* of the Exchequer, and the Rolls of several sorts in the Tower of

[1] Writing on Sept. 6th, 1706, Hearne remarked: 'Mr. Madox upon a Work which is extracted from Records in the Exchequer etc. Twill be larger than his *Formulare*, and he has taken a great deal more pains in it, having been upon it about 9 years' (*Collections*, I, p. 287).
[2] *Exchequer* (1711), p. iv; cf. Madox to Robert Harley, May 5th, 1711 (*Portland MSS. Rep.*, IV, p. 685).
[3] An index to the *Exchequer* was printed in 1741 and included in some copies of *Baronia Anglica*. A second edition of the *Exchequer* with the index was published in 1769 in two volumes.

London. All which Records having been written by Publick officers and by publick authority at the time when the things recorded therein were Done carry in them a full and undoubted credit. Great regard is indeed to be had to the Annals or history contained in Registers of Churches; and in the Manuscript collections of Ancient Writers; particularly in relation to things done in their Own life-time or lying within their personal knowledg. But no doubt the Publick Records of the Crown and Kingdom are the most important and most authentick of All. And These are the Foundation which sustain the whole Fabrick of this History. A Foundation solid and unshaken.[1]

When such methods were applied not to a restricted subject but to a vast tract of English medieval history, it was inevitable that the resulting book, which itself dealt with a wholly new range of original material, should prove at once intrinsically important and extremely influential. In particular, it was hardly surprising that the extensive citations laboriously collected from the very membranes of Exchequer Rolls should in their fullness and accuracy have supplied the impetus, and the material, for very much of the work of a later age. But what was perhaps even more surprising was that Madox was himself fully conscious that this would be so. His 'request to the Gentle reader' was prophetic in its significance; for it requested that 'when he peruseth this Book he will please to read not only the Narration or Text, but also the Testimonies couched in the Margin: For they are in my opinion the most Valuable part of the Work; and by consequence the most Worthy to be read'.[2] In so far as the reply of the twentieth century to the nineteenth in the matter of medieval research has been a greater emphasis on the record, as opposed to the narrative, sources of history, Madox must be regarded as more 'modern' than either Freeman or Green.

The *Exchequer* discussed almost all the aspects of medieval financial administration in England, and as an appendix to the work, with a separate preface addressed to Charles, Lord Halifax, Madox printed for the first time an original treatise which Maitland called 'a unique book in the history of medieval England and perhaps in the history of medieval Europe.'[3] This was the famous text usually known as the *Dialogus de Scaccario* – the Dialogue of the Exchequer – wherein Richard fitz Nigel, Bishop of London, and Treasurer in the reign of Henry II, explained the detailed working of the royal exchequer in his day. The existence of this invaluable source had not been unknown to earlier scholars but they had not recognized its importance. It had been

---

[1] *Exchequer* (1711), p. iv.   [2] Ibid., p. v.
[3] POLLOCK and MAITLAND: *History of English Law*, I, p. 140.

assigned to Gervase of Tilbury, and with wilder inaccuracy to William of Occam, and though quotations had been made from it, the treatise itself had remained unprinted and uncriticized. When, in the early years of the eighteenth century, it fell under the attention of Madox, he at once realized its extraordinary importance, and within a few years he was responsible not only for assigning the book to its true author but also for presenting to the public the first edition of this fundamental source of English history.[1]

It is instructive to watch Madox at work upon this subsidiary labour whose results would of themselves have made the reputation of any lesser man. First, he obtained from Lord Somers two modern copies of the treatise and from these he constructed one version. Then he called in George Holmes to his aid, and the two men set out to collate their copy with the versions in the *Black* and *Red Books of the Exchequer*, the one scholar reading from the original whilst the other made the necessary corrections in the copy.[2] The result was the production of a workmanlike text of a document whose publication gave an immediate impetus to English historical studies. As an edition it was not perfect since there was another MS. which needed also to be collated, and the text which Madox created was in some respects untrustworthy. But it was the edition of Madox which with scarcely any alteration was copied in all subsequent editions of the book down to the twentieth century, and all the scholars who have used the treatise with such advantage owe more to Madox than to any other single man. When in 1902 a standard edition of the *Dialogus* was at last produced by three officials of the Public Record Office, it was fitting that it should be dedicated to Thomas Madox and that the first and last sentences of its learned introduction should contain his honoured name.[3]

The best summary of the importance of the *Exchequer* of Madox is to say that it exactly fulfilled the dual object to which its author aspired, and that the book has served not only as the definitive history of a great governmental department in medieval England but also as a 'Promptuary' to all subsequent students of English medieval antiquities. 'My Ambition', he said, 'was to form this History in such a manner that it may be a Pattern for the Antiquaries to follow, if they please . . . For I think it is to be wished that the Histories of a Countrey so well furnished with Records and Manuscripts as Ours is should be grounded throughout as far as is practicable on proper Vouchers. And for my

---

[1] POOLE: op. cit., pp. 5, 6, 11; *Dialogus de Scaccario*, ed. HUGHES, CRUMP and JOHNSON (1902), pp. 1-3.
[2] MADOX: *Dialogus de Scaccario* (in *Exchequer*, 1711), p. 59.
[3] CRUMP, HUGHES and JOHNSON, op. cit.

Q

own part I cannot look upon the History of *England* to be compleatly written till it shall come to be written after that manner.'[1] It was the new ideal of historical scholarship, and to few scholars has it been given to formulate so lofty an ambition and to come so near to its attainment. It is true that Madox might have made a clearer distinction between the *Exchequer* as it was before and after the accession of Henry III, and that he was at times in danger of being overwhelmed by the very mass of the materials with which he dealt. It is true also that he sometimes hesitated to expose fallacies current among men less informed than himself and that there were some gaps even in his own wonderful erudition. But when perhaps the most learned medievalist in twentieth-century England turned his own attention to the subject which Madox had investigated, he gave it as his considered opinion that this book of 1711, 'the product of ripe learning and profound study', was 'never likely to be superseded'. As 'a storehouse which will always be consulted with profit for the fullness the precision and the certainty of the materials which it contains', it 'remains a monument of erudition of which any country might be proud'.[2]

Few scholars possess the distinction of Madox in having produced two separate publications each of which marked an epoch in a distinct and important branch of historical learning. But even the *Formulare* and the *Exchequer* did not exhaust the output of this extraordinary man. In 1722 he issued in his *Firma Burgi* the one outstanding work on medieval municipal history which appeared in England before the nineteenth century, and after his death there was published a short treatise on tenures under the title *Baronia Anglica*. Important as these books were, however, they do not enhance the reputation of Madox as firmly established in his previous work. The *Firma Burgi* dealt almost exclusively with but one aspect of English burghal growth, and the feudal essay bears all the marks of a posthumous publication that would have undergone a drastic revision had its author been alive. It is known also that Madox contemplated a history of English feudalism, and there can be little doubt that this is one of the great unwritten books of English scholarship. For Madox with his immense knowledge of English charters, and his unique familiarity with the Exchequer records, was ideally fitted to put such a plan into execution, and the ninety-three volumes of his valuable collections which now repose in the British Museum display the scope of his laborious preparations. But Madox died on January 13th, 1726/7, at the age of sixty. And posterity (which

---

[1] *Exchequer* (1711), p. v.
[2] POOLE: op. cit., pp. 2, 17, 18; cf. NICHOLS: *Literary Anecdotes*, I, pp. 245, 246.

likes not manuscript collectanea) is left to contemplate his achievement in the two greatest books which he published.[1]

These were in truth more than sufficient to single out Thomas Madox from among nearly all his contemporaries and to demonstrate that in him was displayed scholarship of a special quality. None of his fellow scholars except Humphrey Wanley could claim to be scientific in the same sense, and it is the mark of his greatness that, even to-day, he seems to move among the moderns as if, apart from the immensity of his production, he were one of themselves. His books may still be criticized as if they were written yesterday; and his aims and methods, except in respect of their successful consummation, were no different from those of ourselves. Madox in his own age had a special task to perform. 'I think', he wrote at the beginning of his career, 'one may say in general that for want of a close Inspection and Use of the Ancient Records and Memoirs of this Kingdom, many crude and precarious Things have been advanced concerning our Old Laws and Constitutions: Men having been tempted, as it seems, to frame hypotheses concerning the Ancient State of Things from either Modern or Present Appearances.'[2] It was in truth the prevalent defect in English scholarship, and Madox gave his life to supply the remedy until at last in his *Exchequer* he could sum up the motives and the achievement of his life's work. 'The writing of History', he concluded, 'is in some sort a Religious act. It imports solemnity and sacredness: and ought to be undertaken with purity and rectitude of mind. Wilfully to misrepresent, and to offer at putting Fallacies upon the Publick is to violate Common Faith and the decent Respect due to Mankind.'[3] The words may seem almost commonplace today. But neither Hickes nor Wharton, nor Brady nor Hearne, would have spoken of religion in this sense, or described their own labours under similar terms. This man is speaking rather in the language of a distant generation. Janus-wise he looks both ways: back to the fierce industry and to the immediate zeal of his predecessors; forward to the objective science which was later to become an ideal. For this reason Thomas Madox may here be regarded as the first of the moderns; and his career may fittingly symbolize the climax and the conclusion of the greatest age of English medieval scholarship.

---

[1] TAIT: *Medieval English Borough* (1936), p. 339; NICHOLS: *Literary Anecdotes*, I, p. 247. A second edition of *Firma Burgi* was published in 1726. *Baronia Anglica* was published in 1736 and reissued in 1741. Madox's collections are contained in B.M. Add. MSS. 4479-4572.

[2] MADOX: *Formulare*, Preface, Sect. viii.

[3] *Exchequer* (1711), p. iii.

CHAPTER XII

THE FRIENDS OF CLIO

A GREAT movement in scholarship depends to an especial degree upon the generous support of an educated public, for if general literature may in fortunate circumstances subsist upon the rewards of widespread demand, erudition must of necessity be addressed to a limited class in the community. 'Till the men of curiosity encrease their number,' remarked White Kennett in 1693, 'this must be the fate of the best books that they shall not bear the charges of their own Impression.'[1] Since his time, historical scholars of less distinction, who have been prone to forget that books are meant to be read, have nevertheless found little difficulty in persuading themselves that it was only the excellence of their work which prevented its sale. Though it has seldom been warranted by the facts, it has always been the cherished complaint of English scholars that 'England is not worthy to have learned men'.[2] 'What else', asked one of these in the reign of Queen Anne, 'was the reason that most of our old Historians were first printed beyond the seas; but only that cheaper methods and quicker sale made the Editors to gain abroad what they must have lost at home?'[3] Hickes could inform even Robert Harley that young Wanley had not here received the encouragement that he would have met with had he been born in Europe.[4] It may, however, reasonably be doubted whether such complaints have ever had general justification, and in particular it is probable that medieval scholarship has never enjoyed a more discriminating endowment than in England between 1660 and 1730.

The neglected scholar has always been a favourite object of generous indignation, and he has lived in all the centuries. It is a picturesque legend that Sir Walter Ralegh threw the second part of his *History of the World* into the fire as a punishment for the way an ungrateful public had treated the first, and Sir Henry Spelman was right to feel aggrieved when his publisher would not offer him even five pounds for the concluding sections of his great *Glossary*. But these were men of substance, and a far less pleasant picture was painted by a German visitor to Oxford in 1710 who found the foremost medievalist then in residence at

---

[1] KENNETT: *Life of Somner* (*Gavelkind*, 1726), p. 96.
[2] HEARNE: *Collections*, I, p. 197.
[3] KENNETT: op. cit., p. 97.
[4] *Portland MSS. Rep.*, IV, p. 16.

the University eager to show visitors round the Anatomy School for
the sake of the tips he might receive. 'This *Hearne*', he added, 'is a man
of 30 and very mean to look at but exceeding diligent. He is the lowest
of the Librarians and from the Library he has only £10'.[1] Nor was
Hearne alone in his misfortunes even at Oxford. Some fifty years
earlier the first Camden Reader of History had left behind him a
widow and children who were so poor that it became a matter of
malicious conjecture 'whether the females lived honestly',[2] and at a
later date several of the scholars suffered similar hardship. Before the
Revolution, William Fulman was persistently cheated of proper recognition, and after it Henry Wharton complained that preferment would
be withheld from him until a time when he could no longer be of service to the learned world. Both the *Monasticon* and Somner's Saxon
Dictionary – two of the most important works of the time – failed to
sell when they first appeared, and White Kennett used this as the basis
of bitter generalizations, exclaiming: 'It is this has stifled the conception
of many glorious designs, to see exquisite Volumes thrown back upon
an Author's empty hands while Plays and Pamphlets reward the
trifling writers.'[3] He could, moreover, have found further examples of
greater hardship among his more immediate acquaintance. Rymer's
poverty was a reproach to the age in which he lived. Among the Saxon
scholars, William Elstob had reason to lament 'evil days cold patrons
and neglected efforts', and his misfortunes paled into insignificance
beside those which his greater sister Elizabeth was later to endure.[4]

But was it really true at this time that such was 'the very usual fate
of men of letters attached to abstruse and unfashionable literature'?[5]
Neither the intellectual interests of the period nor the immense output
of works of erudition would suggest it. Even in exceptional cases the
neglect endured by scholars was often not as severe as they themselves
suggested in times of discouragement. White Kennett might voice the
grievances of learned men, but he himself easily scaled the ladder of
preferment to become Bishop of Peterborough. Dugdale lived to receive a knighthood and to be one of the most respected figures in
Restoration England, and the later research of William Somner was
generously endowed by lay munificence. In some cases a personal
explanation of individual misfortunes was not far to seek, for some of
the scholars, who complained most bitterly, gratuitously outraged the

[1] UFFENBACH: *Diary* (in MAYOR: *Cambridge under Queen Anne*), p. 386.
[2] WOOD: *Ath. Oxon.*, III, col. 219.
[3] KENNETT: op. cit., p. 96.
[4] NICHOLS: *Literary Anecdotes*, IV, p. 139.
[5] See RICHARDSON: *Reprints of Rare Tracts*, vol. I, p. 14.

feelings of those who wished to help them, and even so received a fair
measure of support. Thus Hearne, who was no easy man to befriend,
after starting his career in indigence died leaving over a thousand
pounds concealed in his room, and Humphrey Wanley who as a
young man consistently flouted academic authority later received from
outside his University the patronage which his accomplishments
deserved. The ecclesiastics who after the Revolution dealt harshly with
Henry Wharton had some reason to complain of 'pertness and immodesty' in a young man who in the days of his prosperity had held two
rectories in absence.[1] It would be as misleading as it would be easy to
argue from loud complaints made in exceptional circumstances. A
wider survey suggests that between 1660 and 1730 scholarship in
general, and medieval research in particular, received from both clergy
and laity a consistent and an enlightened support.

The Anglican Church remained throughout this period the chief
repository of English learning, and clerical endowments were regularly
used to foster medieval scholarship. The ecclesiastical control of the
Universities of England was used to this end, but even more noticeable
was the extent to which clerical benefices were allotted to those who by
holding them could best promote the interests of learning. In part this
was due to the old connection between historical study and ecclesiastical
argument, for it was still widely held among Anglican divines that 'a
little skill in Antiquity inclines a man to Popery; but depth in that
study brings him about again to our religion'. But even this conviction
would not of itself explain the learned production of the Anglican
clergy during this age, or the zeal with which the Church fostered
medieval erudition. An extraordinary enthusiasm pervaded the great
prelates of the time, and while many of these were scholars of the first
importance themselves, many more made it their business to promote
scholarly production in others. The extensive correspondence of
Thomas Gale, William Nicolson, Edmund Gibson and White Kennett
would of itself suffice to illustrate the antiquarian interests of the contemporary Church and the degree to which these were consciously
directed towards the investigation of medieval England. 'Next to what
concerns the preservation of our Established Religion and Government, peace here and salvation hereafter', observed William Nicolson
shortly before his death, 'I know nothing that hath greater share in my
thoughts and desires than the promotion of the Septentrional Learning.'[2] 'How happily would it spread the glory of the *English* Church and

[1] NICOLSON: *Epist. Corr.*, p. 20.
[2] Ibid., p. 650.

Nation', added the Bishop of Peterborough, 'if among Divines addicted to these studies some one were preferred to a dignity in every Collegiate Church on condition to employ his talent in the History and Antiquities of that Body of which he was a grateful and useful Member.'[1] 'A sober Scholar', it was remarked, 'was always welcome to his Study and sure of his Countenance and Encouragement.'[2]

When this spirit animated the leaders of the Church there was little danger that medieval scholarship would fail to receive an adequate support out of ecclesiastical revenue. The abuses which were then to be found in clerical life were, generally speaking, not of a character to hamper the ecclesiastical patronage of letters, or to diminish the immense services which the Church was rendering to learning. A disappointed man might complain that he would give anything to be a lord's son since such a one with ordinary learning and morality could not eventually escape some good preferment; and there was truth, as well as unconscious humour, in the observation of Jeremy Collier that in the clerical profession 'the honour of the family continues and the heraldry is every jot as safe in the Church as twas in the State'. If, however, as Anthony Wood remarked, Holy Orders offered 'the readiest way for preferment for the younger sons of noblemen', it was also true that literary distinction of itself usually succeeded in receiving in the Church at least a dignified means of subsistence. Plebeian birth was a handicap, but if it was coupled with scholarly ability, it was, in this period, no insuperable obstacle to ecclesiastical advancement.[3] Even the prevalent practices of pluralities and absenteeism must, from the point of view of the growth of scholarship, be regarded with leniency when they enabled men to undertake research to which all subsequent inquirers have been indebted. Clerical sinecures are deplorable; but they were less to be condemned at a time when the Church was still willing to employ its revenues to promote the scholarship. Aristocratic influence on ecclesiastical appointments is an evil; but it was mitigated when it was used with a wise discrimination to foster erudition.[4]

The immense contribution made by the Anglican Church to medieval scholarship during this epoch was limited far more by disputes within that Body than ever it was by lay influence exercised upon it from outside. In this respect, the period after the Revolution of 1688

[1] KENNETT: op. cit., p. 26.
[2] Life of White Kennett (1730), p. 189.
[3] Cf. OVERTON: Life in the English Church, pp. 297, 300, 301; Lives of the Norths (1890), II, p. 276.
[4] In 1856 Emerson remarked (English Traits, ed. 1883, p. 210): 'The clergy for a thousand years have been the scholars of the nation.' When did this cease to be so?

compared unfavourably with the decades which preceded it. The English episcopate has probably never been adorned with more splendid examples of learning, devotion, and princely munificence than during the reign of Charles II, and since these men were especially interested in the early history of their Church, their influence was particularly favourable to historical study. So long as they remained in control there was little doubt that antiquarian scholarship would receive the full benefit of their sympathetic enthusiasm. But already before the reign of James II new opinions were beginning to appear within Anglicanism. The habits of mind represented, for example, so diversely, in the Cambridge Platonists, in the 'Men of Latitude' and in the clerics who were early members of the Royal Society, were by no means in accord with the interests of the older generation.[1] The new temper thus to be discerned in ecclesiastical opinion was indifferent rather than hostile to many of the scholarly concerns of the Laudian school. On the one hand, the scientific preoccupations of such men made the patronage of research more objective than it had been before, but on the other hand, antiquarian studies loomed less largely in their intellectual life. It would be wholly false to consider that the concern of the Church for historical work was unduly diminished, when men like Gibson and Wake who supported the new regime were highly influential patrons of history. But it is none the less true that changes in ecclesiastical opinion were, before the end of the seventeenth century, beginning to affect the attitude of the Church towards medieval scholarship.

It was partly for these reasons that the Non-juring Schism was an event of the first importance in the development of English medieval erudition since it tended to draw away from the Establishment just those elements in the Laudian tradition which were most favourable to historical learning. The ejection of this group from the Establishment probably diminished the sum of medieval scholarship sponsored by the Anglican Church since it deflected patronage from channels into which it might otherwise profitably have flowed. The personal distinction of the Non-jurors made the extension of their influence a formidable threat, and those in authority became increasingly chary of dispensing preferment in quarters which might possibly be suspect. For many years a large number of the inferior clergy remained at heart sympathetic to the ejected ministers, and the Lower House of Convocation was notoriously lenient towards them.[2] The Bishops, newly appointed

---

[1] SYKES: *Church and State in England in the Eighteenth Century*, pp. 16-25.
[2] OVERTON: *Life in the English Church*, pp. 12-14; BIRCH: *Tillotson*, p. 191.

WHITE KENNETT

Engraved by James Fittler in 1818 from an original portrait then in the
possession of the family of Sir John Bayley, one of White Kennett's
descendants. The 'Black Patch' (see page 249) will be noted

after 1688, in their desire to strengthen the Revolution settlement, therefore felt themselves constrained to watch all clerical promotions, and whatever might be their own scholarly sympathies to refuse preferment to clerks who, however learned, might be suspected of Non-juring beliefs. A new spirit of political faction thus entered a Church which before the Revolution had been united at least in its attitude towards the State. It found its expression in many extraordinary forms. White Kennett, for example, the Whig Bishop of Peterborough, had in early life suffered from an unfortunate accident.

> In January 1689 by the Discharge and Breaking of a Gun with which he was shooting at a Bird ... a Splinter of the Barrel made a grievous Wound in his Forehead and broke through both the Tables of his Skull: which occasioned his wearing a large black Patch of Velvet on that Part ever after.[1]

The subject doubtless leant itself to caricature, but, when many years later an altar-piece representing the Last Supper was set up in White-chapel, it was hardly necessary for Judas Iscariot to be

> drawn sitting in an elbow chair dressed in a black garment, between a gown and a cloak, with a black scarf and a white band, a short wig, and *a mark on his forehead between a lock of hair and a patch*.[2]

Such episodes were not conducive to dignity, and their effect upon the learned activities of the Church was aptly illustrated when the greatest editor in contemporary Oxford was, on account of his Non-juring principles, denied access to the Bodleian and to all the College Libraries.

The promotion of scholarship by the Anglican Church was seriously hampered when, after the Revolution, the control of the ecclesiastical system became as never before a matter of contention between the two great political parties in the State. Whigs as well as Tories were now the supporters of Anglicanism and set themselves to use this vastly influential Corporation for their own party purposes with results that were inevitably unfavourable to clerical learning. It was not that a Whig might not be as fine a scholar as was his opponent. It was rather that intellectual distinction was no longer considered as of itself sufficient to ensure promotion. To this cause, many years later, Samuel Johnson directly attributed the decline of scholarship in England. 'Few Bishops', he said, 'are now made for their learning. To be a Bishop a man must be learned in a learned age, factious in a factious age but always of eminence', and 'no man can now be made a Bishop for his

---

[1] *Life of White Kennett* (1730), p. 7.
[2] NICHOLS: *Literary Anecdotes*, I, p. 397.

learning and piety'. If the censure was unduly severe even for the last
quarter of the eighteenth century, it exactly represented the results of a
process which began in the Anglican Church after the Revolution of
1688.[1]

An estimate of the debt of scholarship to the Anglican Church
during the seventy years which elapsed after the Restoration must
therefore make some distinction between the period which preceded
the Revolution and that which followed after. But, speaking generally,
it was, throughout, a support as consistent as it was munificent. So
enthusiastic was the encouragement of medieval studies on the part
of the Anglican ecclesiastics of this age that it is remarkable that so little
was done officially at this time to foster this erudition in the two great
Universities which were exclusively under Anglican control. To enter
the teeming academic world, described so vividly by Baker, Wood and
Hearne, is to discover great academic enthusiasm in many quarters but
little corresponding endowment of medieval research on the part of
the academic authorities. Partly, this was due to conservatism, for the
older systems of study at the Universities, though moribund, were
firmly established, and it was difficult to find in them any place for
historical scholarship. David Gregory, the first Regius Professor of
History at Oxford, was right when he informed Lord Townshend in
1728 that the two Universities had been in some measure defective since
they were obliged to adhere so much to the rules laid down by their forefathers', and that 'the old scholastic learning had been for some time
despised, but not altogether exploded, because nothing had been substituted in their place'.[2] Men like Thomas Sprat, who was Bishop of
Rochester from 1684 to 1713, did not hesitate to point out that the
Universities were lagging behind the great intellectual movements of
the age.[3] And if many of the censures levelled at the Universities at this
time were exaggerated, it was none the less true that official opinion at
Oxford, and even also at Cambridge, was bound by a rigid conservatism which was inimical to new ideas, and hostile to schemes of study
that lay outside the circumscribed limits of an outworn curriculum.[4]

The political events of the age also reacted very unfavourably upon
this aspect of University life. Anthony Wood and Roger North, both
zealous supporters of monarchy, were united in the opinion that the
Restoration introduced an unhealthy epoch at both Oxford and Cambridge, and if Zachary von Uffenbach, the German diarist who visited

[1] Cf. SYKES: op. cit., pp. 33-41.
[2] Quoted in Sykes, *Gibson*, p. 106.
[3] SPRAT: *Royal Society, passim.*
[4] AMHERST: *Terrae Filius* (1726), pp. xviii, xix; *Spectator*, No. 43.

both Universities in 1710, was in many ways a prejudiced witness, he none the less confirmed in the early years of the eighteenth century many of the charges which had been brought against the preceding generation.[1] In its turn, the attempt of James II to catholicize the Universities had introduced fresh dissensions, and these were vastly increased when later the Non-juring Schism grievously divided the Colleges. These conditions were not favourable even to intellectual honesty. It was bitterly pointed out that at Oxford a man was deprived of office unless he took the oaths to one king, and debarred from social recognition unless he drank to his deposition by another.'[2] The Universities at this time were in fact too much occupied with their own dissensions to pay a proper attention to fostering scholarship, and academic patronage in consequence became very dependent upon factious influence from outside. Colleges, like Christ Church under Atterbury, were divided for long years by bitter feuds, and every important academic appointment became the subject of scurrilous abuse.[3] 'I have known', remarked *Terrae Filius* in 1726, 'a profligate *debauchee* chosen Professor of *moral* Philosophy, and a fellow who never looked upon the *Stars soberly* in his life Professor of *astronomy*.'[4] Such diatribes need not perhaps be taken too seriously, but undoubtedly many appointments at this time were made for scandalous reasons, and certainly, the prevalence of this factious temper goes far to explain the surprising fact that the ecclesiastical patronage of scholarship during this period so seldom took the obvious form of the creation of University posts to promote historical learning.

Long before the Restoration, it is true, some steps had been taken at both the Universities to satisfy this crying need in English academic life. In 1622 William Camden had founded at Oxford the Chair of History which now bears his name, appointing as its first occupant Degory Wheare whose zeal was a happy augury for the future.[5] Two years later Fulke Greville, Lord Brooke, followed his example by setting up at Cambridge a Chair of History and politics. In both cases, however, the benefactions failed substantially to benefit English medieval scholarship. The Cambridge Professorship was doomed to early extinction,[6] and though no such disaster befell the Camden Chair at

[1] UFFENBACH: *Diary* (MAYOR: op. cit.), *passim.*
[2] AMHERST: *Terrae Filius* (1726), p. 248.
[3] See the letters from Dr. Stratford, Canon of Christ Church, to Edward Harley in *Portland MSS. Rep.*, vol. vii.
[4] AMHERST: *Terrae Filius* (1726), pp. 47, 48.
[5] See *Life of Camden* (Britannia, ed. Gibson, 1772, I, p. xxv); H. STUART JONES, *The Foundation and History of the Camden Chair* (*Oxoniensia*, IX, pp. 170-192).
[6] Samuel Ward to James Ussher, May 16th, 1628 (PARR: *Life of Ussher*, 1686, p. 393).

Oxford, it soon received its modern characteristic of being entirely devoted to ancient history. How far the author of *Britannia* foresaw this development when he made his benefaction is uncertain, for though he certainly charged his Professor with giving readings from ancient historians, Wheare's admirable inaugural lectures apparently covered a much wider field by including a discussion of many topics relating to the medieval history of England.[1] It is possible that if Brian Twine, the Oxford antiquary, had lived to enjoy his promised succession to the office,[2] the history of the Chair might have been different. As it was, the Professorship became almost exclusively concerned with classical antiquity, and though Wheare numbered among his immediate successors men who were personally distinguished, their appointment did not of itself contribute to the advancement of English medieval study.

The absence of any official organization of medieval scholarship in the English Universities between 1660 and 1730 tempts speculation how far a great movement of erudition is dependent upon the regimentation of research. The Spelman lectureship at Cambridge which so profitably assisted the labours of Wheloc and Somner[3] was by far the most successful academic endowment of English history made during the seventeenth century. But shortly after the Restoration it was allowed to lapse; and though William Nicolson later attempted to establish at the same University a similar endowment of Anglo-Saxon learning so that David Wilkins actually enjoyed for a time what he called his 'Saxon pension', this in its turn proved but a temporary expedient.[4] Generally speaking it may be said that the most prolific movement which English medieval scholarship has ever witnessed took place without any great assistance from Professors of History.

Nor were these conditions substantially improved even in 1724, when through the efforts of Edmund Gibson there were established at Oxford and Cambridge the Regius Chairs of Modern History and Languages. Gibson himself was certainly moved in part by a genuine desire to enlarge the University curriculum, and he rightly thought it a duty of the Universities to train men for the service of the State as well as of the Church. The new Professors and their assistants were therefore charged with the instruction of forty scholars carefully selected by the Government. These, it was thought, might be trained as suitable members of the Civil Service, and a detailed report of their

---

[1] Translated with elaborations in 1698 and thus published under the title: *Method and Order of Reading Histories*.
[2] *Life of Camden* (*Britannia*, ed. Gibson, 1772, I, p. xxvi).
[3] See above, p. 61.
[4] NICOLSON: *Epist. Corr.*, p. 447.

progress was to be forwarded annually to the Secretary of State. It is hardly surprising that historical learning did not benefit largely from such a scheme which was part of a design to win over the Universities to the House of Hanover. The business of the new Professors was conceived as the training of competent civil servants whose loyalty to the Government would be unquestioned, and the quality of the early occupants of these Chairs was not such as might extend the restricted scope of their duties. The Government, it was observed, was resolved to keep David Gregory, the Oxford Professor, strictly to his good behaviour, while Samuel Harris, his Cambridge colleague, indignantly denied that his business was anything so pedantic as to foster a school of historical research. Very soon even the limited usefulness of the original project diminished with the advent of abuses, and when the Government allowed the appointment of the scholars to lapse the Professors were allowed to enjoy for the remainder of the eighteenth century the undisturbed repose of an academic sinecure.[1]

In these circumstances the continuous production of works of medieval erudition produced at this time by men trained at Oxford and Cambridge must be regarded as a most remarkable illustration of the prevailing trend of ecclesiastical opinion. So great indeed was the number of learned editions which poured from the University presses at this time that it was made a specific ground of complaint against the English universities by some of their foreign critics. 'All Europe', remarked one of these, 'admires the fine editions of ancient authors which from time to time are published in these Universities, and it is certain that when the English do seriously apply themselves to anything they succeed perfectly in what they undertake; yet all the Protestant part of Europe expects something more than this from Universities so famous.'[2] In his turn, an English writer poured scorn on the 'new accurate Editions of primitive *Fathers* and ancient *Chronicles*' which were the chief production of the Oxford Press – 'the *midwife* in ordinary to *Alma Mater*'.[3] Posterity, however, has had much reason to be thankful for the activity which was thus condemned. Any observer who handles to-day the editions of Bede which were published at Cambridge in 1644 and 1722, or, for example, the Oxford edition of Hickes's *Thesaurus*, will share the admiration of contemporaries for an activity which was so notable an expression of the prevalent zeal for medieval research.

---

[1] SYKES: *Gibson*, pp. 95-105; FIRTH: *English Historica Review*, Jan. 1917.
[2] LE CLERC: *Life of Burnet* (1715), pp. 30-32.
[3] AMHERST: *Terrae Filius* (1726), pp. 53, 54.

The books thus produced were for the most part written by clerics. In many cases their authors were to rise to high places in the Church, and their accomplishment is to be considered as a result of the enthusiasm for these studies which filled the contemporary Establishment. The success of their work depended not on official encouragement given to their studies by academic authority, but rather upon private enterprise backed by ecclesiastical patronage. This patronage was exercised, moreover, far more by means of a judicious allocation of benefices in the country at large than through specific endowments within the Universities. No scholar of outstanding distinction in this period occupied a Chair of History in England, and the growth of historical erudition for which these men were responsible derived not from the creation of such ineffective posts as were originally the Regius Professorships, but from the sustained enthusiasm of individuals who, while yet training as clerics at College, looked out into the world to see the highest dignitaries in the Church acting as the munificent patrons and the zealous exponents of history.

Stupor Mundi Clerus Britannicus:[1] there is, at least in the sphere of historical learning, no reason to dispute the admiring dictum as a description of the Church of England between the Restoration and the death of George I. A modern observer feels inclined to share the despair of a contemporary who found it impossible to do justice to the Anglican achievement in erudition because of 'the great multitude of incomparable scholars therein to be commemorated'.[2] To name such as Hickes, Stillingfleet, John Smith, Humphrey Hody, Henry Wharton and Thomas Gale is itself sufficient to indicate the magnitude of the Anglican accomplishment in this field during these years. These men, moreover, were only part of a larger company which included busy prelates, indefatigable collectors, and a multitude of lesser men working assiduously throughout England. They were drawn from all the contending parties in the Church, and they poured out their conflicting erudition against each other. But it was a common enthusiasm for medieval antiquities which brought together opponents, such as Atterbury and Hody, Hickes and Kennett, into a scholarly community which was a glory to the ecclesiastical fold in which they were all reared. At no other period, before or since, has the Anglican Church been more distinguished as a nursery of medievalists who were a wonder to Europe.

The Anglican Church in the seventeenth century was the natural

---

[1] The version given by Humphrey Hody (*English Councils*, 1710, Preface).
[2] T. PLUME: *Life of Hacket*, Preface.

THE FRIENDS OF CLIO

home of antiquarian learning, but the movement in scholarship which was there fostered was never exclusively ecclesiastical. It received enthusiastic support from English laymen, and in particular it derived much of its vitality from its close association with the interests of the gentlemen of England. At the beginning of this period for example everything possible had been done to stimulate in William Dugdale the scholarly proclivities of the heir to a small but considerable estate, and shortly after its close Browne Willis, the wealthy owner of Whaddon Hall near Bletchley, was to be found so immersed in antiquarian pursuits that, as was said, he 'ruined his fine estate' to support them in others, and at the end of his life was compelled to dress so meanly that many mistook him for a beggar.[1] Some years earlier, Abraham de la Pryme, the historian of Hull who was possessed of a good property in Lincolnshire, had given evidence of a similar enthusiasm:

> 'My zeal for old MSS, antiquities, coins and Monuments' – he wrote – 'almost eats me up so that I cannot prosecute the search of them as I would. I am at very great charges in carrying on my studies of antiquities in employing persons at London, Oxford etc. to search records etc. even to the danger and hazard of my own ruin, and the casting of myself into great debts and melancholy.'[2]

These were but extreme manifestations of a fervour which was very prevalent in the class to which these men belonged. On the eve of the Restoration it certainly informed the activities of the Norfolk associates of Sir Thomas Browne as they appear in the pages of *Hydriotaphia*. Thus one of these was making himself 'no slender master of antiquities' so that 'he could daily command the view of so many imperial faces', and another was busy excavating his fields at Caistor; a third was unearthing gold and silver coins, and yet a fourth was concerning himself with the Roman antiquities of Brancaster.[3] These were the preoccupations of a considerable section of the East Anglian gentry at a time when a bloody Civil War was barely ended, and the English squirearchy was facing a crisis in its history. Nor did the zeal, which was thus exhibited, wane in the years which followed. To turn from the Norfolk of Thomas Browne into another district and into another generation is to encounter the same enthusiasm. When Ralph Thoresby at the beginning of the eighteenth century undertook his peregrinations through the north of England, he was able to record at house after house a critical interest in antiquities; and the large contemporary cor-

[1] NICHOLS: *Literary Anecdotes*, VI, pp. 186-211.
[2] A. DE LA PRYME: *Diary* (Surtees Society, vol. LIV), p. xx.
[3] *Hydriotaphia* (1658), Preface and pp. 14, 18, 19.

respondence of the Gales shows that the northern gentry were every whit as curious in such matters as were their fellows in the south.[1] If such letters were produced by but one section of this class, their number, their scattered provenance and their character suggest that the section was a large one and the antiquarian culture which they reflected was widespread. It even involved some of the foremost ladies of the land. About 1673, for example, the Countess of Huntingdon and the Marchioness of Dorchester were giving contentious evidence of the zeal with which they had studied Baker's *Chronicle*,[2] and when in 1720, Ralph Thoresby paid a visit to Lady Elizabeth Hastings, the benefactress of Queen's College, he and his hostess spent 'the whole time from afternoon prayers till supper' . . . 'perusing some ancient court rolls and charters that her ladyship wanted to understand more fully'.[3] It does not seem too much to suggest that antiquarian studies were a dominant intellectual interest of the English gentry during this period. Nor is it surprising that such a pervasive enthusiasm created an atmosphere peculiarly favourable to the growth of historical scholarship.

The influence of country gentlemen, who drew a lively inspiration to study antiquity from the familiar promptings of local patriotism, was partly responsible for the fine actuality which the more professional scholarship of the age derived from its close association with local investigations. The advance made during these years by English topography and local history forms no part of the subject of this book, but it deserves emphasis how consistently the great medievalists of this period fortified their work by means of local inquiry. At the beginning of this period, for example, it seemed possible that the connection between Dugdale and Thomas Browne might produce a really great history of Norfolk,[4] and though this was never to be written, the finest book from the pen of the former scholar was in fact to be a county history. Dugdale's *History of Imbanking*, again, took its place in an extensive literature relating to the eastern Fens, and in like manner the antiquities which were studied by George Hickes were strictly related by him to the districts from which they came. Wanley interested himself in the history of Essex; Joseph Sparke's edition of chronicles was inspired by the fact that these were derived from Peterborough; and John Smith combined his epoch-making work on Bede as if naturally with the collection of materials for a history of Durham. William

---

[1] THORESBY: *Correspondence, passim; Bibliotheca Top. Britt.*, No. ii.
[2] F. M. POWICKE: *Notes on the Hastings Manuscripts (Huntingdon Library Quarterly)*, I, p. 260.
[3] THORESBY: *Diary*, II, p. 302.
[4] Cf. Dugdale *Correspondence* (HAMPER, pp. 337-352).

Nicolson, whose *Historical Libraries* were long to subserve the needs of students of national history, concerned himself, especially in his *Leges Marchiarum*, with the antiquities of the Border, and Tanner who, before he began his long labours on the *Bibliotheca*, issued his plans for a history of Wiltshire. Similarly (to cite a final example) White Kennett, who wrote a much discussed volume of the *Compleat History of England*, and examined at length the relations between Convocation and Parliament in the Middle Ages, achieved his most enduring work in a book of much more restricted scope. 'Next to the immediate discharge of my holy office,' he wrote, as a country vicar, in 1695, 'I know not how in any course of studies I could better have served my patron, my people and my successors than by preserving the memoirs of this parish . . . which before lay remote from common notice and in a few years had been buried in unsearchable oblivion.'[1] He thus justified his interest in 'Parochial Antiquities', and introduced his fine *History of Ambrosden and other Adjacent Parts*. Not the least important lesson bequeathed by these men to posterity lay in their teaching that neither in the circumscription of purely local interests nor yet in theories divorced from detailed application is to be found the truth of history.

The pious examination of the antiquities of the English countryside made at this time by a multitude of country gentlemen and country clergy thus had its effect upon the scholars with whom this book is concerned, and the enormous production of works of local history which resulted is here to be noted merely as a reflection of the highly instructed public which was ready to sustain the scholars, and to exercise upon them the influence of an informed criticism. Thus was created the atmosphere which made possible their work, and the common interest which linked the scholars to those who supported them was thus admirably exhibited in the new *Britannia* which was a fitting product of the age. The famous book which Camden had originally written in Latin, had passed even before 1607 through numerous editions in England, and it had since been reissued abroad. In 1610, a translation had been made by Philemon Holland, but though Camden himself revised the proof sheets it inadequately represented the original, and when it was reissued in 1637 many injurious alterations were introduced. Apart from this, the original work was ceasing to represent the state of English topographical knowledge, and in 1658 Thomas Browne clearly saw that a revised *Britannia* would fill a wide gap in English scholarship.[2] Towards the end of the century Edmund Gibson,

[1] KENNETT: *History of Ambrosden* (1695), Preface.
[2] *Hydriotaphia* (1658), Preface.

R

then a young man in his twenties at Oxford, undertook the task. His book appeared in 1695, and in it he sought to present Camden to English readers in the form which would be most useful to them, to correct the mistakes which were in the original work, and to supplement the revised edition from printed publications which had appeared since Camden's death. The enterprise was at once recognized as being of considerable importance, and when the second edition appeared in 1722 it was brought further up to date by the inclusion of additional material. It was a comprehensive project and it achieved a large measure of success. The editor of the edition of the *Britannia* which in 1789 was at last to supersede that of Gibson aptly summed up the importance of his predecessor:

> The republick of letters – he wrote – has great obligations to Bishop Gibson. For if Camden first restored antiquity to Britain, and Britain to antiquity, his lordship restored Camden to himself, rescuing him from the confusion of that universal translator *Philemon Holland*, and building on his latest and most improved edition a valuable superstructure.[1]

The value of Gibson's edition of the *Britannia* and in particular its significance as a reflection of the prevailing antiquarian interests of the English public, were to be found in the fact that this was a co-operative work. Gibson was quite incapable of undertaking the task single handed, and he sought and obtained a wide collaboration. Thus, Hugh Todd, the friend of Henry Wharton, contributed to the account of Cumberland, and Tanner to that of Wiltshire. White Kennett dealt with the translation of the part relating to Oxfordshire; Nicolson with Durham and Northumberland; and Cambridgeshire received the attention of Echard. Thoresby concerned himself with the East Riding of Yorkshire; the papers of Sir Henry Spelman were used for the account of Norfolk; and 'the account of the Arsenals for the Royal Navy in Kent with the additions to Portsmouth and Harwich so far as they relate to the Royal Navy were communicated by Mr. Pepys'. Others also contributed, and in no way could the spirit which animated the antiquarian revival in England during the latter half of the seventeenth century be better appreciated than by the contemplation of this distinguished and disinterested company who thus placed their services under the youthful editorship of Gibson. By so doing they produced a work which exactly corresponded to the tastes of the large public in England which was eager to foster medieval research.[2]

[1] R. Gough in his edition of *Britannia*, I, p. ix.
[2] SYKES: *Gibson*, pp. 14-18.

The enthusiasm of the most influential classes in English society for medieval study set an example to men in other walks of life and stimulated an antiquarian curiosity in the most unlikely quarters. Thus Dugdale in recommending a gardener to his friend Lady Archer noted that the 'poore fellow hath a great inclinacion to the love of Armes and Antiquities but the want of meanes and learninge doth keepe him under', and at a later date scholars were called upon to admire the erudition of a penurious tailor in Norwich.[1] Such men were of necessity rare but an equally astonishing manifestation of the prevailing taste was surely supplied when Edward Manlove, a lawyer of Ashbourne in Derbyshire, composed 'in meteer' a treatise on the *Liberties and Customs of the Lead Mines* containing references to original medieval texts. The antiquarian interests of the English gentry were in fact shared by others throughout the length and breadth of the land. While lawyers turned naturally towards precedent, an apothecary could write a history of Halifax[2] and architects like Inigo Jones and Webb could quarrel learnedly about Stonehenge.[3]

There was one profession which was especially affected by this powerful trend in English public opinion. Following the example of Thomas Browne, the doctors of England turned with a surprising readiness from the ministration of the sick to the problems of historical scholarship. Sometimes the transition was easy as when Dr. E. Wilson produced his *Spadocrene Dunelmensis* or 'Short Treatise on an Ancient Medicinal Fountaine or Vitroline Spaw near the City of Durham', but when just before the Restoration Dr. Thomas Witherby started his excavations in the fields of Walsingham,[4] he must surely have left all thought of his patients behind. 'To preserve the living, and make the dead to live', remarked Thomas Browne, 'is not impertinent unto our Profession whose study is Life and Death',[5] and Dr. Robert Thoroton, the historian of Nottinghamshire, in 1677 repeated the same sentiments if with less elegance. 'The Art of Physic', he remarked, '(which I have professed with competent success in this county) not being able for any long time to continue the People living in it, I have charitably attempted, notwithstanding the Difficulty and almost Contrariety of the study, to practise upon the Dead, intending thereby to keep all which is, or can be left of them, to wit the Shadow of their Names (better than precious Ointment for the Body) to preserve their Memory as

---

[1] Dugdale *Correspondence* (HAMPER, p. 152); *Bodleian Letters*, I, p. 271.
[2] See *Dict. Nat. Biog.*, sub. Briercliffe, J.
[3] NICOLSON: *English Historical Library* (1736), p. 26; cf. *A Fool's Bolt soon shot at Stonage* (HEARNE: *Peter Langtoft*, II, p. 481).
[4] *Hydriotaphia* (1658), p. 14.   [5] Ibid., Preface.

long as may be in the World'.[1] Frequently, of course, it must have been difficult to produce books 'composed by snatches of time, as medical vacations, and the fruitless importunity of *Uroscopy* would permit',[2] but the attempt was often made and with great success. Robert Brady and Robert Thoroton are notable among the doctors of this time whose historical studies have outlived in reputation their skill in general practice, but they were members of an extensive company. Here, once again, the great scholars of the age found a sympathetic and critical audience to which they could address their work, and it is remarkable to note the number of doctors who subscribed to the historical treatises of the period.

Between 1660 and 1730 there was thus a large public, lay as well as ecclesiastical, in England eager to welcome and competent to criticize the work of the scholars. Just as in a former age, politicians had turned from the practical affairs of everyday life to investigate the problems of medieval history, so now Sir William Temple could spare time to write his admirable essay on the Norman Conquest, and Lord Halifax could compose a treatise on the Plantagenet kings. These were examples of a concern for antiquities which had come to pervade the society of country gentlemen and the aristocracy of England. The great works of medieval scholarship produced at this time when they come, to-day, into the market, frequently contain the book plate of some contemporary family of distinction. Indeed this interest became so widespread that in 1722 Dr. Samuel Jebb, a physician at Mansfield and later in London, who had already written a biography of Hody, saw fit to engage upon a remarkable venture. Together with Joseph Wasse, then Rector of Aynhoe, he started to produce a periodical devoted to classical and medieval antiquity which by combining articles of a technical character with a discussion of the 'labours of the learned' foreshadowed the modern scholarly review. The length of Wasse's articles was to ruin the project, but between 1722 and 1724 ten numbers of this *Bibliotheca Literaria* appeared, and in their notices of 'what works of Value are preparing for the Press abroad or at home' they attempted to keep an interested public in touch with the outstanding developments of English and continental scholarship. In themselves they provide a striking illustration of contemporary taste.[3]

This widespread interest in medieval antiquity could in fact be illustrated in many ways, but to encounter an aristocratic enthusiasm for

---

[1] THOROTON: *Antiquities of Nottinghamshire* (1677), Preface.
[2] BROWNE: *Vulgar Errors*, Preface.
[3] *Bibliotheca Literaria*, esp. the Introduction to the first number; cf. NICHOLS: *Literary Anecdotes*, VIII, pp. 129, 366, 367; IX, p. 490.

these studies hardly to be paralleled elsewhere in English history it is unnecessary in conclusion to do no more than visit Paternoster Row on Saturday afternoons in the reign of Queen Anne. There, through the winters, the Duke of Devonshire, and the Earls of Oxford, Pembroke, Winchelsea and Sunderland were wont to meet for book hunting expeditions through London. There too, these prominent members of the English nobility were frequently joined by Thomas Britton, 'the musical small-coal man', dressed in his blue smock and carrying the coal sack with which he had in the morning been hawking his wares about the London streets. He was a welcome addition to the party as he was himself an enthusiastic book-collector and the proud possessor of a manuscript copy of Robert of Gloucester.[1] Further comment appears superfluous. And in the contemplation of that strange company moving off in search of the manuscript treasures left by medieval England it becomes perhaps possible at last to penetrate into the very atmosphere which fostered the most fecund growth ever attained by English medieval scholarship.

In these circumstances, a work of pure erudition devoted to a medieval theme stood, at the end of the seventeenth century, at least as good a chance of a remunerative sale as it does to-day. It was a long list of country gentlemen that White Kennett recorded as having done 'honour to their country and to their Families by serving the interest of Mr. Somner',[2] and when Hickes, as a political outcast, issued at a very high price his three huge folios of difficult Latin on the origins of the Teutonic languages he was able to add to them a list of subscribers, headed by twenty-six peers of the realm, longer and more distinguished than could now be found for any similar work. Hearne sold his numerous editions of medieval texts by subscription at half a guinea a volume and amassed a small fortune in the process, and such financial success on the part of a man too busy with the problems of scholarship, and too cantankerous in character to be efficient in business, would have been quite impossible if there had not existed in England a public zealous to read works of technical erudition. If the lists of subscribers to the works of Hearne, Madox and Hickes (to name no others) were assembled together a fair picture would be obtained of the enlightened and generous public which in their time supported the study of English medieval history.

From this company the great patrons of the age stood out only by

---

[1] CAULFIELD: *Remarkable Persons* (Revolution to George II), I, pp. 71-81; HEARNE: *Robert of Gloucester* (1724), I, p. lxxii; HEARNE, *Collections*, V, pp. 103, 104.
[2] KENNETT: *Life of Somner*, pp. 134, 135.

reason of their greater wealth or more sustained enthusiasm. Two generations of Derings in Kent, and two generations of Townleys in Lancashire, were eminent as supporters of medieval learning, and both Dugdale and Joseph Sparke owed much to the family of Brudenell. Sir Henry Spelman, himself a great scholar, was an active supporter of scholarship in others, and his son John inherited his patronage if he did not succeed to his ability. Christopher Hatton the first Baron was noted for his munificence, and his son, the first Viscount, not only studied Anglo-Saxon but left at the last his valuable manuscripts to the Bodleian Library. In 1673 the seventh Earl of Huntingdon when twenty-three years of age offered Dugdale the use of his family papers,[1] and if the Duke of Lauderdale won for himself a sinister reputation in politics, a competent observer could describe him as 'a very learned man and a great favourer and encourager of all such'.[2] In 1713 it was Lord Chief Justice Parker who 'was so munificently indulgent as to be at the expense of cutting a new sett of Saxon types for Mrs. Elizabeth Elstob's Saxon grammar'.[3] The list could in fact be extended to wearisome length. For the fostering of medieval scholarship by the aristocracy of England, which was exemplified in 1644 when Lord Fairfax spared the Records in St. Mary's Tower at York, and stood the friend of Dodsworth[4], never flagged until after the death of George I.

It might perhaps appear that as the seventeenth century drew to its close this encouragement of medieval learning became the affair of a smaller group of persons who acted with a quasi-regal lavishness. In part this impression is created by the extent of the munificence of such as Lord Somers, Lord Halifax and Robert Harley. Somers as Whig Lord Chancellor befriended the Jacobite Hickes, and he later became the consistent patron of Madox. Halifax was chiefly responsible for the undertaking which resulted in Rymer's *Foedera*, and when that work was in danger of languishing for lack of funds, Harley and Somers came to the assistance of the outraged editor. And if the great dynasties of Cotton and Harley must be considered primarily in connection with the magnificent libraries which they founded, their immense services to scholarship were not confined to flinging these open to scholars. They were often the friends of the men whom they supplied with the materials of study. Sir Thomas Cotton placed Dugdale personally in his debt,[5] and his son John admitted Anthony Wood into his domestic

---

[1] POWICKE: op. cit., p. 250.
[2] *Lives of the Norths* (1890), II, p. 302; HEARNE: *Collections*, I, p. 268.
[3] NICHOLS: *Literary Anecdotes*, I, p. 67.
[4] Cf. J. HUNTER: *Three Catalogues*, p. 73.
[5] HAMPER: op. cit., p. 24.

privacy.[1] In the next generation the whole company of scholars looked up to Robert Harley, Earl of Oxford, as the great Maecenas of English medieval learning, and they were right to do so, for he was the correspondent and benefactor of very many of them, and he deserved their gratitude as surely as he earned through his book-collecting the thanks of posterity.

In no way did medieval scholarship at this time derive greater benefit than through the generosity with which the English aristocracy placed at the disposal of scholars the great libraries which they were building up with unexampled zeal. The magnificent library of manuscripts formed by Sir Robert Bruce Cotton in the early years of the seventeenth century, remained an abiding treasure house for historical scholars, but even the supremacy of the Cottonian Library was challenged by the collection which in the early years of the eighteenth century the Harleys amassed at notable speed through the agency of Humphrey Wanley, who by 1715 had so augmented it that it contained more than six thousand manuscripts and about thirteen thousand charters and rolls.[2] Such collecting inevitably outdistanced rivalry, but it had become something of a fashion for the English nobility to vie with each other for the possession of rare volumes, and the libraries of Somers and Halifax, of the Earls of Sunderland, of Cardigan, of Derby and of Carlisle were already, for example, justly famous. Competition became acute. When, for instance, the agent of the Earl of Sunderland secured for his master the Zarottus Virgil after a struggle he threw up his hat in the auction room, and Wanley bitterly complained that such competition was sending up book prices to unreasonable heights.[3] But shrewd observers like William Nicolson were quick to see the importance of such collecting when it was inspired by the enthusiasm of munificent patrons of learning. 'The laudable Emulation', he remarked, 'which is daily increasing amongst the Nobility of England, vying with one another in the Curiosities and other rich Furniture of their respective Libraries, gives chearful Hopes of having the long hidden Monuments of ancient Times raised out of their present Dust.'[4] He was justified in his optimism; for the growth of medieval erudition in England was to owe very much to the activities of noble collectors of books who were the patrons of the scholars who could best use them.

To assess the debt of medieval scholarship to the families of Cotton

[1] WOOD: Life and Times, ii. p. 109.
[2] TURBERVILLE: Welbeck, I, p. 361.
[3] Cf. Wanley's Diary (Lansdowne MS. 771, fol. 50); NICHOLS: Literary Anecdotes, I, p. 90.
[4] NICOLSON: English Historical Library (1736), p. xii.

and Harley would be to trace the course of English historical research from the foundation of these collections to the present day when they repose in the British Museum. But it may at least be noted that both these great libraries were reasonably accessible to students when they were in private ownership. The correspondence of the age, and the diaries of such as Humphrey Wanley, show a long succession of scholars seeking admission to these libraries, and very seldom being turned away. Formed as private ventures, maintained often with difficulty, these great collections seem always to have been regarded by their possessors as something of a public trust to be held in the interests of learning, and in both cases their final and hazardous transference into the hands of the nation seems to have conferred little immediate benefit on scholars since the transition had long been prepared by the generous way in which they were conducted. 'I hope you do me the justice to believe', wrote the daughter of Edward Harley when the public purchase of the library was mooted, 'that I do not consider this a sale for an adequate price. But your idea is so right and agreeable to what I know was my Father's intention that I have a particular satisfaction in contributing all I can to facilitate the success of it.' Here was exactly expressed the motives of men who were throughout acutely conscious of the responsibilities as well as of the joys of collectorship. 'Some tribute of veneration', exclaimed Samuel Johnson some years later, ought surely to be paid to these men and 'to that generous and exalted curiosity which they gratified with incessant searches and immense expense'. It only remains for the modern commentator to add that without their open-handed encouragement of learning the whole development of medieval scholarship in England would have proceeded on other and far less advantageous lines.[1]

The libraries of the aristocracy at this time completely overshadowed that of the King which, presided over by Richard Bentley and his assistant David Casley, could offer no comparable assistance to English learning. Indeed the resources and the conduct of the libraries of the English nobles contrasted very favourably with those formed under other auspices. A German scholar who came to Oxford and Cambridge in 1710 was properly overwhelmed by the number of Old English texts at Cambridge, but nothing seems to have struck him more forcibly than the sorry condition of most of the College Libraries. He was a jaundiced observer. But his complaints of the ignorance and discourtesy of librarians (more noticeable at Oxford than at Cambridge), of the paucity of books, and of the neglect of manuscripts, must have had

[1] EDWARDS: *Founders of the British Museum*, pp. 131-139, 234-244.

some justification in fact.[1] They were echoed by other commentators. Wood's earlier explorations into the libraries of Oxford Colleges had revealed strange interiors,[2] and in a later generation, to judge from contemporary descriptions, conditions had not improved.[3]

Even the University Libraries themselves did not escape a widespread criticism which was the more remarkable since they were vastly enriched during these years. Cambridge in 1715 acquired its famous royal gift of the great collection made by Bishop Moore, and the Bodleian, which had but recently received most of the books of Selden, acquired between 1660 and 1724 not only the collections of Dodsworth and Junius but also valuable additions from other libraries. But, despite these benefactions, the University Libraries played a smaller part in the promotion of medieval learning than did their rivals in the metropolis. In the case of the Bodleian some explanation of this may perhaps be found in the quality of their management. Thomas Hyde, who was Bodley's Librarian from 1665 to 1701 was a learned man, but neither he, nor his successor John Hudson, were well fitted to introduce efficiency into the Library over which they presided,[4] and their assistants, who on occasion seem to have preferred race meetings to their duties, were not always reluctant to make money out of the volumes committed to their charge. When Wanley as Librarian to the Earl of Oxford was offered a gratuity in return for special privileges to examine the Harleian collection, he replied that he would by no means sell his lord's favour.[5] At Oxford things might be different. 'You cannot touch any book in the Bodleian', exclaimed an indignant visitor, 'nor see anything but what the under-librarians choose to show you for a tip.'[6] In view of the work done in the Bodleian during these years it would be unwise to take the complaint too seriously, but in assessing the debt of English scholarship to private patronage the comparison is none the less instructive.

It was the good fortune of English learning that just at the time when the private collections of an earlier generation were being amalgamated into larger libraries, these in their turn were made available to scholars by a cultured aristocracy. Elsewhere the student had to take his chance of being permitted to examine his material, and sometimes

---

[1] WORDSWORTH: *Scholae Academicae*, pp. 2-11; Uffenbach *Diary* (MAYOR: op. cit., pp. 158, 374, 375).
[2] WOOD: *Life and Times*, vol. ii, *passim*.
[3] Cf. AMHERST: *Terrae Filius* (1726), pp. 186, 187.
[4] Cf. MACRAY: *Annals of the Bodleian* (1890), pp. 128-208; cf. *Bodleian Library Record* vol. iii, No. 29 (1950), pp. 40-45.
[5] Lansdowne MS. 771, fol. 31.
[6] Uffenbach *Diary* (MAYOR: op. cit., pp. 374, 375).

he was unfortunate. When James Wright compiled in 1684 his History of Rutland he found many of the local gentry 'very Shy in discovering the Evidences and Conveyances of their several Estates',[1] and when Hearne contemplated his edition of the *Textus Roffensis* in 1720, he was informed that the Dean of Rochester was apprehensive lest publication should make the manuscript itself less valuable.[2] The Muniment Rooms of the Cathedrals were probably then, as now, the least explored, and, with some exceptions, the least accessible of all the great repositories of records, but, in general, the prevailing temper among both clergy and laity was such that the libraries of individuals were freely opened to scholars. Laymen such as Samuel Pepys or John Evelyn were enlightened as well as successful collectors,[3] and though, after Stillingfleet's books had gone to Dublin, and Moore's to Cambridge, few prelates could boast of libraries as distinguished as those which many of the laity were forming, they were mostly eager that their books should be used. White Kennett, for instance, conceived 'the Design of Gathering together an Antiquarian and Historical Library',[4] for the use of his Cathedral Church at Peterborough, and he was not unique in such activities. Sancroft bequeathed part of his Library to his native village of Fressingfield in Suffolk;[5] Catherine North gave many of her books to Rougham in Norfolk;[6] and if the parochial libraries which were being established in England at the beginning of the eighteenth century[7] hardly affected the growth of English medieval scholarship, the private benefactions which created them at least testified to the willingness of the aristocracy to provide for the less fortunate the means of study.

During this period the student of medieval England could scarcely complain of the manner in which materials for his study were, by means of private generosity, made available for his use. His difficulties lay rather in his attempt to discover where his sources lay; and for this reason the notable librarians of the age were men of the first importance in the development of scholarship. The great catalogues which they compiled marked a stage in the growth of medieval erudition. Here once again the aristocracy, both lay and ecclesiastical, performed a signal service, for with the exception of Bernard's Catalogue, and the Bodleian catalogue wrongly attributed to Hudson, all the more important catalogues of the time were undertaken at their instigation. Thus

---

[1] J. WRIGHT: *Antiquities of Rutland* (1684), Preface.
[2] Cf. HEARNE: *Textus Roffensis*, Preface.
[3] Cf. EVELYN: *Diary*, April 29th, 1699; May 7th, 1699; NICOLSON: *Diary* (Cumberland and Westmorland Antiq. Soc.), II, II, p. 40.
[4] *Life of Kennett* (1730), p. 148   [5] D'OYLY: *Sancroft*, II, p. 90.
[6] *Lives of the Norths* (1890), I, p. 7.
[7] Cf. for example OVERTON in *Dict. Nat. Biog.*, sub. Bray, Thomas.

at Lambeth, Wharton worked to the orders of Sancroft, and Wilkins to those of Wake. Thomas Smith, the Non-juror, produced in 1696 the first adequate catalogue of the Cottonian collection, and Wanley's work on the Harleian MSS. which still to-day retains its value, was begun and continued at the express command of his noble patrons. Such labours made the task of the medievalist far easier than it had ever been before; and the great catalogues of the age sponsored by the aristocracy of England made smooth for all subsequent inquirers an approach to research.

No more striking illustration of the services rendered at this time to medieval scholarship by the great private libraries of England could be found than in the contrast which these presented to the public repositories of documents. Though the connection between the Public Records and medieval research was constant through the seventeenth century, it was far less satisfactory at its close than at its beginning. Already by the time of James I scholars had become conscious that in the Public Records, then deposited at Westminster and the Tower, there existed an almost inexhaustible supply of material ready for their need, and already something had been done to make this available for students. Arthur Agarde, Deputy-Chamberlain in the Exchequer, had, for example, compiled before 1615 a description of the records in the Four Treasuries of Westminster, and this was printed in 1631 by Thomas Powell in a volume called the *Repertorie of Records* together with a catalogue of certain Chancery records lying at the Tower. In 1627 the office of General Remembrancer had been established[1] partly, at any rate, to assist the inquiries of investigators. These measures were not without results. Certainly, the great scholars before the Restoration such as Dodsworth and Spelman made abundant use of records, particularly those of the Chancery, and their activities suggest that in the days of Charles I access to the Public Records, and research among them, were not so difficult as might be supposed.[2]

After the Restoration conditions here changed lamentably for the worse. The Civil Wars had led to much loss and more confusion in the Public Records, and, during the Commonwealth, these had been scandalously neglected. When, therefore, in 1661 William Prynne was made Keeper of the Records at the Tower, he found that vast numbers of valuable documents 'through negligence, nescience, and sloathfullness had for many years then past layen buried together in one confused chaos under corroding putrifying cobwebbs, dust, and filth in the

---

[1] AYLOFFE: *Calendars* (1774), pp. xxxi, xxxii.
[2] POWICKE: *Sir Henry Spelman and the Concilia*, pp. 12, 37.

darkest corners of Caesar's chapel in the White Tower'.[1] It was perhaps only his fortunate appointment that rescued an important section of the public archives from complete destruction. Prynne belongs to an earlier age than that with which this book is concerned, and his great work on English archives had already been in all essentials completed before the Restoration. He must therefore make his appearance in these pages simply as an official labouring during the last eight years of his prolific and chequered career to remove from a later generation of scholars one of the greatest impediments to the successful prosecution of their work. Better acquainted with the documents under his charge than was any other man in England, he spared no efforts in his new task. 'I employed', he remarked, 'some soldiers and women to remove and cleanse them from their filthiness; who soon growing weary of this noisome work left them almost as foul as they found them. Whereupon I and my clerks spent many whole days in cleansing and sorting them into distinct confused heaps in order to their future reducement into method, the old clerks of the office being unwilling to touch them for fear of endangering their eyesights and healths by the cankerous dust and evil scent.'[2]

Prynne's labours at the Tower received a proper commendation from subsequent critics who were none the less forced to admit that 'his indefatigable industry' did not 'conquer a tenth part of the work', and in 1703 there were still 'in Caesar's chapel, under the leads of the White Tower, Multitudes of Records laid in confused Heaps . . . in great Danger of utter perishing'.[3] When in November 1704 William Nicolson visited the Tower in the company of the Bishop of Chichester, he was appalled at what he saw. 'When we got into the Chapple', he wrote in his Diary', "twas a great trouble to me to see so many Waggon Loads of Records as are here in the most Dirty and perishing Condition imaginable; many peeping out of Heaps of Dust and Rubbish a yard or two in Depth'.[4] Such conditions elicited a modified approval from a conscientious Government Commission so that it can be imagined what was the situation in the other record offices. The State Paper Office in Whitehall was for example mismanaged throughout this period, and in 1709 it was discovered that 'some records in the Chapter House at Westminster' and 'all in the Office of the Old Court of Wards in Fish Yard' were in a 'perishing condition.'[5]

---

[1] AYLOFFE, op. cit., p. xxxvi.
[2] See EDWARDS: *Founders of Libraries*, pp. 265-268.
[3] NICOLSON: *English Historical Library* (1736), p. xv.
[4] NICOLSON: *Diary* (Cumberland and Westmorland Antiq. Soc.), II, p. 213.
[5] Cf. AYLOFFE: *Calendars* (1774), p. xl.

The historical student of the period might thus well despair of making any proper use of the Public Records, and his difficulties were increased by the fact that even when his documents could be discovered for him, he was liable to be charged large fees before he could inspect them. Conditions had not yet reached the state discovered at the beginning of the nineteenth century by Lord Langdale who, as Master of the Rolls, found that the Public Records were 'dispersed in upwards of sixty different places of deposit all more or less under different management and having as many rules and regulations for their governance'.[1] But the confusion was already great, and it had become clear that it could never be properly removed until the number of repositories was lessened and some sort of centralized control established.

It was left once again to the aristocracy to come to the rescue of the scholar. The same group among the nobility who maintained in their own libraries such a very different state,[2] strove also to effect among the Public Records a reform in the interests of learning. Soon after the accession of William III Halifax turned his attention to the Public Records, and by 1703 a committee of the House of Lords including Somers and Harley was formed under his Chairmanship 'to inspect the method of keeping records in offices and to consider of ways to remedy what should be found to be amiss'. This Committee was for some time annually renewed, and through its recommendation and in particular through the appointment of four additional assistant clerks, some improvement was made in the conditions at the Tower. In 1704, for example, Nicolson could watch 'the new-appointed clerks sorting the long neglected and confused records into Baskets',[3] and on January 21st, 1709-10, Ralph Thoresby, having walked to the Tower, professed himself 'mightily pleased with the new and excellent method the Records are put into'.[4]

The same group in the House of Lords concerned itself with the other record offices also. In 1705 a petition was made to the Queen to reform the State Paper Office, and four years later yet another committee attacked the abuses of the Westminster chapter house. Nor did the efforts of these men cease after 1714. A commission presided over by Lord Macclesfield reported in 1719 on the conditions at Westminster, and after the fire at the Cotton Library in 1731, a new committee

[1] T. D. HARDY: *Memoirs of Lord Langdale* (1852), II, p. 143; cf. ibid., II, pp. 111-194.

[2] In June 1702 Nicolson recorded in his *Diary* that he visited the library of Samuel Pepys and found it 'arranged in 9 cases finely gilded and sash glassed'. 'The Books', he added, 'are so well ordered that his Footman after looking at the catalogue could lay his finger on any of 'em blindfold' (NICOLSON: op. cit., II, p. 40).

[3] NICOLSON: op. cit., II, p. 214.

[4] THORESBY: *Diary*, II, p. 26.

was set up to inquire into the whole state of the public records.[1] The work performed by these committees has been unduly disparaged because they failed to prevent the abuses of a later generation, but their immediate influence was notable and beneficent. It was mainly owing to them that in spite of all difficulties much research into the public records was in fact actually carried out between 1660 and 1730, and that in particular the outstanding performance of Rymer and Madox was made possible. During this period, the contents of the Public Record Offices became better known than they had ever been before. By comparison with the great private libraries of the time, the state of these offices was lamentable, but the same men who so enthusiastically sponsored the growth of learning in the spheres directly under their control, sought also to ameliorate the conditions of medieval research in official quarters that were as yet unresponsive to their high ideals.

The character of the support given to English medieval scholarship between 1660 and 1730 was unique in Europe. It attracted the attention of continental scholars who were quick to see how widely it differed from that supplied abroad. It was characteristic of this country that a great movement in erudition should thus have depended upon individual enterprise backed by private munificence. The English production in works of medieval scholarship during this period was at least as prolific as that of France, but it consisted of the work of individuals and not of official publications. It was, moreover, not only the nature of the English encouragement of this branch of learning that won the admiration of foreigners but its success. When, for example, a learned German was shown by Thwaites a copy of Hickes's *Thesaurus*, he exclaimed: 'By God, France never produced anything more sumptuous or more magnificent than this even under the patronage of Louis the Great.'[2] In truth, the English aristocracy both lay and ecclesiastical here played much the same part as that assigned in France to Versailles, for, after the Revolution, the Crown was never in a position to concentrate in itself the responsibilities of learned patronage. It is noteworthy that the official favour extended to Rymer was intermittent, and compared very badly with that exercised by private persons on behalf of other scholars. With the partial exception of the *Foedera*, England between 1660 and 1730 saw nothing comparable to the series of historical works which poured from the French press 'with the privilege of the King'. Here as elsewhere the great gentlemen of England

---

[1] *Report of the Lords' Committees* (1719); AYLOFFE: *Calendars* (1774), pp. xxxvi-xl; GALBRAITH: *Public Records* (1934), p. 68.

[2] 'Per Deum, nihil Gallia sub auspiciis Ludovici Magni magnificentius aut augustius edidit.' Quoted in a letter of Hickes to Charlett, Dec. 29th, 1713 (*Bodleian Letters*, I, p. 267).

seized upon the prerogatives of the Crown, and admirably discharged a function which they regarded as an honour as well as a duty. 'It is observed', wrote Madox in 1711, 'that the Science of Antiquities hath in this last age been cultivated in England with more industry and success than in several ages before', and he gave it as his opinion that the chief explanation of this was the 'Encouragement which hath been given to These Studies by several Persons of Eminent Learning and Superior Order in the Realm'.[1] Certainly, the rapid growth of English medieval scholarship during this period owed very much to the English aristocracy who had no reason to feel ashamed of the results of their munificence.

It is very easy to ridicule the circumstances that attended the private patronage of letters in the early years of the eighteenth century, and the fulsome compliments of contemporary dedications have nourished the self-satisfaction of an age which prefers the flattery of a large public to the delectation of a patron. But hasty writing designed to extract money as rapidly as possible from the largest number of pockets is not necessarily a better means of producing good books than the effort to please the exigent taste of a cultured and wealthy class. The ideal lies, doubtless, somewhere between the two extremes. If Gibbon was right when he declared that literature thrives best when it is half a trade and half an art, the same is even more true of scholarship which needs, not only some contact with public opinion, but also some freedom from the exigencies of supply and demand. The endowment of unremunerative learning has been a constant concern of modern England, and the means taken to achieve this laudable end have each carried with them their own defects. But the closing years of the seventeenth century will stand comparison in this respect both with the periods which preceded them and with those which followed. For then the Church was ready to use its large endowments to promote the learning they were designed to foster; and then the laity were capable of supplying a class of patrons who were both munificent and discriminating. The scholars of this age had sometimes to endure the buffets of ecclesiastical faction, and of aristocratic caprice. But, in the main, they had no reason to complain of the reception of their work or of the manner in which they were encouraged. They were sustained on a wave of public enthusiasm for the studies to which they gave their lives. And the greatest age of English medieval learning was conditioned not only by the appearance of a long series of pre-eminent scholars but by the warm approval and the critical support given to their work by a large section of educated England.

[1] MADOX. Exchequer (1711), p. i.

CHAPTER XIII

THE END OF AN AGE

Comfort me by a solemn assurance, that, when the little parlour, in
which I sit at this instant, shall be reduced to a worse furnished box, I
shall be read with honour by those who never knew nor saw me, and
whom I shall neither know nor see.

FIELDING: *Tom Jones*, Bk. XIII, Chap. 1.

THE scholars who are commemorated in this book came from
two, or at the most three, generations of Englishmen, and their
achievement covered the span of but one man's life. Less than
half a century separated the deaths of Dugdale and Madox, of Philipps
and Wanley, or of Brady and Hearne, and during the intervening
period, the younger men had been linked to their elders by an intimate
exchange of thought. Opposed on many burning questions of faith
and policy, they had been united in their approach to the past. Their
research had a common quality which enabled them to profit by every
discovery which they made, and each to take his own share in an endeavour that was general to them all. They contended together, but,
so to speak, in the same language; and their differences ensured rather
than impaired the continuity of their inquiries. The torch was passed
easily among them, and the younger men arrived appositely to shoul-
der the burdens which their predecessors had laid down. The investigations of Dugdale, Brady and Rymer were as intimately connected
as were those of Somner, Thwaites, and Wanley, and while the editorship of Fulman and Gale supplied the starting point for the labours of
Hearne, so also did Spelman, Tanner, and Wake form a close succession
in the study of ecclesiastical antiquities. A community of learned
interests, a harmony of scholarly aims bound these men together, and
it was an uninterrupted effort which was above all else responsible for
their corporate achievement.

But as the eighteenth century advanced, the surviving members of
this succession began one after another to disappear. Their co-operative
effort proceeded with gradually decreasing momentum, and the din of
their controversies gave place to an ironic silence. Thwaites died in
1711, Rymer in 1713, and Hickes two years later. Wanley's death in
1726 was followed by those of Madox and Nicolson in the next year,
and the succeeding decade removed Tanner, Hearne, and Wake. These

men had been knit together in their concern for antiquity, and their related efforts had sustained without pause a great movement in scholarship. They left few successors, and their passing marked the end of a period.

Medieval scholarship in England underwent during the eighteenth century not a development but a reaction. These studies between 1730 and 1800 made no advance comparable to that which had been achieved in the previous seventy years. The stultifying of so promising a growth, the slackening of an endeavour which had been marked by such devoted labour was a phenomenon in the development of English culture which was very remarkable. In all the branches of a research which had for so long occupied many of the best minds of England there appeared a decreased effort. The line of great 'Saxonists' which had been graced by Hickes and Wanley came to an end so that, with the solitary exception of the *Dictionary* compiled by Edward Lye and published in 1772, no outstanding contribution was made to Old English studies in the latter part of the eighteenth century.[1] The efflorescence in the study of ecclesiastical history which had marked the Convocation Controversy and had produced the *Concilia* of 1737, ceased with the establishment of new relations between Church and State.[2] The editing of medieval texts which had so long occupied the attention of men like Thomas Gale and John Smith suddenly stopped. 'Ever since the time of Thomas Hearne', wrote a contributor to the *Gentleman's Magazine* in 1788, 'the publication of our old historic writers has been discontinued.'[3] He was scarcely exaggerating. 'The age of Herculean diligence which could devour and digest whole libraries is passed away,'[4] wrote Gibbon in his old age when referring to the writers of the previous century. He was lamenting the disappearance of 'those heroes whose race is now almost extinct'.

This sudden sterility excites surprise. It commands explanation. For more than a hundred years the intellectual temper of England had encouraged the growth of a flourishing school of medieval study, and there are few more notable changes in the development of English culture than that which rapidly transformed this climate of opinion so that by the middle of the eighteenth century the leaders of English taste had come to profess almost a hatred of the past, and a disdain for those who explored it. In the year of Hearne's death, Bolingbroke saw fit to express 'a thorough contempt for the whole business of these learned

---

[1] Cf. D. N. Smith: *Warton's History of English Poetry* (1929), p. 8.
[2] W. Stubbs: *Seventeen Lectures* (1900), p. 381.
[3] See Gibbon: *Misc. Works*, III, p. 595.
[4] Gibbon: *Address recommending Mr. Pinkerton (Misc. Works*, III, p. 571).

lives; for all the systems of chronology and history that we owe to the immense labours of a Scaliger, a Bochart, an Ussher, or even a Marsham'.[1] Devotees of Reason were content to use the labours of their predecessors, but they relied upon a criticism which was fundamentally unhistorical. Locke and Butler had learnt little from Dugdale and Rymer, and had nothing to teach them.[2] Political speculation produced a social contract incapable of historic proof, and the quest for precedent became wearisome to those who found in the existing English constitution the best mechanism ever devised to satisfy the temporal needs of man. In the State, complacency saw no advantage in investigating the growth of political structure at less fortunate periods. In the Church, the place once occupied by Stillingfleet and Wake was taken by men who professed an open contempt for ecclesiastical history. Historical investigation withered in an atmosphere of abstract Cartesianism which neglected development, and by insisting upon the uniformity of human thought, discouraged the study of the distinguishing growth of diverse nations.

Any division between epochs must of course admit modification. The opinions which at a later date were to be so deleterious to medieval scholarship in England had been freely expressed in this country before the beginning of the eighteenth century, and in the writings of Burnet, of Atterbury and of Temple there could be found plentiful evidence of the approaching change in English intellectual life. Conversely, in the years which followed the accession of George II, research into English medieval history still found some devoted adherents. It was not until 1767 that George, Lord Lyttelton, began to publish his massive life of Henry II, and Abraham Farley's great edition of Domesday Book which appeared in 1783 would have been a monument to the medieval scholarship of any learned age. The literary and antiquarian societies of the time met the needs of an interested public which read the *Gentleman's Magazine*, and the investigation of local antiquities was continued in many of the country houses of England. The eighteenth century was to produce its own great contribution to the antiquarian description of the counties of England, and in the sphere of local history the break between the two epochs was less marked than elsewhere. In many ways the influence of the earlier scholars – their concern with the past and their respect for tradition – was to persist into an age which reacted against their preoccupations. It was significant that Edward Gibbon, as a representative English man of letters, should

[1] BOLINGBROKE: *Study of History* (*Works*, ed. 1754, II, pp. 261-262).
[2] Cf. R. H. GRETTON: *History*, p. 14.

give his life to 'making literature out of dead empires',[1] and a few years after his death the preponderating opinion of his countrymen was that the cap of liberty should be fashioned slowly out of ancient stuff.

Nevertheless, when all proper qualifications have been made, it remains impossible to escape the conclusion that, about 1730, the development of English medieval scholarship underwent profound modification; and, when due note has been taken of the performance of individuals, the general contrast between these two ages of English learned culture still appears pronounced. The impulse which had driven the earlier scholars to their work weakened and died, and research languished with the decay of the motives which had inspired it. To men of the temper of Dugdale and Hickes, the mainspring of inquiry had been that in the exploration of the past was to found alike the justification of religious belief and the guide to patriotic action. But an Age of Enlightenment could afford to be ignorant of the centuries which had preceded it, and the minute investigation of history became an occupation unworthy of a man of sensibility. History which had been styled 'fundamentum doctrinae' now entertained the dilettanti. Horace Walpole might amuse himself with a panegyric of Richard III, but he and his like were chiefly concerned to dress up the products of antiquarian research in attractive garb, and to parade the result as a new toy. Even as he studied the past, he jested at those who made it a serious business. 'We antiquarians', he murmured, 'who hold everything worth preserving merely because it has been preserved!'[2] The fiery zeal of the scholars degenerated into a prying devoid of reverence, into a mild curiosity destitute of serious purpose.

Scepticism of the value of all historical evidence came, in its turn, to blight production. From the time of the Restoration it had been an object of English medieval scholarship to set up more exacting standards of criticism. 'This is the *Work* we propose to be encouraged', wrote Thomas Sprat in 1674, 'which at once regards the discovering of new *Secrets* and the purifying and repairing all the profitable things of *Antiquity*.'[3] In historical study the labours of John Smith on Bede, and of Hickes on charters, had marked an epoch in this respect, and the lives of Wanley and Madox had been given to testing the sources of history by minute criticism. To amateurs of abstract theory, however, such investigations seemed hardly to justify the labour they entailed.

[1] Cf. G. M. YOUNG: Gibbon, p. 76.
[2] *Historic Doubts on the Life and Reign of King Richard III* (1768); cf. GIBBON: *Misc. Works*, III, pp. 331-349; SOMERS: *Tracts*, III, pp. 316 *sqq.*
[3] SPRAT: *Royal Society* (1784), p. 436.

We must consider – said Dr. Johnson – how very little history there is; I
mean real authentick history. That certain Kings reigned and certain battles
were fought we can depend upon as true; but all the colouring, all the philosophy of history is conjecture.[1]

The discussion which ensued illustrated a reaction far more severe than
that which in historical scholarship had taken place at the Restoration.
Then, the rebellion against authoritarian tradition had served not to
discourage medieval research but to increase its objectivity. Now, such
research was not merely criticized for its methods: its very usefulness
was denied. At times the new scepticism could be as uncritical as the
credulity it sought to correct. Bolingbroke's vague assertions were
often less 'scientific' than those of the antiquaries he derided, and even
Gibbon, when he wrote of feudalism, composed an essay[2] that is now
more obsolete than that which Henry Spelman had written more than
a hundred years before. The fashion of disbelieving testimony served
on occasion for the exposure of legend, but it led more frequently to
superficial performance. It discouraged detailed criticism at the same
time as it lauded the virtues of doubt.

The failure of eighteenth-century England adequately to develop
the medieval scholarship it inherited is partly also to be explained by
the form in which that legacy was received. The mighty achievement
of a hundred years of self-effacing effort was not to be lightly mastered
by mildly curious gentlemen of culture who, then as now, wandered
about the outer corridors of that majestic house of learning, and were
surprised to find them a trifle cold. The stark presentation of learning
which had seemed proper to Wharton and Wake repelled superficial
study, and the arbiters of Augustan elegance were quick to denounce
what to them was 'impolite'. 'I know, my Lord,' wrote Madox as early
as 1711, 'the Lovers of Antiquities are commonly looked upon to be
men of a Low unpolite genius fit only for the Rough and *Barbarick*
part of Learning.'[3] 'That of low Genius', added Elizabeth Elstob, 'is
not the worst Charge which is brought against the *Antiquaries*, for
they are not allowed to have so much as Common Sense, or to know
how to express their Minds intelligibly.'[4] The 'literary' historian of the
Enlightenment was more anxious to be a man of taste than a man of
learning. He performed good work in denouncing research whose end
might be merely compilation, but if, at his best, he could extend the

---

[1] BOSWELL: *Life of Johnson* (ed. Hill, 1887), II, pp. 365, 366.
[2] GIBBON: *Du Gouvernement Féodale surtout en France* (*Misc. Works*, III, 183-202).
[3] MADOX: *Exchequer* (1711), p. ii.
[4] *Rudiments of Grammar* (1714), p. xxx.

scope of history as a form of intellectual inquiry, the elegance of his work was frequently achieved at the expense of depth. The best criticism of the intellectual movement which produced him came from one who towered above him in the very excellences to which he aspired. Edward Gibbon was the greatest historical stylist of his age. He could take a detached view of English national culture, and he cultivated a 'humanity' which made him unsympathetic to the earlier scholars whose work he used. But, a scholar himself, he could temper his admiration of Voltaire with censure of a mentality that disdained erudition, and he ruefully contrasted 'the taste for true learning which prevailed in the seventeenth century with the present taste uniting much indifference about theology with superficiality of learning and boldness in philosophy'.[1]

A great age of medieval scholarship in England inevitably closed when the most representative exponents of English history became so disdainful of the culture of their predecessors as to refuse to follow them in a detailed investigation of the past. The fierce desire of the elder scholars to discover in antiquity the foundation of belief faded away to leave nothing in its place to serve as a stimulus to research. Elegance rather than accuracy became the ideal of historians who could scarcely approach the books of their forerunners without the patronizing smile proper to superior beings. Historical details once so eagerly sought came to be regarded (in Voltaire's phrase) as 'the vermin which destroy books', or as useless lumber detrimental to intellectual clarity.[2] Philosophic generalization begat a contempt for erudition, and the men who had given their lives to the service of exact scholarship were despised as at best the drudges who had collected material for the lofty speculations of men of sensibility. 'These men', wrote Bolingbroke with sublime impertinence, 'court fame as well as their betters by such means as God has given them to acquire it. They deserve encouragement while they continue to compile and neither affect wit nor presume to reason.'[3] It was a measure of the magnanimity of Gibbon, and of his intellectual stature, that almost alone among his fellows he could confess his debt to men whose spiritual temper was so different from his own. But even Gibbon could not escape the condescension of his generation. 'The antiquary who blushes at his alliance with Hearne', he remarked, 'will feel his profession ennobled by the name of Leibnitz.'[4] Technical research had ceased to be a proper occupation for a

[1] Cf. YOUNG: op. cit., pp. 72, 77.
[2] Cf. DAWSON: *Edward Gibbon* (1934), p. 4.
[3] BOLINGBROKE: *Study of History* (*Works*, ed. 1754), II, p. 261.
[4] GIBBON: *Address recommending Mr. Pinkerton* (*Misc. Works*, III, p. 568).

gentleman; it needed the apology of a light excuse. 'The view of so many manuscripts of different ages and characters', wrote Gibbon of his visit to Paris in 1763-4, 'induced me to consult the great Benedictine works, the *Diplomatica* of Mabillon and the *Palaeographia* of Mont-faucon. I studied the theory without attaining the practice of the art; nor should I complain of the intricacy of Greek abbreviations and Gothic alphabets since every day in a familiar language I am at a loss to decypher the hieroglyphics of a female note.'[1]

This decline of technical research was of itself sufficient to check the further progress of English historical studies. But the end of the epoch of antiquarian erudition was marked more specifically by a conscious neglect of the particular subject which these scholars had made their own especial province. These men had established the study of medieval England, but after their passing there were few who aspired to build upon the foundations which had been so securely laid down. 'All history', said Voltaire, 'is almost equal for those who merely wish to store their memories with facts. But whoever thinks or (what is more rare) whoever possesses taste only counts four centuries in the history of the world.'[2] This limitation of interest to the age of Pericles, the epoch of Augustus, the Italian renaissance, and the reign of Louis XIV, was accepted by many of Voltaire's English contemporaries, and long before his time prejudice had been growing in certain quarters that the Middle Ages in particular were unworthy of the attention of men of culture. 'The Authors of those barbarous and illiterate Ages are few and mean,' wrote Sir William Temple in 1695, 'and perhaps the rough Course of those lawless times and Actions would have been too ignoble a Subject for a good Historian.'[3] Much later, Hume, misrepresenting the sense of Milton, quoted him with approval as deriding the history of Saxon England: 'Such bickerings to recount met often in these our Writers what more worth is it than to Chronicle the Warrs of Kites or Crows flocking and fighting in the Air?'[4] The study of the Middle Ages was not merely 'impolite'; it was positively to be forbidden as a waste of time tending to degrade culture. Horace Walpole expressed the wish that Gibbon 'had never heard of the Monophysites or Nestorians or any such fools',[5] and Lord Chesterfield, though he

---

[1] GIBBON: *Memoirs of my Life and Writings* (*Misc. Works*, I, pp. 175, 176).
[2] VOLTAIRE: *Siècle de Louis XIV*, quoted Dawson, op. cit., p. 17; TEMPLE: *Introduction to the History of England* (1695), Preface.
[3] TEMPLE: *Introduction to the History of England* (1695), Preface.
[4] HUME: *History of England*, vol. I, chap. i. His misrepresentation of Milton in this passage is commented on by Pinkerton (see GIBBON: *Misc. Works*, III, p. 606). The original sentence is to be found in MILTON: *History of Britain* (ed. 1671), p. 183.
   Cf. DAWSON: op. cit., p. 13.

admitted that Modern History 'begins properly with Charlemagne in the year 800', hastened to add to his schoolboy son that 'a general notion of what is rather supposed, than really known to be, the history of the five or six following centuries seems to be sufficient; and much time would be but ill employed in a minute attention to those legends'.[1] The advice was in strict harmony with the instruction of Bolingbroke who when speaking of the sixteenth century could confidently assert:

> To be entirely ignorant about the ages that precede this aera would be shameful. Nay some indulgence may be had to a temperate curiosity in the review of them. But to be learned about them is a ridiculous affectation in any man who means to be useful to the present age. Down to this aera let us read history: from this aera and down to our time let us study it.[2]

Certainly 'a temperate curiosity' was not the emotion which had driven the scholars to their enduring achievement.

While such sentiments pervaded lay society a similar transformation took place in the intellectual interests of the Anglican Church. 'The Monks finished what the Goths began'; and as the epithet 'Gothic' came, until the advent of a new romanticism, to be applied in disdain to all things medieval, so did the adjective 'monkish' serve to excuse in ecclesiastics their neglect of the learning of their immediate predecessors. As early as 1693 Burnet had professed himself 'not at all out of countenance to own that I have not much studied these Authors. The little that I have studied did not encourage me to go further than to convey to my mind a true view of the state of the Church in those times from which I might be able to judge of the Necessity of a Reformation.'[3] Burnet was given his answer by Henry Wharton, and his attitude was not allowed to prevail in the church of Stillingfleet and Thomas Gale. Not until the latter years of the primacy of Wake did such a temper begin to be predominant in Anglican opinion. The future was with Hoadly; and Hoadly was, in reality, antipathetic not only to the Non-juring High Churchmen whom he specifically denounced, but also to the great medievalists among the Whig bishops who had but recently brought to its climax the most productive period in the study of English church history. Burnet had 'raked together all the Dirt he could to throw at the Monasteries'. His later successors in the Church adopted a more intransigent attitude in advocating ignorance concerning those centuries to which they felt so superior. 'Church History making an important part of our theologic studies',

---

[1] CHESTERFIELD: *Letters to his Son*, No. cxiii.
[2] BOLINGBROKE: *Study of History* (*Works*, ed. 1754, II, p. 360).
BURNET: *Letter to the Bishop of Coventry and Litchfield* (1693), p. 15.

wrote one of the most influential of Georgian prelates, 'the antiquarian who delights to solace himself in monkish owl-light sometimes passes for the Divine.'[1] It was the direct negation of the temper which had made the Anglican Church for a hundred years the nursery of medievalists, and its prelates the outstanding patrons of History.

Medieval English scholarship was thus stifled during the eighteenth century by the deliberate neglect of an Age of Enlightenment. It was also stultified by the scorn of those who, nurtured in an earlier tradition, looked somewhat wistfully across the 'arid wastes' which separated them from the lofty heights of classical culture. When Gibbon, who was a child of the Renaissance rather than a disciple of Voltaire, sought with all the resources of his splendid intellectual equipment to drive a road across the intervening centuries, it was significant that he should record the decline and fall of the old civilization rather than the process by which the long pathway of the Roman genius merged into the Via Sacra of the Cross. Gibbon was as incapable of appreciating the positive achievements of medieval culture as he was of assessing truly the significance of Byzantine history, and it was fortunate that he did not amplify in his great book the sketch of the thirteenth century which he included in his early essay on the History of the World. His approach to the sources of medieval history was far more informed than that of most of his contemporaries, but it was tinged with the same condescension. 'I am *almost* a stranger to the voluminous sermons of Chrysostom,' he wrote, 'my personal acquaintance with the Bishop of Hippo does not extend beyond the *Confessions* and the *City of God*.' The irony discounted the implied modesty, and no one among the seventeenth-century scholars would have referred his readers to Ussher 'for all that learning can extract from the rubbish of the Dark Ages'.[2] It was perhaps symptomatic of contemporary taste that Gibbon never followed his early inclination to write the history of medieval England, but it seems possible that his opinions on the subject, and his judgments of the men who had investigated it, mellowed and changed.[3] Towards the close of his life he sought to inaugurate the Publication of our Latin Memorials of the Middle Ages, and his final comments deserve emphasis as perhaps the best summary of the decline of English medieval studies during the age which he adorned:

[1] FIGGIS: *William Warburton* in *Typical English Churchmen from Parker to Maurice*, pp. 219-220.
[2] GIBBON: *Decline and Fall*, ed. Bury, III, pp. 375, 407.
[3] Compare the tone of the *Outlines of the History of the World*, written between 1758 and 1763 with that of the *Address recommending Mr. Pinkerton*, written in 1793. (*Misc. Works*, III, pp. 1-156 and pp. 559-578.)

The consideration of our past losses – he wrote in 1793 – should incite the
present age to cherish and perpetuate the valuable relics which have escaped,
instead of condemning the MONKISH HISTORIANS silently to moulder in the
dust of our libraries; our candour, and even our justice, should learn to estimate their value and to excuse their imperfections.[1]

His advice was soon to be followed in England when shortly after the
beginning of the next century the official publication of medieval
records began in earnest, and the sponsors of that movement found it
necessary to link up their work not with the culture of the eighteenth
century but with the learning of the earlier scholars.

Men are wont to accord a readier sympathy to the prejudices of their
grandfathers than to the pre-occupations of their parents; and the
criticism by any age of the intellectual tastes of its immediate predecessor is a recurrent phenomenon in the history of thought. But at
certain times, and with particular subjects, the reaction may be accen-
tuated, and the reception of medieval learning by England in the
eighteenth century may thus be regarded. Men concerned to deride a
scholarship which had become uncongenial found little difficulty in
exposing the defects of an erudition which they could not emulate.
The earlier scholars had without doubt sometimes confused the antiquary with the historian; doubtless, too, though more rarely, they had
forgotten interpretation in the accumulation of fact; and in their books
they certainly neglected to present the results of their labour attrac-
tively. They needed the reminder that the search for historic truth may
be expanded into a survey of civilization, and that the immediate purpose which inspires it must be controlled by objective detachment.
History, as Gibbon insisted, is not only a branch of literature, it is also
'a science of cause and effect.'[2] His advice was apposite. But historians
who were more representative of the opinions of eighteenth-century
England went far further than in supplying such salutary correction. In
the name of culture they disdained the motives, and despised the
labours, which alone can fructify medieval research. There is a happy
mean in scholarship between the lowest degree of credulity compatible
with learning, and the highest pitch of scepticism consistent with effort.
That condition was probably approached in England far more nearly
between 1660 and 1730 than during the seventy succeeding years.

Between the Restoration and the death of George I circumstances in
England had been peculiarly favourable to the prosecution of medieval
studies. Some consideration of the magnificent achievement which

[1] GIBBON: *Address recommending Mr. Pinkerton* (*Misc. Works*, III, p. 561).
[2] *Essai sur l'Etude de la Litterature* (*Misc. Works*, IV, pp. 63 sqq.).

resulted has been attempted in these pages, and if it has been necessary to
protest against the neglect with which this has sometimes been treated,
it has also become apparent how surely this learning became embedded
in the work of a later age, when, after the eighteenth-century reaction,
an interest in medieval antiquities was again revived in England. No
informed student of Old English history can, to-day, afford to neglect
his debt to Hickes and the great 'Saxonists', and no worthy investigator
of ecclesiastical antiquities is likely to forget his obligation to Wake and
to Wilkins. Brady and Philipps illuminated the Anglo-Norman period,
and if modern editions have largely (though not entirely) supplanted
the books of Wharton, Hearne, John Smith, and Thomas Gale, their
very excellence has in great part derived from the labours of these
scholars. In the successful application of exact criticism to medieval
materials Wanley, Tanner, and Madox differed from their best modern
successors only in the immensity of their production. The results of
this scholarship, which was so extensive and so profound, were attained
in the teeth of difficulties of which the modern student has no experience; its success was achieved by means of labour of which he is incapable. The quality of a great age of learning can only be appreciated
by a study of the books it produced, and of the men who made them.
It may be added, however, that students are wont to find their admiration increasing in proportion to their own proficiency and knowledge.
Certainly, the warmest praise which has here been cited of the work of
these scholars has come from those best qualified to pass judgment
upon them. In modern times the greatest English medievalists have
been precisely those who have held seventeenth-century scholarship
in the highest esteem.

The scholars of that time left behind them a contribution to medieval
erudition which, in its full content, has not yet been superseded. But
their influence was not circumscribed even by the range of their immense learning. They were men of importance, and their research was
intermingled with the affairs of their country. By force of character
and vigour of action they compelled the respect of their fellows, and
their intrepidity was woven into the strenuous life of their age. Thus
Dugdale had gone into exile, Brady had faced the ire of Parliament,
and Hickes, himself a proscript, had given to his friends a last fare-
well at the gibbet. The lesser men in this company were also of such
character that they could not be ignored. Fabian Philipps defying the
London crowd, Hearne hurrying with his note-books through the
Oxford streets, Wharton standing at work in his study, were figures
which demanded attention. An air of personal distinction surrounded

them, and they were fashioned in no common mould. In their successful prosecution of research they can challenge comparison with their
fellows in any age, but it was not solely through their books that they
exercised their influence upon England.

They fostered qualities in the English character which have in no
small measure been responsible for the greatness of this land. They
reflected in the nation a reverence for the past, and during an age of
change they taught her to rely upon traditional wisdom rather than
novel doctrine. Whether Parliamentarian or Royalist, whether Whig
or Tory, they were all concerned to insist, throughout an era of critical
transformation, that political structure and public policy must be based
upon the essential character of the nation as discovered in its past history. Both the Non-jurors and the Whig Bishops who opposed them
approached even the problems of Revolution through the study of
antiquity. English stability has gained much from this insistence upon
tradition. Her social customs have acquired a special vitality from being
the outcome of slow growth; her political structure has been founded,
not on clear-cut theories claiming universal validity, but on com-
promises derived from precedents eagerly sought. During the seventeenth century an enduring stamp was set upon the English character,
and though during that momentous age this country passed through
many upheavals, she never then or since experienced a revolution based
upon doctrinaire principles. She owed much to her scholars, and her
debt to them is perhaps not yet exhausted. They bequeathed to the
nation a sense of development that might be proof against the fascina-
tions of the temporary phase.

These scholars who made the motives of public policy depend so
strictly upon an examination of past history, who made even change
subserve an inherent continuity, fortified the mind of England. A dis-
trust of abstract theory, a reliance upon national experience, has been
a source of English strength. The English have seldom profited by
systems of thought; they have combined a vigorous grasp of facts with
a comparative indifference to theory. Suavity of expression has rarely
for itself carried conviction among them, and neat generalizations they
have been prone to fear. They tend to demand evidence for dogma,
and, unimpressed by eloquence, they have set more value upon the
hard-won products of research than on the wide doctrines of detached
reasoning. Bolingbroke might praise the theorist at the expense of the
man 'who declines the business of the world that he may dedicate his
whole time to the search for truth',[1] but it is very doubtful whether he

[1] BOLINGBROKE: *On the True Use of Retirement and Study* (*Works*, ed. 1754, II, p. 520).

here expressed an opinion native or congenial to his own country. With more benefit to themselves the English have hearkened rather to those who taught them that the 'search for truth' is itself a condition of happy human fulfilment, and that by pursuing knowledge a man may become wise.

These scholars prized historical inquiry as a road to spiritual perfection, and for this reason, also, they became fit instructors of the nation from which they sprang. The serious purpose which drove them to their work inspired them with a sense of its intrinsic value, and the subjection of their research to the exigencies of temporal government they thus resisted as the last outrage upon individual integrity. 'We are not Magisterial in opinions', exclaimed one of them, 'nor have we Dictator-like obtruded our conceptions . . . and therefore opinions are free, and open it is for any to think or declare the contrary.'[1] They deserve thus an especial commemoration at a time when new attempts are being made to remove political institutions from the scope of historical criticism, and when the ideals of independent scholarship are once more threatened with widespread destruction. It is even possible that the future of the civilization which these scholars helped to build up may in some measure depend upon the survival of their belief in the moral justification of unfettered inquiry. They won through their books that immortality which adheres to discovery, but the antiquity which they explored was none the less, for them, a guide to conduct. They sought for truth in precedent, and it was in relation to eternity that they studied time.

They have their memorial. Their folios remain as the proper monument to their erudition, and by their successors in medieval scholarship they must be regarded as masters and as pioneers. But their influence persists also in the habitual temper of the nation which they taught. Linking research to action, they associated both with morality, and since their day it has seldom been the practice of their countrymen to divorce the adventures of the mind from the problems of right living. Inasmuch as this people has been guided by experience rather than theory, inasmuch as there prevails in England the conviction that policy should be judged by moral standards, so far have the labours of these men been woven into the fabric of the national life. The enduring texture of their work derived from its own inherent quality, and the reward of the scholars was to inspire in their English posterity an abiding consciousness of the living past.

[1] THOMAS BROWNE: *Vulgar Errors*, Preface.

INDEX

Addison, Joseph, 15, 88
Ælfric the grammarian, 66, 90, 98
Agarde, Arthur, 225, 237, 267
Aldhelm, 144
Aldritch, Henry, 194
Alford, Michael, 197
Amherst, Nicholas, 181, 251, 253
Anglia Sacra, 17, 140, 144–52, 195
Anglican Church:
  Contribution of, to medieval studies, 19,
    20, 71, 195–218, 246–54
  Decline of, during eighteenth century,
    279, 280
Anglo-Saxon:
  Charters, 23, 63, 91–4
  Dictionaries, 38, 49, 52–7, 68, 71, 93, 99,
    118, 245, 273
  Laws, 61, 68, 69, 87, 90, 122, 211
  Manuscripts, Criticism of, 91–2, 102, 109–
    118
  Scholarship, 15, 16, 52–181
    Defence of, 19
    Patronage of, 52–5, 71
Anglo-Saxon Chronicle, 61, 68, 69–71, 109,
    166, 173, 176
Anstis, John, 47
Antiquaries, Society of, 105–8, 175, 234
Archer, Simon, 31–3
Arles, Council of, 199
Arthur, 199, 200
Asser, 164, 165, 199
Aston, John, 96
Atterbury, Francis, 203–8, 212, 213, 274
Atwood, William, 122
Aubrey, John, 160, 170

Bagford, John, 107
Baker, Richard, 134, 256
Baker, Thomas, 222, 250
Bale, John, 157, 162, 163, 177
Bandinel, Bulkeley, 39
Barnes, Joshua, 133, 134
Baronage, 45–7
Bede, *Ecclesiastical History* of, 15, 61–4, 68,
    90, 118, 165, 166, 177
Bedford, Hilkiah, 96, 132, 133
Bedford Thomas, 176
Benson, Thomas, 56, 66

Bentley, Richard, 102, 183, 213, 264
Bernard, Charles, 67
Bernard, Edward, 60, 61, 111–3, 159
Beverley, Alured of, 185, 186
Bibliography, Monastic, 140, 153, 156–64.
    See also *Anglica Sacra*
Bibliotheca Literaria, 184, 260. See also Jebb,
    Samuel; Wasse, Joseph
Bilston, John, 181
Birch, Thomas, 141
Birchington, Stephen, 147
Bliss, Philip, 169
Blomfield, Francis, 159
Blount, Thomas, 49
Bodleian Library, 31, 76, 100, 102, 112–4,
    160, 179, 181, 182, 190, 249, 265
Boethius, 66
Boethius, Hector, 198
Bolingbroke. See St. John
Bollandists, 60, 148
Book-collecting, 104, 261, 262–4, 266
Boston, John, 156, 162, 163
Bourchier, John, Lord Berners, 13
Brady, Robert, 16, 124–38, 189, 237, 243,
    260, 272, 282
Britannia, 20, 21, 25, 63, 159, 187, 257–8.
    See also Camden, William; Gibson,
    Edmund
Britton, Thomas, 261
Brome, William, 83
Browne, Thomas, 28, 29, 49, 255, 256, 257,
    284
    His *Hydriotaphia*, 28, 29
    His *Vulgar Errors*, 29, 284
Burnet, Gilbert, 50, 129, 145, 151–3, 169–71,
    200, 207, 274, 279
Burton, Annals of, 171, 172
Burton, William, 31, 47

Caesar, Sir Julius, 225
Caius, John, 187
Caius, Thomas, 187
Calamy, Edmund, 141, 226
Caley, John, 39
Cambridge, University of:
  Anglo-Saxon Lectureship at, 53, 54, 57,
    252
  See also Spelman, Henry

Stillingfleet, Edward, 196, 198–200, 221, 254,
    266, 274, 279
  His *Origines Britannicae*, 198–200
Stratford, William, 105, 217, 218
Stubbs, William, 148, 151, 155, 210, 220
Surius, L., 216
Swift, Jonathan, 205
Sydenham, Thomas, 125
Syme, James, 67

Talman, John, 107
Tanner, Thomas, 36, 99, 141, 156–64, 183,
    186, 214, 218–20, 257, 272, 282
  His *Notitia Monastica*, 109, 161–4
  His *Bibliotheca*, 158–60
Tate, Francis, 136
Taylor, Jeremy, 18
Temple, William, 16, 123, 260, 274, 278
Tenison, Thomas, 142, 212
Terrae Filius. See Amherst, Nicholas
Textus Roffensis, 73, 188, 190, 266
Thesaurus Linguarum Septentrionalium, 88–95,
    103, 113–7, 183, 253, 270
Thomas, William, 79
Thoresby, Ralph, 73, 84, 87, 106, 174, 183,
    227, 255, 258
Thorotin, Robert, 42, 259
Thwaites, Edward, 15, 56, 64, 66–8, 88, 92,
    94, 118, 270, 272
  His *Heptateuchus*, 66, 90. *See also Thesaurus*
Tilbury, Gervase of, 241
Tillotson, John, 141
Tindal, Nicholas, 135
Todd, Hugh, 149
Tonson, Jacob, 230
Tout, T. F., 239
Townley, Christopher, 262
Trivet, Nicolas, 177
Twine, Brian, 178
Twysden, Roger, 36, 55, 56, 167, 168, 173,
    177
Tyrrel, James, 16, 134, 135

Uffenbach, Zachary von, 244, 245, 250,
    251
Universities. *See* Cambridge; Glasgow;
    Leyden; Oxford; St. Andrew's
Ussher, James, 25, 55, 60, 62, 64, 65, 142,
    167, 196, 197, 199, 274

Vatican Library, 114
Vergil, Polydore, 60
Vertue, George, 180

Voltaire, 277, 278
Vossius, Isaac, 210

Wake, William, 17, 19, 24, 196, 204,
    208–21, 248, 267, 272, 274, 276, 279,
    282. *See also Concilia*
Walker, Edward, 35
Waller, Edmund, 223
Walpole, Horace, 275
Walsingham, Thomas, 165
Wanley, Humphrey, 15, 16, 23, 26, 27, 51,
    52, 68, 72, 76, 84, 86, 88, 92, 98–118,
    174, 186, 187–9, 219, 228, 234, 237,
    243, 256, 263, 265, 267, 272, 273, 282.
    See also Antiquaries, Society of; Har-
    leian Library; *Thesaurus*
Wanley, Nathaniel, 98
Ward, Thomas, 142
Warton, Thomas, 113, 187
Wasse, Joseph, 260
Wats, William, 166, 167, 177
Waverley, Annals of, 173
Webb, P. C., 137
Wharton, Henry, 17, 19, 27, 139–55, 171,
    174, 178, 219, 243, 244, 245, 248, 254,
    258, 267, 276, 279, 282. *See also Anglia
    Sacra*
Wheare, Degory, 251, 252
Wheloc, Abraham, 15, 54, 55, 61, 62, 68–70,
    173, 252
Whitaker, T. D., 37, 42
Wilfrid, Life of, 60, 61
Wilkins, David, 17, 69, 163, 217–20, 252,
    267, 282. *See also* Anglo-Saxon Laws;
    Concilia
Williamson, Joseph, 225
Willis, Browne, 255
Wilson, E., 259
Wisbech, antiquarian society at, 108
Wise, Francis, 187, 197
Witherby, T., 259
Wonders of the Little World. See Wanley,
    Nathaniel
Wood, Anthony, 18, 30, 37, 38, 41, 45, 49,
    51, 145, 159, 160, 163, 168–70, 182, 197,
    247, 250
Worcester, antiquarian society at, 108
Wotton, William, 92, 93
Wright, James, 39, 266
Wulfstan, Life of, 147, 150–1
Wycherley, William, 230

Zodiac Club, 108